SPY CHIEFS

Volume 1

T0352787

SPY

CHIEFS

Volume 1

INTELLIGENCE LEADERS

in the United States and United Kingdom

CHRISTOPHER MORAN

MARK STOUT

IOANNA IORDANOU

PAUL MADDRELL

Editors

Foreword by
Lt. Gen. PATRICK M. HUGHES,
USA (Ret.)

GEORGETOWN UNIVERSITY PRESS / WASHINGTON, DC

The publisher is not responsible for third-party websites or their content. URL links were active at time of publication.

Library of Congress Cataloging-in-Publication Data
Names: Moran, Christopher R., editor. | Stout, Mark, 1964– editor. | Iordanou, Ioanna, editor. | Maddrell, Paul, editor.
Title: Spy chiefs / Christopher Moran, Mark Stout, Ioanna Iordanou and Paul Maddrell, editors.
Description: Washington, DC : Georgetown University Press, 2018. | Includes bibliographical references and index. | This book grew out of two academic meetings. The first was a panel, organized by Paul Maddrell, on Intelligence Leaders in International Relations at the 55th annual convention of the International Studies Association in Toronto, Canada, in March 2014. This led to a second, a conference entitled Spy Chiefs: Intelligence Leaders in History, Culture and International Relations, which was organized by Christopher Moran and his colleagues at Warwick University and held at the Palazzo Pesaro Papafava in Venice, Italy, in May of that year. The purpose of these meetings was to discuss the leadership of intelligence and security agencies; what good leadership of such agencies is and what impact it has had on the performance of the agencies concerned—Preface to volume 1. | Description based on print version record and CIP data provided by publisher; resource not viewed.
Identifiers: LCCN 2017008735 (print) | LCCN 2017012716 (ebook) | ISBN 9781626165182 (volume 1 : hc : alk. paper) | ISBN 9781626165199 (volume 1 : pb : alk. paper) | ISBN 9781626165205 (volume 1 : eb) | ISBN 9781626165212 (volume 2 : hc : alk. paper) | ISBN 9781626165229 (volume 2 : pb : alk. paper) | ISBN 9781626165236 (volume 2 : eb)
Subjects: LCSH: Intelligence service—Congresses. | Intelligence service—History—Congresses. | Espionage—Congresses. | Espionage—History—Congresses. | International relations—Congresses. | Leadership—Case studies—Congresses.
Classification: LCC JF1525.I6 (ebook) | LCC JF1525.I6 S635 2018 (print) | DDC 327.12092/2—dc23
LC record available at https://lccn.loc.gov/2017008735

♾ This book is printed on acid-free paper meeting the requirements of the American National Standard for Permanence in Paper for Printed Library Materials.
19 18   9 8 7 6 5 4 3 2 First printing

Printed in the United States of America

Cover design by Faceout Studio, Spencer Fuller. Cover image of Richard Helms courtesy the National Archives and Records Administration and of the London map by Shutterstock.

This book is dedicated to the memory of
Professor Keith Jeffery (1952–2016),
a leading light and voice of inspiration to the intelligence studies
community.

CONTENTS

FOREWORD

It has been my good fortune to spend some forty-five years in the intelligence business. As a US Army officer, my service included tactical, operational, and strategic intelligence positions from captain through lieutenant general. This culminated in a series of senior assignments, including the positions of director of intelligence at US Central Command, director of intelligence for the Joint Staff, and director of the Defense Intelligence Agency (DIA). After retiring from the army, I served as assistant secretary of homeland security for information and analysis (intelligence), and I also have worked as a corporate officer and private consultant dealing with intelligence issues.

For people in my business, the changes in the world since the end of World War II have been dizzying. They have included the creation and then frequent restructuring of many elements of the US intelligence community; the division of the world into hostile camps that clashed in places as diverse as Korea, Vietnam, Central America, Africa, Bosnia, the Middle East, and Afghanistan; the abrupt end of the Cold War; the "normalization" of relationships with Russia and the former Warsaw Pact nations; the evolutions in China that took it from a power that was even more radically Communist than the Soviet Union to one that is still Communist albeit in less definitive ways; the advent of terrorism and long and inconclusive wars; and the emergence of amazing technologies that held (and delivered) the promise of a revolution in intelligence affairs. At the core of these sweeping changes were intelligence leaders with great insight, exceptional technical knowledge, and vision.

The power of intelligence knowledge—to know the secrets of the world and to know the hidden, fleeting truth—compels the rise to leadership and motivates the best and the brightest to seek the highest positions. In any attempt to write about intelligence leadership, this realization should be close at hand.

Leaders and Secret Knowledge

This does not mean that intelligence leaders know everything, let alone control everything. It goes without saying that the conspiracy theorists' view that the director of the CIA controls history, current affairs, and much more besides is wrong. However, even sober historians can overemphasize the importance of intelligence leaders. They often focus on intelligence leaders to try to understand what really happened during those leaders' tenure. In fact, it is unsupportable to believe that intelligence leaders always know everything their organizations are doing—or even everything they are personally responsible for. It is more realistic to assume that intelligence leaders know generally what is happening and the rest is dependent on the trust and confidence they have in their associates, who are usually trustworthy and dependable—but not always. God knows we've had our own traitors and incompetents.

There are other reasons why it is wrong to assume that intelligence leaders know everything about their own organizations. Leaders cannot, and should not, know everything all the time because to do so is to become overloaded, overwhelmed, and overcome by the demands of daily and hourly events. Intelligence is—after all—a complex business.

A fundamental element of most intelligence work is the practice of compartmentalization, a system in which a person's access to information is determined by an assessment that such access is appropriate and necessary to the tasks at hand. Compartmentalization means that no one knows everything and thus no one can give away everything (whether purposely or by accident) to the adversary. Sometimes even subsets of a given activity are put in separate compartments. While it is sensible and necessary, compartmentalization is a double-edged sword, and in the leadership of intelligence organizations, the friction of this "need to know" mechanism becomes obvious. Sometimes failure has occurred simply because the right hand did not know or understand what the left hand was doing. Compartmentalization has been particularly troublesome when an intelligence leader did not know—and in some cases was not allowed to know—specific details of an intelligence operation. This is hard for the nonprofessional observer to come to grips with because on its face it seems improper and contrary to the principles of effective management. Nevertheless, the realities of intelligence work do not always fit the standard mold or the business school example.

The Burdens of Leadership

Though it can be dangerous for intelligence leaders not to know, knowledge is also a burden. One may know too much, and one may know things that are so sensitive and so restricted that they become a burden in thought and expression and sometimes in personal action. This sets intelligence officers apart from the "regular" person, and while intelligence leaders do not know everything that is "known" within their own organization, they know a great deal.

Like many other fields, intelligence work involves putting some people in harm's way. What makes an intelligence officer's sacrifices unusual is that, if found out, his or her fate is thought to be a terrible procession of events: incarceration, isolation, psychological attack, torture, interrogation, and potentially death. During this expected course of inhumane treatment, the intelligence officer is to rely on training and will to resist (to the death). One can only hope for the ability to resist—but one cannot know until the test comes. Intelligence leaders know the possibilities—and they hold the responsibility for such events and their effects on family and friends and on professional compatriots in their kit bag of leadership challenges. We should give them credit for this great burden. Similarly, most intelligence leaders, honorable and devoted as they are, will have encountered the spy in their midst and have borne the heavy burden of the aftermath of deception, subversion, and betrayal. This, too, is a form of institutional death. Dealing with such emotion-laden events is yet another defining quality of intelligence leaders.

Other Leaders

During my years of service, I have been fortunate to come to know many intelligence leaders, both American and foreign. Most were honorable and devoted to their service and country. Their perspectives were often somber and pessimistic, in part because they were products of their own history and they had learned to expect disasters around every corner. If some happier eventuality occurred, they could rationalize that as a form of fate, but if they stuck to their view of dark threats and troubling possibilities, the uncertain and menacing horizon was more dependable than forecasting rosy outcomes.

Though intelligence is a very secret world, certain bonds connect intelligence leaders across international boundaries. It is not unusual for intelligence leaders of different countries to have a long history with each other, either through personal contact or shared experiences. For instance, as a young officer I was assigned to an activity in Washington, DC, that required me to collect information about what were then our enemies, personified in the military attachés of the Warsaw Pact countries and Union of Soviet Socialist Republics (USSR). The interaction with these officers—especially peers in rank and age among the foreign attachés—included gathering information that might be useful in the future. One attaché and his spouse were especially warm and welcomed my wife and me to a social event at their apartment in one of the suburbs of Washington. We went—only to find ourselves in the uncomfortable position of being the only Americans present. In fact, everyone else was from the "countries of intelligence interest." It was a social event, but everyone in that room was also at work. During our interaction with this attaché, his photograph was taken and duly logged in a file.

Flash forward nearly twenty years. The Cold War has ended. This officer has risen to be the head of military intelligence for his country, and I am the director of the DIA. In short, he and I are friendly counterparts. He invites me to visit his country, and later I reciprocate. In the course of these visits, gifts are exchanged and memories of the bad old days are recounted. One of the gifts, presented as a side event, quietly and very personally, is the photograph taken of him when he was a young "enemy" attaché in Washington, DC, and I was his opponent in the great game. You cannot put into simple words the knowing surprise, the emotion, and the broad element of shared understanding and subsequent cooperation that this simple event produced.

Not all such interactions are so positive. As a young officer I was assigned to duty as an intelligence program adviser in Vietnam during the war. I worked against the Vietcong infrastructure. Like most advisers, I became attached to the people, the culture, and the place, the green beauty of it all against the stark nature of war.

Flash forward twenty years. I travel to Hanoi as an early American guest of the director of military intelligence for the Vietnam People's Armed Forces, my direct counterpart. We meet in his office in a brief and tense encounter during which he berates me for having served in Vietnam during the war. Then he admits that he was the North Vietnamese military intelligence chief in the Central Highlands and, by virtue of his position, played a role in the deaths of many American and South Vietnamese soldiers and civilians. But now the war is over, and our job is to bandage the wounds and help them heal.

Later that day we meet for dinner in a typical North Vietnamese setting, a French-style two-story building with a seating area upstairs, the entire building probably controlled by the Vietnam intelligence service. We are facing our hosts, including the intelligence general, and he seems alternately interested and dismissive of our presence. At some point during the dinner, he asks me what I did during the war, a question he had not posed at the earlier meeting.

It was a surprise that he did not already know—maybe he did. I tell him I fought as an infantry platoon leader and later as an adviser working against the Vietcong infrastructure. He scowls and launches into a tirade against the war and the toll it took on Vietnam. We bid good evening to each other in Vietnamese. The dinner ends unhappily.

In that case the Vietnam War was long behind us. Sometimes, however, it is necessary for intelligence leaders to meet an adversarial counterpart in time of war or crisis. This entails clandestine travel and furtive meetings but often produces results that no other type of interaction could provide. Personality and perception are vital components of such meetings—and the intelligence leaders involved seek to know whatever they can about their opposite number. In my experience, these occasional meetings were the highest form of intelligence endeavor between and among intelligence leaders. They happen for good reasons, but they are seldom discussed or acknowledged. "Honor among spies" is a reliable concept under the right circumstances.

Honorable Duty

Another distinguishing characteristic of intelligence leaders is an exceptional level of dedication to their profession and an impressive devotion to the ideals and values of the system of government and the national character in which they do this demanding work. It is no greater than some other examples of the constancy of dedication and devotion of others—military professionals and civilians who devote their life to work in the national security structure of their nation, for example—but it is noteworthy and valuable in its best manifestations.

We are all products of our own experiences; our defining character was sown into us when we were developing as youthful citizens and maturing as engaged adults. This may be an important quality of the stories in this volume—about how leaders were formed emotionally and cognitively.

The Human Qualities of Intelligence Leaders

One of the features of intelligence leadership is that you can come to believe that you hold some form of power in the information you possess. This is sometimes true, but the point of interagency and interorganizational cooperation is to share that knowledge and to use it collectively for the common good. This noble purpose is of course affected by ego, personal experiences, relationships, and the motivation of the leaders involved. What these leaders knew—and perhaps more important, what they didn't know—is tangled up in the stuff of their humanity.

Thus, it is important for historians to understand that they are writing about human beings. Intelligence leaders are also students, lovers, parents, employees, and teachers, not to mention members of an extended community of family, friends, and professional associations and citizens of the countries and governments they serve. Intelligence leaders are filled with the stuff of humanity themselves—and it would do them a disservice to fail to recognize that fact.

An Anglo-American Community of Leaders

This volume discusses some of the most important intelligence leaders of the United States and the United Kingdom. While it addresses them individually, it is also worth thinking about them as a group. One of the key elements of this volume is the effect of leadership—with all that word entails—on those who were led and on professional friends and allies. Leadership can have enduring effects. For instance, Maj. Gen. William "Wild Bill" Donovan (chapter 1) inspired great loyalty (and in a few cases distaste) among his subordinates. Aspects of his leadership style and his personal foibles (of which there were many) have influenced American intelligence ever since and are key to understanding the evolution of our national intelligence efforts.

In fact, the great old hands who held the title of director of central intelligence—among them Allen Dulles (chapter 4), Richard Helms (chapter 5), William Colby, and William Casey (chapter 6)—were all connected to each other. The foundation of their shared relationships and common efforts can be found in their compelling common history in World War II and their service with General Donovan, as has been so ably described by Douglas Waller in his landmark book, *Disciples*. Many British intelligence chiefs were similarly influenced by the Second World War and their relationships with US intelligence. It is worth remembering that many of the people mentioned in this volume knew each other. Sometimes they got along well, other times they did not (see Richard Aldrich's discussion of William Odom's relationship with his British counterpart at Government Communications Headquarters in chapter 8), but they always influenced each other.

Necessary Work

The work of intelligence is vital to our collective well-being and national survival. We must ensure that we select the best, the brightest, the most dependable, and the most capable leaders for this necessary and demanding work. Perhaps if this volume has merit, it will be found in the examples of leadership that the authors write about and in the recounting of the lives and achievements of these fine people who for the best of reasons chose to labor in the intelligence services of their countries.

With great respect and admiration for those of you who provide information for the benefit of our nation and the security of our people and for those who have stuck with us as dependable counterparts and allies over the past tumultuous years.

Patrick M. Hughes, Lieutenant General, US Army (Retired)

ACKNOWLEDGMENTS

The editors would like to thank Georgetown University Press, in particular senior acquisitions editor Don Jacobs for his enthusiasm, patience, and backing. This project, which sprouted and budded from Paul Maddrell's International Studies Association conference panel in Toronto in 2014, benefited from generous funding by the British Academy (BA)—under the auspices of Christopher Moran's BA Postdoctoral Fellowship—and Warwick University's Institute of Advanced Study (UK). We would also like to acknowledge the anonymous reviewers for their thoughtful and constructive feedback. Naturally, we are greatly indebted to our contributors for their commitment to this volume and their exemplary scholarship. The whole project proved somewhat more time-consuming than we anticipated; accordingly, we would like to express our gratitude to our respective families for their support and patience throughout the process.

ABBREVIATIONS

AC(O)	Official Committee on Communism (Overseas)
AEC	Atomic Energy Commission
AEI	Atomic Energy Intelligence
AFSA	Armed Forces Security Agency
AFSAAB	Armed Forces Security Agency Advisory Board
CIA	Central Intelligence Agency
CIG	Central Intelligence Group
CIP	Catholic International Press / Center of Information Pro Deo
COI	Coordinator of Information
COMINT	communications intelligence
COMSEC	communications security
COS	Chiefs of Staff
CSS	Central Security Service
DCI	director of central intelligence
DDCI	deputy director of central intelligence
DDIR	deputy director
DIA	Defense Intelligence Agency
DIRNSA	director of the National Security Agency
DNI	director of naval intelligence
DOD	Department of Defense
FBI	Federal Bureau of Investigation
FISA	Foreign Intelligence Surveillance Act
FSO	foreign service officer
GC&CS	Government Code and Cipher School
GCHQ	Government Communications Headquarters
GCSB	Government Communications Security Bureau
HUMINT	human intelligence
IA	information assurance
IAB	Intelligence Advisory Board
IC	intelligence community
IRIS	Interim Research and Intelligence Service
ISA	Intelligence Support Activity

ITC	Independent Television Corporation
JCS	Joint Chiefs of Staff
JIC	Joint Intelligence Committee
MED	Manhattan Engineer District
MI5	Security Service
MI6	Secret Intelligence Service (more formally known as SIS)
MID	Military Intelligence Division
MIS	Military Intelligence Service
NATO	North Atlantic Treaty Organization
NIA	National Intelligence Authority
NIE	National Intelligence Estimate
NSA	National Security Agency
NSC	National Security Council
ONI	Office of Naval Intelligence
OPC	Office of Policy Coordination
OPEC	Organization of the Petroleum Exporting Countries
ORE	Office of Reports and Estimates
OSO	Office of Special Operations
OSS	Office of Strategic Services
PRB	CIA's Publications Review Board
PUSD	Permanent Undersecretaries Department
R&A	Office of Strategic Services Research and Analysis Branch
RAF	Royal Air Force
RNVR	Royal Naval Volunteer Reserve
SCA	service cryptologic agency
SCC	service cryptologic component
SIGINT	signals intelligence
SIS	Secret Intelligence Service (informally known as MI6)
SOE	Special Operations Executive
SSU	Strategic Services Unit
TAL	Tube Alloys Liaison
USAF	US Air Force
USCYBERCOM	US Cyber Command
USIB	US Intelligence Board

Introduction

Spy Chiefs: Power, Secrecy, and Leadership

Christopher Moran, Ioanna Iordanou,
and Mark Stout

At a climactic moment in the 1990 action spy thriller *The Hunt for Red October*, the director of the Central Intelligence Agency (CIA), played by James Earl Jones, causes a major plot twist when he unexpectedly emerges from the shadows in the combat information center of a US Navy ship and presses a red button, prematurely detonating a torpedo racing toward a Soviet submarine. Then he quietly but sternly says to the young officer over whose workstation he stands, "Now, you understand, Commander, that torpedo did not self-destruct. You heard it hit the hull. And I was never here."

This fictional moment encapsulates a common and romantic view of spy chiefs: that they are immensely powerful and secretly manipulate the world to be not as it appears. This perception is neither new nor limited to cinematic representations. Throughout history there have been many cases of intelligence professionals being intimidated by and in awe of spy chiefs of rival intelligence agencies.[1] Wilhelm Stieber (1818–82), head of intelligence for Otto von Bismarck, had such a fearsome reputation among the intelligence personnel of Germany's rivals that his successors enjoyed its benefits for decades after his death. During the Cold War James Jesus Angleton, the longtime head of the CIA's counterintelligence staff, attributed nearly godlike powers of espionage and deception to the KGB leadership.[2] Among Western intelligence services, Markus Wolf (1923–2006), the head of the East German Hauptverwaltung Aufklärung (HVA), the foreign intelligence component of the Stasi, had an outsized reputation for power and obscurity.[3] In the twenty-first century spy chiefs are often seen as powerful and secretive. Italian street artist Paulo Cirio has described them as the "Napoleons of today," especially the high-ranking officials who preside over vast surveillance superstructures such as the National Security Agency (NSA), purportedly inspecting every aspect of our digital lives.[4] In a bid to bring them out of the shadows and reveal them to be as digitally helpless as the people they supposedly watch,

Cirio finds private photos of prominent spy chiefs on Plugins such as Photo Hack and then pastes them guerrilla-style on city walls and buildings around the world—reversing the gaze.

The claim that spy chiefs are powerful actors who operate in near total secrecy deserves a serious scholarly investigation. In our view it would be easy but unfair to dismiss spy films as nothing more than cheap entertainment, to remark that Stieber's reputation was wholly undeserved and that Angleton was utterly wrong and possibly clinically paranoid. Arising out of an idea of Paul Maddrell—who planned and organized a panel on Intelligence Leaders in International Relations at the Fifty-Fifth Annual Convention of the International Studies Association in Toronto in March 2014, which was followed up by a conference at the Palazzo Pesaro Papafava in Venice in May—this volume, as well as its companion volume on intelligence leaders in the wider world, seeks to broaden and deepen our understanding of the role and contribution of the spy chief globally. Written by experts in the fields of intelligence, international history, and international relations, chapters examine and reflect on what it means to be an intelligence leader in diverse national and institutional settings and explore how the job has evolved as threats to national security have changed and agencies confront challenges such as increased public pressure for transparency. At the core of this book and its sister volume are six key questions:

- How do intelligence leaders operate in different national, institutional, and historical contexts?
- What role have they played in the conduct of international relations?
- How much power do they possess?
- How secretive and accountable to the public have they been?
- What qualities make an effective intelligence leader?
- Does popular culture (including the media) distort or improve our understanding of intelligence leaders?

Central to both volumes are three components: power, secrecy, and leadership. Let us introduce them in order.

Power

There have been times, of course, when spy chiefs must have felt tremendously powerful. A prominent example would be Frank Wisner (1909–65), the head of the CIA's Directorate of Plans during the 1950s under Director Allen Dulles. Wisner liked to boast that he could use covert action to influence events around the world with the power and precision of an organ master sitting at a "Mighty Wurlitzer." In retrospect, however, Wisner, who was sinking into mental illness at the time, clearly overestimated his influence. As scholar Hugh Wilford has shown, the CIA might have called the tune, but the piper did not always play it, nor the audience dance to it.[5] Nevertheless, sometimes the self-assessment is warranted. By any yardstick Stieber was enormously powerful. He enjoyed private dinners with Bismarck and, during the bitter Franco-Prussian War of 1870, quite literally had a license to kill, personally overseeing the execution of many alleged enemy spies. During the siege of Paris, after a young Frenchman had been brought to his headquarters at Versailles, he ordered that the man "must be executed," despite one of his officers reportedly protesting, "But he is innocent, and he was married only two days ago."[6] Edward Travis (1888–1956), the operational head of Britain's Government Code and Cipher School (GC&CS), doubtless felt powerful when GC&CS, at Bletchley Park, had its event-influencing successes against German cipher systems during World War II.[7] One also wonders whether Gen. Keith Alexander (1951–), who served as the director of NSA from 2005 to 2013, felt the same way as he presided over what has been called a new golden age of signals intelligence.[8] Christopher Curwen, head of Britain's Secret Intelligence Service (SIS), surely sensed his power when, under his aegis, the service successfully engineered one of its most impressive achievements: the safe exfiltration from Moscow of KGB colonel Oleg Gordievsky in 1985.

But intelligence is a difficult business, so the job of being a spy chief must often induce a sense of fighting against long odds. For instance, covert actions are notoriously hard to implement successfully for the reason that the partners of the intelligence agencies, and the people in the target country, are not simply automatons who have no choice but to cooperate when the CIA or KGB or Inter-Services Intelligence (ISI) comes calling. The law of unintended consequences dictates that a short-term covert action success can lead to long-term problems. The history of the CIA's covert actions in Chile in the early 1970s is testament to this: by abetting the fall of Salvador Allende, the agency contributed to the rise of Gen. Augusto Pinochet, who duly brought a reign of terror on the Chilean people.[9] As mentioned previously, even Wisner's fabled program of support for front groups and the noncommunist left in Europe and elsewhere was not without its problems. While some, like Frances Stonor Saunders, have claimed that the agency had tight control over the intellectual agenda of the cultural forces it bankrolled (otherwise known as the "puppet master" thesis), others, like Wilford and Helen Laville, convincingly show that the CIA often failed to dictate how its disbursements were spent, meaning that covert subsidies were used for purposes that had no connection to the Cold War ideological struggle for hearts and minds.[10]

The business of collecting information about what is going on in the world and then analyzing it to help policymakers and military commanders optimize their decision making is also daunting. To borrow the terminology of Richard Betts, there are many "enemies of intelligence," and all of them constrain the power of the spy chief.[11] First, there are the "outside enemies"—for instance, the foreign governments that obsessively guard their secrets. In seeking to steal the information of an adversary, the spy chief is always fighting from a disadvantageous position. He or she must find a way to purloin well-protected secrets, usually on the target's home turf, where the target government has all the advantages, including domestic counterintelligence infrastructure. Furthermore, the best sources are usually very "fragile" as the British call them or "sensitive" in American terminology. This means that the slightest indiscretion or slip will result in the spy being arrested (or worse yet doubled), or the vulnerable cipher system being changed, or the imagery signature becoming hidden or ended.

Second, there are what Betts calls the "innocent enemies" of intelligence. These are people or institutions within the spy chief's own country who support the chief's overall goal of protecting national security through intelligence but who thwart his or her work nonetheless. Treasury officials or appropriations committees who do not provide the resources that an intelligence leader deems necessary, or bureaucrats who create rather than cut red tape, fall into this category. So too do politicians, journalists, and citizens who seek to limit the power of intelligence agencies on the grounds of civil liberties or legal objections.[12] One thinks here of the challenge faced by the directors of the CIA during the late 1960s and early 1970s as they were faced with a drumbeat of media leaks and protests over alleged and actual improprieties that led to unprecedented levels of congressional scrutiny. Then there are whistleblowers. One can only imagine the degree of frustration that would prompt the leaders of NSA to ban their subordinates from even referring by name to Edward Snowden, at least if Washington scuttlebutt is to be believed. Today we also see spy chiefs being undermined by a new category of "innocent enemy"—the tech industry—as illustrated by the stance of Apple CEO Tim Cook, who, in early 2016, took a stand against his firm helping the Federal Bureau of Investigation (FBI) to access encrypted data on a cell phone owned by the shooter who killed fourteen people in San Bernardino the year before. Battles between intelligence leaders and Silicon Valley are likely to increase as tech companies continue to lobby for more tightly drawn rules on what data they are required to turn over to law enforcement bodies.

Spy chiefs are also often constrained by their superiors, their peers, and sometimes their subordinates. In the 1990s CIA director James Woolsey (1941–) had little power because he had essentially no relationship with

President Bill Clinton. Indeed, when a deranged pilot crashed a propeller-driven Cessna airplane onto the south lawn of the White House in September 1994, the joke circulated that it was Woolsey trying to get the president's attention. Woolsey initially hated the story, but in time he became so accustomed to not seeing the president that he began to tell it himself.[13] The spy chiefs in the Soviet satellite states, even the great Markus Wolf, were virtual lackeys of the KGB in Moscow. More dramatically, the leaders of the Soviet People's Commissariat for Internal Affairs (NKVD) knew that they had to work carefully and with an eye on Stalin lest they end up arrested and executed. Saddam Hussein's intelligence chiefs worked in a similar environment, undermining their freedom of thought and action.

Spy chiefs' relationships with peers are seldom as dangerous in the sense of life or death but can restrict their power. Allen Dulles (1893–1969) was remarkably fortunate because most of his time as director of the CIA coincided with the tenure of his brother, John Foster Dulles (himself a military intelligence officer during World War I), as secretary of state.[14] Having been close since childhood and sharing a visceral hatred of Communism, the two siblings championed the right of the United States to intervene overseas to advance its interests, including, if the situation demanded it, the right to overthrow governments. Historian Stephen Kinzer has written that the Dulles brothers "turned the State Department and the CIA into a reverberating echo chamber for their shared certainties," perhaps best described as a form of brotherly groupthink.[15] The Dulles era, however, was unusual. Typically, the CIA and the State Department are competitors in the dog-eat-dog world of Beltway politics. In recent decades the secretary of defense, with his enormous budget, has been a serious rival to both directors of the CIA and directors of national intelligence. A similar situation prevailed in the United States during World War II, when Gen. William Donovan (1883–1959), head of the Office of Strategic Services (OSS), had to fight endless battles with J. Edgar Hoover's FBI and the intelligence components of the armed services.[16] As a result of these skirmishes, the OSS was almost entirely denied access to signals intelligence information. Moreover, its reputation suffered as departmental rivals, especially Hoover, leaked damaging stories about botched operations and waste of human talent and lives.

Subordinates, too, can restrict the freedom of action of a spy chief. Many directors of NSA have been frustrated by the "warlords" within the agency who jealously guard the prerogatives of their own particular sections of the agency (see chapter 7).[17] Military officers heading civilian intelligence agencies are often frustrated by their inability to run the agency in question like a military staff. There are also many examples of spy chiefs being unpopular with their subordinates, to the detriment of the chiefs' ability to implement their own agendas. The enormous respect commanded by career intelligence officer Richard Helms, then deputy director of the CIA, was such that his boss, the director of central intelligence (DCI), Adm. William Raborn (1905–90), had reduced authority. Raborn quipped, "I thought for a time when I was Director that I might be assassinated by my Deputy."[18] At the CIA there was great discontent, especially in the Directorate of Operations, with Adm. Stansfield Turner (1923–), who sharply reduced the size of the clandestine service, firing some eight hundred officers, and who shared President Jimmy Carter's concern about the propriety of much of what the CIA had previously done. At agency headquarters in Langley, Virginia, notice boards featured vile anti-Turner messages and caricatures.[19] The so-called Turner Purge even led some disgruntled former officers to consider filing a civil action lawsuit against their old boss. In the British context the "gentlemanly" senior officers of the Security Service (MI5) resented being led after World War II by burly ex-policeman Sir Percy Sillitoe (1888–1962), whom they dismissed as a "plod." To his frustration they mischievously wrote letters in Latin as a weapon of bamboozlement, knowing that he could not understand it.[20]

Secrecy

The idea that even the spy chiefs of the leading nations are vastly powerful must, then, be treated with a great deal of caution. But what of secrecy? In many countries today spy chiefs are the public face of intelligence. They speak to the media, appear before public inquiries and committees, write books (typically with impunity, in contrast to the undercover rank and file), and in retirement, become honorary professors on college campuses. Gen. Michael Hayden (1945–), a former director of the CIA and the National Security Agency, is a public commentator on intelligence matters and writes a biweekly column for the *Washington Times*. Dame Stella Rimington (1935–), a former head of MI5, was the first serving spy chief in Britain to be publicly named and the first to pose openly for the cameras. She now writes spy novels and is held as the blueprint for Dame Judi Dench's "M" in the James Bond films: much like her real-world inspiration, Dench sported a closely cropped "silver pixie" haircut, wore collarless jackets of three-quarter length, and hated male chauvinism. A recent head of SIS, Sir John Sawers, even earned popular notoriety as the "Speedo Spy" after family photographs of him relaxing on the beach appeared on Facebook.[21] Moreover, it is increasingly common, in the United Kingdom and the United States at least, for prime ministers and presidents to talk about their spy chiefs.[22] In November 2015, for example, in the House of Commons, David Cameron referred explicitly to the views of MI5's director general and the chairman of the Joint Intelligence Committee (JIC) in making his case for British air strikes to defeat the Islamic State of Iraq and the Levant (ISIL) in Syria. Tony Blair had done the same in the lead up to the invasion of Iraq in 2003.

Not too long ago such things would have sent shivers down the spine of the majority of secret services. In the past certain intelligence agencies did not even "officially" exist. The existence of the United States' National Reconnaissance Office was not declassified until 1992. Britain did not publicly acknowledge the existence of MI5 until 1989, and only put SIS and Government Communications Headquarters (GCHQ) on the statute book in 1994. Clearly, the leaders of such organizations were not going to have significant public profiles either.

Whether their agencies were secret or not, spy chiefs have often been a shadowy lot. For most of the twentieth century, the heads of agencies in Britain were appointed and worked in secret: their names and roles were not announced to the public, and when they died, their obituaries would contain only short references to "H.M. Diplomatic Service." Individuals who dared to disclose the identity of spy chiefs risked violating D-Notices or, worse still, the Official Secrets Act. In 1932 the First World War intelligence officer Compton Mackenzie was prosecuted and fined £100 for his book *Greek Memories*, which, among other offences, revealed the name of the first chief of SIS, Sir Mansfield Cumming, who by that time had been dead for nine years.[23] Roger Hollis, a former director general of MI5, had such a passion for secrecy that he left instructions for his cremated remains to be stowed behind an unmarked stone in a churchyard wall: anonymity, even in death.[24] Even when their names were not secret, spy chiefs could be very publicity shy. Markus Wolf cultivated his "Man without a Face" persona, and Reinhard Gehlen (1902–79), his West German opposite number, was almost as secretive. As discussed, Stella Rimington was the first head of MI5 to be publicly named on appointment, but the British government originally did not intend to release her photograph and only did so after a newspaper published one of its own.

In the Western world the heads of the intelligence components of the various armed services have typically been low-profile individuals who have attracted little public attention, at least during their lifetimes. Some of them, as scholarship has revealed, have been hugely important. One example is Adm. William Reginald Hall (1870–1943). Nicknamed "Blinker" on account of a chronic eyelid twitch, Hall headed the Royal Navy's intelligence department during World War I and not only provided outstanding intelligence support to the Royal Navy and the national leadership but also helped push the United States into the war with the decryption and public release of the Zimmerman telegram. Another example is Col. Ralph H. Van Deman (1865–1952), the father of American military intelligence, who headed the US War Department's intelligence division during the early part of the US involvement in World War I.

Elsewhere, military intelligence chiefs can be major and extremely public players. Indeed, some go on to enjoy political careers. Abdel Fattah el-Sisi (1954–), the president of Egypt and a former director of military intelligence in the country (2010–12), is perhaps today's most prominent example. In African countries, especially those under authoritarian rule, spy chiefs are seldom out of the news. It is not uncommon for them to be publicly fired as a show of strength by insecure or scheming presidents. In September 2015, for example, the KGB-trained General Toufik, head of Algeria's fearsome Intelligence and Security Directorate, was very publicly "retired," with speculation being that his departure was an attempt by the ailing seventy-eight-year-old President Abdelaziz Bouteflika to "demilitarize" the country and usher in a new generation of civilian leadership and business oligarchs. Unheard of among spy chiefs in the West, African spy chiefs have even launched coups. In late 2015, for example, Burkina Faso was plunged into crisis when the head of the presidential guard, Gen. Gilbert Diendéré, arrested the leadership and the next morning announced himself on live television as the country's new ruler, just three weeks before planned elections. Within a week—following civilian resistance, violent clashes on the streets, and intervention from regional heads of state—the iron-fisted general's seizure of power had been defeated.[25]

Leadership

While spy chiefs oscillate somewhere between secrecy and transparency, they cannot escape the pitfalls of leadership, as they are in charge of large institutional operations. But what exactly is leadership in the field of intelligence, and whom does it depend on? Does it depend on the actual leader? Or rather on the leader's subordinates? Or on the operation? Or the organization that commands the operation? In other words, does the organization make the leader, or does the leader make the organization? Are leaders determined by their subordinates, or are the subordinates determined by their leaders? These are some of the questions and debates that the authors in this volume are engaging with.

Before we move on to explore these pertinent issues, it is important to ask a basic question: what is leadership? "Leadership" is a contested term that has been attributed countless definitions in both theory and practice. Still, to this day there is no consensus as to its basic meaning, let alone its effect and evaluation.[26] To understand what leadership is, it might be easier to first discard what leadership is not. Leadership is not management—that is, overseeing the processes and procedures that a number of individuals carry out in order to complete a task.[27] Leadership should also not be misperceived as command, or giving direct orders at a time of crisis in order to solve an imminent problem that calls for swift and urgent decision making.[28] But if leadership does not entail following standard operating procedures (management) or making urgent (and authoritarian) decisions in time of crisis (command), what exactly does it involve?

Leadership is inextricably linked with uncertainty. In essence, it deals with problems that have no obvious solutions. Thus, the leader's primary responsibilities are to ask the right questions that will generate the appropriate solutions to an issue and to mobilize those related with the issue to work toward solving it. In consequence, the leader's job is not to find the right answer but to come up with the appropriate questions that will mobilize others to take action.[29] President John Kennedy's approach during the Cuban Missile Crisis offers a good example of leadership. Despite pressure imposed by his military advisers to come up with instant decisions, Kennedy persisted in asking his civilian assistants questions that required time for reflection. Had he succumbed to the entreaties of hawkish elements, humanity might have witnessed a nuclear war.[30]

Following this explanation of leadership, another important question arises: what are the key attributes of a leader? In the realm of intelligence, for instance, one of Allen Dulles's primary accomplishments as CIA director was his creation of an atmosphere of missionary zeal to combat the spread of Communism, as James Lockhart explains in chapter 4. As Andrew Hammond shows in chapter 6, DCI William Casey's leadership centered on an authoritarian attitude that he used to bully key figures in Congress in order to fund his covert missions in the name of good versus evil. Comparing these two intelligence leaders, what is it that determines their leadership: the result, as in the case of Dulles, or the process, as in the case of Casey?

This last question, which is redolent of Machiavelli's distinction between *fortuna* (luck, circumstance, constraint) and *virtù* (skill, ability, audacity), encapsulates the practical complexities of reaching a common understanding (and definition) of leadership.[31] This is because leadership can be viewed and assessed from different perspectives. The primary four, as leadership scholar Keith Grint explains them, are the following:

- Leadership as *position*: does *where* leaders operate render them leaders?
- Leadership as *person*: is it *who* leaders are that makes them leaders?

- Leadership as *result*: is it *what* the leaders accomplish that determines their acceptance as leaders?
- Leadership as *process*: is it *how* leaders achieve things that renders them leaders?[32]

This dissensus in the way we view leadership need not cause further confusion if we are clear as to what form of leadership we are talking about. Importantly, rather than trying to elide the differences, it might be more helpful to consider the common denominator of these diverse perspectives of leadership: its relational element—that is, the relationship between the leader and the follower. In fact, the simplest definition of leadership describes it as "having followers."[33]

Stemming from this definition, a rather nonessentialist explanation of leadership presents leaders as capable of persuading their followers to face up to complex collective problems and take responsibility for them.[34] This presupposes that the followers have accepted their position as followers and are receptive to being led by the leader. Leaders, therefore, cannot exist in isolation without followers. In other words, a leader's authority is sanctioned by the followers' identification and self-acceptance as followers.

According to this definition, leadership is premised on two prerequisites: the creation of a group that followers can feel part of and wittingly situate themselves in and the mobilization of the group to proceed to certain actions that the leader deems necessary.[35] When Adolf Hitler mobilized the majority of the German population to accept his political views, for instance, not every German was a Nazi.[36] Leadership, therefore, goes beyond overseeing the organization and operation of a process or a mission. In fact, Hitler was a gifted motivator, not an organizer, as his steadfast refusal to take up the post of the Nazi Party chair in 1921 indicates.[37] Thus, leadership presupposes the social construction of the context that legitimizes a certain action by a group at a specific point in time.[38]

This is particularly pertinent in intelligence organizations, where overseeing the smooth running of intelligence operations and analysis depends on the connivance of a number of people who are directly or indirectly related to the organization or even the state, as several intelligence leaders occupy a prominent position within the realm of statecraft. Major decisions on national and international security, including the answer to the critical question of whether a nation should resort to war, are partially dependent on these spy chiefs' verdicts. Without the consent of the followers, however (followers in this context can be peers, subordinates, the citizens, or even the head of a nation), the leader's authority is obsolete. This consent does not have to rely on a unanimous endorsement of the leader. The followers' unwillingness to challenge the leader's position will suffice. In other words, "the mobilization of a society or an organization does not depend upon a consensual identity; rather it rests on an identifiable solidarity."[39] In the pertinent question of war involvement, for example, it is the intelligence leader's role to construct a convincing image of the enemy that followers will also construe as an enemy. If this endeavor is successful, the leader is sanctioned.

This brings us back to the issue of power. Max Weber's original idea of power centered on a person's ability to achieve certain goals even against the opposition of others.[40] Weber identified a primary distinction between power (which he called *macht*) and authority—or in this context, leadership—(which he called *herrschaft*). While the latter is legitimate in the eyes of the followers, the former need not be.[41] The effectiveness of the leader, therefore, lies in his or her ability to construct and articulate a common purpose that will "mobilize the fanatics and immobilize the sceptics."[42] This will determine whether the leader will use or abuse power, interpret or misinterpret the law, and engage or disengage with the status quo. By most accounts inaugural SIS head Mansfield Cumming (1859–1923) was a highly charismatic figure whose strength of personality, strong work ethic, and even eccentricities galvanized his staff.[43] Reportedly, he cruised around Whitehall corridors on a child's scooter and, when interviewing potential recruits, would stab his wooden leg through his trousers with a letter opener, to see their reaction and test whether they had the stomach for intelligence work.[44] Still, his underlings overlooked his eccentricities. The Cumming example shows that legitimacy is the most effective instrument of power and, certainly, more cost-effective than bullying or buying.[45]

But what happens when leaders err? It is undeniable that leaders' decisions have the potential to shape both the present and the future. Indeed, exploring history as it unravels through the centuries, one need only consider a slight variation in the decision-making processes of a specific individual that would have led to a different future. What would have the course of history been, for example, if Adolf Hitler had not pursued the stern course of action that he did? The key issue here is that if leaders are wrong—and as human beings they are bound to be at times—but do not recognize the error, then their followers and organizations can be exposed to great risk.[46] For example, it is often claimed that Sir Maurice Buckmaster, head of the F Section of the Special Operations Executive (SOE) during the Second World War, sent brave agents to their arrest or even death by ignoring compelling evidence that SOE networks had been penetrated by the Germans.[47] A critical difference, then, between success and failure in leadership lies in the extent to which subordinates are asked and are able to compensate for the errors of their leaders.[48] The successful leader is the one that recognizes the error and empowers the followers to rectify it, not to pay for it.[49] Leaders, therefore, have the capacity to *invent* the future, and this is a great responsibility indeed.

All these and more issues are explored and analyzed further in this volume. Importantly, the chapters present all forms of leadership discussed here: leadership defined as position, person, result, and process. In chapter 5, for instance, Richard Helms's leadership is defined by his position as director of the CIA, with a particular focus on his affinity for the agency's fervent espousal of the credo of secrecy. As shown in chapter 3, Leslie Groves, the stern head of the Manhattan Project between 1942 and 1945, was also notorious for his passion for secrecy. It was this particular personal attribute that consolidated his perception as leader in the eyes of others. In chapter 4 Allen Dulles's methodical and successful accomplishment of fending off the encroaching forces of Communism is a key characteristic of his leadership of the CIA. Finally, as we shall see in chapter 7, several NSA directors with untimely careers in the agency can be seen as exemplars of ineffective leadership practices. The chapter's authors attribute this ineffectiveness to the agency's prohibitive bureaucracy and insular organizational culture that interfered with the process of effective leadership. These are only a handful of instances of intelligence leaders in Britain and the United States that are presented and discussed in this volume.

Structure

The decision was made to split the project into two volumes, with the present volume focusing on spy chiefs in the United States and the United Kingdom and the second looking at spy chiefs globally. Intellectually, it made sense to group American and British intelligence leaders together. As Philip Davies has shown, intelligence communities in the United States and the United Kingdom share certain formal structural characteristics.[50] In the context of liberal democracies, both perform a similar function—namely, to gather, analyze, and disseminate intelligence to cabinet-level political elites. They also possess what he calls "common morphological traits."[51] In both countries intelligence is carried out by highly specialized covert collection agencies, supported by comparable formal management structures and executive machinery, and peopled by career-minded officials with a vested interest in protecting their own department. In Washington and London there is a broad-based acceptance that intelligence analysis should be politically and policy neutral, in contrast to the view in many non-Western countries where any assessments opposing the regime's objectives would be undesirable. Intelligence communities in the United States and the United Kingdom typically face analogous enemies and threats that cut across functional and institutional lines. More-over, they both adhere to the philosophy of "intelligence exceptionalism"—the idea that intelligence has a special place within government because it is secretive, because it involves breaking the laws of other countries, and because it is fungible, used for a variety of purposes.[52]

This is not to say, of course, that the two systems are identical. Notwith-standing the obvious disparity in terms of budgets and staff, there exists what Davies astutely identifies as informal cultural differences. It is generally acknowledged that there is a greater degree of interdependence, collegiality, and consensus in the British system, whereas intelligence in the United States is invariably dogged by competition and bitter turf wars. Historically, the UK definition of intelligence is "narrow" in the sense that it is largely concerned with clandestine collection. In contrast, US conceptualization foregrounds all-source analysis and is therefore broader.[53]

This volume is itself divided into two parts: the first consisting of chap-ters that address US spy chiefs and the second comprising contributions that consider the UK context. For intellectual coherence and consistency, the spy chiefs who feature in this volume were chosen on the basis that they all oper-ated at the national or strategic level, with direct access to the most senior offi-cials, including presidents and prime ministers. The first three chapters relate to US intelligence leaders who operated during or immediately after World War II. In chapter 1 Michael Graziano looks at the influence of Catholicism on the leadership of OSS head Gen. William "Wild Bill" Donovan. The son of poor Irish Catholic parents, Donovan cultivated a close relationship with Pope Pius XII; indeed, in July 1944 the pontiff decorated him with the Grand Cross of the Order of Saint Sylvester, the oldest papal knighthood. Through this per-sonal relationship, Graziano argues, the Vatican became a prize intelligence asset for the Allies, despite its declared policy of neutrality. Chapter 2, by Mark Stout, reflects on the career of one of Donovan's great rivals, Col. John Grombach, the head of a completely unacknowledged espionage organization from 1942 to 1955, known as the "Pond." Grombach, a pugnacious ex-Olympic boxer who kept a black poodle under his office desk, hated the larger-than-life publicity hound Donovan and his "Oh So Social" agency, believing instead that intelligence services should be absolutely secret, analogous to Britain's SIS. Astonishingly, there is no evidence that President Harry Truman even knew the Pond existed. As Stout shows, Grombach's story resonates with debates relevant today, including the role of contractors in protecting national security and the question of how open agencies should be to be able to do their job securely and effectively. Secrecy is also a major theme in chapter 3, by Matthew Fay, which reflects on the career of Leslie Groves, who headed the Manhattan Project from 1942 to 1945. During this period, no major breaches of security occurred, a reflection of Groves's obsession about secrecy. Every employee had a rigorous background check by the FBI and was required to wear a badge with their picture, job, and level of clearance at all times. All mail entering and leaving the project sites was meticulously vetted. After the war, however, Groves's rigid application of the "need to know" principle became counterproductive. By refusing to share vital intelligence, even with his superiors, Groves was partly responsible for agencies such as the Central Intelligence Group (CIG) and later the CIA producing woefully inaccurate estimates of Soviet atomic bomb development.

Chapters 4, 5, and 6 deal with three titans of the US intelligence community: CIA directors Allen Dulles (1893–1969), Richard Helms (1913–2002), and William Casey (1913–87). In chapter 4 James Lockhart provides fascinating new evidence to reveal how Dulles, the consummate cold warrior, transformed the CIA in the 1950s from an organization that was content to sit quietly and cogitate on the Soviet threat to an "action-oriented" body infused with missionary enthusiasm to fight the spread of Communism, in any corner of the globe. In chapter 5 Christopher Moran sheds light on the retirement years of the legendary Helms. Known by the epithet "the man who kept the secrets," Helms believed for most of his life that intelligence professionals should take their secrets to the grave, a conviction that in the late 1970s saw him run afoul of federal prosecutors who discovered that he had lied to Congress about the CIA's role in trying to bring about regime change in Chile. As biographer Thomas Powers has argued, "Of course, everyone in the American intelligence community believes in secrets in theory, but Helms *really* believed in secrets."[54] In the 1990s, however, the octogenarian retired spymaster surprised everyone by writing a memoir. Using Helms's private papers, Moran suggests that the aging Helms did not abandon secrecy but rather came to realize the importance of intelligence agencies communicating their mission and history to the public, to correct misconceptions and build public support.

In chapter 6 Andrew Hammond examines the directorship of Casey, the crusty and driven New York lawyer who is often held as the most powerful DCI in history and who is credited with leading the agency through a "second golden age," redolent of the freewheeling days of the 1950s. Recognizable by his heavy, oversized, Yves St. Laurent glasses and marble-mouthed speech (some contend he mumbled purposely to disguise his statements), Casey, argues Hammond, used a combination of bullying tactics and sweet talk to get big appropriations from Congress to fund extensive covert actions. His abrasive leadership style, Hammond claims, reflected his harsh Manichean worldview of good versus evil and evoked the spirit of his hero, General Donovan.

Part 1 of the volume concludes with two chapters on directors of NSA. In chapter 7 Betsy Smoot and David Hatch provide a fast-paced overview of the people who have headed NSA from 1952 to 2014, reflecting on the profile of individual directors, their impact, and leadership typology. Smoot and Hatch point out that NSA directors have historically had to manage the needs and sensitivities of three constituencies: their masters within the executive branch, especially the Department of Defense (DOD); the NSA workforce; and outsiders, including the legislative branch and, increasingly, in a post-Snowden world, the general public. Fascinatingly, they argue that many directors have struggled to make meaningful organizational changes, since their time at NSA is typically short-lived and the fiercely insular fiefdoms that make up the internal civilian bureaucracy have invariably clung to the status quo to protect their own power and influence. It is also interesting to note from Smoot and Hatch's analysis that, with the exception of Adm. Michael Rogers, appointed in 2014, no director in the agency's history has been a career cryptologist. Moreover, only a few had any prior service with NSA before taking the role. In short, the job of NSA director has historically been filled by outsiders and intelligence neophytes.

In chapter 8 Richard J. Aldrich provides a case study of one particular director, Gen. William Odom. Described as "a fighter and an intellectual" by President Jimmy Carter's national security adviser Zbigniew Brzezinski, under whom he once served as military assistant, Odom demonstrated both these qualities during his time at NSA.[55] Aldrich reveals how Odom rarely saw eye to eye with his opposite number, Peter Marychurch in Britain's GCHQ, and even questioned whether Britain, in an age of expensive supercomputers, any longer had a place at the "Five Eyes" top table. Aldrich also shows how Odom managed the problem of defectors, like Ronald Pelton, and press leaks, including efforts to prevent *Washington Post* journalist Bob Woodward from printing details about Operation Ivy Bells, the attempt by NSA, CIA, and the US Navy to place listening devices around Soviet underwater communication cables in the Sea of Okhotsk.

Part 2 of the collection, on British spy chiefs, opens with three chapters that deal with individuals who had a profound impact on the British intelligence community. Chapter 9 by Michael Goodman explores the career of Eric Welch, who, from 1941 to 1945, was head of the Norwegian Section of SIS. Known for the close personal relationships he forged with his agents, many of whom regarded him as a surrogate figure, Welch blazed a trail in the field of atomic intelligence. During the war, shows Goodman, he played an instrumental role in monitoring, assessing, and thwarting German atomic bomb development, including coordinating commando raids on the heavy water plant in Vemork. In chapter 10 Rory Cormac explores the origins of British covert action by reflecting on the career of Stewart Menzies, chief of SIS from 1939 to 1952. Covert action, argues Cormac, came of age in the British context under the watchful eye of Menzies. A key reason for Menzies's success, the author contends, was his sure-footedness in the slippery bureaucratic corridors of power. Adroitly, he made friends with people that really mattered, most notably the prime minister, the foreign secretary, and the senior civil servants in the Foreign Office. In chapter 11 Danny Steed looks at the seven years Patrick Dean spent as chairman of the Joint Intelligence Committee (JIC), Britain's preeminent intelligence assessment and evaluation body. In 1957 Dean was a prime mover in transferring the JIC from being a subcommittee of the Chiefs of Staff to a cabinet committee within the Cabinet Office. This bureaucratic change, argues Steed, ranks in importance with any operational success, since it put the JIC at the heart of the British machinery of government.

The final two chapters of the volume shift the focus to the important issue of representation. Rightly or wrongly, public perceptions of spy chiefs have been to a certain degree influenced by what people read in the newspapers or see on their television sets and in movie theaters. This is a natural consequence of the power of popular culture as a persuasive tool but is also reflective of the lamentable fact that information about spy chiefs from other (perhaps more reliable) sources has historically been in short supply. Put another way, culture has filled a vacuum. The most famous fictional spy chief has undoubtedly been James Bond's superior "M." Chapter 12, by Ian Fleming Foundation president Mike VanBlaricum, reveals the fascinating backstory to "M" by discussing the man widely held to be Ian Fleming's model for the character: Adm. John Henry Godfrey, director of British Naval Intelligence during World War II. Drawing on Fleming's private papers and unseen signed copies of his books, VanBlaricum shows that M was likely an amalgam of the old sea dog Godfrey and intelligence leaders Mansfield Cumming and William Melville, head of Scotland Yard's Special Branch in the late nineteenth and early twentieth centuries.

In Britain there is a long and celebrated tradition of spy television series, from *The Avengers* in the 1960s to the twenty-first-century *Spooks*, broadcast in the United States under the title *MI-5*. In chapter 13 Joseph Oldham provides a summary of how intelligence leaders have been represented in British spy television, suggesting that the portrayal has evolved in three waves. Originally, the dominant image of the fictional spy chief was that of an all-knowing, largely deskbound figure whose main purpose is to brief the agent and, in doing so, legitimate the mission. Typically, this individual was authoritarian, determined to hold his staff to the highest professional standards, but also paternal, anxious to ensure that his agents return safely from the field. By the mid-1970s, however, the spy chief starts to assume a much more important role in the plot as the office of the intelligence bureaucracy—not the field—becomes the main site of the drama. In this depiction the leader is presented as being cold and corrupt, with hidden agendas. According to Oldham, the last decade has witnessed a third representational wave characterized by shared leadership, with missions being planned and controlled by teams, not a singular authority. In fiction the implication seems to be that national security is better served by leadership that is broadly distributed.

The volume concludes with some reflections by the editors on the lessons from this study for contemporary spy chiefs.

Notes

1. See Paul Maddrell, ed., *The Image of the Enemy* (Washington, DC: Georgetown University Press, 2015).

2. See Tom Mangold, *Cold Warrior: James Jesus Angleton, the CIA's Master Spy Hunter* (New York: Simon & Schuster, 1991); Michael Holzman, *James Jesus Angleton, the CIA, and the Craft of Counterintelligence* (Amherst: University of Massachusetts Press, 2008); David Robarge, "The James Angleton Phenomenon: 'Cunning Passages, Contrived Corridors': Wandering in the Angletonian Wilderness," *Studies in Intelligence* 53, no. 4 (2009): 43–55.

3. For analysis of Western intelligence assessments and perceptions of East Germany and its rulers, see Paul Maddrell, *Spying on Science: Western Intelligence in Divided Germany, 1945–1961* (Oxford: Oxford University Press, 2006). Among the only details that were known about Wolf was his strategy of using sex to gain secrets, including the use of seductive "Romeo" agents to entice lonely office secretaries in the West with access to classified information. See Adam Bernstein, "Markus Wolf, 83, East German Espionage Chief," *Washington Post*, November 10, 2006.

4. Laura Mallone, "Shaming Spy Chiefs by Plastering Them All over the World," *Wired*, July 8, 2015.

5. Hugh Wilford, *The Mighty Wurlitzer: How the CIA Played America* (Cambridge, MA: Harvard University Press, 2009).

6. "Nasty Wilhelm Steiber Was Bismarck's Ruthless Spy Chief," *Look and Learn* (blog), August 23, 1975, http://www.lookandlearn.com/blog/18355/nasty-wilhelm -stieber-was-bismarcks-ruthless-spy-chief/.

7. There are of course countless histories of Bletchley Park and its operational head Sir Edward Travis, but for an excellent recent overview, see chaps. 1–5 of Richard J. Aldrich, *GCHQ: The Uncensored History of Britain's Most Secret Intelligence Agency* (London: HarperCollins, 2010).

8. James Risen and Laura Poitras, "N.S.A. Report Outlined Goals for More Power," *New York Times*, November 22, 2013.

9. For a good summary of CIA interventions in Chile, see Zakia Shiraz, "CIA Intervention in Chile and the Fall of the Allende Government in 1973," *Journal of American Studies* 45, no. 3 (2011): 603–13.

10. Frances Stonor Saunders, *Who Paid the Piper? The CIA and the Cultural Cold War* (London: Granta, 1999); Helen Laville, *Cold War Women: The International Activities of American Women's Organizations* (Manchester: Manchester University Press, 2002).

11. Richard Betts, *Enemies of Intelligence: Knowledge and Power in American National Security* (New York: Columbia University Press, 2009).

12. Jack Goldsmith, *Power and Constraint: The Accountable Presidency after 9/11* (New York: W. W. Norton, 2012), makes this argument about the American national security apparatus generally, though the intelligence agencies are a particular focus.

13. Michael Warner, *The Rise and Fall of Intelligence: An International Security History* (Washington, DC: Georgetown University Press, 2014), 260.

14. See Peter Grose, *Gentleman Spy: The Life of Allen Dulles* (Boston: Houghton Mifflin, 1994); James Srodes, *Allen Dulles: Master of Spies* (Washington, DC: Regnery, 1999); Bevan Sewell, "The Pragmatic Face of the Covert Idealist: The Role of Allen Dulles in US Policy Discussions on Latin America, 1953–61," *Intelligence and National Security* 26, no. 2 (June 2011): 269–90; Stephen Kinzer, *The Brothers: John Foster Dulles, Allen Dulles, and Their Secret World War* (New York: Times Books, 2013).

15. Gordon Goldstein, "Book Review: 'The Brothers,' on John Foster Dulles and Allen Dulles, by Stephen Kinzer," *Washington Post*, November 14, 2013.

16. Douglas Waller, *Wild Bill Donovan: The Spymaster Who Created the OSS and Modern American Espionage* (New York: Free Press, 2011).

17. Matthew Aid, *The Secret Sentry: The Untold History of the National Security Agency* (New York: Bloomsbury, 2009).

18. Christopher Moran, *Company Confessions: Revealing CIA Secrets* (London: Biteback, 2015), 116.

19. Ibid., 195.

20. Christopher Moran, *Classified: Secrecy and the State in Modern Britain* (Cambridge: Cambridge University Press, 2013), 289–94.

21. Kim Sengupta, "A Spy in Speedos: Wife Blows Cover of MI6 Chief on Facebook," *Independent*, July 9, 2009.

22. Richard Aldrich and Rory Cormac, *The Black Door: Spies, Secret Intelligence and British Prime Ministers* (London: HarperCollins, 2016).

23. Moran, *Classified*, 66.

24. Ron Morgans, "The Head of MI5 and a Traitor's Grave," *Ron Morgans* (blog), June 23, 2011, http://ronmorgans.blogspot.co.uk/2011/06/head-of-mi5-and-traitors-grave.html.

25. "The Rise and Fall of Burkina Faso's Coup: What You Need to Know," *Guardian*, September 24, 2015, http://www.theguardian.com/world/2015/sep/24/burkina-faso-coup-rise-and-fall-of-what-you-need-to-know.

26. Keith Grint, *Leadership: A Very Short Introduction* (Oxford: Oxford University Press, 2010), 1.

27. Keith Grint, "Problems, Problems, Problems: The Social Construction of Leadership," *Human Relations* 58 (2005): 1467–94; Keith Grint, "The Cuckoo Clock Syndrome: Addicted to Command, Allergic to Leadership," *European Management Journal* 28 (2010): 306–13.

28. William B. Howieson and Howard Kahn, "Leadership, Management and Command: The Officer's Trinity," in *Air Power Leadership: Theory and Practice*, ed. Peter W. Gray and Sebastian Cox (Norwich: HMSO, 2002).

29. Grint, "Problems."

30. For an analysis of Kennedy's leadership during the Cuban Missile Crisis, see ibid., 1481–83.

31. Niccolò Macchiavelli, *The Prince*, trans. George Bull (London: Penguin, 1999), 17–31.

32. Grint, *Leadership*, 4–5.

33. Ibid., 2

34. Grint, "Cuckoo Clock Syndrome," 307.

35. Grint, *The Arts of Leadership* (Oxford: Oxford University Press, 2000), 6–7; Grint, "Problems," 1469.

36. For an analysis of Adolf Hitler's leadership, see Grint, *Arts of Leadership*, 289–358; Grint, *Leadership, Management and Command: Rethinking D-Day* (Basingstoke: Palgrave Macmillan, 2008).

37. Ian Kershaw, *Hitler 1889–1936: Hubris* (London: Penguin, 1998), 156.

38. Grint, "Problems," 1570–71.

39. Grint, *Arts of Leadership*, 350.

40. Max Weber, *Economy and Society* (Berkeley: University of California Press, 1978).

41. Ibid. See also Grint, *Leadership*, 94.

42. Grint, *Arts of Leadership*, 410.

43. Alan Judd, *The Quest for C: Mansfield Cumming and the Founding of the Secret Service* (London: HarperCollins, 1999).

44. Richard Norton-Taylor, "Sir Mansfield Cumming, First MI6 Chief, Commemorated with Blue Plaque," *Guardian*, March 30, 2015.

45. Richard J. Samuels, *Machiavelli's Children: Leaders and Their Legacies in Italy and Japan* (Ithaca, NY: Cornell University Press, 2003), 9.

46. Grint, *Arts of Leadership*, 350–51.

47. Sarah Helms, *A Life in Secrets: Vera Atkins and the Lost Agents of SOE* (London: Abacus, 2006), 295–96.

48. Grint, *Arts of Leadership*, 351.

49. Ibid., 415.

50. Philip H. J. Davies, *Intelligence and Government in Britain and the United States: A Comparative Perspective*, 2 vols. (Santa Barbara, CA: Praeger, 2012).

51. Ibid., 2:2.

52. See Michael A. Turner, "A Distinctive U.S. Intelligence Identity," *International Journal of Intelligence and Counterintelligence* 17, no. 1 (2004): 42–61; Michael A. Turner, *Why Secret Intelligence Fails* (Washington, DC: Potomac Books, 2005).

53. Michel Herman, *Intelligence Power in Peace and War* (Cambridge: Cambridge University Press, 1996); Philip H. J. Davies, "Ideas of Intelligence: Divergent Concepts and National Institutions," *Harvard International Review* 24, no. 3 (Fall 2002): 62–66.

54. Thomas Powers, "The Rise and Fall of Richard Helms," *Rolling Stone*, December 16, 1976.

55. Matt Schudel, "William Odom: Obituary," *Washington Post*, June 1, 2008.

PART I

American Spy Chiefs

1 Studying Religion with William Donovan and the Office of Strategic Services

Michael Graziano

William "Wild Bill" Donovan remains a legendary figure in American intelligence history. As one of Donovan's colleagues, echoing the sentiment that would come to be associated with his memory, later recalled, "Bill Donovan is the sort of guy who thought nothing of parachuting into France, blowing up a bridge, pissing in Luftwaffe gas tanks, then dancing on the roof of the St. Regis Hotel with a German spy."[1] Donovan lived an eventful life: he won the Medal of Honor in World War I, argued cases before the US Supreme Court, and of course, led the Office of Strategic Services (OSS). President Dwight Eisenhower famously called him "the last hero."[2]

This essay considers a different side of the OSS chief, one not as often discussed: William Donovan, scholar of religion. Under Donovan's leadership the OSS worked with religious groups and came to think about "religion" as a category of strategic concern in American intelligence. Donovan's actions during World War II illustrate the value placed on religious intelligence by the OSS. Donovan presided over an intelligence organization that prioritized the study of religion and its applications in intelligence work. Yet while the OSS developed close working relationships with religious groups and institutions, the information gleaned from this intelligence was filtered through intelligence officers who often denigrated foreign peoples and ideas even as they sought to understand them. As a result, the OSS was occasionally hamstrung by the very assumptions it sought to promote.

The species of religious information sought by Donovan and the OSS does not necessarily refer to knowledge of the theological, dogmatic, or doctrinal (though knowledge of these things had their place in intelligence gathering, to be sure). Donovan was broadly interested in cultural intelligence, particularly the relationship between religion and society. Donovan and his senior officers assumed religion to be key in understanding any population since it provided one way to access knowledge of the institutions, rules, and groups that structured social life in foreign areas of the world in which the OSS, and the military it supported, operated.[3] Donovan's experiences during the war convinced him that religious intelligence would be a growth industry in the postwar world. Donovan's interest in religious intelligence was part of the larger relationship between the American defense establishment and American religious institutions during World War II and the Cold War. Early versions of these relationships were present in Donovan's organization of operations in Italy and North Africa during the Second World War, especially those involving religious groups. Donovan's interest in religion stemmed in part from his early life and career.

Donovan's Religious Background

Born and raised a Catholic, Donovan was a product of the last great systematized attempt to keep American Catholics out of political power in the United States. Donovan's family heritage traced to Ireland by way of the Irish shantytowns that dotted nineteenth-century Buffalo, New York. Though his family dropped the "O" from their name—transitioning from the O'Donovans of County Cork to the Donovans of Buffalo—they did not drop their religious affiliation.[4] Donovan was an Irish Catholic and a Republican at a time when that made him something of an oddity among both, and he acquired extensive experience with anti-Catholicism in the US federal government. His legal career took off after President Calvin Coolidge had appointed him to the Justice Department, and Donovan eventually became assistant to the attorney general. The limits of his upward mobility became apparent during the presidential election of 1928. The *New York Times* reported that Donovan was the "prime favorite" to be Republican Herbert Hoover's running mate.[5] Yet party insiders had trouble deciding whether a Catholic on the Republican ticket would hurt or help their chances against the Democratic nominee, the Catholic Al Smith. Eventually, they decided against nominating Donovan. The climate of the general election testified to the wisdom of their decision, as Al Smith's campaign was savaged by anti-Catholic protests and attacks in the media. One joke went that after Al Smith had lost the election, Pope Pius XI received a one-word telegram: "Unpack."[6]

Donovan's fortune failed to improve after the election. As Hoover built his cabinet, Donovan was widely rumored to be the new president's choice for attorney general.[7] Newspapers reported the appointment as all but formally announced, and these rumors sparked a popular backlash against the possibility of a Roman Catholic leading the Justice Department.[8] Hostile editorials in the newspapers and protests by the Ku Klux Klan inflamed these

Photo 1.1 Action Man: With his brash style of leadership, OSS chief General "Wild Bill" Donovan earned admirers and enemies in equal measure. *Library of Congress*

opinions.[9] The idea that a Catholic and an opponent of Prohibition would serve as the nation's highest lawyer was unthinkable to many Americans.[10] Already frustrated by his failure to secure the vice presidential nomination, Donovan had pinned his hopes on the appointment. He had to settle for the position of deputy attorney general instead. This was an experience Donovan would not soon forget. After these disappointments Donovan did not divert attention away from his Catholic identity. He spoke openly of the need for more Catholics, and people familiar with Catholicism, in the US government. Donovan argued that America needed Catholic leaders at a "national" rather than simply a "parochial" level.[11]

This experience had important consequences for Donovan's later career, including his time spent leading the OSS. First and foremost, it led Donovan to appreciate the value of religious information. For example, when Donovan worked in the Department of Justice, he led one of the most successful raids of the Prohibition era, seizing a great deal of illegal alcohol and money. Nonetheless, his detractors pegged him as an anti-Prohibition activist because his religious affiliation was associated with that position. From Donovan's point of view, this assumption on the part of his political detractors was a costly mistake—in assuming that all Catholics behaved a certain way, they lost out on a well-qualified candidate to lead the Department of Justice. (For those familiar with Donovan, it will not come as much of a surprise that Donovan was a firm believer that the best person for any job was Donovan.) And it was not only Protestants who mistook Donovan: when Donovan ran unsuccessfully for the New York governorship in 1932, he discovered that some of his fellow Catholic citizens saw him as insufficiently Catholic. Donovan's lifestyle choices—not least that he was wealthy—made him stand apart from much of American Catholic culture in the interwar period. Donovan married a Protestant, for example, and his children were not educated in parochial schools. There were even whispers that because they had only two children, the Donovans must be using contraception—claims that weakened his Catholic credentials, regardless of their veracity.[12]

The story of Donovan's early career is part of the larger history of the relationships among the United States, the Vatican, and Catholicism. Until World War II these relationships had been marked by a peculiar mixture of apathy and tension. Except during the Spanish-American War and World War I, American leaders had rarely given any thought to the Vatican at an official level.[13] At the same time, American history through World War II was marked with a rich and vibrant history of popular anti-Catholicism that made itself known in American law, politics, and culture.[14] This was not new either: the American republic itself was birthed in the midst of Catholic conspiracies, and the specter of papal scheming was a mainstay of American Protestantism thought in the nineteenth and early twentieth centuries.

Donovan possessed the strategic knowledge that comes from being *in* power but not *of* it, and this understanding contributed to Donovan's effectiveness as an intelligence leader. Appreciating the value of religious information—acknowledging the complexity of religious identity, in this case—allowed Donovan to conceptualize Roman Catholicism and the Vatican in different ways than did many of his non-Catholic colleagues in the upper echelons of American government. Donovan understood that religious identity was not deterministic. From his own experience, he knew that being Catholic did not necessarily make one opposed to Prohibition or supportive of Fascism. The iron-strong link between lay Catholics and the Vatican, often assumed to be unbreakable by those Americans with little to no knowledge of Catholicism, Donovan understood to be far less restrictive.[15] While Catholics' place in American culture would change rapidly after the war, Donovan's Catholicism marked him as an outsider through the 1940s.[16]

As a result, Donovan's leadership had two consequences for the relationship between religion and American intelligence. First, Donovan's actions as head of the OSS helped to normalize defense relations with the Catholic Church, which contributed to the growing sense of the United States as a religiously diverse nation. Second, as religious expertise grew in importance after World War II, the seriousness with which the OSS treated religion and religious knowledge would be called on as a model for future American intelligence endeavors. These developments were visible across a number of OSS operations, but two in particular stand out: Catholicism in Europe and Islam in North Africa.

Religion in Operations

Donovan is often remembered as a zealous man of action in American popular culture and in the history of American intelligence. Make no mistake: Donovan was fond of both cloaks and daggers. But there was another, analytical side to the man. William Colby, an OSS officer and future Central Intelligence Agency (CIA) director, was no stranger to the shadows either. Yet when Colby remembered the ceremony in which Donovan pinned a Silver Star on his chest at war's end, it was Donovan's comments about OSS's brainpower that remained in Colby's memory. "During the final ceremony," Colby recalled, "Donovan referred first to his scholars and research experts in describing the OSS 'team' and only secondly mentioned the 'active units in operations and intelligence who engaged the enemy in direct encounter.' In this he reflected his unique contribution to American intelligence, that scholarship was its primary discipline, that the acquisition of information was to serve it, and that its paramilitary adventures were an adjunct to its authority and expertise in secret machinery."[17] No part of OSS better demonstrated Donovan's idea that scholarship should be the "primary discipline" of American intelligence than the Research and Analysis Branch (R&A).

Of the many scattershot OSS activities, perhaps the most consistently useful was R&A.[18] Donovan himself recalled how "most of our intelligence came from good old-fashioned intellectual sweat."[19] R&A assembled an impressive array of specialties under its roof during the course of the war. The wide variety of OSS operations tasked R&A with acquiring knowledge both broad and deep. The group was run by William L. Langer, the renowned diplomatic historian and chair of Harvard's History Department. Turning to the universities for personnel made sense given the eclectic diversity of information demanded by the OSS. Expertise in Persian history, German economic policy, and Brazilian politics was hard to find outside the ivory tower. Langer and other R&A leaders dispatched letters to their colleagues still in academia, requesting the names of their graduate students and PhDs who would be willing to serve their country—"a few good boys who will ruin their health for about $2,000 per annum."[20] The appeal was successful, and R&A was filled with future intellectual heavyweights. Members of R&A included eight future presidents of the American Historical Association, five future presidents of the American Economic Association, one future director of the American Council of Learned Societies, numerous leading area studies specialists, and two Nobel laureates.[21]

Stanley Lovell, head of OSS's scientific development, explained after the war, "Those of us in applied sciences, working with tangible tools to meet the subtle demands of the resistance forces in Europe and Asia were, I think, inclined to belittle the work of this academic group. How wrong we were. It was intelligence at its best, and it had never been done before—until Bill Donovan created it."[22] Work in R&A was challenging, and not always because of the subject matter. A division chief charged with corralling these unruly academics into productive pursuits wryly observed to his charges, "For reasons I do not profess to understand . . . it appears easier to get out a 250-page epitome of what Europe will be like in 1986, to be delivered tomorrow morning at 830" than "a 2-page summary of what you most want to know about the job you're doing."[23]

Lovell later recalled about R&A, "They assembled an incredible mass of information about practically every nation in the world: its history, geography, political and economic structure, its ethnology, ecology, and other ologies too numerous to mention."[24] Developing religious expertise appealed to the OSS, and the organization used R&A to research and collect religious information on a number of fronts.[25] Chief among these information targets was the Catholic Church. The church was maligned in popular American culture for the very reasons that made it a tantalizing intelligence asset for OSS: it was involved in politics, it had tremendous financial resources, and it had outposts across the globe. The OSS's working experience with the Vatican encouraged further operational relationships with other religious groups. This connection shaped how the OSS thought about religion and about the possibilities for relationships between the American government and religious groups.

Donovan and Catholicism in OSS Operations

From an early stage in the war, Donovan saw religion as a backdoor into fortress Europe. Beyond studying the situation with R&A, Donovan took more active measures as well. Donovan dispatched Allen Dulles to work with various European Protestant groups, including the World Council of Churches.[26]

Yet those relationships did not approach the scale and level of cooperation that the OSS had with Catholic groups and institutions, including (but not limited to) the Vatican. The relationship between Donovan's OSS and the Vatican was extensive and developed over the course of the war. For example, within months of Donovan's appointment as Coordinator of Information—the office that preceded the creation of the OSS—Donovan sent a memo to President Franklin Roosevelt outlining an arrangement that Donovan had worked out with the pope's apostolic delegate in Washington, DC. While the delegate stressed to Donovan that the Vatican's official policy must be "strict neutrality," he also told Donovan that the Vatican would make available to the Americans information from the Vatican's various delegates "all over the world."[27] In describing the delegate's motivation to Roosevelt, Donovan explained that the pope's representative "recognizes that a Hitler victory might well mean a modern Avignon for the Papacy."[28]

The services Donovan rendered were sometimes as useful to the Vatican as they were to the Americans. Donovan responded to a request by Francis Cardinal Spellman, the archbishop of New York and the most prominent Catholic in the United States, to ship "various commodities" to the Vatican. Donovan provided navicerts, a kind of commercial passport that allowed Cardinal Spellman's cargo to pass through the British blockade of Nazi Germany without the costly (and perhaps embarrassing) risk of search and seizure.[29] To be sure, it did not hurt to have Cardinal Spellman and members of the Vatican Secretariat of State grateful to Donovan. These actions also aided the Vatican's own intelligence gathering since one of the greatest challenges the Vatican faced during the war was a lack of communication security.[30] In his review of Vatican intelligence during the war, David Alvarez recounts how before Rome fell to the Allies, Pope Pius XII had often been so out of the loop on world events that his chief source of news proved to be summaries provided by the British ambassador to the Vatican, drawn from the ambassador's listening to BBC News on his personal radio.[31]

As the war progressed, Donovan had several personal audiences with Pope Pius XII. Judging from Donovan's memos to Roosevelt, these audiences could cover a range of topics. In one meeting, Donovan and Pius discussed specific intelligence issues, such as "the question of the Japanese embassy placing their radio transmitter in the Vatican" as well as geopolitical developments more broadly, including "communism, Germany, Russia," and Roosevelt's 1944 reelection campaign (Pius "expressed great interest in your re-election," Donovan wrote to the president).[32] While Donovan could be irritated with much of Pius's perceived "fence-sitting," Donovan admitted that he liked Pius "immensely as a person."[33] For his part, the pope made sure to tell Donovan to pass along to President Roosevelt "all my heart's affection."[34] These actions convinced Donovan and the OSS of the goodwill that the Church felt for the Allied cause.

Even in terms of then-recent history, this marked an abrupt change: during the Spanish-American War and World War I, American leaders had assumed that the Vatican quietly supported America's enemies. While there was much of the same thought in the early days of World War II, Donovan's OSS was instrumental in proving that just the opposite was the case. For example, in a memo of sufficient importance for Donovan to pass it on to President Roosevelt, the OSS assessment of the Vatican by early 1944 was that "the Vatican is a sure source of aid in [the] fight against the Germans. . . . Diplomatically, the Vatican insists on its neutrality. Actually, the Church in Italy is actively pro-Allied."[35] Donovan and his senior staff saw a Catholic Church that was eager to cooperate with American aims, even if that Church could not say so publicly. Roosevelt, reading with interest much of OSS's reporting on the matter, was inclined to agree.

Donovan helped to develop the intelligence relationship between the United States and the Vatican during World War II, and his skills were also called on to maintain the relationship when it came under strain. Perhaps in part because of his Catholicism, Donovan was apt to notice things that his colleagues may have overlooked. When Allied bombs began falling on Italy, Vatican buildings occasionally suffered collateral damage. Though they were not intentionally targeted by Allied Air Forces, Donovan was aware that intentions were not particularly relevant to how Catholics around the world might view the damage. An OSS memo outlines how Axis propaganda was capitalizing on damage to the Vatican and Castel Gandolfo in order to argue that "U.S. troops do not respect Catholic property" and that the once god-fearing nations of the West were now subservient to Soviet atheism.[36] Donovan was keen to avoid this perception, aware that both Vatican neutrality and the popular opinion of American Catholics were necessary to the war effort. The OSS proposed battling against this perception in the news media and drew up a plan to "disseminate news throughout Europe by all available means, including underground channels."[37] Part of the "all available means" drawn up in this plan almost certainly included a Catholic news and intelligence network carefully cultivated by Donovan since the early days of the war. Known variously as the Catholic International Press or the Center of Information Pro Deo (CIP), this represented Donovan's biggest operational success with regard to the Vatican.

Within the OSS, American engagement with CIP was known as Operation Pilgrim's Progress. The CIP was a Catholic journalism network with correspondents scattered across Europe. The group was dedicated to using information management tools to reestablish "the place of God in public life."[38] It was run by the Belgian Catholic priest Father Felix Morlion. Adamantly opposed to Nazi Germany, Father Morlion was forced to flee Belgium after the German invasion of the Low Countries. He soon found himself living in exile in Lisbon, where his attempts to start a new branch of CIP were frustrated by Portuguese authorities. Donovan learned of the priest's plight through friendly contacts in Rome and decided to intervene. With the help of Allen Dulles, Donovan arranged to have Morlion moved from Lisbon to the safety of New York City. Donovan personally met with Morlion and hammered out a working arrangement between their two organizations.[39] Father Morlion reactivated his network of Catholic journalists using the nearly $2,000 per month provided by Donovan.[40]

While this arrangement was certainly a boon to CIP's circulation, it also provided Donovan access to Father Morlion's network of Catholic journalists scattered throughout occupied Europe. Unbeknownst to the journalists working for Father Morlion, their dispatches and unpublished notes were routed through OSS Headquarters, where Donovan and others sifted through them for useful intelligence.[41] Indeed, the OSS often tasked Morlion to acquire specific information from his network of religious journalists, and some of these requests likely struck the reporters as strange. While not all of the reports were useful (they often were suggestive of little more than Catholic theological infighting about the value of things such as public education in Belgium), they represented a window into occupied Europe as well as the papacy. The value of Father Morlion and his network increased when, after the Allies had liberated Rome, the OSS arranged to move Morlion so that he could continue his reporting from the Vatican.[42]

Not everything went according to plan, of course. One of the most embarrassing moments in the OSS's brief existence, the Vessel affair, developed out of its desire to cultivate intelligence on the Vatican. OSS officers bought Vatican documents from a source code-named Vessel—documents that were later proved to be forgeries. In the meantime, though, many in the OSS Rome office put a great deal of trust in the material, sending it along to Donovan. The documents, in turn, were treated with the highest secrecy and wound up on the desk of President Roosevelt.[43] Donovan was an eager consumer of this information and wrote numerous cover letters to Roosevelt introducing each new bit of Vessel insight.[44] Donovan's excitement was understandable since the documents appeared to contain a wealth of geopolitical intrigue. Among much else the reports contained information about Japanese war plans that, if accurate, would have proved incredibly valuable. It was only after an investigation by James Angleton,[45] then head of the OSS counterintelligence branch in Rome, that the Vessel source was deemed problematic.[46] The Vessel affair demonstrated both how difficult it was to get quality information from inside the Vatican and how important this information was in Donovan's OSS.

Donovan and Islam in OSS Operations

Donovan's approach—gathering and exploiting elements of culture that some of his colleagues saw as frivolous or irrelevant—extended beyond Italy and the Catholic Church. North African Islam provides one striking example of how the American government, engaged in total war on a global scale, turned to little-understood religious systems and ideas of foreign peoples in order to incentivize those people to act in accordance with American foreign policy. Yet the OSS's perception of Islam was colored largely by its officers' and informants' tendency to understand non-Christian religions through the lens of Christianity.

Carleton Coon, an anthropologist who worked under cover for the OSS, illustrates many of these conflicting impulses. Early in the course of the war, Donovan sent Coon to North Africa to survey the nomadic Muslim tribes that were then nominally under French rule. Coon's peacetime career in anthropology corresponded neatly with Donovan's image of the ideal spy: "You can hire a second-story man and make him a better second-story man," Donovan explained. "But if you hire a lawyer or an investment banker or a professor, you'll have something else besides."[47] So it was with Coon, who was there to study the local population—studies he pursued alongside his intelligence operations. Coon's position as a well-respected Harvard anthropologist provided an adequate cover for many of the activities the OSS wanted him to perform, such as supplying guns to the French Resistance and taking the political temperature of the indigenous Muslim population.

Coon was far from the only academic Donovan recruited.[48] "Donovan made a fetish of acquiring distinguished college professors," recalled Lovell.[49] Yet Coon's appointment reads like the plot of a particularly bad movie: Coon, an Ivy Leaguer and Social Darwinist with an interest in race science and no background in intelligence, was instructed to "busy myself with Arab affairs, to find out what the Arabs were thinking and how they could best be influenced."[50] The episode, at least by Coon's own account, went far better than one might expect. One representative story from Coon's time in North Africa is his attempt to translate President Roosevelt's Flag Day speech into Arabic. The plan was to distribute this translated address among the various Muslim tribes in Morocco, thereby presumably instilling in them a great deal of loyalty to the Allied cause. Coon remembered how: "Browne [Coon's colleague] and I would reword the English in a more Arabic-sounding way, and Gusus [another colleague] would sing out an Arabic poetical version and then write it down. Every time Mr. Roosevelt mentioned God once, we named Him six times; and the result was a piece of poetry that might have come out of the Koran."[51] Coon does not record the reaction of any Muslims to this message, though it seems doubtful that they mistook the words of Franklin Delano Roosevelt for Qur'anic poetry. Still, Coon remained convinced that Islam was the key to motivating the indigenous population to rise up against the Axis. The text of another one of Coon's propaganda messages, addressed to Moroccan Muslims in anticipation of the Allied landings, is particularly striking in this regard:

> This is a great day for you and for us, for all the sons of Adam who love freedom.
>
> Behold. We the American Holy Warriors have arrived. Our numbers are as the leaves on the forest trees and as the grains of sand in the sea.
>
> We have come here to fight the great Jihad of Freedom.
>
> We have come to set you free.[52]

Coon's attempt to leverage Islamic ideas in the service of the Allied cause failed in its main objective: preparing for the Allied landings in North Africa. Coon prophesied 80,000 Muslims would rise up in Morocco to aid the American army when it washed ashore.[53] That number, needless to say, proved exaggerated.

Coon's haphazard effort to utilize Islam in the service of OSS intelligence-gathering speaks to another issue with the "religious approach" in OSS (and later, CIA) operations. While Donovan seems to have understood that religious identity is not irretrievably bound up with specific behaviors, this realization appears to have applied less to religious groups with which American intelligence officials were less familiar, such as Islam. In his biography of Donovan, Anthony Cave Brown argues that, under Donovan's direction, Coon "controlled" various Muslim tribes "through their religious brotherhood."[54] This is almost certainly an exaggeration born of a misunderstanding of Islam, perpetuated by both Coon and later historians. Still, while Coon's efforts can be fairly understood as clumsy propaganda, the way in which he and his colleagues went about it— self-consciously mimicking the poetical nature of the Qur'an—is a testament to the value that Donovan's OSS placed on systems of religious knowledge.

A "Religious Approach" in Intelligence

By the summer of 1945, planning for the postwar world was well under way. A key concern of Donovan's was the status of American intelligence after the war. Would the OSS be maintained? Would another federal intelligence agency be created in its place? During this time Donovan received a memo about postwar intelligence planning from his OSS colleague Ferdinand Mayer. Mayer wanted to know, "What are we going to do about the religious approach?"[55]

This is, perhaps, not something one would expect Donovan and his team to be discussing as they planned for their institutional future. Yet strange as it may seem, concerns about religion factored into Donovan's considerations. Questions about the role of the "religious approach" in a new postwar intelligence model make sense for an organization that regularly dealt with religious groups and institutions. Donovan and Mayer had both been ardent supporters of Pilgrim's Progress, a plan they saw as providing US decision makers with information unavailable to any other government on Earth. Judging from the exchange between Mayer and Donovan, OSS leaders were eager to continue pursuing religious contacts. Indeed, they had a global religious reach in mind. Mayer wrote to Donovan, "What are we going to do about the religious approach? This includes not only Pilgrim' s Progress and the Catholic world but the ideas Javelin and I have had with regard to the orthodox church, the Mormon picture in Europe in general and Germany in particular and whatever development we can work out in the Moslem and Hindu worlds and indeed throughout the Far East."[56] The perceived importance of "religious approaches" was in no small part due to the dividends paid by Donovan's investments in religious information. For Donovan, religion was more than extraneous cultural details. William Casey, a young OSS officer long before he headed the CIA under President Ronald Reagan, later recalled that Donovan "realized, earlier and better than most, that 'stranded' information was not much good. It had to be analyzed, dissected, and fitted into the larger whole that modern warfare required."[57]

By mid-1945 Donovan was already making arrangements to staff and fund an OSS Religion Office to be headquartered in New York City. Mayer explained to Donovan that while the staff at the Religion Office might start out doing non-religion tasks, once they got into their jobs "my guess is that very shortly this business would claim their full attention."[58] This memo and the plans for an OSS Religion Office are useful artifacts for thinking through the relationship between the OSS and religious institutions during the Second World War. While Donovan's plans were never put into practice—President Truman axed the OSS a few months later—the memo demonstrates that American intelligence leaders' interest extended to the full variety of world religions. The context for this exchange is also important since it occurred during a period of rapid jostling for postwar budgetary spoils. Donovan and his staff were eager to secure a permanent central intelligence organization that could continue the OSS's work once the war was over. Religion, at least for some among the OSS leadership, was key to that plan and to the bureaucratic arguments necessary to secure it. Handling "religion" was understood to be a strength of the OSS, and Donovan foresaw a role for it in any future organization. As Mayer wrote to Donovan, "It remains my view that the religious approach, aspects of which none of the regularly constituted agencies such as State, War, or Navy could effectively or properly operate, is one of the super-secret activities that the Central Agency could best manipulate."[59]

Donovan's concerns were prescient. Religion would quickly become a concern of the OSS's successor, the CIA. Before the decade was out, American intelligence officials would again work with the Vatican, this time to massage the outcome of the 1948 Italian elections.[60] A few years later the CIA found itself in South Vietnam, trying to make sense of Vietnamese Catholicism, Buddhism, and indigenous traditions such as Hòa Hảo and Caodaism.

Donovan's actions had consequences on the home front as well. The actions that Donovan arranged for the OSS—while not expressly aimed at doing so—contributed to lessening anti-Catholicism in the upper echelons of the American defense establishment. American Catholics were understood as strategically valuable in a new way. To be clear, these changes were not made to accommodate Catholics per se. Nor was the OSS the only cause of this change. That Donovan was aware of anti-Catholic sentiment in the US government and American culture, while also buying in to the sometimes overly grandiose assumptions about the intelligence capabilities of the Vatican, is a testament to the curious context in which American Catholicism found itself in the wartime United States. While there was certainly much to recommend the Vatican as an intelligence asset during World War II, the perception of the papacy as the best-informed office on the planet stems in part from many of the same attempts within the United States to exoticize Catholicism as illiberal, undemocratic, and anti-American that cost Donovan the position of vice president. Yet while the lure of the Vatican as a unique intelligence asset draws from the same kind of assumptions that helped fuel American anti-Catholicism, Donovan himself was not given to anti-Catholic conspiracy. It may be more accurate to understand Donovan as an American Catholic who, though a product of his time and place, also knew and understood the institutional value of the Catholic Church on the world stage.

The OSS's interest in religion is best explained by placing OSS within its political, cultural, and bureaucratic context during the war. The wartime relationship between William Donovan's OSS and religious groups is one good example of how scholars of intelligence, and of American history, can come to a sharper understanding of broad changes in American culture by considering the involvement and influence of the American intelligence apparatus since World War II.

Notes

1. Quoted in Walter L. Hixson, *Parting the Curtain: Propaganda, Culture, and the Cold War, 1945–1961* (New York: St. Martin's Press, 1998), 3.

2. Anthony Cave Brown, *The Last Hero: Wild Bill Donovan* (New York: Times Books, 1982), 2.

3. I am drawing on Bruce Lincoln's "polythetic and flexible" definition of religion, focused on what Lincoln takes to be the four most important components of religion: "discourse, practice, community, institution" (ix). See the introduction in Bruce Lincoln, *Holy Terrors: Thinking about Religion after September 11*, 2nd ed. (Chicago: University of Chicago Press, 2003).

4. Douglas C. Waller, *Wild Bill Donovan: The Spymaster Who Created the OSS and Modern American Espionage* (New York: Free Press, 2012), 9.

5. Richard V. Oulahan, "Three Quit Lowden Ranks," *New York Times*, June 11, 1928.

6. Quoted in Robert A. Slayton, *Empire Statesman: The Rise and Redemption of Al Smith* (New York: Free Press, 2007), 309.

7. William J. Vanden Heuvel, "Donovan, William J. (Wild Bill)," in *The Yale Biographical Dictionary of American Law*, ed. Roger Newman (New Haven, CT: Yale University Press, 2009).

8. Richard V. Oulahan, "Morrow Pressed by Leaders to Head Hoover's Cabinet," *New York Times*, January 21, 1929.

9. "Hoover Pays Visit to Coolidge Again," *New York Times*, January 10, 1929.

10. L. C. Speers, "Problems That Confront President Hoover," *New York Times*, March 10, 1929.

11. "Donovan Sees Need for Church Leaders: Holds Spiritual and Cultural Promotion Should Be on Nation-Wide Basis," *New York Times*, March 1, 1935.

12. Cave Brown, *Last Hero*, 124.

13. David Alvarez, *Spies in the Vatican: Espionage and Intrigue from Napoleon to the Holocaust* (Lawrence: University Press of Kansas, 2002), 125.

14. There is a large body of work on this topic within American religious history. See, for example, Philip Hamburger, *Separation of Church and State* (Cambridge, MA: Harvard University Press, 2004); Elizabeth Fenton, *Religious Liberties: Anti-Catholicism and Liberal Democracy in Nineteenth-Century U.S. Literature and Culture* (New York: Oxford University Press, 2011); Tracy Fessenden, *Culture and Redemption: Religion, the Secular, and American Literature* (Princeton, NJ: Princeton University Press, 2006).

15. The history of Catholicism in America is rife with the assumption by majority-Protestant Americans that American Catholics took their orders directly from the Vatican. For the vast majority of US history, this assumption grossly overstated the strength of the relationship between the Vatican and lay American Catholics.

16. For more on these changes, see Kevin M. Schultz, *Tri-Faith America: How*

Catholics and Jews Held Postwar America to Its Protestant Promise (New York: Oxford University Press, 2011).

17. Quoted in William Egan Colby and Peter Forbath, *Honorable Men: My Life in the CIA* (New York: Simon & Schuster, 1978), 55–56.

18. The Research and Analysis Branch is one of the most interesting parts of the OSS; it is also one of the parts least studied. For exceptions to this, see Rhodri Jeffreys-Jones, *Cloak and Dollar: A History of American Secret Intelligence* (New Haven, CT: Yale University Press, 2003), 146; Barry M. Katz, *Foreign Intelligence* (Cambridge, MA: Harvard University Press, 1989).

19. Quoted in Katz, *Foreign Intelligence*, 1.

20. Quoted in ibid., 9.

21. Robin Winks, *Cloak and Gown: Scholars in the Secret War, 1939–1945* (New Haven, CT: Yale University Press, 1996), 495–98; Katz, *Foreign Intelligence*, 203.

22. Stanley Lovell, *Of Spies and Stratagems: Incredible Secrets of World War II Revealed by a Master Spy* (Englewood Cliffs, NJ: Prentice-Hall, 1963), 183–84.

23. Quoted in Katz, *Foreign Intelligence*, 4.

24. Lovell, *Of Spies and Stratagems*, 183.

25. Richard Dunlop, *Donovan: America's Master Spy* (Chicago: Rand McNally, 1982), 325.

26. John C. Hughes to William Donovan, October 17, 1944, Director's Office Records, NARA Microfilm Publication M1642, Roll 80, National Archives and Records Administration (NARA); Allen Dulles to William Donovan, October 7, 1944, Director's Office Records, NARA Microfilm Publication M1642, Roll 80, NARA.

27. William Donovan, Memorandum for the President No. 265, February 18, 1942, Director's Office Records, NARA Microfilm Publication M1642, Roll 22, NARA.

28. Ibid.

29. Francis Spellman to William Donovan, December 3, 1941, Director's Office Records, NARA Microfilm Publication M1642, Roll 105, NARA.

30. Alvarez, *Spies in the Vatican*, 277.

31. Ibid., 274.

32. William Donovan and Franklin Roosevelt, July 3, 1944, Director's Office Records, NARA Microfilm Publication M1642, Roll 30, NARA.

33. Quoted in Waller, *Wild Bill Donovan*, 258.

34. Donovan and Roosevelt, July 3, 1944.

35. OSS Spec. Det. G-2, "The Military Significance of Political Conditions in Rome," February 21, 1944, RG 226, Entry 210, Box 313, Folder 5, NARA.

36. David Williamson to William Donovan, "Suggested U.S. Action to Combat Anti-Allied Sentiment among Catholics Resulting from Vatican Bombings," March 23, 1944, Director's Office Records, NARA Microfilm Publication M1642, Roll 98, NARA.

37. Ibid.

38. Felix Morlion, *The Apostolate of Public Opinion* (Montreal: Fides, 1944).

39. Felix Morlion, "Rapport Sur Les Activities Du Reverend Pere Morlion Dans La Domaine de La Guerre Psychologique," July 4, 1942, Anna M. Brady Papers, Box 2, Folder 24, Georgetown University Manuscripts.

40. Waller, *Wild Bill Donovan*, 257.

41. While in theory the CIP correspondents were ignorant of OSS involvement, the OSS did suspect that occasional lapses in operational security allowed certain correspondents to assume (correctly) broader American involvement in their work. See Frederic Dolbeare to Homer Hall, "'H.J' Reports," April 25, 1945, RG 226, Entry 210, Box 415, Folder 6, NARA.

42. Frederic Dolbeare to Allen Dulles, November 9, 1944, RG 226, Entry 210, Box 363, Folder 4, NARA.

43. For a helpful overview of the Vessel affair, see Timothy Naftali, "Artifice: James Angleton and X-2 Operations in Italy," in *The Secrets War: The Office of Strategic Services in World War II*, ed. George Chalou (Washington, DC: National Archives Trust Fund Board, 1992).

44. Many of these reports (sometimes termed "Black Reports" or "Special Black Reports") bear such introductions. One such example is William Donovan to Franklin Roosevelt, February 16, 1945, Director's Office Records, NARA Microfilm Publication M1642, Roll 119, NARA.

45. Richard Harris Smith argued in 1972, and maintains in his 2005 reprint, that Vessel was not actually an intelligence failure but rather an intelligence coup. Smith argues that the source for Vessel was none other than Cardinal Montini, the future Pope Paul VI. This account relies primarily on Smith's interviews, however, and this interpretation is largely discounted by other histories of the OSS. See Richard Harris Smith, *OSS: The Secret History of America's First Central Intelligence Agency* (Berkeley: University of California Press, 1972). Max Corvo, who worked for the OSS in Rome, wrote a memoir in which he echoes some of the claims made by Smith. While there is little evidence to substantiate these claims, the claims made by Smith and Corvo are representative examples of the politically charged nature of much OSS involvement with the Vatican. See Max Corvo, *Max Corvo: OSS Italy, 1942–1945*, rev. ed. (New York: Enigma Books, 2005), 243–44.

46. Naftali, "Artifice," 232. The Vessel source was only partially discontinued, and its fabricated output was later used to US advantage during the Italian elections of 1948. See Winks, *Cloak and Gown*, 387.

47. Quoted in Evan Thomas, *The Very Best Men: Four Who Dared: The Early Years of the CIA* (New York: Touchstone, 1995), 9.

48. Though the study only addresses graduates of Yale University, a detailed account of the relationship between academics and the OSS can be found in Winks, *Cloak and Gown*.

49. Lovell, *Of Spies and Stratagems*, 183.

50. Carleton Stevens Coon, *A North Africa Story: The Anthropologist as OSS Agent, 1941–1943* (Ipswich, MA: Gambit Publications, 1980), 11.

51. Ibid., 14.

52. Quoted in Cave Brown, *Last Hero*, 252–53.

53. Waller, *Wild Bill Donovan*, 137.

54. Cave Brown, *Last Hero*, 252.

55. Ferdinand Mayer to William Donovan, "'Religious Approach' Memo," July 17, 1945, RG 226, Entry 210, Box 338, Folder 1, NARA.

56. Ibid.

57. Quoted in William H. Webster, "Remarks by William H. Webster, Director of Central Intelligence, at the Dedication of a Statue of General William J. Donovan, CIA Headquarters Building," October 26, 1988, Item #CK3100274754, Declassified Documents Reference System, http://eresources.loc.gov/record=e1000193~S9.

58. Mayer to Donovan, "'Religious Approach' Memo."

59. Ibid.

60. There is a great deal of work on American involvement in the 1948 Italian elections, including James E. Miller, "Taking off the Gloves: The United States and the Italian Elections of 1948," *Diplomatic History* 7, no. 1 (1983): 35–56; see also Kaeten Mistry, *The United States, Italy and the Origins of Cold War: Waging Political Warfare, 1945–1950* (Cambridge: Cambridge University Press, 2014).

2 The Alternate Central Intelligence Agency

John Grombach and the Pond

Mark Stout

> I don't think it is possible to diagnose Col. Grombach's activities
> without being personal, since the very characteristics of the man
> affects his work.
>
> —Office of Strategic Services official, 1942

John Grombach is one of the most remarkable and yet least known intelligence leaders in American history. He headed an organization known informally as the "Pond" that conducted espionage operations for the US government from 1942 to 1955. Senior Central Intelligence Agency (CIA) official Lyman Kirkpatrick accurately described the Pond as "one of the most unusual organizations in the history of the Federal Government. It developed completely outside of the normal government structure, used all of the normal cover and communications facilities normally operated by intelligence organizations, and yet was never under any control from Washington."[1]

Grombach championed a philosophy of intelligence and corresponding intelligence practices that were grounded (he thought) in experience and the intelligence wisdom of the ages. However, his intelligence structures were utterly demolished by the CIA. Not only was Grombach ultimately unsuccessful, he and his ideas about intelligence were almost completely forgotten. Indeed, standard histories of the CIA and American intelligence give Grombach and the Pond scant coverage, often in footnotes, if they mention the topic at all.[2] Grombach appears more frequently in specialized histories.[3] In fact, aside from two articles by the present author and a collaborator, the only published works to go beyond generalities about Grombach have been David Barrett's history of the CIA and Congress, Douglas Waller's biography of William Donovan, and Christopher Simpson's treatment of the American relationship with Nazis after World War II, which mischaracterizes Grombach as excessively sympathetic to the fallen Axis power.[4]

This lack of scholarship can be explained by the fact that before 2010, it was difficult to write anything extensive on Grombach. The records of his organization were not available in the National Archives, having been pruned from the files or never sent to the archives in the first place. Nevertheless, occasional stray documents could be found in the records of other agencies. Christopher Simpson was able to obtain Grombach's personnel file from the US Army via the Freedom of Information Act in the 1980s. However, by the time the present author requested it in the early 2000s, the army was unable to locate the file.[5] An initial request for the Federal Bureau of Investigation (FBI) file on Grombach produced a collection of papers so extensively redacted as to be nearly useless, though a later request produced somewhat more results. There were also penny packets of correspondence to and from Grombach in collections of private papers across the United States. Overall it was not a rich record.

In 2001, however, a sizable collection of papers belonging to the Pond was found in a private building in Virginia and made its way to the CIA, which, in due course, declassified virtually all of them and transferred them to the National Archives, where they were opened to scholars in 2010.[6] Finally, it was possible to write with depth and nuance about Grombach.

Drawing on these records this chapter examines how Grombach developed an espionage capability out of normal channels, how he fecklessly endeavored to thwart the postwar intelligence plans of Harry Truman, and how he developed his organization into a bitter rival to the CIA even while taking the agency's money. Finally, it shows why Grombach's efforts were doomed to failure.

Grombach the Man

Jean (later John) Valentin Grombach was born in New Orleans in 1901 to a French family. At the age of eighteen, he renounced his French citizenship when he went to West Point as part of the Class of 1923. There he was an athletic star, but he also made himself unpopular during his plebe year for challenging upperclassmen to fights over perceived insults.[7] The day before graduation he was found to have eight more demerits than allowed. The authorities decided to give him his bachelor of science degree but deprive him of a commission.[8] Nonetheless, he soon wangled a commission and spent five years on active duty as an infantry officer, including service in the Panama Canal Zone, where he was assistant provost marshal and assistant G-2, his first involvement with intelligence.[9]

Photo 2.1 The Pugilist: Known for his combative approach with rival organizations, boxer, fencer, and businessman John Grombach headed the War Department, later private intelligence organization the "Pond" from 1942 to 1955. *US Government Photograph, Private Collection*

Grombach left the army in 1928 and joined the New York National Guard. In 1929 he went to work for a subsidiary of CBS and Paramount Publix.[10] He later claimed that he had kept his hand in the intelligence business during this time, however, with a "highly confidential secret" project for the State Department in 1937; no details of this work can be found today. Apparently, the project involved a study of British intelligence, and Grombach boasted of connections to Sir Basil Thomson, the disgraced British former police and intelligence officer.[11] In 1941 Grombach was brought back onto active duty in the army's 27th Infantry Division.[12] After Pearl Harbor, however, friends recommended him to the army's G-2, and as a result, he was ordered to Washington and assigned to intelligence duties in February.[13] His intelligence career would last until 1955.

John Grombach was a man's man. In his youth he worked as a bouncer at a brothel in New Orleans.[14] Of imposing physique, he was an accomplished athlete who particularly loved the combat sports. He was an excellent fencer who was active in the sport at the national and international level for decades.[15] He became a fixture at the New York Athletic Club (NYAC). His boxing prowess was legendary at West Point, and the love of the ring stayed with him for the rest of his life. He was a friend of several boxing greats, most notably Jack Dempsey, and shared a financial interest in a young French boxer named Laurent Dauthuille, who fought a legendary title fight against Jake LaMotta. Grombach claimed to have been a stunt double in jousting scenes in Hollywood movies, and he had several wives, none of whom seem to have impinged much on his life.[16]

A 1946 War Department performance appraisal nicely encapsulates Grombach. He got "Superior" ratings on most criteria and the highest possible rating for "Physical Activity and Endurance." However, he got damningly mediocre ratings for "Cooperation," "Intelligence," and "Judgment."[17] In fact, his personal style tended toward the combative and self-important. He was quick to take offense and to question the motives and competence of anyone with whom he disagreed. He was also a virulent anti-Communist who was deeply hostile to the New Deal and flirted with Joseph McCarthy–style conservatism. Grombach had many loyal friends, but the number of people who disliked him was larger. A report from the FBI's New York field office following a meeting with Grombach in 1955 stated that he "loves to talk but . . . constantly emphasizes the clandestine nature of his operations and how important it is that as few persons as possible should learn of them."[18] He was also a wheeler-dealer who, in the words of a detractor, "live[d] on contacts."[19] He was constantly thinking about how to work an "angle"—seemingly one of his favorite words—on whatever issue was at hand.

His masculine persona and political views come through clearly in his extensive writings, almost none of which was about intelligence. For instance, during World War II, he wrote an article for *Infantry Journal* on hand-to-hand combat called "Kill or Get Killed."[20] Later he penned an essay on dueling for *American Mercury*.[21] In 1956 and 1957 he also coauthored a book-length manuscript about Communism titled "Red Rule" that was never published.[22] At work with the Pond, he had a tendency to write long melodramatic letters and memos in which he and his organization were portrayed as aggrieved parties having to suffer through the double dealing and incompetence of others.

Creation of the Pond

Grombach's Pond was a product of the interagency rivalries surrounding William Donovan's Coordinator of Information (COI), which was founded in 1941. The concerned national security agencies had agreed that "secret intelligence" (espionage) would be the purview of COI. However, jealousies quickly began to accumulate, and in early March 1942 the Chiefs of Staff adopted as their position a proposal to abolish the COI and distribute most of its parts among the armed services. Under this proposal, the fate of the secret intelligence function would be decided by the services and the State Department.[23]

The army's G-2, Maj. Gen. George Strong, was especially committed to disestablishing the COI, and as early as 1941 he wanted to encroach on Donovan's turf by creating his own espionage service.[24] Meant to be more discreet than the COI, Strong's service was to work with the State Department and undercut the rationale for a COI clandestine collection unit. In the spring of 1942, Brig. Gen. Hayes Kroner, the head of the War Department's Military Intelligence Service, the operational component of the Military Intelligence Division (MID), was directed to establish a secret intelligence organization. Presumably Strong issued these orders, but it appears that Army Chief of Staff George C. Marshall or his deputy gave the ultimate approval while cautioning that there was to be no written record of the decision.[25] The COI survived the challenge to its existence and by October 1942 had been reorganized as the Office of Strategic Services (OSS). But the organization now had a secret rival.

Kroner selected Grombach to head this new organization "particularly because [he] could take such instructions, that all of this should be done under the terms of the highest secrecy."[26] Soon Grombach had in place a structure that would continue largely unchanged for nearly thirteen years. It operated under the "real cover" of the Contact and Liaison Section and later the Coverage and Indoctrination Branch of the Military Intelligence Service. The Pond's initial budget allocation from the War Department was $150,000 per year, although that grew to $300,000 per year by the end of the war.[27] By contrast the 1943 OSS budget was $35 million and grew somewhat over the next two years.[28] In an unusual move the Pond augmented its wartime-appropriated budget with money from foreign business interests, though the extent of that funding is unknown.[29]

Grombach's Theory of Intelligence

Grombach's personality very much shaped the Pond. So too did his philosophy of intelligence. Of course, this philosophy matured over time, but from the earliest days it had four pillars: experience, secrecy and security, competition, and the use of all available information.

Experience
Grombach emphasized experience in the intelligence business: both personal experience and historical experience. In a draft letter to President Truman, he

expressed the view that "few Military or Naval personnel know either intelligence, international affairs, or possess the flair for intelligence—a fifth sense, like showmanship in the entertainment industry—an innate quality which cannot be acquired but which must be nurtured by lots of experience."[30] Of course, Grombach believed that he had extensive personal experience, dating back to the early 1920s, and rare skills. Given that the FBI presented itself to the public as a manly, all-American agency that had existed since 1908, Grombach unsurprisingly found it to be "an efficient and professional organization." However, he ridiculed the newcomer agencies—the OSS and CIA—for their amateurism and lack of security.[31]

Grombach found the CIA to be run in a manner at variance with the espionage wisdom of the ages. The 1950s are remembered today as a period of freewheeling covert action by the CIA, but Grombach was dealing with the parts of the agency that conducted clandestine espionage operations and reported the resulting information to analysts. This he found extremely frustrating. "Clandestine work . . . from time immemorial has called for imagination, personal initiative, complete independence and innovation [and] is hampered and handicapped by rules, regulations, procedures, red tape and bureaucratic angles," he complained of the CIA in 1954.[32] Another of his continuing complaints was that the CIA's dual role as the sole authorized collector of clandestine intelligence and as an analytic agency was unsound and had been proved misguided by historical experience.[33]

Secrecy and Security

Grombach valued secrecy and security almost to the point of fetish. This becomes clear in his views on British intelligence. Though Grombach was Anglophobic, he had great respect for British intelligence. He believed that the British had been conducting intelligence operations for centuries and that they had been successful largely because the British government had never admitted that it even had intelligence organs. As Grombach put it in 1947, "For a secret intelligence setup up to be really worthwhile it should be really secret."[34] This the publicly avowed OSS and CIA were not. By contrast, the existence of the Pond remained secret long after the organization had ceased to function.

In terms of its internal procedures, the Pond thought it important to apply "super-security," as any "well-trained" espionage organization would. One of the tenets of super-security was not to trust even those who are supposed to be one's friends. A Pond training manual from about 1947 contrasted the group's ways on this point to those of agencies such as the OSS or the CIA: "Normal intelligence's basic assumption is that 'everybody on one side of the fence is all right, and those on the other side of the fence are all questionable but partly all right; the fence is nice and high and big, with no cracks or knotholes to look through, and everyone stays on his own side of the fence.' In S[ecret] I[ntelligence], of course, nothing can be so simple as that."[35]

Grombach's emphasis on security was reflected in the Pond's internal records, which generally used cryptonyms and codewords. The security these offered was often paper-thin, however. For instance, Germany was "Pabst." Grombach was "Mr. Dale." George C. Marshall was "Mr. Ney," a reference to Marshal Michel Ney, one of Napoleon's subordinate commanders, and Congress was "Mound," an apparent reference to Capitol Hill. Grombach's obsession with security was also reflected in his refusal to share the identities of the Pond's sources with the CIA, even when the agency was paying his bills.

Grombach clung to the ideal of secrecy to the very last, as illustrated by an incident in May 1954. The FBI had disseminated a report to the Office of Naval Intelligence (ONI) containing derogatory information about someone of interest to the Navy, but the information had originated with the Pond. ONI went to the FBI seeking more information. Apparently, the FBI asked Grombach if he would speak with the Navy officials. However, even though Grombach knew the Pond would probably soon go out of business (as indeed happened), he refused to meet with ONI officials because he did not want them to know that the Pond existed.[36]

Competition
Grombach's Pond was created to compete with the OSS during World War II. During the second half of its existence, it competed with the CIA. Grombach believed competition with these large agencies was critical because a monopoly on espionage might lead to another Pearl Harbor. "The nature of secret intelligence," he wrote in 1946, "is such that even if the angels went into it they would not coordinate with any other angels that were also . . . operating in this field."[37] A lack of competition in clandestine collection, he argued several years later, "removes the possibility of any check up being made, as to accuracy, upon the lone survivor in that field."[38] He also argued that a "monopoly of covert intelligence collection by one organization" could leave the United States blind for a year or more in case of a security breach. Furthermore, such a disaster was made all the more likely because "a large organization centrally located is easily penetrated."[39]

The Use of All Available Information
Grombach also had well-developed thoughts about what information was gathered by intelligence agencies and how that information contributed to national security. To him, intelligence was "knowledge of what exists and what goes on in the world." This knowledge, he said, "forms the basis for

action and planning for the protection of our national interests and security."[40] Grombach believed that every bit of intelligence might turn out to be useful and thus should be made available to analysts.[41] That last belief led Grombach into searing battles with both the War Department and the CIA, which he thought were far too quick to discard—that is, not disseminate to analysts— reporting that came from doubtful sources, did not seem useful, or ran contrary to an existing analytic line.

Grombach believed that these battles derived in part from other agencies' misunderstanding of the nature of different kinds of intelligence. He noted that intelligence could be overt or covert. The former included open-source material and information gleaned from personal observation or available to State Department officials. Overt intelligence, Grombach thought, formed perhaps 80 percent of what the US government needed to know.[42] Such information from an unspecified source or a source of little standing was not reliable, whereas information from a known and authoritative source was highly reliable.[43] By contrast, covert intelligence was information that the rulers of a target country sought to keep secret and that, therefore, needed to be acquired by clandestine methods. Though covert intelligence made up only a small part of what the government needed to know, it was as important as overt intelligence because it "furnish[ed] the necessary missing pieces to make the jig-saw puzzle of the intelligence picture complete." Furthermore, covert intelligence could not be judged on its face or by the standing of the source but only with reference to the source's track record. "Covert intelligence," Grombach maintained, "can only stem from individuals who obtain it by stealth and who must, for their own safety, keep their identities a secret." Moreover, "frequently, [covert sources] are not . . . reputable persons." They might also be individuals of low status.[44]

How the Pond Operated

The OSS primarily used official cover, usually military but sometimes also diplomatic, for its case officers overseas.[45] As it has long admitted, the CIA also made extensive use of official cover for its case officers.[46] Grombach, however, generally preferred his case officers to have no visible connection with the US government. He described the basic modus operandi of the Pond this way: it employed the "classical British and German indirect method, namely the use of large international business organization[s], prominent business and professional men as the nuclei for systems, nets, and cells of agent observers who, in turn, can employ direct agents and informers."[47] Often these "agent observers" were not Americans. Grombach liked to claim that Pond personnel and their recruited sources worked primarily for reasons of patriotism or anti-Communism, not remuneration. In 1947 he even claimed that the Pond "never purchased" information.[48]

Though the Pond started out as part of the War Department General Staff and later became a private company working on contract for government agencies, its essential methods remained the same throughout its existence. Sometimes, the central Pond office in New York City communicated directly with its personnel overseas through letters and, more often, through State Department channels. (By contrast, the OSS and CIA had their own separate communications channels.) In fact, the department was a vital partner in the Pond's operations throughout the group's existence. However, the Pond did not liaise at all with the State Department's intelligence branch. Instead, during the war the Pond's day-to-day point of contact at the department was the Division of Foreign Activity Correlation (FC), which reported during World War II to Assistant Secretary Adolf Berle, who remained a Grombach ally for many years afterward. Later the Office of Security took over the liaison role.

American embassies in countries in which the Pond operated would usually have one witting foreign service officer (FSO) chosen for his or her discretion. In some cases that FSO would be the Pond case officer. More often the FSO supported the case officers by providing access to the State Department's communications systems, both the diplomatic pouch and the cable system.[49] Cables were double encrypted, first in a Pond cipher and then in a departmental cipher, and sent to FC for passage to the Pond.[50] When Pond headquarters received intelligence information from overseas, it would format it and forward it to the agency for which it was working. This agency would, if it chose, disseminate the report to interested parties without any indication that it came from the Pond, facilitating the seeming nonexistence that Grombach found so important. The original reporting from the field would usually be retained in New York for about six months before it was purged from the files, leaving the source-sanitized reports that the Pond sent to its sponsoring agency as the only record.[51]

Despite its small size and budget, Grombach's organization was quite productive. By early 1946 it claimed to have disseminated 2,807 field reports since its establishment. It also claimed to have a presence in 32 countries and some 800 field personnel.[52] Though the organization suffered some lean years between 1948 and 1951, the overall trend throughout its lifetime was growth in production, geographic reach, and personnel.

The War Department Years: Battling the OSS and War Department

Grombach's vision of intelligence work was infused with the idea of combat, and he fought innumerable battles during the time that the Pond was affiliated with the War Department. Moreover, the post–World War II demobilization hollowed out the Pond just as it did the rest of the defense and intelligence infrastructure. The Pond managed to survive by going even further underground, this time into the private sector, and thanks to the willingness of the State Department—under circumstances that are still unclear—to secretly sponsor it, it survived past 1947, when it should have gone out of business with the establishment of the CIA.

From the beginning the Pond's creators imagined it existing in opposition to the OSS. In Grombach the Pond had a leader who loathed the OSS to his very core and never missed a chance to battle it. Early on, for instance, the Pond wrestled away from the OSS an important cooperative relationship with the Dutch electronics firm N.V. Philips Gloeilampenfabrieken, which had subsidiaries all over the world, including in occupied territory.[53] The OSS was a wartime agency, and thus, its officers had less intelligence experience than Grombach had—at least that was Grombach's opinion. Accordingly, he criticized the OSS harshly for amateurism and insecurity. In fact, a Pond training manual written shortly after the war recommended that Pond trainees read books about OSS operations because "these . . . are generally valuable 'in reverse.' . . . [T]hey often make a tremendous show of 'the wrong way and the wrong attitude.'"[54] Grombach contrasted the secrecy with which the Pond operated with the record of the OSS, which seemed to him to revel in publicity. He described the OSS as a "joke throughout the world" and believed that "the publicity in the US press about the OSS and secret intelligence has resulted in a much closer surveillance of our embassies, legations, and missions throughout the world and made some of our operations more difficult."[55] Grombach further believed that the OSS discovered and compromised some of the Pond's sources to allied and neutral countries.[56] He also believed— correctly—that the OSS was penetrated by Communists and hopelessly insecure.[57] Given the menace that it believed the OSS posed, the Pond kept close tabs and even maintained files on the OSS and its operatives, whom they codenamed "the Dons," an apparent reference to William Donovan.[58]

The culmination of Grombach's rivalry with the OSS came in early 1945. President Franklin Roosevelt solicited a study of the OSS from a member of his staff, Col. Richard Park Jr. It is not clear how Grombach was connected with Park, but Grombach conducted an "ex parte investigation" as input to the Park report. Park's work castigated William Donovan and the OSS for their bumbling and incompetence, and much of the report's content came from Grombach's "monograph." Roosevelt never lived to see the Park report, but it probably played a role in President Truman's decision to abolish the OSS immediately upon the end of World War II.[59]

From his first months in the War Department, Grombach was on the trail of subversion, not only in the OSS but also in the Departments of State and

War. His bête noire was Col. Alfred McCormack, the G-2's director of intelligence. McCormack was a New York lawyer who had been called in by his former law partner, Assistant Secretary of War John McCloy, to study the War Department's signals intelligence (SIGINT) processes after the Pearl Harbor debacle. Having succeeded at that task, McCormack received a commission as a colonel in the Army, making him senior to Grombach, who had far more military experience, a fact that irritated Grombach.[60] Initially made the deputy chief of the unit that analyzed SIGINT materials, McCormack later led a reorganization that brought all-source analysis to the MID. McCormack violated three of Grombach's basic principles of intelligence: He lacked intelligence experience, he violated security by allowing pro-Communist personnel to work for him, and he did not believe it imperative to use all available information.

As the war progressed, Grombach was dismayed to find that the majority of the Pond's reports pertaining to the Soviet Union and Communism were being "eliminated" by McCormack's subordinates, that is, they were not passed on to other analysts or otherwise used. In an effort to confirm his suspicions, Grombach struck a deal with the sergeant who ran McCormack's incinerator and thereby collected the eliminated reports so that he could read the comments that McCormack and his staff had written on them.[61] Then in 1945 the MID did a study that cast doubt on the utility of much of the Pond's reporting. Grombach and his associates responded with charges that the negative ratings on much of their reporting resulted from the pro-Communist leanings of many of McCormack's people. Grombach also called for an inspector general investigation of his opponent and for good measure accused numerous officials throughout the government of being pro-Communist. The officials he targeted included some who were later proved to have been Soviet agents, such as Alger Hiss and Harry Dexter White, as well as Maurice Halperin and Carl Marzani of the OSS. Grombach also included some figures who were later controversial, such as John Service and Owen Lattimore, as well as a great number of others who almost certainly were innocent, including future Supreme Court Justice Abe Fortas, then a senior official at the Department of the Interior. Grombach accused two subordinates of McCormack of being Soviet agents.[62] Not long thereafter, suspecting that McCormack was receiving unauthorized information from inside the Pond, Grombach set up a sting by leaving phony derogatory information about himself available to two of his own subordinates whom he distrusted. When McCormack used that information against him, Grombach sacked his disloyal subordinates.[63]

Grombach seemed out of control, so his superiors hauled him on the carpet on June 15, 1945, and accused him of discrediting an officer of the Military Intelligence Service to outsiders and of disclosing classified information without authorization. Grombach denied both allegations, and nothing further came of the matter.[64] However, Grombach was not chastened.

Postwar Battles: The Central Intelligence Group and the National Security Act, 1945-47

The end of World War II led to a massive demobilization of intelligence organizations. Most dramatically, President Truman ordered the OSS disestablished as of October 1, 1945. Nonetheless, he wanted to continue to have a robust national intelligence capability. Specifically, he envisioned an intelligence community with the State Department as its center. While the details were worked out, the OSS's Secret Intelligence (espionage) and X-2 (counterintelligence) Branches were given to the War Department under the name of the Strategic Services Unit (SSU). Meanwhile, the Research and Analysis and the Presentation (graphics) Branches went to the State Department, where they formed the Interim Research and Intelligence Service (IRIS). At the suggestion of Undersecretary of State Dean Acheson, Alfred McCormack was dispatched to the State Department to head IRIS.[65] Truman's plan for a community centered on the State Department soon ran into massive opposition, of which Grombach was a part.

The marriage at the State Department of McCormack and the OSS outraged Grombach, and he immediately fought back. Though Acheson supported the move, some members of Congress were concerned, and many people within State, including Assistant Secretary for Administration Donald Russell and a great many FSOs, opposed it, some on ideological grounds and some on the grounds that the Foreign Service was its own intelligence service and did not need outsiders to tell it what was going on in the world. Grombach attacked on both of these fronts. Already sensing that the Pond might not have a lasting home in the War Department and hoping to lodge the organization in the State Department, Grombach lobbied Russell and also H. Ralph Burton, general counsel for the House Military Affairs Committee, about the benefits of the Pond and the failings of McCormack and the OSS. Grombach appears to have passed to State Department opponents of the plan the story that McCormack had ordered his MID analysts to take a soft line on the Soviet Union.[66] He also shared with the Military Affairs Committee a copy of his input to the Park report and the names of fifteen G-2 officers who had followed McCormack to the State Department whom he suspected of disloyalty.[67] He sent to allies on Capitol Hill a "suggested letter" to Secretary of State James Byrnes objecting to the transfer of Alfred McCormack and OSS personnel to the department without further security checks and again naming certain OSS personnel who had "provable Communist records," as he had in his intra-MID dustup.[68] In March 1946 the House committee made Grombach's charges public, though without naming him. Congress cut all appropriations for IRIS. In April its components were farmed out piecemeal to the regional policy offices at the State Department, and McCormack resigned and went back into private law practice.[69]

With the State Department clearly not inclined or able to take the lead on intelligence, Truman on January 22, 1946, ordered the creation of the Central Intelligence Group (CIG) to coordinate the country's intelligence efforts, particularly strategic analysis and the coordination of intelligence policy across the various agencies.[70] The CIG was advised by the Intelligence Advisory Board (IAB), consisting of the heads of the intelligence agencies, and it operated under the overall aegis of the National Intelligence Authority (NIA), consisting of the secretaries of state, war, and the navy plus the nonvoting director of central intelligence (DCI). Meanwhile, Washington began to debate the terms of legislation that would reform the entire national security apparatus.

As this was going on, the Pond itself felt the impacts of the postwar demobilization. The Pond was far smaller than the OSS and was extraordinarily secret. In fact, there is no evidence that President Truman even knew that it existed. Hence, it slipped under the radar, able to survive owing to the discreet support of senior officials in the War and State Departments even despite Grombach's difficult personality. The Pond was officially deactivated in November 1945, though remnants of its network continued coasting along for some time.[71] In January Grombach was relieved as head of the Coverage and Indoctrination Branch, within which the Pond had last been hidden, and left active duty. He promptly embarked on a dispute about his medical benefits.[72]

This was not really the end of the Pond, however. According to Grombach, in early February 1946, the War Department G-2, Lt. Gen. Hoyt Vandenberg, gave authority for the Pond's reactivation "at least to span the void of one or two years . . . and possibly for continuation either under G-2 and State or under the Central Intelligence [Group] thereafter." Grombach added that Vandenberg "did not desire to know any details of this setup."[73] The Pond was formally reactivated in reorganized form on March 22, 1946.[74] It retained a few personnel in G-2 as a "secret inside liaison and administrative group," but the real headquarters moved to private companies in New York City.[75] The main headquarters seems to have been in a newly created "Universal Service Corporation," which Grombach incorporated in 1947 and which helped him hide intelligence activities underneath legitimate international business consulting.[76]

Though the Pond had secured its position with the War Department, its existence was challenged from outside. Precisely what happened is unclear, but in February 1947 Grombach wrote to a friend at the FBI to complain that the CIG was surveilling him and inquiring with associates about his activities.[77] He blustered that he would go to the press or bring legal action if CIG snooping endangered his business ventures.[78]

Then the Pond found itself in even more dire straits. In mid-1946, after only a few months as G-2, General Vandenberg was named DCI and started to consolidate power in the recently created CIG. In particular, he sought to bring clandestine collection under the auspices of the CIG. Vandenberg took the matter to the IAB, which consisted of the intelligence chiefs of the services, the State Department, and the FBI. The G-2, Maj. Gen. Stephen Chamberlin, opposed the idea but found himself outmaneuvered. In late June the IAB unanimously agreed that centralization should take place, and in early July the NIA agreed.[79] In theory the Pond could have been brought under CIG auspices, but bothered by an alleged security breach within the Pond and probably influenced by Grombach's personality, Vandenberg had no desire to do so. Though he had given the Pond a new lease on life just a few months previously, he now favored its death.[80]

With General Chamberlin's support, Grombach refused to take the Pond out of business. Grombach believed—not without reason—that a number of intelligence failures during World War II, particularly the surprise at Pearl Harbor, had come about because of shortcomings in the sharing and analysis of intelligence. Accordingly, he accepted the idea of the CIG, coordinating intelligence activities and evaluating intelligence. Nevertheless, he was bothered by what he saw as inexperience among CIG personnel.[81] Furthermore, he was utterly unwilling to stand by idly while DCI Vandenberg created a "gigantic, monolithic, all-powerful intelligence trust" by taking over all espionage.[82]

This situation continued into the spring of 1947. In April of that year, Vandenberg and Adm. Roscoe Hillenkoetter (Vandenburg's soon-to-be successor) signed a joint letter to the G-2 that said its secret intelligence operations "should be discontinued with the least practicable delay."[83] Somebody associated with the Pond leaked word to the *New York Times* that the NIA had "compelled the War Department to liquidate its world-wide secret intelligence network" in favor of the CIG and that the dissolution would be "difficult and expensive."[84] Grombach denied responsibility for the leak. In June 1947 Grombach, General Kroner, and another Grombach ally testified before Congress in hearings on the National Security Act of 1947 against allowing the CIA to conduct espionage. They maintained that conducting espionage would warp the CIA's analytic functions and lead to a dangerous monopoly on clandestine collection.[85] The testimony was to no avail. Truman signed the National Security Act of 1947 on July 26, and the CIA supplanted the CIG on September 18, 1947, and became the country's premier espionage organization. Grombach resigned as head of the Pond effective September 30, 1947, though the Pond continued to wind down its business for the next couple of months. The organization formally ceased to exist on December 31, 1947.[86]

Or so it seemed. Actually, Grombach had already found a secret way of keeping the Pond alive. As the Pond was coming to an end as a secret appendage of the War Department, Grombach took his case to the State Department. He briefed Christian Ravndal, the director general of the Foreign Service, and as Grombach recorded afterward, Ravndal "banged the table" and said that the Pond must not be allowed to die. Ravndal allegedly took the case to John Peurifoy, the deputy assistant secretary of state for administration, who had responsibility for security at the department. Peurifoy, impressed with the large number of FSOs already involved, was agreeable.[87] There is no other evidence about internal State Department deliberations on the question of the department taking over the Pond. However, the secretary of state at this time was George Marshall, who had been army chief of staff when the Pond was created and probably was involved in its creation. Now, it seems, Marshall condoned acting behind the CIA's back.[88]

State Department Interregnum (1948-51)

Though the State Department had rescued the Pond from extinction, the group operated on a much-reduced budget. To keep the organization afloat, some of its members worked for no compensation. In addition, the Pond continued its rather unorthodox practice of seeking outside financial support.[89] Although it was inexpensive, the Pond was controversial at the State Department, at least among the few people who knew about it. The fact that the State Department was not supposed to have any such organization must have been of major concern. Foreign Service Officer James McCargar, who had worked with the Pond in Hungary in 1947, recalled that the Pond was the "subject of some burning discussions at the top levels of the Department." Apparently, the department was having trouble hiding the Pond's budget within its own. Ravndal at one point asked McCargar to brief a skeptical Norman Armour, assistant secretary for political affairs, on the merits of the Pond.[90]

The State Department gradually increased the Pond's budgets, though they never approached the levels they had been at during the War Department period. Grombach attributed these budget increases to the high quality of the product provided.[91] However, he also told Adolf Berle, who was now in private legal practice, that he was having a difficult time finding places in the government where his intelligence could safely be used because the Truman administration, like the Roosevelt administration, leaked badly.[92] In any event, by the fall of 1950, the bloom was definitely off the rose in Grombach's relationship with the department. Grombach had a serious dispute with the State Department's intelligence arm, the R Area (the successor to IRIS), which was apparently accusing him of some sort of malfeasance. In September 1950 a diatribe in Grombach's diary described the matter as a hoax, a frame-up, or a Communist plot. He pledged to "deny everything" and warned the R Area against "starting [the] whole business without proper proof," blustering, "We cannot be responsible for blown fuses, arrests, compromise, serious embarrassments to State nor any . . . necessary actions we may have to take to protect ourselves [and] our people."[93]

That same month Grombach approached the G-2 and offered to work for the army again, adding that if the army wasn't interested, perhaps it could recommend to DCI Walter Bedell Smith that the CIA pick up the contract. The army took Grombach's offer seriously but in January backed off after a consultation with J. Raymond Ylitalo, assistant chief of the State Department's Security Division, which by this time had inherited the Pond liaison role. Asked to evaluate the Pond's material, Ylitalo responded that "in all frankness [he] could describe it in only one word, 'crap.'"[94] So, instead of returning to the army, Grombach turned to Adolf Berle. On March 22 Berle gathered Grombach and his deputy; Allen Dulles, deputy director for plans of the CIA; Lyman Kirkpatrick, executive assistant to the DCI; a representative of the deputy undersecretary of state for management; and Ray Ylitalo. In less than a day, a tentative agreement was initialed. The contract was finalized the next month, and the Pond had a new sponsor.[95]

The CIA Period (1951–55)

It must have been difficult for Grombach to subordinate himself to the CIA. He had ridiculed its high public profile, and it was, after all, populated with many OSS veterans. Moreover, working for the CIA involved subordinating himself to Allen Dulles, the head of the CIA's operations side (later deputy director and then DCI). Grombach loathed Dulles, who had supported the centralization of intelligence in 1947, and thought that although Dulles had significant intelligence experience, the Gestapo had "covered him like a tent" when he was the OSS station chief in Switzerland during World War II.[96] In private correspondence Grombach complained bitterly about the "egomania of a really very stupid and morally dishonest tho [*sic*] allegedly religious family": the Dulleses.[97] Throughout the Pond's tenure with the CIA, Grombach was in active correspondence with friendly journalists, members of Congress, and the FBI about agency operational incompetence. He routinely pointed out CIA failures, security breaches, and tradecraft missteps and regularly called for investigations of the CIA and for its role to be limited to analysis so that the various executive branch departments could conduct their own espionage operations abroad.[98]

Nevertheless, the relationship with the CIA was tolerable for a time. Initially, the Pond reported to the Contact Division in the Office of Operations, a relatively overt part of the agency whose job was to ensure that domestic sources of foreign intelligence were exploited. However, in January 1952 the Office of Special Operations (SO)—the component responsible for espionage overseas—took over handling the Pond account, and the relationship quickly soured.[99] The Pond provided SO with reporting from its agents overseas, and SO reports officers would then decide whether the reports should be reformatted and disseminated to analysts around the intelligence community.

Soon, however, SO began to routinely "eliminate" the Pond's reports—that is, they did not disseminate them to analysts—and tempers flared over this and a host of other issues. Among the immediate issues were what Grombach saw as interference with a Pond attempt to recruit the Hungarian minister in Switzerland.[100] Among the deeper issues was that the CIA wanted to have greater visibility into the Pond's operations and impose its methods of operations on the group. Another serious bone of contention was that Grombach and his inner circle continued to be concerned about the security of the CIA and of its operations.[101]

As he had during World War II, Grombach took the decision to eliminate Pond reports as an affront and a sign of incompetence. There were several reasons for the eliminations, all of them disputed. First, the CIA's reports officers saw no value in disseminating reports that duplicated already reported information. In contrast, Grombach saw this as useful confirmation of previous reporting. Second, the CIA sometimes would not disseminate unconfirmed reports. At one point this led Grombach to ask rhetorically, "Shall every report concerning a new fact be eliminated? On the other hand, if that fact has already been reported, our report has to be eliminated because already known."[102] Third, agency reports officers saw no value in disseminating information that seemed trivial. Grombach, on the other hand, believed that it was impossible to judge a priori what information might turn out to be useful in the future; hence the agency needed to be liberal in what it disseminated.[103]

Fourth, Grombach believed that SO declined to disseminate reports that cast a bad light on the CIA or its recruited sources.[104] However, even before the Pond was transferred to SO, Grombach had already started a line of "Dirty Linen" reports on Americans, especially those with CIA connections. These Grombach sent to whomever he deemed appropriate, often including the FBI, the CIA's great rival. The first Dirty Linen report in June 1951 said that "the

CIA in Switzerland is a hotbed of sexual perversion with its principal members all homosexuals" who had been compromised by Soviet intelligence and had betrayed American cipher systems.[105] The CIA ordered the Pond to stop forwarding its reports to the bureau. Grombach did not comply.[106]

Fifth, Grombach believed that the CIA was ideologically biased, inclined to be skeptical of information that cast the USSR, Communists, Socialists, and organized labor in a negative light or that came from sources known for their anti-Communism. Grombach attributed this to the fact that the CIA was disproportionately populated by "college professors." Such people were naive and "because of their background and struggle for existence and their low income naturally tend toward liberal if not Marxist principles."[107]

Sixth, and most important, the Pond's approach to evaluating sources contrasted with that of the CIA. Grombach thought that a source's track record or "box score" was especially important.[108] However, the CIA, having been burned by many fabricators, both individuals and organized "paper mills," liked to examine the operational circumstances that led to information being given to US intelligence. It also liked to scrutinize the source's access to the information.[109] This entailed knowing the source's identity. However, for Grombach the identity of the source was sacrosanct, and to reveal it was a breach of faith. As he had from the very beginning, he steadfastly refused to "card" the Pond's sources and share that information with any outside agency.[110]

Lyman Kirkpatrick, who received the unenviable assignment of liaison to the Pond, later wrote that the group tended to change source descriptions on "the rather paranoid grounds that we would be able to discover the real source if they provided identical descriptions on each report from that source."[111] Grombach also thought that identifying sources would lead to them being taken over by the agency, which "would also destroy the [Pond's] usefulness as a secret intelligence collecting agency and independent check."[112]

The Pond and the CIA contended for the loyalties of one important Hungarian, Dr. László Bartók, a Hungarian diplomat from 1919 to 1947 who dabbled in counterintelligence work. During World War II he was the Hungarian representative to Germany's Croatian puppet state and then a secret envoy sent to Switzerland to contact the Western Allies. With the approval of the Hungarian prime minister, he passed information about the German military to Allen Dulles. After the war he was appointed Hungarian minister to Vienna, where Pond records hint that he maintained "very close contact with the US minister . . . and . . . [the] chief of the CIA in Vienna." The CIA reportedly helped him defect to the West after the Communists took over Hungary in 1947. Under circumstances that are not clear, Bartók started working for the Pond in October 1948.[113] He stayed in Europe until 1951, when he moved to Uruguay still in the Pond service.[114] There he ran operations in Uruguay, Argentina, and Brazil against Communists, Peronists, and Nazis.[115]

However, the CIA spiked much of the reporting from Bartók's network in South America. Particularly irksome to Grombach was the agency's rejection of a stream of reporting indicating that a particular Uruguayan official, whom Grombach believed to be a CIA source, was a Communist. The CIA sent back comments such as "conjecture based on source's evident bias against [the official] who, according to the weight of evidence here, is definitely anti-Communistic." Ultimately, the CIA instructed the Pond to desist "until source sends some proof." Grombach was enraged. In his telling the Uruguayan was later shown to be a Communist.[116] By the fall of 1953, Grombach was complaining to his diary about "falsehoods" about Bartók and blaming the CIA chief in Uruguay for the fact that Bartók could never be sent back to Montevideo because he was "irrevocabl[y] absolutely burned."[117] Oddly, sometime in that year Bartók switched sponsors over to the CIA, taking two agent nets with him. In late 1954, however, he abruptly quit working for the agency. Grombach told the FBI that it was because the Hungarian found the agency "impossible to work with" given their rules, red tape, and poor tradecraft. Grombach complained to Dulles about the matter and hinted darkly that Congress might hear about it, though in fact nothing further came of the dispute.[118]

The End of the Pond

By January 1953 tension was so high that Grombach feared that the CIA might not renew its annual contract, which was up in August. His inclination was to appeal to DCI Smith, with whom he had a generally positive relationship. However, Smith's health was failing, and Grombach decided to wait until a successor was named.[119] Unfortunately for him Allen Dulles took over as DCI on February 26, 1953. The result was a new agreement in August 1953 that cut the Pond's budget by 46 percent.[120] Grombach knew the situation was dire, so he turned to Congress. He took the matter up with conservative Republican senator Styles Bridges of New Hampshire.[121] Grombach also suggested to his friend columnist George Sokolsky—a confidant of Sen. Joseph McCarthy and his right-hand man, Roy Cohn—that if the contract with the CIA expired, "I would like to place my experience, contacts and abilities, and perhaps my organization, at the disposal of Congress."[122] These blandishments soon came to the attention of the CIA, which was already at odds with McCarthy.[123] In July 1953 McCarthy gave the agency a list of twelve alleged security risks among its employees. Kirkpatrick studied the list and realized that "some of the phrases were identical to so-called 'dirty-linen' reports that the [Pond] had fed to us about our own people, and some of the names were identical with those that the [Pond] regarded as sinister."[124] Then, the Pond and the agency entered a vitriolic dispute over the authenticity and importance of some cryptographic materials stolen from an eastern bloc target.[125]

In 1954 the CIA decided that it had had enough of Grombach's scheming and questionable products and would not renew the Pond contract when it ended on August 15. The group was allowed a few months to wind up its business. Kirkpatrick decided to have it out with Grombach, however, and confronted him about his contacts with McCarthy. Kirkpatrick recalled that "after a bit of blustering and blowing," Grombach admitted that he had given information to McCarthy and said that it was his responsibility to do so. He reportedly further admitted that he had offered to put the Pond to work for the junior senator from Wisconsin investigating US government employees.[126]

In late 1954 and into 1955, Grombach tried to find new sponsors, even pitching an old fencing buddy on President Eisenhower's staff and the State Department's R Area. These efforts were unsuccessful. Aside from two last operations that continued into April, the Pond ended its conflict-filled existence on January 1, 1955.[127]

Assessing Grombach

It is interesting to compare Grombach to his rival, William Donovan. Both headed embattled intelligence organizations that ran contrary to business as usual. In Donovan's case this was because the OSS was a largely independent entity that reported directly to the president. As such it was a direct threat to the power and prerogatives of the State, War, and Navy Departments and the FBI. The historical trajectories of the Pond and the OSS were quite different, however. The Pond survived the post–World War II demobilization but lost in the long run and was all but forgotten. By contrast Donovan's organization did not last out 1945 but won in the long run, bequeathing vital components and many personnel, as well as a culture, to the CIA, a truly centralized independent agency that reports to the president.

How do we explain these different outcomes? The OSS came to grief in 1945 for many reasons: it had a high profile, it was opposed by every major department and agency of the government involved in national security, its director was a conservative Republican, and it had drawn heavy fire from the press for, among other things, being a proto-Gestapo.[128] However, Donovan's suggestion that the OSS carry on was an apt proposal owing to the problems that the United States faced in the emerging Cold War. Given the sprawling nature of the Cold War, the huge amounts of intelligence needed to keep the nation safe, and the lessons of Pearl Harbor, it is hard to imagine the United States getting far into the Cold War without a central intelligence organization of some kind. Once Donovan was out of the picture, the government moved swiftly to create the CIA, finishing the job in less than two years.

Grombach, by contrast, ably guided the Pond through the postwar demobilization simply by slipping under the radar, an easy task given the organization's small size and extreme secrecy. Certainly Grombach had enemies, but they were individuals, not cabinet departments, and although Grombach was probably even less in sync politically with President Truman than Donovan was, there is no evidence that Truman knew that Grombach and the Pond existed. In the long run, however, Grombach's Pond solved no pressing problem for the US intelligence community or national security apparatus and indeed posed considerable risks with its uncoordinated operations and potential for falling prey to deception and intelligence hucksters.

Ultimately, how should we assess Grombach as a leader? Arguably, he was a good leader internally. His faith in himself never slipped, and he put together a cohesive group. Certainly he created an organization in his own image. In fact, in reading the records of the Pond, it is impossible to tell where Grombach leaves off and the organization itself begins. Also, he was able to maneuver his organization effectively in a tactical sense. He also showed remarkable leadership and resourcefulness in bringing the Pond through so many hard times, though many of those hard times were of his own making.

Ultimately, however, Grombach was a failure. The Pond went out of existence, and his philosophy of intelligence did not take root in the US intelligence community. Grombach's failures were in part the result of structural factors exacerbated by his philosophy of intelligence. One problem was that many of the factors that allowed the Pond to survive in 1945 contributed to its demise when it gained a powerful enemy in the CIA. The Pond was small and inexpensive and therefore lacked clout compared to the CIA and other agencies that were evolving in a different direction from what Grombach proposed. In addition, the premium he placed on secrecy meant that the organization could not vie for public support in the ways that the OSS and the FBI did, though it did cultivate a few allies in Congress.

Even more damaging was Grombach's personality and lack of strategic skill. Because he led a small organization that propounded views on intelligence that were directly contrary to those of the larger agencies, he should have eschewed conflict. A less confrontational leader might have been able to keep his or her organization alive at the sufferance of the bigger organizations, which, after all, were not fundamentally threatened by the little Pond.

Grombach had a knack for alienating almost everyone who did not work for him. Alpha male sportsman that he was, he never missed an opportunity to lead the Pond into fights. Many of these fights were mere personality clashes that could have been avoided. Others could have been avoided only at the cost of compromising Grombach's philosophy of intelligence. For instance, had Grombach dissolved the Pond in 1947, when the CIA asserted its monopoly over espionage, or had he acquiesced in the 1950s, when the CIA wanted him to divulge the name of his sources, he might have made the right decision, but he would not have been memorable, and the Pond still might not have survived.

In the long run, however, the Pond was probably doomed whatever the quality of Grombach's leadership because of the quality of the reporting produced with Grombach's unusual methods. It is hard to independently judge the quality of a large body of intelligence reporting, particularly from a remove of multiple decades, but it is telling that all three of the agencies that the Pond worked for questioned the quality of its product. Certainly the Pond had no golden human sources to rival a Fritz Kolbe or an Oleg Penkovsky.

In John Grombach, then, we find a flawed leader fighting a probably unwinnable fight. American intelligence was moving in a certain direction and was going to run over any individual who stood in its way.

Notes

The Central Intelligence Agency has reviewed this chapter to ensure that it contains no classified material. The chapter reflects only the views of its author.

Epigraph: Read [?] to Goodfellow, July [8?], 1942, CIA FOIA Electronic Reading Room (CIAFERR), http://www.foia.cia.gov/document/0005374688.

1. Lyman Kirkpatrick, *The Real CIA* (New York: Macmillan, 1968), 148.

2. A few general histories mention Grombach and the Pond briefly. These include Thomas F. Troy, *Donovan and the CIA: A History of the Establishment of the CIA* (Frederick, MD: Aletheia Books, 1981); Tim Weiner, *Legacy of Ashes: The History of the CIA* (New York: Doubleday, 2007); Burton Hersh, *The Old Boys* (New York: Scribner's, 1992). Others, including John Ranelagh, *The Agency: The Rise and Decline of the CIA* (New York: Simon & Schuster, 1986) and Rhodri Jeffreys-Jones, *Cloak and Dollar: A History of American Secret Intelligence* (New Haven, CT: Yale University Press, 2002), do not mention him at all.

3. Peter Grose, *Gentleman Spy: The Life of Allen Dulles* (Amherst: University of Massachusetts Press, 1996) and Charles Gati, *Failed Illusions: Moscow, Washington, Budapest, and the 1956 Hungarian Revolt* (Stanford, CA: Stanford University Press, 2006) both have very brief discussions of Grombach.

4. Mark Stout, "The Pond: Running Agents for State, War and the CIA," *Studies in Intelligence* 48, no. 3 (2004): 69–82; Mark Stout and Katalin Kádár Lynn, "'Every Hungarian of Any Value to Intelligence': Tibor Eckhardt, John Grombach, and the

Pond," *Intelligence and National Security* 31, no. 5 (2016): 699–714, doi:10.1080/02684 527.2015.1088691; David M. Barrett, *The CIA and Congress: The Untold Story from Truman to Kennedy* (Lawrence: University Press of Kansas, 2005); Douglas Waller, *Wild Bill Donovan: The Spymaster Who Created the OSS and Modern American Espionage* (New York: Free Press, 2011); Christopher Simpson, *Blowback: America's Recruitment of Nazis and Its Effects on the Cold War* (New York: Weidenfeld & Nicolson, 1988).

5. I am grateful to Professor Christopher Simpson for sharing with me materials he gathered on Grombach from the US Army through the Freedom of Information Act. Hereafter cited as Simpson papers.

6. Randy Herschaft and Christian Salazar, "Before the CIA There Was the Pond," *Sand Diego Union Tribune*, July 29, 2010, http://www.sandiegouniontribune.com /news/2010/jul/29/ap-impact-before-the-cia-there-was-the-pond/.

7. J. Phoenix, "A Past Olympian Called 'Frenchy,'" *Gray Matter*, August 7, 2008, http://www.westpointaog.org/page.aspx?pid=2916; Earl "Red" Blaik, *The Red Blaik Story* (New Rochelle, NY: Arlington House, 1960), 33–34.

8. "Outline of (Jean) John V. Grombach," Box 6, Folder "Grombach," Charles G. Stevenson Papers, US Military Academy Library Special Collection (hereafter cited as Stevenson Papers).

9. Stout, "Pond," 70; Rose to President, Examining Board for Officers, January 31, 1928, CIAFERR, http://www.foia.cia.gov/document/0005374645.

10. "Outline of (Jean) John V. Grombach."

11. Grombach to the National Intelligence Authority [1946–47], RG 263, Entry P12, Series 1, Box 20, Folder 1, National Archives and Records Administration (NARA). All archival sources in this chapter are from NARA RG 263 except as specifically noted.

12. "Outline of (Jean) John V. Grombach."

13. LaVarre to Miles, December 8, 1941; Grombach to "Bill" [LaVarre], January 31, 1977; Smith to Personnel Officer, G-2, January 24, 1942; Smith memorandum to Adjutant General, February 16, 1942, all in Simpson papers.

14. John Bakeless, "John Valentine Grombach," *The Assembly* 42, no. 1 (1983): 132–33.

15. "History," *USA Fencing*, 2015, http://www.teamusa.org/USA-Fencing/About -Us/History; Photo 111-SC-489385, RG 111, NARA; Fédération Internationale d'Escrime, "History," http://www.fie.ch/download/en%20bref/en/historique%20FIE %20ang.pdf.

16. Grombach to Stevenson, March 25, 1960, Box "Corresp. 1960–1962," Folder "1960," Stevenson Papers.

17. Blocker to Director of Information, March 19, 1946, Simpson papers.

18. SAC, New York to Director, FBI, August 6, 1955, NY 66-6301-45, obtained through the Freedom of Information Act.

19. McGivern to Smullin, March 30, 1953, Simpson papers.

20. John V. Grombach, "Kill or Be Killed," *Infantry Journal*, February 1943, 46–48.

21. John V. Grombach, "Who's a Sissy?" *American Mercury*, August 1955, 31–33.

22. John Bakeless Diaries, entries from October 1 and 13, 1957, December 12, 1956, January 4 and 12, 1957, John Bakeless Papers, New York Public Library.

23. Bradley F. Smith, *The Shadow Warriors: OSS and the Origins of the CIA* (New York: Basic Books, 1983), 117–19.

24. [Grombach], "Draft," [~1946], Entry P12, Box 20, Folder "PP File—Intelligence."

25. "Suggested Memorandum for Mr. Ney [Marshall]," July 15, 1947; Clayton Bissell, note for record, February 27, 1944, Entry P12, Box 20, Folder "PP, 1943–1948 (folder 1 of 2)."

26. *National Security Act of 1947: Hearing Before the Committee on Expenditures in the Executive Departments*, 80th Cong., 54 (1947).

27. Grombach Diaries, August 9, 1949, John V. Grombach Papers, US Military Academy Library Special Collection.

28. Walter Laqueur, *The Uses and Limits of Intelligence* (New Brunswick, NJ: Transaction, 1995), 224.

29. Untitled undated [1947] memo, Entry P12, Box 20, Folder "PP, 1943–1948 (folder 1 of 2)."

30. "My Dear Mr. President," n.d. [1947?], Entry P12, Box 20, Folder "PP File—Intelligence."

31. Ibid.

32. Memorandum to Pat, December 8, 1954, Entry P13, Box 3, Folder "Dahl."

33. "Intelligence: A Study of the Central Intelligence Agency," Box 074083, Folder "CIA—Confidential Memo 1953 & 1954," Styles Bridges Papers, New Hampshire State Archives, Concord, NH (hereafter cited as Bridges Papers).

34. Draft Letter to Mr. Baldwin, [1947], Entry P12, Box 27, Folder "Transcript and Memos."

35. "The Training Division," [~1947?], Entry P12, Box 27, Folder "The Training Division."

36. [Redacted] to SAC, NY, May 17, 1954, NY 66-6301-28, FBI, obtained through FOIA.

37. Dale [Grombach], "(CIG Directive No. 15)," n.d. [1946], Entry P12, Box 20, Folder "PP File—Intelligence."

38. "Intelligence," Bridges Papers.

39. Ibid.

40. Ibid.

41. Blind memorandum, October 14, 1952, Box 57, Folder 1, George E. Sokolsky Papers, Hoover Institution Archives, Stanford, CA (hereafter cited as Sokolsky Papers).

42. "Intelligence," Bridges Papers.

43. "Evaluation Report," Box 074083, Folder "CIA—Confidential Memo 1953 & 1954," Bridges Papers.

44. "Intelligence," Bridges Papers.

45. Michael Warner, *The Office of Strategic Services: America's First Intelligence Agency* (Washington, DC: Central Intelligence Agency, 2002), https://www.cia.gov/library/publications/intelligence-history/oss/art03.htm.

46. See, e.g., Richard Stolz, "A Case Officer's First Tour," *Studies in Intelligence* 37, no. 1, https://www.cia.gov/library/center-for-the-study-of-intelligence/kent-csi

/vol37no1/html/v37i1a04p_0001.htm; Deputy Director (Support) to DCI, March 4, 1957, CIAFERR, http://www.foia.cia.gov/sites/default/files/document_conversions /5829/CIA-RDP80B01676R004300160109-0.pdf.

47. "Aide-Memoire," [1945], Entry P12, Box 19, Folder "Papers to Be Available in Washington."

48. Untitled memorandum, [1947], Entry P12, Box 20, Folder "PP, 1943–1948 (folder 1 of 2)."

49. Stout, "Pond," 72.

50. "Training Division."

51. "Dear Friend," March 10, 1954, Entry P13, Box 2, Folder "Pedro (Montevideo)."

52. [Grombach] to Director of Information, February 18, 1946, Entry P12, Box 20, Folder "PP File—Intelligence."

53. Director of Strategic Services to Joint US Chiefs of Staff, January 22, 1943; Cook to Bruce, January 19, 1943, RG 226, Entry 210, Box 359, Folder 1, NARA.

54. "Training Division."

55. "Aide-Memoire," [1947?], Entry P12, Box 19, Folder "Papers to Be Available in Washington."

56. [Grombach], "Draft," [ca. 1946] Entry P12, Box 20, Folder "PP File—Intelligence."

57. Memorandum No. 69 to the State Department, July 19, 1944; Memorandum No. 44 to Mr. Lyon, January 13, 1944, Entry P12, Box 26, Folder "State Liaison, 1943–46"; "Memorandum on High Level Intelligence," June 13, 1947, Entry P12, Box 29, Folder "Washington File." John Earl Haynes, Harvey Klehr, and Alexander Vassiliev, *Spies: The Rise and Fall of the KGB in America* (New Haven, CT: Yale University Press, 2009), is the most comprehensive account of Soviet espionage in the United States during the period. See especially chapters 4 and 5.

58. See especially RG 263, Entry P12, Boxes 5 and 6, NARA. Grombach contemplated similarly tracking CIA officers, though no traces of such files remain, if they ever existed. "Memorandum re Dale's Trip to Washington March 4 and 5, 1947," Entry P12, Box 20, Folder "PP File—Intelligence."

59. "OSS," [1945], Entry P12, Box 18, Folder 1: "Monograph on OSS 1942–1945"; "My Dear Mr. President," [1947?], Entry P12, Box 20, Folder "PP File—Intelligence"; [Grombach] to the National Intelligence Authority (Through the Director), Entry P12, Box 20, Folder "PP, 1943–1948 (folder 1 of 2)"; Michael Warner, "The Creation of the Central Intelligence Group," *Studies in Intelligence* 39, no. 5 (1996): 112–13. A comparison of the "monograph" and the Park report indicates that large portions of the latter are taken nearly verbatim from the former. The Park report can be found in the Rose A. Conway Files at the Harry S. Truman Presidential Library.

60. Grombach to Reid, April 14, 1946, Entry P16, Box 1, Folder "1641 File."

61. Stout, "Pond," 73.

62. Ibid., 73–74; Grombach to Director of Information, April 20, 1945; "Note to Colonel Cox," June 9, 1945; "Persons in Key Government Positions," Entry P16, Box 1, Folder "Draft—Supplement to Answer to Project 1641," Grombach Papers.

63. "Dear Friend," June 18, 1945; "Attached Is Copy of . . . ," [June, 1945]; C to J,

June 18, 1945; "Memorandum for Colonel Stevenson," June 15, 1945; Grombach to Director of Information, June 15, 1945, Entry P16, Box 1, Folder "Draft—Supplement to Answer to Project 1641."

64. Stout, "Pond," 74.

65. R. Harris Smith, *OSS: The Secret History of America's First Central Intelligence Agency* (Berkeley: University of California Press, 1972), 334.

66. Martin Weil, *A Pretty Good Club: The Founding Fathers of the U.S. Foreign Service* (New York: W. W. Norton, 1978), 244.

67. State Department Memorandum No. 123, August 10, 1945; State Department Memorandum No. 134, November 8, 1945; State Department Memorandum No. 138, November 30, 1945, Entry P12, Box 26, Folder "State Liaison, 1943–46"; Grombach to H. Ralph Burton, May 8, 1946; Grombach to Burton, September 18, 1946, Entry P12, Box 20, "Folder 3 "PP File—Intelligence"; Grombach Diaries, notes for a letter to "Bill" on pages for April 20–25, 1946.

68. "Draft of a Suggested Letter," RG 46, Records of the Senate Internal Security Subcommittee, name file "McCormack, Alfred," NARA.

69. "House Group to Drop 'Pro-Soviet' Hearings," *New York Times*, March 26, 1946, 24; "Denies Bureau Aides Have Pro-Soviet Bias," *New York Times*, March 21, 1946, 12; Smith, *OSS*, 334.

70. Truman to Secretaries of State, War and Navy, January 22, 1946, in *Foreign Relations of the United States, 1945–1950: Emergence of the Intelligence Establishment* (Washington, DC: US Government Printing Office, 1996), 178–79 (hereafter cited as *FRUS*.)

71. [Grombach] to "Pat," February 20, 1947, "Draft," Entry P12, Box 20, Folder "PP File—Intelligence."

72. [Grombach] to "Pat," February 20, 1947, Entry P12, Box 20, Folder "PP File—Intelligence"; [Grombach] to James Wadsworth, July 16, 1947, Entry P12, Folder "PP, 1943–1948 (folder 1 of 2)."

73. [Grombach] to Director of Information, February 18, 1946, Entry P12, Box 20, Folder "PP File—Intelligence."

74. Blind memorandum, September 4, 1946, Entry P12, Box 20, Folder "PP File—Intelligence"; "Draft," Entry P12, Box 20, Folder "PP File—Intelligence."

75. [Grombach] to Director of Information, February 18, 1946, Entry P12, Box 20, Folder "PP File—Intelligence."

76. Grombach Diaries, 1947 frontispiece; "Freddy" [Lyon] to Fullerton, July 24, 1947, Entry P12, Box 20, Folder "PP, 1943–1948 (folder 1 of 2)."

77. [Grombach] to Ladd, February 19, 1947, Entry P12, Box 20, Folder "PP File—Intelligence"; [Grombach] to Van[denberg], not sent, February 19, 1947, Entry P12, Box 20, Folder "PP File—Intelligence."

78. [Grombach] to "Pat," February 20, 1947.

79. *National Security Act*, 6, 46; *FRUS*, 369–92.

80. *National Security Act*, 8.

81. "(CIG Directive No. 15)," [1946], Entry P12, Box 20, Folder "PP File—Intelligence."

82. "Intelligence," Bridges Papers.

83. Quoted in Stout, "Pond," 76.

84. Quoted in ibid., 76–77; Grombach to Chamberlin, Entry P12, Box 20, Folder "PP, 1943–1948 (folder 1 of 2)."

85. *National Security Act*, 33, 51, 56.

86. Grombach to Director of Intelligence, War Department General Staff, August 27, 1947, Entry P12, Box 20, Folder "PP, 1943–1948 (folder 1 of 2)"; "Monograph on Project 12-A," Entry P12, Box 19, Folder "(Old) PP."

87. Blind memorandum, Entry P12, Box 20, Folder "PP, 1943–1948 (folder 1 of 2)."

88. Grombach drafted a letter to Marshall on the subject, but it is not clear if he sent it. "Suggested Memorandum for Mr. Ney," July 15, 1947, Entry P12, Box 20, Folder 1 "PP, 1943–1948 (folder 1 of 2)."

89. "Informational Memorandum," June 9, 1953, Box 074083, Folder "CIA—Confidential Memo 1953 & 1954," Bridges Papers.

90. Stout, "Pond," 77.

91. "Informational Memorandum," June 9, 1953, Bridges Papers.

92. Adolf Berle Diaries, September 28, 1948, University of Maryland Library.

93. Grombach Diaries, September 8, 1950.

94. Stout, "Pond," 77.

95. Berle Diaries, March 22, April 6 and 12, 1951.

96. Grombach to Sokolsky, July 22, 1954, Sokolsky Papers.

97. Grombach to Sokolsky, November 6, 1956, Sokolsky Papers.

98. "Intelligence," Bridges Papers. For Grombach's complaints about CIA incompetence, see "Otto John," July 27, 1954; Clement to Bridges, July 28, 1954; "Evaluation Report," Box 074083, Folder "CIA—Confidential Memo 1953 & 1954," Bridges Papers.

99. "Informational Memorandum," June 9, 1953, Bridges Papers.

100. Report for the Director, Central Intelligence Agency, [August 5, 1952], Entry P12, Box 4, Folder "Eyes Only Report to General Bedell Smith 1952."

101. Berle Diaries, August 10, 1951; Untitled notes, also "Statement by Dr. Laszlo Boros Concerning Mr. Eugene Gonda," September 23, 1952, Entry P12, Box 7, Folder "Eckhardt"; Jeff [Eckhardt] to Dale [Grombach], August 26, 1953, Entry P12, Box 12, Folder 5 "Interoffice J Memoranda—1953."

102. "Memorandum concerning Handling of Our Counterintelligence Reports from Uruguay," August 11, 1952, Box 074083, Folder "Confidential Reports on CIA (O'Brien & Grombach) 1954," Bridges Papers.

103. Blind memorandum, October 14, 1952, Box 57, Folder 1, Sokolsky Papers.

104. Stout, "Pond," 78.

105. "Report Dirty Linen #1," June 15, 1951; "Data on American Intelligence in Switzerland," June 16, 1951, P12, Box 5, Folder "Dirty Linen—Z Reports."

106. Stout, "Pond," 79.

107. "Evaluation Report," Bridges Papers.

108. "Intelligence"; "Evaluation Report," Bridges Papers.

109. "Evaluation Report," Bridges Papers; Mark Stout, "Émigré Intelligence

Reporting: Sifting Fact from Fiction," in *Handbook of Intelligence Studies*, ed. Loch Johnson (New York: Routledge, 2006), 264–65.

110. Stout, "Pond," 78; "Intelligence," Bridges Papers; [Grombach] to Director of Information, February 18, 1946, Entry P12, Box 20, Folder "PP File—Intelligence."

111. Kirkpatrick, *Real CIA*, 150.

112. Quoted in Stout, "Pond," 78.

113. "Dr. Laszlo Bartok," May 29, 1953, Entry P12, Box 12, Folder "Interoffice J Memos 1952"; Czikann-Zichy to Eckhardt, August 3, 1951, Entry P12, Box 7, Folder "Eckhardt."

114. "Dr. Laszlo Bartok," May 29, 1953.

115. Untitled document, December 15, 1954, Entry P13, Box 3, Folder "Dahl."

116. Stout, "Pond," 78.

117. Grombach Diaries, September 14, 1953, and October 14, 1953.

118. [Grombach] to Pat [FBI], December 8, 1954, Entry P13, Box 3, Folder "Dahl"; Grombach to Dulles, December 9, 1953, Box 074083, Folder "Clements, John, re CIA-State Dept 1954," Bridges Papers.

119. Grombach to Sokolsky, January 20, 1953, Sokolsky Papers.

120. "Confidential Memorandum to Be Furnished to Senator Styles Bridges Pursuant to His Request," April 7, 1954, Folder "CIA—Confidential Memo 1953 & 1954," Bridges Papers.

121. O'Brien and Grombach to Bridges, June 29, 1954, Folder "CIA—Confidential Memo 1953 & 1954," Bridges Papers.

122. Grombach to Sokolsky, January 20, 1953, Sokolsky Papers.

123. Grombach Diaries, May 10, 1953.

124. Kirkpatrick, *Real CIA*, 151–52.

125. "Confidential Memorandum to Be Furnished to Senator Styles Bridges."

126. Kirkpatrick, *Real CIA*, 152–53.

127. Stout, "Pond," 81; Frenchy [Grombach] to Craig, November 24, 1954, CREST, CIA-RDP80-01446R000100120030-1, NARA; Armstrong to Murphy, March 16, 1955, RG 59, Entry 1561, Box 11, Folder "Inactive Files on Outsiders," NARA.

128. Waller, *Wild Bill Donovan*, chap. 30.

3 The Atomic General's "One-Way Street"

Leslie R. Groves and the Manhattan Engineer District Foreign Intelligence Section, 1945–47

Matthew H. Fay

As commanding officer of the Manhattan Engineer District (MED), Brig. Gen. Leslie R. Groves thrived under the secrecy required to construct the first atomic bombs. "Compartmentalization" was, according to the atomic general's biographer, a key element of Groves's leadership style. It was, in fact, his "organizing principle . . . allow[ing] him to wield a great deal of power based on his knowledge of various organs acting independently of one another."[1] Secrecy served Groves well during World War II. It allowed him to manage the scientists working on the bomb, keep the project mostly out of sight of the American public, and direct espionage against the enemy's efforts to build their own absolute weapon.

Secrecy is a prerequisite for intelligence leadership, but it must be balanced against the need to share information. Cooperation with other organizations is often necessary in both the collection and analysis of intelligence. More important, intelligence collected and analyzed matters only insofar as it can influence the decisions of policymakers.[2] Groves failed to balance the competing needs to maintain secrecy and to share intelligence. Following World War II Major General Groves's dedication to secrecy hampered American efforts to discover who might next build an atomic bomb.

Groves's direction of the atomic intelligence efforts of the MED Foreign Intelligence Section followed his wartime pattern of compartmentalization. With limited resources available following the war, MED relied heavily on outside agencies to collect intelligence. However, following the lead of their commanding officer, Manhattan Project intelligence officials rebuffed efforts by those same organizations to obtain information from MED. Moreover, Groves himself made decisions based on his desire to maintain secrecy that hampered intelligence-collection efforts. Furthermore, the atomic general ensured that what intelligence was collected remained within his office—not even sharing it with his superiors charged with making decisions about future

Photo 3.1 The Atomic General: Leslie Groves, who directed the Manhattan Project, was a passionate believer in the "need to know" principle. *US Department of Energy*

American policies regarding atomic energy. This dedication to secrecy led Gen. Hoyt Vandenberg, at the time the director of central intelligence, to dub the MED's intelligence arm a "one way street."[3]

Groves's role as an intelligence leader has garnered only limited scholarly attention. As Barton Bernstein noted, until recently analysis of Groves as a historical figure was for the most part a product of larger histories of the atomic bomb. Many of these works did not hold the general who oversaw the Manhattan Project in high esteem.[4] This trend changed with Robert Norris's biography. "Groves was the indispensable person in the building of the atomic bomb," Norris argued, "a larger-than-life figure, a person of iron will and imposing personality who knew how to get things done."[5] Looking specifically at Groves the intelligence leader, Norris claimed the intelligence apparatus Groves developed to spy on Nazi Germany's atomic project was a precursor to America's postwar national security state.[6] However, Norris did not delve into Groves's postwar role as an intelligence leader.[7] In this oversight he is not alone. Scholars have generally ignored the MED's postwar intelligence efforts.[8] While it is quite clear from Norris's work that Groves was a capable and even brilliant leader of the wartime efforts to build the atomic bomb, the absence of his postwar intelligence leadership from this analysis leaves an incomplete picture of his legacy.

This chapter proceeds in three parts. The first offers a brief overview of the origins of the Manhattan Project's atomic intelligence efforts in World War II and of the way Groves used compartmentalization and secrecy to spy on the Nazi atomic project. The second looks at the culture of secrecy that Groves encouraged in the MED Foreign Intelligence Section and the way it affected efforts to cooperate with other intelligence organizations in collecting atomic intelligence after World War II. The third section examines the consequences of Groves's unwillingness to share information with either the new Central Intelligence Agency or policymakers deciding on the future of the atomic bomb.

Groves and Atomic Intelligence in World War II

Although Groves was named commander of the MED in September 1942, it would take another year before he became an intelligence leader. Initial efforts to ascertain the extent of Nazi atomic developments had largely fallen to the British, with American contributions coming from the army assistant chief of staff for intelligence (G-2). There was certainly reason to suspect that Nazi Germany was on its way to building a bomb. Germany had some of the leading physicists in the world at its disposal, particularly the Nobel Prize–winning theoretical physicist Werner Heisenberg. Shortly before the establishment of the Manhattan Project, Vannevar Bush, head of the Office of Scientific Research and Development, warned that America needed to urgently construct an atomic bomb because it was likely the Germans were already six to twelve months ahead of the Allies.[9]

Despite Bush's warning, it was the general lack of information about their adversary's atomic developments—a theme that would persist after the war—that concerned American leaders most. From what little information they had, Allied leaders believed the Germans would use the captured Norsk Hydro reactor at Vemork, Norway, to produce heavy water in their efforts to build an atomic bomb. The Allies launched five separate attacks against the facility during the war. The third, a February 1943 attack by Norwegian commandos, destroyed the heavy water section of the plant—the most important part of the facility. With that British intelligence became convinced the Germans could not produce an atomic bomb.[10]

British assurances, however, did not persuade US Army Chief of Staff George Marshall, and he wanted further proof that the Nazis would not manufacture a bomb before the Allies did. Marshall turned to Groves, who shared his skepticism over British estimates.[11] In September 1943 the chief of staff put the atomic general in charge of coordinating atomic intelligence efforts against Nazi Germany.[12] Groves, in turn, delegated responsibility for the project to Robert Furman, a twenty-eight-year-old major with whom he had worked on construction of the Pentagon.[13]

Groves put the expertise of the Manhattan Project's scientists at Furman's disposal as he began to organize the intelligence mission. The most important of these scientific advisers was the Manhattan Project's scientific director, Dr. Robert Oppenheimer. The man who later became the father of the atomic bomb outlined the requirements for Furman's intelligence mission, providing a list of key items for which intelligence-collection efforts would have to account. Oppenheimer instructed Furman to identify potential sources of raw materials—specifically uranium but also graphite, heavy water, and beryllium—that could act as regulators in atomic reactors. Production plants using between 100,000 and 1 million kilowatts of power, as well as those located near plentiful water supplies or large chemical industries, also needed to be located.[14]

Oppenheimer stressed that the most important thing MED intelligence efforts could accomplish was locating German scientists involved in atomic research. He wrote in a letter to Furman in September 1943, "Clearly one of the most important points to be investigated is the whereabouts and activities of the men who are regarded as specialists in this field and without whom it would be difficult to carry out a program effectively."[15] Specifically, he highlighted the need to locate Heisenberg.

Who would do all this looking remained an open question. In what would become a recurring problem for MED atomic intelligence collection, Groves and Furman needed personnel. The atomic general, never satisfied with a single path to solving a problem—evident in the multiple methods of uranium enrichment he insisted on—organized two independent intelligence missions.[16] For the first Groves and Furman approached Gen. William "Wild Bill" Donovan of the Office of Strategic Services (OSS) for assistance. Intrigued, Donovan agreed to help, and together they created Project Larson. The lead operative for the mission was a Princeton graduate and former Major League Baseball player named Moe Berg.[17]

The mission began in Italy in late 1943 with the ostensible purpose of meeting Italian scientists to determine German advancements in rocketry. That cover story facilitated Berg's efforts to locate Italian physicists Edoardo Amaldi and Gian Carlo Wick through a source code-named "Flute"—later discovered to be Swiss physicist Paul Scherrer.[18] These sources suggested that the German atomic program had not advanced nearly as far as previously believed, at least in part because they believed that Heisenberg, while a loyal German, did not support the Nazi regime.[19]

The second mission conducted under MED's auspices highlighted Groves's penchant for both secrecy and compartmentalization. Organized in late 1943, this mission consisted of elements of G-2, the Office of Naval Intelligence, and the OSS. Whereas Project Larson used an OSS intermediary, Howard Dix, to pass information from Berg to Groves, this second mission reported solely to Groves.[20] At the head of this second mission, Groves placed Lt. Col. Boris Pash—a Hungarian émigré and virulent anti-Communist.[21] Pash's appointment served two purposes for Groves. It provided the atomic general with a capable field commander, and it kept Pash away from Oppenheimer, who the lieutenant colonel was convinced was a Communist spy. Capable leader or not, Pash quickly angered his commander when he and his subordinates dubbed their mission "Alsos"—which in Greek literally means "the grove."[22] Groves thought the name would alert outsiders to his involvement should it be discovered. However, he decided against changing it given that a last-second modification was more liable to draw unwanted attention.

While OSS intelligence efforts in Italy and Switzerland continued in 1944, Alsos was only just beginning. With Pash's team in London to prepare for the coming cross-channel invasion of Europe, Oppenheimer sent another letter to Furman providing guidance for the mission. He described the type of installations the Alsos teams needed to locate and reiterated the importance of identifying which physicists worked at each installation, warning him once again about the importance of Heisenberg.[23]

Groves's predilection for secrecy was evident in the way both missions communicated their findings to him. Groves insisted that documents be carried by hand to his office in Washington or, when that was not possible, sent using the Army Signal Corps's teletype equipment in codes known only to the atomic general and his assistant, Mrs. O'Leary.[24] Dix handled all of Berg's findings and forwarded them directly to Groves himself.[25] Alsos findings were sent directly to Groves in sealed envelopes. Not even Gen. George Strong, army chief of staff for intelligence—and known as "King George" because of his importance in intelligence matters—was allowed to open them.[26]

Ultimately, what those envelopes contained did not amount to much. Nazi Germany's atomic program never truly recovered from the Norwegian commando raid on the Norsk Hydro Reactor in 1943, as British intelligence argued at the time. Still, officials considered the wartime atomic intelligence mission conducted under Groves's leadership a success. Pash's men conducted Operation Harborage in 1945, locating several thousand tons of missing Belgian uranium.[27] More important, as the war came to an end, Alsos operatives located Heisenberg and other prominent German physicists—thus ensuring that the Soviets did not find them first.[28] As Groves later recalled in his memoir, he wished to maintain Alsos as an atomic intelligence unit after the war, but the army disbanded it on October 15, 1945—not long after the OSS had met a similar fate.[29]

Groves and the Culture of Secrecy

Despite Alsos and the OSS being disbanded, an atomic intelligence mission remained, and it remained Groves's to conduct. In December 1945 the Department of War issued a directive on intelligence to the agencies under its authority. The directive included an addendum on "Atomic Energy (Nuclear Physics)" that laid out fourteen areas of interests for atomic intelligence collection, many of which concurred with the priorities Oppenheimer had provided Robert Furman just two years prior. Personnel, scientific institutions, industrial plants, and raw materials all took top priority.[30] But the directive was adamant regarding the role of War Department intelligence agencies in atomic intelligence efforts. They were to investigate the point laid out in the addendum "SOLELY in the nature of leads."[31] Agencies other than MED were forbidden from conducting independent investigations.

Despite having sole authority for conducting atomic intelligence, Groves lacked the same resources for intelligence collection he and Furman needed to find during the war: personnel. As the atomic general noted in his diary at the end of the war, personnel at MED were uneasy about the future. Shortly after the war, discussions began in Congress over legislation to transfer control of the atomic bomb to a civilian atomic energy commission. From an organizational standpoint, though, there was immediate concern about the need to compete for talented personnel on the open market with the war effort no longer serving as a motivating force.[32] The MED Foreign Intelligence Section specifically faced a precipitous decline in personnel. According to one postwar estimate, its home office included only a colonel, a lieutenant colonel, a major, and several civilian employees—with no apparatus for evaluation or dissemination of collected intelligence.[33]

While the lack of an apparatus for evaluation and dissemination persisted throughout Groves's postwar tenure, the atomic general solved his personnel shortages for collection by co-opting the efforts of other intelligence agencies. In practice, army and navy intelligence agencies passed the "leads" specified in the December addendum through the attaché system to Groves's representatives. The Federal Bureau of Investigation, with its wartime jurisdiction over Latin America intact, passed information directly from Director J. Edgar Hoover.[34] The Strategic Services Unit (SSU), successor to the operational branch of the OSS, passed intelligence from Europe and Asia through a new liaison to Groves's representatives in the attaché system, who then communicated it to MED.

Despite the lack of resources, Groves maintained many of the practices of secrecy and compartmentalization he had developed during the war. He took measures to ensure that information from the various organizations working on his behalf was routed only to himself or his subordinates. Groves also ensured his preferred method of physically communicating intelligence remained intact after the war. As he told the military attaché in Rio de Janeiro, Brig. Gen. Hayes Kroner, any information or correspondence on matters related to atomic issues should be sent directly to Groves's Washington office via secure pouch. Groves explicitly stated that he wanted to ensure that "material of interest to my organization will have no other distribution."[35]

Groves's correspondence with Kroner also demonstrated how the Manhattan Project commander continued to keep other intelligence leaders away from matters relating to atomic intelligence. In Kroner's original letter to Groves, the attaché referred to an intelligence operative whom Groves had dispatched to Brazil. When asked whether G-2 should be informed of the operative's presence, Groves replied, "In view of the peculiar background of his mission I did not think it necessary to inform [G-2]."[36]

Groves rarely found it necessary to inform G-2 of his intentions, and "King" George Strong's successor, Maj. Gen. Clayton Bissell, proved compliant with that practice. Shortly after the war, when the Military Intelligence Service (MIS) challenged Bissell's responsibility for atomic intelligence collection in Europe, Bissell turned to Groves for guidance on how to respond. Groves explained to Bissell that he should inform MIS that G-2 was responsible for intelligence on "nuclear physics" in Europe, with all information "channelized" to MED representatives to ensure proper handling.[37] Bissell's response to MIS followed Groves's instructions nearly verbatim.[38]

The actions of Groves's subordinates suggest that the atomic general's desire for secrecy and practice of compartmentalization became standard operating procedure for the rest of his organization. This tendency was certainly true with regard to communications between his subordinates in Washington and his representatives abroad. For example, early in 1946 Col. William Shuler of MED warned Lt. Col. Edgar Dean—Groves's representative in the military attaché's office in London—not to communicate with MED headquarters via cable. He reasoned that the circulation of cables was not limited and that others might have access to them even if they were designated "Top Secret." Instead, Shuler requested that Dean send only letters because their distribution could be controlled.[39]

Groves's subordinates did not limit their emulation of their commanding officer's practices to communications. They also ensured that information was not shared even with agencies collecting atomic intelligence on their behalf. Illustrative of that tendency was a January 1946 telephone call between a Lieutenant Clarke of MED and a Colonel Marland, the deputy director of the Planning Division at MIS. As Clarke later reported to his superior, Marland expressed interest in cooperating with MED on atomic intelligence efforts, but Clark informed him that, while MIS was expected to share any intelligence on foreign atomic developments, MED would share nothing in return. The lieutenant further informed the colonel that, because Manhattan Project intelligence would not share information, any reports MIS produced independently would necessarily be incomplete and "probably not wholly accurate." He concluded the conversation with the explanation that MED "realized its position was somewhat embarrassing but hoped for the best of cooperation from MIS in the future as in the past."[40]

While Groves's practice of compartmentalization may have become standard operating procedure among his subordinates, MED's authority over atomic intelligence did not provide its personnel carte blanche in dealing with other agencies. Lieutenant Colonel Dean, for example, felt the need to assure his superiors in Washington that, while he would keep any remarks on atomic intelligence as brief as possible, he could not avoid the subject entirely at an upcoming conference of military and naval attachés. Dean explained to Lt. Col. Richard Free at MED that, while his first loyalty was to Groves, he could not completely alienate his fellow attachés by remaining silent. Free agreed but, foreshadowing Vandenberg's later characterization—and demonstrating the degree to which secrecy was a part of MED culture—warned his colleague not to divulge any more information than absolutely necessary. "We have a reputation for being a sort [*sic*] of one-way intelligence agency—a receptacle," Free wrote, "and if other agencies find a lucrative spot for information, such as yours, you could expect them to start bearing down on you."[41]

While Dean might have felt some obligation toward his fellow attachés, he and his colleagues at MED shared a common contempt for the SSU. Formed from two of the operational branches of the OSS, SSU was a pale shadow of the wartime organization. It remained, however, under War Department authority following Japan's surrender—providing Groves with access to SSU personnel for atomic intelligence collection. Like MED intelligence, though, SSU experienced a drastic reduction in personnel after the end of the war.[42]

Moreover, few thought SSU would survive its parent organization's demise—thus, few wished to support its operations.[43]

Despite its limited capabilities, SSU conducted intelligence for MED in both Europe and Asia—channeling its atomic intelligence reports through Lt. Col. Selby Skinner and using the word "Ramona" to reference atomic matters.[44] The reports themselves described a variety of purported atomic activities—from famed French physicists Frederic and Irene Joliot-Curie's attempts to establish an atomic program in France to Red Army efforts, to commandeer German and Austrian scientists and scientific facilities, to atomic developments in China and the possibility that the Nationalist government of Chiang Kai-shek sought an atomic program of its own.[45] As at least one SSU report conceded, though, SSU intelligence was often "sketchy and incomplete" because the organization lacked resources.[46]

MED intelligence officials treated SSU's reports with scorn, with much of the derision centered on reports about Soviet activity at the Joachimsthal mine in Czechoslovakia. Dean referred to as "pure imagination" one SSU report that claimed Soviet plans to lease property near the mine were for a "resort center" for the Red Army, not to extract uranium. In a handwritten note attached to another Ramona report, Dean expressed anger that Skinner, the SSU liaison, failed to "clarify his own info"—ignoring the fact that MED prohibitions on information sharing made that task essentially impossible. Dean referred to another paragraph as "meaningless" because it did not reach a firm conclusion on whether Czechoslovakian officials had negotiated with the Soviets over the property near the mines even as Skinner acknowledged that "Russian control would be a simple twist of the wrist."[47]

Perhaps the most damning criticism of SSU intelligence on the mine came in a June 1946 review of intelligence on Soviet atomic activities at Joachimsthal compiled by MED intelligence official Henry S. Lowenhaupt.[48] In an attempt to synthesize twenty-eight intelligence reports on activities near Joachimsthal, Lowenhaupt argued that the Soviets had pursued a propaganda campaign to foster the idea that control of the mine had been returned to the Czechs. He underlined the conclusion of the report: "SSU reports from Prague closely follow the propaganda line."[49]

Intelligence on the mine was of particular importance to a wartime program that Groves oversaw to corner the global market on uranium and thorium deposits. According to his memoir, Groves opened a private bank account into which the War Department deposited $37 million to fund the Anglo-American Combined Development Trust.[50] The purpose of the trust was to purchase as much fissionable material available on the open market as possible. During the war, with intelligence agencies focused on Germany and Japan, Groves contracted Union Carbide and Carbon's subsidiary Union Mines Development Corporation to survey worldwide uranium and thorium deposits. The atomic general was quite pleased with the effort. Writing to Secretary of War Robert Patterson on December 3, 1945, Groves claimed the trust controlled 97 percent of world uranium output, with only low-grade ores remaining in the United States, India, Russia, and Argentina—and potential sources available in China, Manchuria, and West Africa posing no threat owing to the lack of industrial capacity in those countries.[51]

Groves, however, miscalculated in two important ways that led to an oversight about the importance of Joachimsthal. First, he wrongly believed that low-grade uranium was relatively useless for enrichment.[52] Second, he misunderstood how comprehensive his initial survey of worldwide uranium deposits had actually been. According to historian Jonathan Helmreich, the discovery of uranium deposits in Sweden forced Groves to refocus intelligence efforts on locating further available ore. In the early part of his reassessment, Groves failed to understand that the uranium available at Joachimsthal made his effort to corner the market essentially worthless.[53] The dysfunctional efforts of MED intelligence and the SSU provided little information useful in correcting this misapprehension.

If lack of knowledge about Soviet access to raw materials stemmed largely from miscalculation, Groves's obsession with secrecy was primarily to blame for MED's inability to gain intelligence on the Soviet scientific community. During the summer of 1945, Moe Berg requested permission to attend a Soviet scientific "jubilee" in Moscow to collect intelligence on Soviet scientists. Groves, however, denied the request. The atomic general cited fears that the mere presence of American personnel with any connection to the atomic bomb project might unwittingly provide the Soviets with information to further their own program.[54]

It is unclear exactly what information Groves feared the Soviets might glean from Berg's presence in Moscow, though. Moreover, Groves was already well aware that Soviet spies had infiltrated the Manhattan Project. In a December 30, 1944, meeting with President Franklin Roosevelt and Secretary of War Henry Stimson, the MED commanding officer acknowledged "that there was every evidence that the Russians were continuing to spy on our work, particularly at Berkeley."[55] Given that Groves's notes following the meeting characterize his statement as coming in response to a question from the president, it is clear the matter had been raised previously.

While the reasons behind Groves's prohibition on Berg's attendance at the Moscow jubilee are uncertain, the result was the beginning of an ongoing problem that left American intelligence bereft of personnel in Russia capable of gaining a better understanding of the Soviet scientific community.[56] Though it did not have any personnel inside Soviet territory, the SSU provided a number of reports on Soviet scientific activities—particularly on Moscow's interest in German scientists.[57] According to one report, the Soviets relocated "the Physikaliche Insitut of Baron Manfred von Ardenne," an institution devoted to atomic research, to the Black Sea in late 1945.[58] Another report, in 1946, highlighted Soviet interference in the operations of the Austrian Radium Institute. According to the institute's director, Dr. Hertha Karlik, a Red Army colonel offered $10 million for one Austrian physicist to relocate to Russia.[59]

There is only limited evidence available to indicate how Groves's subordinates viewed these SSU reports, but what there is suggests they treated them with only slightly less contempt than that directed at the organization's reports on Joachimsthal. Dean, for example, was willing to acknowledge that one SSU report on leading Soviet physicist Peter Kapitza provided a "fair biographical sketch." However, he ultimately dismissed the report as containing "no intelligence data."[60]

That MED officials were so dismissive of the intelligence work of other organizations was not surprising given the way Groves actively worked to ensure intelligence agencies remained uninformed, even as they collected intelligence on behalf of MED. Groves's subordinates were even willing to concede the "one way" nature of their organization, as Lieutenant Colonel Free did in his conversation with Dean about the attachés conference. Other times, though, MED personnel seemed oblivious to how the practices their commanding officer instituted affected their relations with other intelligence organizations. In early 1946, for example, a Groves subordinate wrote parenthetically on a routing slip to Lieutenant Clarke, "It seems darn strange to me that liaison between us and other Govt [*sic*] agencies (State Dept., e.g.) is so lousy."[61] It is unclear from the remainder of the routing slip's text whether Clarke's correspondent was writing sardonically. It is clear, however, that the reputation of Groves's intelligence section as a "one way" agency was well earned.

The Consequences of Groves's Unwillingness to Share Information

The atomic general's practice of compartmentalization and predilection for secrecy did not simply frustrate other War Department intelligence agencies. It also hampered the ability of the burgeoning postwar intelligence community to estimate future development of the atomic bomb in the Soviet Union. The Central Intelligence Group (CIG) and its successor, the Central Intelligence Agency (CIA), produced flawed estimates that routinely relied on guesswork due to a general lack of information. While Groves does not bear sole responsibility for the problems the newly formed intelligence agency faced in estimating Moscow's ability to develop an atomic bomb, his secrecy contributed greatly to a vacuum of reliable information about the duration of America's atomic monopoly.

The importance of atomic intelligence was evident to a number of civilian and military officials in the aftermath of World War II. Shortly before President Harry Truman disbanded the OSS, Moe Berg's former conduit to MED, Howard Dix, wrote to General Donovan suggesting that "plans be made to gauge atom power development by scientists of all countries."[62] Military officials also cited atomic intelligence as a leading reason why a postwar intelligence system was necessary. In a report on the future of warfare using atomic weapons, later popularized as an article in *Life* magazine, Gen. Henry H. "Hap" Arnold, commanding general of the US Army Air Forces, called for "development of the Intelligence necessary for the effective application of our military to whatever job it may be called up to do."[63] Similarly, the Joint Chiefs of Staff noted, "No defense of the United States against [atomic] attack is possible without a thoroughly adequate intelligence system. . . . We must without further delay set up the most effective intelligence system it is possible to devise."[64]

Though the need for a postwar intelligence system was widely acknowledged, creating one remained difficult because of public fears that it might become an American Gestapo and because of efforts to protect bureaucratic fiefdoms within the government. Truman rejected a proposal from Donovan, whom he personally disliked, to continue the OSS after the war.[65] After several proposals for a central intelligence agency under control of either the Department of State or the Department of War proved too controversial, Secretary of the Navy James Forrestal and his longtime collaborator Ferdinand Eberstadt proposed a palatable system that placed the new CIG under the auspices of the National Intelligence Authority (NIA), consisting of the secretaries of state, war, and the navy, as well as a "personal representative" of the president. On January 23, 1946, Truman appointed Rear Adm. Sidney Souers as the first director of central intelligence (DCI).[66] Souers, however, agreed only to a temporary appointment and gave way after six months to Gen. Hoyt Vandenberg of the Army Air Forces.

One intelligence historian has described General Vandenberg as an "empire builder," and the new DCI certainly intended for atomic intelligence to be part of his imperial project.[67] Vandenberg envisioned CIG as an "intelligence staff" for the newly created Atomic Energy Commission (AEC). He wrote to the NIA in August 1946, arguing that, because atomic developments abroad "constitute a paramount field of intelligence related to national security" and because the AEC was set to take over all functions previously under the authority of the Manhattan Project, the DCI should be in charge of coordinating atomic intelligence.[68]

While there is little evidence to suggest that Groves actively resisted Vandenberg's efforts to incorporate atomic intelligence functions into his growing empire, the atomic general's secrecy presented an obstacle of its own. It was not until its eighth month of existence that the NIA even learned of MED's atomic intelligence efforts. At the August 21, 1946, meeting of the authority, the DCI revealed Groves's intelligence efforts to his colleagues. During that same meeting, Vandenberg quipped that the MED intelligence outfit was a "one-way street." Secretary of War Robert Patterson sarcastically added, "If General Groves had information that the Russians were prepared to use atomic bombs, the members of the NIA would not even know about it."[69]

Groves could not maintain his wall of secrecy forever, though, and the days of the MED were numbered by the time Vandenberg argued for control of atomic intelligence at the August 21 NIA meeting. On August 1, 1946, President Truman signed into law the McMahon Act—creating the AEC to take control of American atomic energy matters beginning in 1947. Groves had spent the early part of 1946 fighting for a military voice in the proposed AEC. Not only had his testimony before Sen. Brien McMahon's committee been particularly contentious, the atomic general faced public condemnation from a number of the scientists charged with building the atomic bomb over his often authoritarian leadership methods.[70]

Though Truman put off a decision on responsibility for atomic intelligence during the fall of 1946, Groves preemptively wrote to the AEC in November of that year to endorse Vandenberg's claim on atomic intelligence.[71] Norris writes in his biography that the latter part of that year was perhaps Groves's most challenging as he prepared to transfer MED responsibilities to the AEC and its new director, David Lilienthal—with whom he shared a great deal of mutual animosity.[72] Thus, Groves's letter to the commission arguing for CIG control of atomic intelligence is difficult to take at face value. "I have long thought," the MED commanding officer wrote, "CIG has the best resources for this intelligence collection and dissemination and for procuring and retaining personnel capable of serving the Atomic Energy Program [sic] in the future."[73] While it is possible Groves had "long thought" CIG an organization well suited for atomic intelligence, that he kept his intelligence mission a secret from its leaders for so long suggests otherwise. His doubts about Lilienthal and the AEC outweighed any reservation he may have held about CIG though.[74]

The timing of Groves's belated endorsement of CIG was ironic because the intelligence organization released its first estimate on when Moscow might develop an atomic bomb a month before his letter. As part of Vandenberg's empire-building project, the DCI created the Office of Reports and Estimates (ORE) within CIG to coordinate "national policy intelligence."[75] ORE was not set up to conduct its own intelligence collection but rather to coordinate and evaluate intelligence provided by various entities at the Departments of War, State, and Navy and at the AEC.[76] It would then produce estimates on topics of "national concern," a category the Soviet atomic program certainly fell into—thus making ORE responsible for producing the "best judgment" on when Moscow might test its first atomic bomb.[77]

CIG's first estimate of the Soviet Union's ability to produce an atomic bomb left much to be desired. ORE 3/1, "Soviet Capabilities for the Development and Production of Certain Types of Weapons and Equipment," concluded, "It is probable that the capability of the USSR to develop a weapon based on atomic energy will be limited to the possible development of an atomic bomb to the stage of production some time between 1950 and 1953."[78] As problematic as the conclusion was, the methodology was even more dubious. Given that Groves's organization had yet to share even the limited intelligence it had gathered on Soviet scientists, facilities, or potential uranium sources, ORE 3/1 relied on, in its own words, "educated guesswork." Two main pieces of evidence made up ORE's guesswork: "the past performance of Soviet and Soviet-controlled German scientists and technicians" and the American experience building its first atomic bombs.[79]

Inability to access MED intelligence was one of a number of reasons that "educated guesswork" was the best ORE could muster to estimate Soviet production of an atomic bomb. Despite Vandenberg's imperialism, CIG's budget remained miniscule. Moreover, ORE was overwhelmed with requests to produce "current intelligence"—which Truman preferred over long-term estimates.[80] The trend that began with Groves's decision to prohibit Berg from attending the Moscow scientific jubilee in 1945 continued as human intelligence sources inside the Soviet Union remained elusive. ORE 3/1 and subsequent estimates therefore relied heavily on a combination of captured German documents and deductive reasoning.[81]

These issues did not end with Groves's letter to the AEC. Manhattan Project intelligence files remained out of CIG's reach until March 1947, when the MED Foreign Intelligence Section became the Nuclear Energy Group for ORE's Scientific Branch.[82] By that time it was clear there were severe problems in the country's atomic intelligence enterprise. In July of that year, Sidney Souers issued a report on shortcomings in atomic intelligence. He highlighted in particular the need for close cooperation between the AEC and the proposed CIA.[83] Still, the creation of the CIA did not ameliorate the problems that CIG had previously experienced. Despite Groves's professed belief in CIG's ability to conduct atomic intelligence, the reality others experienced in dealing with the CIA was far from satisfactory. Vannevar Bush, then chair of the military Research and Development Board, argued in December 1947 that the "CIA is not yet in a position to meet its responsibilities" for atomic intelligence.[84] David Lilienthal at the AEC complained that intelligence on Soviet atomic developments remained in the realm of "educated guess." He argued that the CIA atomic intelligence was "five percent information and ninety-five percent construction . . . in my opinion sources of information about Soviet progress are so poor as to be actually merely arbitrary assumptions."[85] John Ohly, assistant to Secretary of Defense James Forrestal, noted as late as March 1948 that high-level intelligence consumers were "increasingly concerned about our intelligence setup for the handling of nuclear matters."[86] Later atomic intelligence estimates continued to reflect these sentiments.[87]

Groves's intelligence leadership did not cause all the problems in CIA intelligence estimates, but it did help create the intelligence vacuum that enabled them. With his knowledge of the Combined Development Trust and control over MED intelligence, Groves was free to make bombastic statements—to policymakers, the president, and the public—about when the Soviet Union might develop its own atomic bomb. Arguing that Russian industry could never replicate "the magnificent achievement of the American industrialists, skilled labor, engineers and scientists who made the Manhattan Project a success," Groves predicted it would take Moscow "ten, twenty, or even sixty years" to build an atomic bomb.[88] Given these confident statements and Groves's unwillingness to share what little his intelligence division knew of foreign atomic developments, the surprise policymakers, right up to the president, felt when the Soviets tested their first atomic bomb in August 1949 is understandable.

Conclusion

By the time of the Soviet atomic test, Lt. Gen. Leslie Groves had retired from active duty, his career having stalled after his public battle against the AEC. Regarding Soviet atomic developments, a variety of bureaucratic obstacles stood in the way of proper intelligence collection, and a variety of psychological obstacles and personal peccadillos stood in the way of the ability of various policymakers to update their threat perceptions.[89] However, the information vacuum left by the atomic general's intelligence leadership compounded those problems.

Leslie R. Groves deserves recognition for his accomplishments as the wartime director of the Manhattan Project. However one feels about the decision to build and use the atomic bomb, Groves enabled one of the most important scientific and military breakthroughs in human history. His wartime intelligence leadership had much to commend about it as well. The culture of secrecy and insistence that information about foreign atomic developments remained under his control, however, helped hamper postwar atomic intelligence efforts leading up to the Soviet atomic test. The atomic general rightly deserves praise for his wartime accomplishments, but the failure of his postwar intelligence leadership cannot go overlooked when assessing his legacy.

Notes

1. Robert S. Norris, *Racing for the Bomb: General Leslie R. Groves, the Manhattan Project's Indispensable Man* (South Royalton, VT: Steerforth Press, 2002), 254.

2. Mark M. Lowenthal, "The Policymaker-Intelligence Relationship," in *The Oxford Handbook of National Security Intelligence*, ed. Loch Johnson (New York: Oxford University Press, 2010), 437–52.

3. Minutes of the Sixth Meeting of the National Intelligence Authority, August 21, 1946, in *Foreign Relations of the United States: Emergence of the Intelligence Establishment, 1945–1950* (Washington, DC: US Government Printing Office, 1996), 395–400 (hereafter cited as *FRUS: 1945–1950*).

4. Barton J. Bernstein, "Reconsidering the 'Atomic General': Leslie R. Groves," *Journal of Military History* 67, no. 3 (2003): 883–920. The best overview of the Manhattan Project is Richard Rhodes, *The Making of the Atomic Bomb* (New York: Simon & Schuster, 1986). For histories of the atomic bomb with negative assessments of Groves, see Martin J. Sherwin, *A World Destroyed: Hiroshima and Its Legacies*, 3rd ed. (Stanford, CA: Stanford University Press, 2003); and Gregg Herken, *The Winning Weapon: The Atomic Bomb in the Cold War, 1945–1950* (New York: Vintage Books, 1982).

5. Norris, *Racing for the Bomb*, x–xi.

6. Ibid., 253–55. Garry Wills later echoed this claim, arguing that Groves's demand for secrecy provided the foundation for the postwar national security state. See Gary Wills, *Bomb Power: The Modern Presidency and the National Security State* (New York: Penguin Press, 2010), 7–56.

7. For an overview of US atomic intelligence efforts against Nazi Germany, see Rhodes, *Making of the Atomic Bomb*; and Jeffrey Richelson, *Spying on the Bomb: American Nuclear Intelligence from Nazi Germany to Iran and North Korea* (New York: W. W. Norton, 2006), 17 –61.

8. The exception is Richelson, *Spying on the Bomb*, 62–77, 201–2.

9. Vannevar Bush to Vice President Henry A. Wallace, Secretary of War Henry L. Stimson, and Gen. George C. Marshall, memorandum, December 16, 1942; Correspondence of the Manhattan Engineer District, 1942–1946; "Bush-Conant Files," File 25, RG 77, microfilm publication M1109, National Archives and Records Administration (NARA).

10. Richelson, *Spying on the Bomb*, 32–33, 43.

11. Norris, *Racing for the Bomb*, 283.

12. Ibid., 287.

13. Ibid., 287–88.

14. Richelson, *Spying on the Bomb*, 33.

15. Norris, *Racing for the Bomb*, 290.

16. Ibid., 289–90.

17. For the story of Berg's life and exploits, see Nicholas Dawidoff, *The Catcher Was a Spy: The Mysterious Life of Moe Berg* (New York: Pantheon Books, 1994).

18. Ibid., 161, 177–81, 197–98.

19. Ibid., 181.

20. Richelson, *Spying on the Bomb*, 51–52.

21. Norris, *Racing for the Bomb*, 286.

22. See Rhodes, *Making of the Atomic Bomb*, 605. For a detailed account of Alsos from the perspective of its leader, see Boris T. Pash, *The Alsos Mission* (New York: Award House, 1969).

23. J. Robert Oppenheimer to Major Robert Furman, June 5, 1944, General Case File, Box 34, Folder 17, Correspondence with Robert R. Furman, 1943–1944, Library of Congress.

24. Norris, *Racing for the Bomb*, 272–73.

25. Ibid., 290.

26. Ibid., 286–87.

27. Richelson, *Spying on the Bomb*, 58–59.

28. Ibid., 59–61.

29. Leslie R. Groves, *Now It Can Be Told: The Story of the Manhattan Project* (New York: Da Capo Press, 1983), 248–49.

30. "Department of War Intelligence Directive Addendum: Atomic Energy (Nuclear Physics)," December 11, 1945, RG 77, Entry 22, Box 170, Folder 32.60, NARA.

31. Emphasis in the original. See ibid.

32. Groves Office Diary, September 14, 1945, RG 200, Entry A1 7, Box 3, NARA. At one point Lt. Col. Richard Free, a Groves subordinate in Washington, DC, informed the MED representative in London that he expected the Manhattan Project to survive another year despite the creation of the AEC, but he did explain that his colleague could resign if he would like to. See Lt. Col. Richard H. Free to Lt. Col. Edgar P. Dean, Office of the Military Attaché, American Embassy London, "Personnel of MED London Office," June 13, 1946, RG 77, Entry 18, Box 144, NARA.

33. General G. A. Lincoln to General Norstad, "Problem of Atomic Intelligence," JCS 1477/10, July 22, 1946, RG 165, Entry 421, Box 566, ABC File 471.6 Atom (17 Aug 45) Sec 2, NARA.

34. Correspondence between Hoover and MED intelligence regarding uranium deposits in South America is sprinkled throughout the Manhattan Project intelligence files. At least one postwar letter refers to "previous correspondence." For examples, see J. Edgar Hoover to Col. William R. Shuler, "Re: Monazite Shipment, Brazil," June 7, 1946, Box 163; J. Edgar Hoover to Col. W. R. Shuler, "Re: Activity on the Atomic Field—Santiago, Chile," August 26, 1946, Box 174; and J. Edgar Hoover to

Colonel William R. Shuler, "Re: Shipment of Monazite," December 6, 1946, Box 163. All available in RG 77, Entry 22, NARA.

35. Maj. Gen. L. R. Groves to Brig. Gen. Hayes Kroner, Military Attaché, American Embassy, Rio de Janeiro, Brazil, May 5, 1945, RG 77, Entry 22, Box 163, NARA.

36. Ibid.

37. Maj. Gen. L. R. Groves to Maj. Gen. Clayton Bissell, Assistant Chief of Staff, G-2, "Assignment of Collecting Tasks, War Department Intelligence," October 8, 1945, RG 77, Entry 22, Box 170, Folder 32.60, NARA.

38. Ibid.; Maj. Gen. Clayton Bissell, GSC A.C. of S., G-2 to the Assistant Chief of Staff, G-2, US Forces, European Theater, "Collection of Intelligence on Nuclear Physics," October 25, 1945, RG 77, Entry 22, Box 170, Folder 32.60, NARA.

39. Col. W. R. Shuler to Lt. Col. E. P. Dean, Office of the Military Attaché, American Embassy, London, "Use of Cables," January 21, 1946, RG 77, Entry 18, Box 144, Folder 6, NARA.

40. Lt. C. F. Clarke to the File thru Colonel Shuler, "Colonel Marland," January 4, 1946, RG 77, Entry 22, Box 170, Folder 32.60, NARA.

41. Lt. Col. Richard H. Free to Lt. Col. E. P. Dean, Office of the Military Attaché, American Embassy, London, "Conferences of Military Attaches and Naval Attaches," June 6, 1946; and Lt. Col. Richard H. Free to Lt. Col. E. P. Dean, Office of the Military Attaché, American Embassy, London, "MIS Inquiries on Atomic Energy," April 15, 1946. Both in RG 77, Entry 18, Box 144, Folder 6, NARA.

42. "Memorandum from Director of Strategic Services Unit, Department of War (Magruder) to the Assistant Secretary of War (McCloy)," October 25, 1945, in *FRUS, 1945–1950*, 243–45. Another estimate put the number of SSU personnel as low as 750 at one point. See Bradley F. Smith, *The Shadow Warriors: O.S.S. and the Origins of the C.I.A* (New York: Basic Books, 1983), 408.

43. For example, the Department of State was reluctant to house SSU personnel at foreign embassies, knowing its termination might be imminent. See "Memorandum from the Acting Director of the Office of Controls, Department of State (Lyon) to the Secretary of State's Special Assistant for Research and Intelligence (McCormack)," November 13, 1945, in *FRUS, 1945–1950*, 245–46.

44. Maddox thru Shepardson to Magruder, "Liaison with Major Groves Unit," January 7, 1946, RG 226, Entry 210, Box 421, Folder #1, NARA.

45. See Lt. Col. S. M. Skinner to Col. W. R. Shuler, "Joliot," February 15, 1946; and SAINT, JJ/1 from SAINT, BG/1, "High Commissariat for Atomic Energy (in France)," April 18, 1946. Both in RG 226, Entry 210, Box 42, Folder #1, NARA.

46. "Ramona" Report from Strategic Services Unit China Theater, X-2 Branch, June 24, 1946, RG 226, Entry 210, Box 314, Folder 1, NARA.

47. Lt. Col. Edgar P. Dean to Colonel W. R. Shuler, "New Report on the Situation at Joachimsthal," April 17, 1946, RG 77, Entry 22, Box 1963, NARA.

48. Lowenhaupt subsequently went on to be a CIA analyst working on the Soviet nuclear program. See Henry S. Lowenhaupt, "On the Nuclear Scent," *Studies in Intelligence* 11, no. 4 (Fall 1969): 13–29.

49. H. S. Lowenhaupt, "Joachimsthal Summary Analysis," Draft, May 6, 1946, RG 77, Entry 22, Box 1963, NARA.

50. Groves, *Now It Can Be Told*, 137.

51. Jonathan Helmreich, *Gathering Rare Ores: The Diplomacy of Uranium Acquisition, 1943–1954* (Princeton, NJ: Princeton University Press, 1986) 69.

52. Groves's belief that the Soviets had access only to low-grade ores led to a misguided assumption in some quarters that Groves believed Russia to be bereft of uranium altogether. See Charles A. Ziegler, "Intelligence Assessments of Soviet Atomic Capability, 1945–1949: Myths, Monopolies and Maskirovka," *Intelligence and National Security* 12, no. 4 (1997): 4.

53. Helmreich, *Gathering Rare Ores*, 42, 60–70.

54. Edgar Dean at the London attaché's office also recommended Groves send Berg to Moscow. See Cable from US Military Attaché, London, England to War Department, Cable 43786, May 31, 1945, RG 77, Entry 22, Box 160, NARA. On Groves's denial, see "Azusa," 154, Dix and Buxton to Berg, "Reference Your #30844 (in 14558) and Our #26094 (Out 13280)," June 5, 1945, RG 226, Entry A1134, Box 219, Folder 1371, NARA.

55. Maj. Gen. L. R. Groves, "What Occurred during a Meeting at the White House between 12:30pm and 1:00pm, Above Date, at Which the Following Were Present: The President, the Secretary of War, Major General L.R. Groves," December 30, 1944, RG 77, microfilm publication M1109, NARA.

56. Groves had also prevented physicist Edward Condon from attending the event, going so far as to have the New York City police stop his plane at La Guardia Airport. His justification was the same he gave for prohibiting Berg's presence, but his reason seems more plausible in regard to Condon because he was a physicist who had actually worked on the bomb at Los Alamos. See Norris, *Racing for the Bomb*, 458–59.

57. OSS provided an estimate in August 1945 that the Soviet Union had 175 "top notch" physicists. See Azusa Cable from 109 and Dix, August 18, 1945, RG 226, Entry 134, Box 219, Folder 1371, NARA.

58. "Movement of Ardenne Atomic Energy Institute to USSR," December 14, 1945, RG 226, Entry 210, Box 421, Folder 1, NARA. On Von Ardenne's role in the Soviet atomic bomb project, see David Holloway, *Stalin and the Bomb: The Soviet Union and Atomic Energy, 1939–1956* (New Haven, CT: Yale University Press, 1994), 190.

59. "RAMONA," To Mr. Richard Helms from Security Control Division, Austria, June 29, 1946, RG 226, Entry 210, Box 314, Folder 1, NARA.

60. Lt. Col. Edgar P. Dean to Lt. Col. Richard H. Free, Room 4181, New War Department Building, Washington, DC, "SSU Report on Peter Kapitza," June 6, 1946, RG 77, Entry 18, Box 144, NARA.

61. Ryan to Lt. Clarke, Memo Routing Slip, February 24, 1946, RG 77, Entry 22, Box 63, NARA.

62. Col. H. W. Dix to Gen. W. J. Donovan, "Influence of Atomic Bomb in Indirect Methods of Warfare," September 4, 1945, RG 226, Entry 210, Box 422, Folder 2, NARA.

63. The report, titled "Third Report of the Commanding General of the Army Air Forces to the Secretary of War," and also known as the Arnold report, was completed November 12, 1945. The need for intelligence is discussed on page 72. A detailed description of the subsequent *Life* magazine story, including a link to the Arnold report itself, is available at the blog *Restricted Data: The Nuclear Secrecy Blog*. See Alex Wellerstein, "The 36-Hour War: *Life* Magazine, 1945," *Restricted Data: The Nuclear Secrecy Blog*, April 5, 2013, http://blog.nuclearsecrecy.com/2013/04/05/the-36-hour-war-life-magazine-1945/.

64. Joint Chiefs of Staff, Joint Strategic Survey Committee, "Overall Effect of Atomic Bomb on Warfare and Military Organization," October 30, 1945, 13, Item # NP00007, Digital National Security Archive.

65. David F. Rudgers, *Creating the Secret State: The Origins of the Central Intelligence Agency, 1943–1947* (Lawrence: University Press of Kansas, 2000), 19–46. See also Thomas F. Troy, *Donovan and the CIA: A History of the Establishment of the Central Intelligence Agency* (Frederick, MD: Aletheia Books, 1981). On the fear of an American Gestapo, see Rhodri Jeffreys-Jones, *The CIA and American Democracy* (New Haven, CT: Yale University Press, 2003), 30.

66. Rudgers, *Creating the Secret State*, 90–92.

67. Ibid., 114–15.

68. Memorandum from the Director of Central Intelligence (Vandenberg) to the National Intelligence Authority, August 13, 1946, in *FRUS, 1945–1950*, 394–95.

69. Minutes of the Sixth Meeting of the National Intelligence Authority, August 21, 1946, in ibid., 395–400.

70. Norris, *Racing for the Bomb*, 460–62.

71. Richelson, *Spying on the Bomb*, 72.

72. Norris, *Racing for the Bomb*, 464.

73. "Memorandum from the Commanding General of the Manhattan Engineer District, Department of War (Groves) to the Atomic Energy Commission," November 21, 1946, in *FRUS, 1945–1951*, 458–59.

74. Richelson, *Spying on the Bomb*, 72.

75. Richard H. Immerman, *The Hidden Hand: A Brief History of the CIA* (Malden, MA: John Wiley & Sons, 2014), 15–17.

76. Donald P. Stuery, "How the CIA Missed Stalin's Bomb," *Studies in Intelligence* 49, no. 1 (2005), https://www.cia.gov/library/center-for-the-study-of-intelligence/csi-publications/csi-studies/studies/vol49no1/html_files/stalins_bomb_3.html.

77. Ibid.; and Lawrence Freedman, *U.S. Intelligence and the Soviet Strategic Threat*, 2nd ed. (Princeton, NJ: Princeton University Press, 1986), 16.

78. Central Intelligence Group, Office of Records and Estimates, "Soviet Capabilities for the Development and Production of Certain Types of Weapons and Equipment," ORE 3/1, October 31, 1946, 1, Item #CK3100533980, Declassified Documents Reference System.

79. Ibid., 1; and Steury, "How the CIA Missed Stalin's Bomb."

80. Freedman, *U.S. Intelligence and the Soviet Strategic Threat*, 14–16. On Truman's preference for current intelligence, see Immerman, *Hidden Hand*, 14–15.

81. Military Intelligence Division, "Intelligence Estimate of the World Situation for the Next Five Years," August 21, 1946, 1, RG 319, Box 78, NARA. See also Richelson, *Spying on the Bomb*, 69–71.

82. "Minutes of the 10th Meeting of the NIA," June 26, 1947, in *FRUS, 1945–1950*, 766–76; and Richelson, *Spying on the Bomb*, 72–73.

83. Sidney W. Souers to the Commissioners, Atomic Energy Commissions, "Atomic Energy Intelligence Requirements," July 1, 1947, RG 326, Box 107, Folder 350.09, NARA.

84. "Memorandum from the Chairman of the Research and Development Board (Bush) to Secretary of Defense Forrestal," December 5, 1947 in *FRUS, 1945–1950*, 817–18.

85. Quoted in Michael S. Goodman, *Spying on the Nuclear Bear: Anglo-American Intelligence and the Soviet Bomb* (Stanford, CA: Stanford University Press, 2007), 28, see also 33.

86. Quoted in Rudgers, *Creating the Secret State*, 155.

87. See, for example, Central Intelligence Agency, "Threats to the Security of the United States," ORE 60-48, September 28, 1948, CIA FOIA Electronic Reading Room, http://www.foia.cia.gov/sites/default/files/document_conversions/89801/DOC_0000258368.pdf.

88. Quoted in Norris, *Racing for the Bomb*, 475–76. This estimate varied depending on the audience Groves spoke to, with fifteen to twenty years being one estimate he offered, while "no earlier than 1955" was another, see 674n8.

89. Matthew J. Connelly et al., "'General, I Have Fought Just as Many Nuclear Wars as You Have': Forecasts, Future Scenarios, and the Politics of Armageddon," *American Historical Review* 117, no. 5 (2012): 1431–60.

4 The Dulles Supremacy

Allen Dulles, the Clandestine Service, and PBFortune

James Lockhart

This chapter highlights Director of Central Intelligence (DCI) Allen Dulles's influence in the formative history of the Central Intelligence Agency (CIA), emphasizing PBFortune, his failed effort to arm Nicaragua's Somoza dictatorship against Guatemala in 1952.[1] Historians have long contextualized PBFortune as a dress rehearsal for Operation PBSuccess, which overthrew the Jacobo Árbenz administration, and as yet another instance of American intervention in the Caribbean.[2] In explaining PBSuccess, realists have emphasized US national security concerns, while revisionists have stressed the United Fruit Company's interests. Multicausal explanations presently prevail.[3] This chapter, however, foregrounds Dulles's leadership and his approach to intelligence during the agency's early years, and it extends the discussion into Guatemala.

Dulles remains indispensable to any understanding of CIA operations in Latin America and, indeed, the larger world in the 1950s. He was an Office of Strategic Services (OSS) legend, the most respected civilian authority on intelligence of his time, an insider who confidently strode the corridors of power in bureaucratic Washington. He joined the CIA in the winter of 1950–51 and in January 1953 became the Dwight Eisenhower administration's DCI, a position he held until the Bay of Pigs fiasco in 1961. He possessed a well-defined intelligence doctrine, and he shaped the agency's institutional identity, priorities, and organizational culture through it. He, more than anyone else, conceived and reified the Clandestine Service, then guided several ambitious paramilitary and psychological warfare operations through the national security bureaucracy, beginning in Guatemala and Iran. These operations enabled Dulles to break President Harry Truman's mold of a quiet CIA that primarily produced national intelligence and discreetly performed limited covert operations from time to time to create a new mold premised on a higher profile, far more activist agency.

This chapter approaches this history through bureaucratic politics theory, particularly its appreciation for factions, negotiated outcomes, and irrationality in American foreign relations.[4] It follows this model and proceeds in three chronologically overlapping parts. First, it introduces the leading participants in this history: Truman, Walter Bedell Smith, and Dulles. Second, it reviews "the rules of the game"—the laws, policies and procedures, and practices that delimited the possible in bureaucratic Washington in Dulles's era. And third, it reconstructs PBFortune as an incident that reveals Dulles's leadership and his approach to intelligence.

The Participants

Truman created the CIA in 1947.[5] He explained from retirement, "I decided to set up a special organization charged with the collection of all intelligence reports from every available source, and to have those reports reach me as President without departmental 'treatment' or interpretations"—in other words, national intelligence. "I never had any thought that when I set up the CIA," he continued, "that it would be injected into peacetime cloak and dagger operations."[6] Truman's behavior as president remained consistent with this narrative, and he appointed DCIs, particularly Lt. Gen. Walter Bedell Smith, who shared his objectives, which remained constructing a quiet agency that primarily produced national intelligence, even though it would perform other secondary functions, including covert operations.

Thus, Truman tasked the CIA "to perform such other functions and duties related to intelligence affecting the national security as the National Security Council [NSC] may from time to time direct."[7] Clark Clifford, one of the president's closest advisers, clarified, "The 'other' functions the CIA was to perform were purposely not specified, but we understood that they would include covert activities. We did not mention them by name because we felt it would be injurious to our national interest to advertise the fact that we might engage in such activities. We intended that these activities be separate and distinct from the normal activities of the CIA."[8]

Rear Adm. Sidney Souers, the first DCI, and then the president's representative to the intelligence community, concurred. According to Souers, "Truman regarded the CIG (and CIA) as his personal intelligence service. His conception of CIG's functions was extremely simple. It was to keep him personally well informed of all that was going on in the outside world."[9] Souers added, "I always felt strongly that CIG and CIA had no business to get involved as a principal in Covert Operations of a para-military type."[10] Thus, the administration prioritized national intelligence when conceiving and drafting the agency's charter, but it included limited covert operations as a secondary and separate function that might even lay dormant for years at a time.

Truman selected Bedell Smith to replace embattled DCI Rear Adm. Roscoe Hillenkoetter in the spring of 1950. Neither the Pentagon nor the Department of State's representatives in the intelligence community cooperated with Hillenkoetter, particularly with respect to sensitive information. Bedell Smith was reluctant to accept this position, partly because he was suffering health problems. The president nevertheless remained confident that Bedell Smith, "an able and forceful organizer and manager," was the right man for the job and persuaded him to take it.[11]

Unlike the relatively low-ranking Hillenkoetter, Bedell Smith had served Gen. Dwight Eisenhower as chief of staff and wore three stars (soon four). Truman believed the Pentagon would cooperate with his new appointee, and as Bedell Smith had recently served as ambassador to Moscow, the president hoped the Department of State would respect him as well. The Senate confirmed him unanimously.

Bedell Smith studied the CIA's situation and consulted key people when he assumed the directorship. He accepted NSC 50, described later, as Truman's directive to him. He worked fast, sending the agency's first all-source intelligence summary, which Truman called "the jackpot," to the president on February 28, 1951.[12] Bedell Smith would begin presiding over the national intelligence system he had set out to create approximately a year later.[13]

Bedell Smith also appointed Dulles deputy director for plans. According to the CIA's declassified history, Bedell Smith "valued Dulles's experience and skill as a clandestine operator and thought to make use of those qualities, while retaining policy control in his own hands."[14] Thus, he delegated supervision of covert operations and espionage to Dulles. Bedell Smith did this after Truman and Souers had rejected Dulles as a candidate for director. "Dulles's interest and experience," the declassified history explained, "were too narrowly confined to clandestine operations, a minor and incidental part of the DCI's responsibilities."[15] Bedell Smith named Dulles to this important position even though he "took an instant and permanent dislike" to the man.[16]

Dulles conceived the CIA's purposes differently than Truman, and he sought to reshape the agency accordingly. He considered intelligence a warfighting activity; he could not imagine an intelligence service that did not support resistance groups behind enemy lines or anywhere the enemy might penetrate. He began articulating this doctrine while chairing the Dulles Survey, tasked to review the CIA's performance in 1948.[17] "Secret operations," he advised the NSC, "particularly through support of resistance groups, provide one of the most important sources of secret intelligence, and the information gained from secret intelligence must immediately be put to use in guiding and directing secret operations."[18] So while Truman was asking, "Where's my newspaper?"[19] Dulles was proposing to merge the Office of Policy Coordination (OPC), the government's nascent covert operations arm, and the Office of Special Operations (OSO), the agency's espionage branch, forging the Clandestine Service.

This represented a watershed. As Director of Policy Planning Staff George Kennan, who had created and was distantly managing the OPC,[20] warned his superiors, "the implications . . . are so far-reaching that I think they should be discussed by you and [Secretary of Defense] Mr. [James] Forrestal rather than in the lower levels of NSC."[21] The NSC supported Kennan, directing that the OPC "shall operate independently of other components of [the] Central Intelligence Agency."[22]

However, Dulles expected Republican Thomas Dewey to defeat Truman that November and anticipated becoming the new administration's DCI. He was advising Dewey's campaign while he chaired the Dulles Survey, which he planned to use as his blueprint.[23] The president, however, won the election, and Dulles's report, in his biographer's words, "landed almost irrelevantly on the crowded desks of the reelected Truman administration."[24]

Others influenced this history, not merely Truman, Bedell Smith, and Dulles. Kennan authored the containment doctrine and directed some of the government's earliest covert operations in the Cold War. Kennan's OPC, occupying a gray area between the Department of State and the CIA, reported both to the secretary of state and the DCI until 1952. Paul Nitze, who succeeded Kennan at the Policy Planning Staff, militarized containment after 1950. He urged using all available means to weaken the Kremlin. The Pentagon, "the hub of U.S. national security policy in 1951–52," according to historian Melvyn Leffler,[25] pressed the OPC to expand the scope and pace of its paramilitary operations after the Korean War began. And Frank Wisner, another OSS veteran who shared Dulles's intelligence doctrine, led the OPC, expanding its operations. In former DCI William Colby's recollection, "Wisner landed like a dynamo . . . and set out to form a clandestine force worldwide. By hard work and brilliance, and by reaching widely for similarly activist OSS alumni, he started it operating in the atmosphere of an order of Knights Templars."[26]

Rules of the Game

Truman, Congress, and the national security bureaucracy—the Department of State, the Pentagon, and the armed services—wrote the rules of the game, laws, policies and procedures, and practices that delimited the possible in Washington in Dulles's era. This bureaucratic community fell into rivalry, confusion, and disarray with respect to grand strategy, national intelligence, and covert operations in the Cold War's early years. The Truman administration created the NSC, which produced government-wide directives to better manage this community and the foreign policy issues it was grappling with.

But as Leffler concluded, Truman rarely presided at the NSC, preferring to delegate to his principal subordinates instead.[27] Historian Sarah-Jane Corke, while explaining Truman's failure to choose either containment or rollback in Albania and elsewhere in Eastern Europe, concurred. She found "that Truman never brought the full power of the presidency to bear on the one problem that was tearing his administration apart . . . the United States simply did not have a coherent or unified strategy for waging the Cold War."[28]

This worsened after McCarthyism wounded the administration. "Throughout most of his last fifteen months in office," Leffler observed, "Truman was a harassed, frustrated, irascible man."[29] In March 1952 the president announced he would not seek reelection, and Kennan, the next ambassador to Moscow that spring, found him unresponsive to attempts to solicit instructions.[30]

Meanwhile, the NSC modified its directives on covert operations at least five times in as many years, particularly with respect to OSO and the OPC. Although this partly reflected an evolving Cold War, the busy secretaries of state and defense were barely more involved than the president. They, too, delegated to their subordinates. This left the CIA adrift in stormy seas.

According to the CIA's declassified history, "the National Security Council really had no time and attention to give to understanding the problems of the CIA and to supervising its management. What the NSC wanted was for somebody in whom it had confidence to take charge and run the show, without all this bickering and contention."[31] This meant that strong-willed personalities such as Kennan and Nitze, representing the Department of State, and General Joseph McNarney, representing the secretary of defense, wrote the NSC's directives.

Meanwhile, Dulles remained focused on implementing his intelligence doctrine and creating the Clandestine Service. The Dulles Survey's final report challenged the NSC's earlier decision to keep OSO and the OPC separate. According to Dulles, NSC 10/2 "did not go as far as we had recommended, with the result that the Office of Policy Coordination (secret operations) and the Office of Special Operations (secret intelligence) are not bound together by any special relationship and operate as entirely separate Offices."[32]

Forrestal accepted the report as a guidebook. But he was experiencing emotional distress at the time, and he resigned and committed suicide in the spring of 1949. Louis Johnson replaced him, but he lacked familiarity with the issues and did not evaluate the report himself. He delegated it to McNarney instead. McNarney's recommendations reflected the Pentagon's pressing concerns about what appeared to be becoming the next world war and met no opposition from the Department of State, which was eager to replace Hillenkoetter. McNarney endorsed most of Dulles's report, including his suggestion to merge covert operations and espionage.[33] Secretary of State Dean Acheson and Johnson transformed McNarney's recommendations into NSC 50 on July 1, 1949.[34]

The national security bureaucracy resisted this well into 1950, however. The larger issues remained the same ones that had been plaguing the CIA since 1947. The departments and services supported the agency's responsibility for covert operations. But they, particularly the Pentagon, did not wish to lose control over their own intelligence responsibilities, and they did not wish to report to the DCI and lose their direct access to the NSC and the president either. This rendered Hillenkoetter ineffective until he left the CIA.

Meanwhile, Bedell Smith brought the OPC firmly into the agency's organizational structure when he replaced Hillenkoetter. The DCI asserted his control over the OPC, clarifying the director's position as the highest authority and last word in the OPC's chain of command. He hoped to contain its operations and protect the CIA's primary mission. He explicitly rejected Dulles's proposed OPC-OSO merger.[35] As he explained, this would transform the CIA into "a cold war department."[36] "The Agency's primary mission," he insisted, "was intelligence and . . . he would do nothing that militated against accomplishing this objective."[37]

Bedell Smith persuaded the NSC to suspend the Pentagon's authority over the OPC's rapidly growing covert operations in January 1951. He asked it to reassess the situation. He specifically asked the NSC to clarify exactly what it understood covert operations and guerrilla warfare to entail, plus how much time and resources the CIA should dedicate to them.[38] These operations were transforming the agency. OSO's Lyman Kirkpatrick was reporting, for example, that his branch's rapidly increasing tactical support missions were overwhelming it, subordinating it to the OPC, and undermining "the major mission of establishing a long-term clandestine espionage organization."[39]

According to the CIA's declassified history, "Dulles took care to avoid a flagrant violation of Smith's orders, but nevertheless worked steadily toward the eventual accomplishment of his own purpose in disregard of Smith's known policy."[40] He had begun, for example, synchronizing the OPC and OSO's geographical divisions as a preliminary step toward merging them early in his tenure as deputy director for plans.[41] The OPC located Italy in its Western European area, for example, but OSO placed it in its Mediterranean division.

Dulles's caution notwithstanding, he soon attracted Bedell Smith's anger. "During 1951 he had Jackson 'survey' (investigate) the offices under Dulles's supervision. With reason, he came to suspect that Dulles and Wisner were actually pursuing a policy contrary to his own. In exasperation, he visited upon them more violent manifestations of his wrath than he did upon anyone else."[42] Dulles simply brushed this aside—"The General was in fine form this morning, wasn't he?"—and carried on.[43]

Bedell Smith, however, was fighting a rearguard action by this time. Given the Pentagon's growing budget and influence, he could not likely have stopped or even slowed the OPC's increasing paramilitarization and its increasing importance within the agency no matter what he argued. As CIA historian Nicholas Dujmovic recognized, "It seems that Smith felt trapped into acquiescing to CIA's paramilitary role despite his deep misgivings about it."[44] The OPC's operations soon spanned the entire Soviet perimeter and included many in the People's Republic of China and North Korea, and Dulles and Wisner were planning to support an even larger war by spring 1951.[45]

Bedell Smith asked the Joint Chiefs of Staff (JCS) to assume responsibility for these operations and to assign its own personnel to them to no avail; he was outnumbered on this issue—probably more than he understood at the time. Dulles duly reminded the chiefs in one meeting, probably with a wink and a nod, that the "CIA had no wish to continue the conduct of such large-scale operations and that General Smith had pointed this out repeatedly and had offered to divest himself of this responsibility if only the JCS or someone else would pick it up." General laughter followed, and the chairman replied "(with a smile and bow towards Mr. Dulles) that he saw no reason to revise the present situation or alter the responsibilities as they now stand."[46]

Bedell Smith recognized that the United States was confronting extraordinary wartime conditions and that the Cold War, NSC 68, and what he called the JCS's "high degree of wishful thinking and unreality . . . as to what could be accomplished by special operations in wartime,"[47] and not Dulles and Wisner, were ultimately driving the OPC's operations and changing the CIA. He expressed his dismay with "the variety and magnitude of the covert action operations that he was called upon to conduct,"[48] writing that "the responsibilities which are being placed upon us under our Charter and under NSC directives, particularly in the field of planning and execution of guerrilla warfare activities, go beyond our current capabilities and indeed embrace operations of such magnitude that they threaten to absorb the resources of this Agency to a point which might be detrimental to its other responsibilities."[49]

Bedell Smith remained dissatisfied with the JCS's response and brought the issue to the NSC's attention again in May 1951.[50] He repeated this several weeks later, warning that "the operations tail is now starting to wag the intelligence dog."[51] In the face of this problem, he suggested the Pentagon create a new command dedicated to guerrilla warfare, leaving the agency to focus on national intelligence and more-limited covert operations elsewhere. The NSC ruled against him, however, ordering an expansion of the OPC's operations.[52] He complied, explaining that the CIA was conducting these operations as a wartime measure, acting as the service's executive agent because no other department or agency could or would.[53]

He also withdrew his objections to Dulles's merger and inaugurated the Clandestine Service in July 1952.[54] "Regrettably, (from my personal viewpoint)," he reported, "it seems impracticable for reasons of coordination and security, to divorce these from other covert operations."[55] The particular circumstances explaining this remain elusive. Tantalizing information exists, however. According to the CIA's declassified history, "the turning point in Bedell Smith's attitude toward integration was the NSC's adoption of [eight lines deleted]. He promptly withdrew [deleted] from further consideration."[56] "Thus," it continues, "Bedell Smith yielded, regretfully, to the doctrine of Allen Dulles that clandestine intelligence collection and covert 'psychological warfare' were inseparable, [two lines deleted]."[57] He hoped the NSC's Psychological Strategy Board would properly supervise the Clandestine Service thereafter.[58]

Whatever explains this, Dulles, now deputy director of central intelligence, wasted no time consolidating the Clandestine Service and covert operations' primacy at the CIA. He reaffirmed Wisner's assignment as deputy director for plans, and he placed Kirkpatrick, Richard Helms, and others from OSO in subordinate offices, a pattern he reconfirmed when he promoted his covert action protégé Richard Bissell over Helms several years later. The Directorate of Intelligence, the agency's analytic component, became, in one deputy director for intelligence's estimation, "the unknown CIA," "a stepchild."[59] In other words, to borrow Immerman's metaphor, Dulles, the former OPC, and the Clandestine Service "colonized" the agency.[60]

Dulles explained these realities to Helms later:

> We have to face the fact that because espionage is relatively cheap it will probably always seem inconsequential to some of our less informed friends on the Hill. . . . They're accustomed to dealing in billions. What kind of impression can it make when I come along and ask for a few hundred thousand dollars and a bag of pennies? Believe me, I know the way they think up there. If there's no real money involved, it can't be important, and they just won't pay much attention to us.[61]

Dulles, having prevailed in assembling and empowering the Clandestine Service, now intended to showcase its unique capabilities. This would guarantee the CIA's continuing existence while increasing its budget, profile, and influence in bureaucratic Washington. He had seen Truman dissolve the OSS with the stroke of a pen, witnessing "the conniving and blood spilling that went on when we were trying to sort things out in 1946. . . . Would there even be a service?"[62] He needed to secure the agency against this happening again.

Indeed, many in government thought in these terms. When then–secretary of the navy Forrestal observed the US Marines taking Mount Suribachi and raising the American flag there, he turned to a nearby general and commented, "The raising of that flag . . . means a Marine Corps for the next 500 years."[63] Dulles shared his contemporaries' anti-Communism and their traditional concern to generally protect Americans' investments abroad, but he was also seeking the agency's Suribachi when his gaze fell on Guatemala during the summer of 1952.

The NSC and Latin America

Latin America remained an unlikely arena in which to showcase the Clandestine Service, and indeed Dulles overreached when he first attempted it. The Department of State's Bureau of Inter-American Affairs had the freedom to produce clear and straightforward rules of the game there; it was not a war zone subject to the JCS. The bureau continued to behave as a good neighbor committed to nonintervention. The Truman administration indeed joined the Organization of American States (OAS) and codified this in inter-American law in 1948.

Further, the administration perceived "a potential rather than immediately serious" Soviet threat in Latin America and saw no Chinese threat there at all.[64] Kennan, responding to the OAS's final resolution at its inaugural meeting in Bogotá, which had condemned Communism, advised Secretary of State George Marshall to oppose any multilateral anti-Communist agreement to operate internally within the Western Hemisphere and also any bilateral agreements.[65] Although Latin America's professional officer corps, landowning elites, and Church remained staunchly anti-Communist, Kennan regarded their politics as opportunistic posturing. They used "anti-Communism" to suppress all opposition, Communist or not, and if the United States supported them, this would alienate large numbers of non-Communists in the region.[66]

The administration still organized Latin America's conventional defenses in case the Cold War escalated into world war. It signed the Inter-American Treaty of Reciprocal Assistance—the Rio Treaty—in 1947. It began negotiating bilateral military agreements and increased aid two years later. Pentagon planners recalled the troops and resources they had been obliged to divert to the region during the Second World War, and they wished to empower Latin America's armed forces to secure their own nations.[67]

The administration also began cultivating Latin Americans' identification with US Cold War objectives. Some regional governments tended not to share Washington's views, however. Further, many had expected the United States to attend their postwar regional economic conferences and provide generous aid. They experienced bitter disappointment when this did not happen. As the Brazilian foreign minister explained to one official at the Department of State, his government's response to the Korean War would probably have been more favorable had the administration offered Latin America something comparable to the Marshall Plan.[68]

PBFortune

Dictator Jorge Ubico had seized power in Guatemala during the Depression and ruled the country until 1944. Ubico revitalized Guatemala's economy but at the expense of reinforcing long-standing socioeconomic inequalities. The Boston-based United Fruit Company, for example, continued dominating banana production and virtually every related industry during his rule. Meanwhile, an increasingly assertive middle class arose and demanded democratization and an end to the dictatorship. Ubico finally fled the country. Presidents Juan José Arévalo (1945–51) and Jacobo Árbenz (1951–54) inaugurated a new reformist era.

Arévalo and Árbenz made several enemies. Their reforms empowered Guatemalan labor and the peasantry against traditional interests and United Fruit. When Guatemalan courts ruled against the company in one dispute and the administration seized some of its land, United Fruit began a public relations campaign against the government, characterizing it as Communist. Arévalo and Árbenz had also antagonized several Caribbean dictators, particularly Anastasio Somoza and Rafael Trujillo, by supporting the Caribbean Legion, a loosely organized group of multinational exiles that had attempted to overthrow them. Although Árbenz ceased supporting the legion, the damage was done. Somoza and Trujillo wanted an end to "the Guatemalan revolution."

Somoza supported Lt. Col. Carlos Castillo Armas, one of several Guatemalan dissidents who planned to seize power. Castillo Armas contemplated a Caribbean Legion–style sea, air, and land invasion, with large infantry units armed with mortars, heavy machine guns, and flamethrowers converging on Guatemala City from Mexico, Nicaragua, and the Guatemalan coast.[69] He claimed to command overwhelming forces inside and outside the country. Trujillo agreed to support Castillo Armas "with arms, aircraft, men, and money."[70] But he conditioned this on Castillo Armas murdering four Dominican exiles (probably associated with the Caribbean Legion) in Guatemala

City. Castillo Armas was "glad to carry out the executive action."[71] Somoza and Trujillo's resources remained limited, however. They required American support. But they were dissatisfied with the Department of State's response.[72]

The evidence regarding the Truman administration's involvement, particularly the president's involvement, in PBFortune, the CIA's cryptonym for this conspiracy, remains scant and inconclusive. The agency's involvement, however, clearly began when Dulles responded to the company's pleas. Thomas Corcoran, United Fruit's lobbyist, approached Stuart Hedden, the CIA's inspector general, proposing the agency support his client, sometime in the winter of 1951–52. Corcoran and Hedden may have known each other from Wall Street, where both had worked before they came to Washington.[73] The OPC began following Castillo Armas's progress.[74]

Then Somoza approached Col. Cornelius Mara, an assistant military aide to Truman, in July 1952. Somoza was seeking medical treatment in New England and visiting the United States unofficially; Mara accompanied him back to Managua as a matter of protocol. Somoza offered "to clean up the Guatemala regime with 10,000 rifles and one millions rounds" without further involving the United States at some point during these travels. He also recommended that "the State Department should decide on some stringent action and implement it in a sudden move" against Árbenz. Mara forwarded his suggestions to the president in three memorandums.[75] Somoza subsequently bragged to Trujillo and others throughout the Caribbean that he and the president had reached an understanding on Guatemala. According to one of Somoza's versions, they had discussed it in the White House kitchen.[76]

Somoza's bragging confused Assistant Secretary of State for Inter-American Affairs Edward Miller. Miller, knowing nothing of any such understanding, later asked Wisner and the CIA's director of Latin American operations, J. C. King, what they knew about it. They "gave assurances that General S had gotten no such approval from representatives of the Agency," speculating that "General S's statements could be based only upon remarks made to him by members of the White House staff."[77]

Miller could not imagine any other explanation either. He later judged that Truman must have directed Bedell Smith to support Somoza against Árbenz without consulting the Department of State and further speculated that the president must have initialed one of Mara's memorandums, which would have become the CIA's written authorization. Journalist Herbert Matthews reported this in his memoir two decades later. Neither he nor Miller, however, ever produced any evidence.[78]

Mara could indeed have spoken for the president, and he could also have made unauthorized promises to Somoza. More likely, however, Somoza could have just plain lied. He would have lied for the same reasons he lied when bragging to journalists that President Franklin Roosevelt (1933–45) had admiringly called him "our son of a bitch." It associated him with the president and enhanced his prestige, especially inside Nicaragua. His sons repeated this story often, as political scientist Robert Pastor explained, "to show they were tough, but their *partner*, the United States, was even tougher."[79] Somoza's lying would also explain why Truman's initials do not appear on any of Mara's memorandums, neither the originals nor any extant copy. Indeed, the president's response, if he ever did respond, does not appear on the record.[80] What remains is simply a story that Somoza told Trujillo and others in the Caribbean that ultimately reached Miller's ears.

Dulles's response to Corcoran, however, does appear on the record. Dulles joined Hedden and Corcoran on July 15—the same day Bedell Smith formally inaugurated the Clandestine Service. He confirmed that "we looked with favor upon a change of management." He also told Corcoran, "We thought we could be helpful in pointing out where the principals might buy the goods they needed."[81] Corcoran asked the CIA to buy these goods—that is, arms— suggesting United Fruit reimburse it after Castillo Armas seized power. Dulles and Wisner diverted weapons earmarked for other operations to Guatemala soon after this meeting. There is no evidence they consulted higher authority.[82]

Dulles, speaking in circumlocutions, also sought Miller's approval for something vague that July. He asked Miller and his deputy, Thomas Mann, "Would the State Department like to see a different government in Guatemala? Would the State Department oppose a government established by the use of force? Does the State Department wish CIA to take steps to bring about a change of government?"[83] Dulles claimed Miller and Mann had somehow implied authorization to support the plan, but Bedell Smith was uncomfortable with this language, and he called Undersecretary of State David Bruce for clarification—curious moves if he indeed possessed a written presidential directive.

Neither Bedell Smith nor Bruce documented this telephone conversation. Dulles later claimed "that the Director had received a satisfactory answer from Bruce."[84] Bruce denied this, insisting "that although he had some telephone conversations with the Director he did not recall having said anything that could be interpreted as approval." Miller recalled that although he had told Dulles and Hedden he did not object to any monetary contributions, he feared military adventures and arms transfers were too risky.[85]

Dulles and Wisner nevertheless claimed that Bruce, Miller, and Mann had approved "the Agency's project to provide certain hardware to a group planning violence against a certain government," but "the Department did not wish to be kept informed of the detailed plans."[86] These details represent the crux of the issue. Miller insisted that he knew nothing about the weapons until the dictator's son approached him in Panama, speaking of "the machinery," which Dulles and Wisner confirmed when they asked him to sign an export permit. He advised Acheson to shut this adventure down immediately, which the secretary did.[87] Acheson's only explanation appears in a personal letter he wrote Truman in retirement, complaining of "this asinine Cuban adventure" after the Bay of Pigs: "I told my informants how you and I had turned down similar suggestions for Iran and Guatemala and why."[88]

Meanwhile, Mann told Somoza's ambassador that neither the president nor anyone else in government supported his conspiracy.[89] Then Bruce, Miller, and Mann confronted Wisner and King.

> The Department approves of many of the activities which the Agency is carry-ing out throughout the world and does not like to be called obstructionist, but in the present case, as it has been called upon to approve an export permit, it is forced to state that it disapproves of the entire deal. . . . The Department can raise no objection to any monetary contribution which the Agency might make as it knows the Agency is constantly passing money for purposes which the Department could not approve of and must do this in order to operate, but it feels that money can be passed securely.[90]

Although Bedell Smith disagreed with this, he accepted it, acknowledging "that this Agency is merely an executive agency to carry out the policies of the Department of State and the Department of Defense, and if they instruct us not to engage in a certain operation, we shall not engage in that operation."[91] Dulles refused to let it go, however, and he preserved what he could. Wisner was defiant, reinterpreting Bedell Smith's language to read, "In the Direc-tor's view, the Agency is purely an executive organization of the Government which carries out missions and conducts activities in support of the foreign policy objectives of the Government."[92] Then he stored the weapons some-where in the Caribbean, probably the Canal Zone, and began paying Castillo Armas a stipend while "considering the next step."[93]

The next step closely followed Eisenhower's inauguration. Dulles informed Eisenhower's NSC that the Soviets were menacing Latin America, particu-larly Guatemala, and the president instructed the council to prepare a new policy statement the next month in turn.[94] NSC 144/1 resulted.[95] It reaffirmed the Truman administration's commitment to organizing the region's conven-tional defenses. It also added new, more interventionist objectives, including "the reduction and elimination of the menace of internal Communist or other anti-U.S. subversion." Dulles remained one step ahead of this. "We now expect to be in a position to proceed," he recorded, as he began planning what would become PBSuccess even before the NSC had approved this paper.[96]

Thus, Dulles not only nursed but breathed new life into a dying plan during the Truman-Eisenhower transition. He declared it "a top priority operation for the whole agency . . . the most important thing we are doing."[97] Indeed, he would personally defend it at the White House when the Department of State challenged it again in 1954.[98]

Years later, Dulles personally confronted Truman in Independence, Missouri, after the president published his column recommending the CIA return to its core mission of intelligence collection and analysis. Dulles dismissed the former president's claim, arguing in the memorandum he wrote afterward that Truman had directed everything the agency had done and, therefore, by implication, consented to, if not intended, all that followed, including the emergence of the Clandestine Service. He characterized the president as a confused, easily misled old man who had probably not even written the column himself.[99]

Dulles's response to Truman deeply imprinted the CIA's institutional memory, particularly its oral traditions, which soon also reflected the unhappiness of many people at the agency with politicians' disavowal of their own policies when expedient, what Immerman called "the CIA's . . . historic role as lightning rod and scapegoat."[100] Case officer Samuel Halpern, aware of the president's column, virtually restated Dulles's reply in an interview decades later.

> That's nonsense. Not only was he aware, he was the guy who put us into what I call the first paramilitary operation. My friends say it wasn't the first, it was the second or third which Truman himself put us into. Truman did not write that column; rather, a staff officer wrote it. As far as we know, Truman never saw it. Both Kirkpatrick and Larry Houston wrote a few years later that they visited Truman and talked to him about this, and it was quite clear Truman never had seen the column.[101]

This remains partly accurate but essentially incorrect. It mischaracterizes Truman's position, and more important, it conceals Dulles's worldviews and actions, which opposed the president's often between 1948 and 1953. Truman, Clifford, and Souers did not disavow the containment doctrine or covert operations per se. None were embarrassed by the operations they had authorized in Europe and East Asia, and none joined the New Left or supported the CIA's other critics, including those who called it a rogue elephant during the 1970s. Rather, they merely restated the president's original concept of a quiet agency that primarily produced national intelligence and discretely

Photo 4.1 Trailblazer: Director of Central Intelligence Allen Dulles (right), pictured receiving the National Security Medal in 1961 from President Kennedy, transformed the agency by championing the use of covert action to contain and rollback Communist regimes abroad. *Cecil Stoughton, White House Photographs, John F. Kennedy Presidential Library and Museum*

performed limited covert operations from time to time. The form the CIA had assumed by the early 1960s, however, particularly its profile in the press, where it appeared as a paramilitary intelligence service engaged in "sinister and mysterious foreign intrigue," worried them.[102] They correctly recognized that this was not what they had intended, even if they did not recognize that they failed to properly supervise the agency and to support Bedell Smith while he was the director.

An undeniably lucid Truman, still in Independence, revisited the question some weeks after Dulles's visit. Deputy Director of Central Intelligence Lt. Gen. Marshall Carter was restating Dulles's position when "Truman broke in on the General's statement to say yes, he knew all that, it was important work, and he would order it to be done again under the same circumstances. He went on to add, however, that he had set up the CIA to pull together basic information required by the presidency but which had been denied him by State and Pentagon handling procedures. He said this was the main purpose."[103]

Conclusion

Dulles remained an active, resolute, and very well-connected intelligence director who influenced outcomes in bureaucratic Washington as few of his predecessors or successors could. His intelligence doctrine prevailed at the CIA, rendering the Clandestine Service the agency's leading directorate and covert operations its paramount function after the summer of 1952. Although many causes explain this, including early Cold War crises, NSC 68, and the JCS's requirements in East Asia during the Korean War, Dulles accomplished this through conscious design and persistence.

Interpretations that emphasize Truman or the NSC's creation of the Clandestine Service and assignment of the covert operations function to the CIA fail to acknowledge Dulles's leadership and agenda. They fail to acknowledge the president's intent that such operations should remain limited and secondary to the agency's primary purpose: the production of national intelligence. And they also fail to appreciate Truman's inability or unwillingness to bring the full power of the chief executive to bear on the problems the NSC's confusion and disarray and Bedell Smith's warnings were presenting by 1952. This ceded the initiative to the JCS and Dulles, enabling Dulles, in one historian's estimation, to "tip the scales" toward covert operations and away from intelligence collection and analysis at the CIA.[104]

This tipping of the scales meant that Dulles, in successfully implementing his intelligence doctrine, undermined Truman and Bedell Smith's efforts, especially in 1951 and 1952, leading the CIA into the future he wanted to create for it but, at the same time, a future the president would recognize and disavow as an unintended outcome several years later. Dulles skillfully allied himself with like-minded officials in the NSC, the Department of State, and the JCS, and he seized the opportunities Guatemala and Iran presented to showcase the Clandestine Service, beginning with PBFortune. Dulles's legacy endured into the mid-1970s, well over a decade after he had retired from the agency, rendering him one of the most effective leaders in CIA history.

Notes

The Truman Library supported this research, and I thank archivist Randy Sowell for his expertise and professional courtesy.

1. On the CIA in Guatemala, see Stephen Schlesinger and Stephen Kinzer, *Bitter Fruit: The Story of the American Coup in Guatemala*, rev. ed. (Cambridge, MA: Harvard University Press, 2005); Richard Immerman, *The CIA in Guatemala: The Foreign Policy of Intervention* (Austin: University of Texas Press, 1982); Piero Gleijeses, *Shattered*

Hope: *The Guatemalan Revolution and the United States, 1944–1954* (Princeton, NJ: Princeton University Press, 1991); Nick Cullather, *Secret History: The CIA's Classified Account of Its Operations in Guatemala, 1952–1954*, 2nd ed. (Stanford, CA: Stanford University Press, 2006); Aaron Coy Moulton, "Building Their Own Cold War in Their Own Backyard: The Transnational, International Conflicts in the Greater Caribbean Basin, 1944–1954," *Cold War History* 15 (2015): 135–54; and *Foreign Relations of the United States, 1952–1954: Guatemala* (Washington, DC: US Government Printing Office, 2003) (hereafter cited as *FRUS, 1952–1954: Guatemala*).

2. Stephen Rabe, *The Killing Zone: The United States Wages Cold War in Latin America*, 2nd ed. (New York: Oxford University Press, 2015), 36–43.

3. Stephen Streeter, "Interpreting the 1954 U.S. Intervention in Guatemala: Realist, Revisionist, and Postrevisionist Perspectives," *History Teacher* 34 (2000): 61–74; and Gleijeses, *Shattered Hope*.

4. Morton Halperin, "The Decision to Deploy the ABM: Bureaucratic and Domestic Politics in the Johnson Administration," *World Politics* 25 (1972): 62–95; and J. Garry Clifford, "Bureaucratic Politics," *Journal of American History* 77 (1990): 161–68.

5. On the CIA's origins, see Arthur Darling, *Central Intelligence Agency: An Instrument for Government to 1950* (1953; University Park: Pennsylvania State University Press, 1990); Michael Warner, ed., *The CIA under Harry Truman* (Washington, DC: History Staff, Center for the Study of Intelligence, Central Intelligence Agency, 1994); *Foreign Relations of the United States, 1945–1950: Emergence of the Intelligence Establishment* (Washington, DC: US Government Printing Office, 1996) (hereafter cited as *FRUS, 1945–1950: Emergence*); *Foreign Relations of the United States, 1950–1955: The Intelligence Community* (Washington, DC: US Government Printing Office, 2007) (hereafter cited as *FRUS, 1950–1955: Intelligence Community*).

6. Harry Truman, "Limit CIA Role to Intelligence," *Washington Post*, December 22, 1963. See also Benjamin Onate, "What Did Truman Say about CIA?" *Studies in Intelligence* 17 (1973): 9–11.

7. National Security Act of 1947, Title 1, sec. 102 (d), paragraph 5, Warner, *CIA under Truman*, document 30.

8. Clark Clifford, *Counsel to the President* (New York: Random House, 1991), 165–71. The CIA's leadership challenged this in 1947, and some historians continue to question it today. Houston to Hillenkoetter, "CIA Authority to Perform Propaganda and Commando-Type Functions," September 25, 1947, in *FRUS, 1945–1950: Emergence*, document 269; and Richard Immerman, *The Hidden Hand: A Brief History of the CIA* (Chichester, UK: Wiley Blackwell, 2014), 19–29.

9. Ludwell Lee Montague, "Interview with Sidney Souers," St. Louis, Missouri, December 4, 1969, RG 263, Box 2, Folder 61, National Archives and Records Administration (NARA).

10. Souers to Montague, June 14, 1971, in ibid.

11. Ludwell Lee Montague, *General Walter Bedell Smith as Director of Central Intelligence, October 1950–February 1953* (1971; University Park: Pennsylvania State University Press, 1992), 55–56.

12. Bedell Smith to Truman, February 28, 1951, in *FRUS, 1950–1955: Intelligence*

Community, document 53; and Truman to Bedell Smith, March 8, 1951, in ibid., document 55.

13. Bedell Smith to NSC, April 23, 1952, in Warner, *CIA under Truman*, document 78; Montague, *General Walter Bedell Smith*, 109–92. See also Ray Cline, *Secrets, Spies, and Scholars: Blueprint of the Essential CIA* (Washington, DC: Acropolis Books, 1976), 107–18; and Russell Jack Smith, *The Unknown CIA: My Three Decades with the Agency* (Washington, DC: Pergamon-Brassey's, 1989), 45–56.

14. Montague, *General Walter Bedell Smith*, 91.

15. Ibid., 56–57; Montague, "Interview with Sidney Souers"; and Souers to Montague, January 11, June 14, and July 19, 1971, RG 263, Box 2, Folder 61, NARA.

16. Ludwell Lee Montague, "Interview with William Harding Jackson," Tucson, AZ, December 8–9, 1969, in ibid.

17. Allen Dulles et al., "The Central Intelligence Agency and National Organization for Intelligence," January 1, 1949, CIA FOIA Electronic Reading Room (CIAFERR), https://www.cia.gov/library/readingroom/docs/CIA-RDP86B00269 R001100090002-8.pdf.

18. Dulles et al. to Souers, "Interim Report No. 2: Relations between Secret Operations and Secret Intelligence," May 13, 1948, reprinted in *FRUS, 1945–1950: Emergence*, document 275.

19. Smith, *Unknown CIA*, 31.

20. George Kennan, "The Inauguration of Organized Political Warfare," May 4, 1948, in *FRUS, 1945–1950: Emergence*, document 269. See "Office of Policy Coordination, 1948–1952," January 4, 1948, CIAFERR, https://www.cia.gov/library /readingroom/docs/DOC_0000104823.pdf.

21. Kennan to Lovett and Marshall, May 19, 1948, in *FRUS, 1945–1950: Emergence*, document 276.

22. National Security Council, NSC 10/2, June 18, 1948, in Warner, *CIA under Truman*, document 43.

23. Peter Grose, *Allen Dulles: Spymaster* (1994; London: André Deutsch, 2006), 257–329; and Montague, "Interview with Sidney Souers."

24. Grose, *Spymaster*, 290.

25. Melvyn Leffler, *A Preponderance of Power: National Security, the Truman Administration, and the Cold War* (Stanford, CA: Stanford University Press, 1992), 447.

26. William Colby, *Honorable Men: My Life in the CIA* (New York: Simon & Schuster, 1978), 73.

27. Leffler, *Preponderance of Power*, 448.

28. Sarah-Jane Corke, *US Covert Operations and Cold War Strategy: Truman, Secret Warfare, and the CIA, 1949–53* (New York: Routledge, 2008), 139.

29. Leffler, *Preponderance of Power*, 448.

30. John Lewis Gaddis, *George F. Kennan: An American Life* (New York: Penguin Press, 2011), 441–45; Dean Acheson, *Present at the Creation: My Years in the State Department* (1969; New York: W.W. Norton, 1987), 632–33; and George Kennan, *Memoirs*, vol. 2, *1950–1963* (Boston: Little, Brown / Atlantic Monthly Press, 1972), 105–11.

31. Montague, *General Walter Bedell Smith*, 62.

32. Dulles et al., "Central Intelligence Agency and National Organization for Intelligence," 132.

33. Darling, *Central Intelligence Agency*, 346–47.

34. "Comments and Recommendations to the National Security Council on the Report of the Dulles-Jackson-Correa Committee prepared by the Secretary of State and Secretary of Defense," NSC 50, in Warner, *CIA under Truman*, document 54.

35. "Minutes of a Meeting of the Intelligence Advisory Committee," October 20, 1950, in *FRUS, 1950–1955: Intelligence Community*, document 29. Also see Montague, *General Walter Bedell Smith*, 62, 90–92, 111–14, 211, 217–27.

36. Office of the Director of Central Intelligence, Staff Conference Minutes, October 22, 1951, in Warner, *CIA under Truman*, document 72.

37. Office of the Director of Central Intelligence, Staff Conference Minutes, October 27, 1952, in ibid., document 80.

38. Bedell Smith to Lay, "Draft of NSC Directive on Covert Operations and Clandestine Activities," January 8, 1951, in *FRUS, 1950–1955: Intelligence Community*, document 38; and Lay to NSC, "Responsibilities of CIA (OPC) with Respect to Guerrilla Warfare" and attachments, January 16, 1951, in ibid., document 42.

39. Lyman Kirkpatrick, "Report on the Office of Special Operations," August 31, 1951, in ibid., document 87.

40. Montague, *General Walter Bedell Smith*, 91.

41. Lyman Kirkpatrick, "Meeting on Integration of O/SO and O/PC," February 14, 1951, in *FRUS, 1950–1955: Intelligence Community*, document 50.

42. Montague, *General Walter Bedell Smith*, 91–92, 96. See also Montague, "Interview with William Harding Jackson."

43. Montague, *General Walter Bedell Smith*, 92.

44. Nicholas Dujmovik, "Drastic Actions Short of War: The Origins and Application of CIA's Paramilitary Function in the Early Cold War," *Journal of Military History* 77 (2012): 797.

45. "Office of Policy Coordination, 1948–1952"; and OPC, "CIA/OPC Strategic War Plan in Support of the Joint Outline Emergency War Plan," April 4, 1951, in *FRUS, 1950–1955: Intelligence Community*, document 61.

46. Wisner to Dulles, "United States Policies on Support for Anti-Communist Chinese Forces," April 10, 1952, in ibid., document 106.

47. Joyce to Nitze, "The Director of Central Intelligence on the Scope and Pace of CIA Activities with Particular Reference to Para-Military Operations and Preparations for Operations," June 21, 1951, in ibid., document 75.

48. Montague, *General Walter Bedell Smith*, 204.

49. Bedell Smith to Bradley, March 2, 1951, in *FRUS, 1950–1955: Intelligence Community*, document 54.

50. Bedell Smith to NSC, "Scope and Pace of Covert Operations," May 8, 1951, attached to Lay to Nitze, Nash, Wooldridge, and Jackson, May 14, 1951, in *FRUS, 1950–1955: Intelligence Community*, document 68.

51. Joyce to Nitze, June 21, 1951.

52. NSC 10/5, October 23, 1951, in Warner, *CIA under Truman*, document 73.

53. Bedell Smith to NSC, April 23, 1952.

54. Bedell Smith to deputy directors, "Organization of CIA Clandestine Services," July 15, 1952, in Warner, *CIA under Truman*, document 79.

55. Bedell Smith to NSC, April 23, 1952.

56. Montague, *General Walter Bedell Smith*, 224.

57. Ibid., 211.

58. Joyce to Bruce, "PSB and General Smith's Proposal," October 15, 1952, in *FRUS, 1950–1955: Intelligence Community*, document 129; and Lay to NSC, "Procedure for NSC 10/5 Matters," November 13, 1952, in ibid., document 135.

59. Smith, *Unknown CIA*, 9.

60. Immerman, *Hidden Hand*, 44.

61. Richard Helms, *A Look over My Shoulder*: *A Life in the Central Intelligence Agency* (New York: Random House, 2003), 105.

62. Ibid., 103.

63. Ronald Spector, *Eagle against the Sun*: *The American War with Japan* (New York: Vintage, 1985), 501.

64. Policy Planning Staff PPS-26, "Problem: To Establish U.S. Policy Regarding Anti-Communist Measures Which Could Be Planned and Carried Out within the Inter-American System," March 22, 1948, in *Foreign Relations of the United States, 1948*, vol. 9, *The Western Hemisphere* (Washington, DC: US Government Printing Office, 1972), 193–201.

65. Ibid., 199.

66. Ibid.

67. "United States Policy toward Inter-American Collaboration," NSC 56/2, May 18, 1950, in Department of State, *Foreign Relations of the United States, 1950*, vol. 1, *National Security Affairs* (Washington, DC: US Government Printing Office, 1977), 628–37.

68. Stephen Rabe, *Eisenhower and Latin America*: *The Foreign Policy of Intervention* (Chapel Hill: University of North Carolina Press, 1988), 23.

69. Unlisted CIA officer to Wisner, "Guatemalan Situation," July 9, 1952, in *FRUS, 1952–1954: Guatemala*, document 12; Unlisted CIA author, "Callegeris' Visit to General Somoza," September 1, 1952, in ibid., document 16; Unlisted CIA officer to CIA, September 12, 1952, in ibid., document 17; and Seekford to King, "Liaison between Calligeris and General Trujillo of Santo Domingo," September 18, 1952, in ibid., document 18.

70. Seekford to King, "Liaison between Calligeris and Trujillo."

71. Ibid.

72. Edward Clark, "Roadbuilding Equipment for Guatemala," February 5, 1952, in *Foreign Relations of the United States, 1952–1954*, vol. 4, *The American Republics* (Washington, DC: US Government Printing Office, 1983), document 409; Clark to Krieg, September 5, 1952, in ibid., document 411; Edward Clark, "Export Control Policy toward Guatemala," October 14, 1952, in ibid., document 415; and Leddy to Cabot, May 21, 1953, in ibid., document 423.

73. Editorial Note, in *FRUS, 1952–1954: Guatemala*, document 1; Editorial Note,

in ibid., document 11; and Unlisted CIA author, "Report," October 8, 1952, in ibid., document 20.

74. Earman to Dennison, "Estimate of Situation in Guatemala," January 14, 1952, in Warner, *CIA under Truman*, document 76.

75. Three memorandums, Mara to Truman, July 11, 1952, President's Secretary's Files, Subject Files, "Foreign Affairs: G.," Harry Truman Papers, Harry S Truman Library and Museum, Independence, MO.

76. Untitled memo to JCK RE Guatemala 1954 Coup, November 4, 1954, CIAFERR, https://www.cia.gov/library/readingroom/docs/DOC_0000914985.pdf.

77. Unlisted CIA author, "Central American Situation," October 8, 1952, in *FRUS, 1952–1954: Guatemala*, document 23.

78. Herbert Matthews, *A World in Revolution: A Newspaperman's Memoir* (New York: Scribner's Sons, 1971), 262–64.

79. Robert Pastor, *Not Condemned to Repetition: The United States and Nicaragua*, rev. ed. (Cambridge: Westview Press, 2002), 3–4. Emphasis in the original.

80. One of Mara's original memorandums bears the handwritten notation "see me" in its upper-right corner. Sowell could not identify the handwriting, but he believed it was not Truman's. Personal communication to author, November 13, 2012.

81. Hedden, "Western Hemisphere Division," July 15, 1952, in *FRUS, 1952–1954: Guatemala*, document 13.

82. Unlisted CIA author, "Report."

83. Unlisted CIA author, "Guatemala," October 8, 1952, in *FRUS, 1952–1954: Guatemala*, document 21.

84. Ibid.

85. Unlisted CIA author, "Central American Situation."

86. Ibid.

87. Mann to Acheson, "Possible Military Action against Guatemala," October 3, 1952, in *FRUS, 1952–1954*, vol. 4, document 413; and Matthews, *World in Revolution*, 262–64.

88. Acheson to Truman, May 3, 1961, in *Among Friends: Personal Letters of Dean Acheson*, ed. David McLellan and David Acheson (New York: Dodd, Mead, 1980), 206–7.

89. Mann, "Nicaragua's Desire for Arms," September 29, 1952, in *FRUS, 1952–1954*, vol. 4, document 599.

90. Unlisted CIA Author, "Central American Situation."

91. J. C. King, "Central American Situation," October 9, 1952, in *FRUS, 1952–1954: Guatemala*, document 25.

92. Frank Wisner, "Central American Situation," October 11, 1952, in ibid., document 28.

93. J. C. King, "Central American Situation," October 10, 1952, in ibid., document 26; and Matthews, *World in Revolution*, 262–64.

94. Rabe, *Eisenhower and Latin America*, 31–33.

95. NSC 144/1, "United States Objectives and Courses of Action with Respect to Latin America," March 18, 1953, in *FRUS, 1952–1954*, vol. 4, document 3.

96. Allen Dulles, "Memorandum Re P.B. Fortune," March 8, 1953, in *FRUS, 1952–1954: Guatemala*, document 36.

97. Unlisted Author, "Contact Report," November 16, 1953, in ibid., document 66.

98. Gleijeses, *Shattered Hope*, 374–75; and Immerman, *CIA in Guatemala*, 168.

99. Dulles to Houston, April 21, 1964, in *Documentary History of the Truman Presidency*, vol. 23, *The Central Intelligence Agency: Its Founding and the Dispute over Its Mission, 1945–1954*, ed. Dennis Merrill (Lanham, MD: University Publications of America, 1998), 418–21; Truman, "Limit CIA to Intelligence."

100. Immerman, *Hidden Hand*, 138.

101. Ralph Weber, ed., *Spymasters: Ten CIA Officers in Their Own Words* (Wilmington, DE: Scholarly Resources, 1999), 119. In fact, Dulles, not Kirkpatrick or Houston, visited Truman and then wrote to Houston afterward.

102. Truman, "Limit CIA to Intelligence." Truman rejected David Wise and Thomas Ross, *The Invisible Government* (New York: Random House, 1964), at the same time. See Truman to Arthur, June 10, 1964, Harry Truman Post-Presidential Papers, Outgoing Correspondence File, Box 643, "Arnold-Arz.," Truman Library.

103. Onate, "What Did Truman Say," 11.

104. Immerman, *Hidden Hand*, 42, 55.

5 CIA Director Richard Helms

Secrecy, Stonewalling, and Spin

Christopher Moran

Richard Helms spent his final hours as director of the Central Intelligence Agency (CIA) in the comfort of his seventh-floor office, overlooking the Potomac River, destroying documents. One eyewitness was John Kenneth Knaus. Writing years later, Knaus, who spent forty-four years with the CIA, including seven as chief of the Tibetan Task Force, recollected that he saw Helms tearing up piles of documents and simply tossing them into a burn bag without comment. Among the items destined for the incinerator were five bulky copies of the CIA's in-house report into the Bay of Pigs fiasco as well as a set of "eight x ten glossies of [U.S. Senator] Ted Kennedy cavorting naked in a Rome whorehouse." Reportedly, Helms joked, "We don't need in Agency files dirty pictures of a U.S. Senator who one day may be President."[1]

Helms's decision to purge the CIA's vaults of incriminating material was entirely in keeping with his reputation as a passionately, even obsessively, secretive public servant. Aptly described by biographer Thomas Powers as "The Man Who Kept the Secrets," Helms believed that intelligence service demanded a lifetime commitment to absolute secrecy, much in the same way that the Mafia expected its members to abide by the code of *omertà*, from which only the grave can bring release.[2] Secrecy came second nature to him; it defined his professional life and leadership style. As CIA director he gave only one speech to a nongovernment audience, while his entry in the American edition of *Who's Who* was less than an inch long and included only the prosaic details that he was a "govt. official" and a member of the City Tavern Association.[3] The late Cameron LaClair, a twenty-one-year CIA veteran, remarked in an interview that Helms was "absolutely first class at not answering questions."[4] Secrecy even governed his personal life. On the night before she married him, Cynthia, his British-born second wife, was told by a friend, half in jest, "not to marry Dick because he doesn't say anything."[5]

Emblematic of his devotion to secrecy, Helms has the unfortunate distinction of being the only CIA director to have ever been convicted of lying to Congress, owing to his disingenuous testimony before the Senate Foreign Relations Committee in 1973, during which he was questioned about whether the CIA had been involved in the overthrow of Salvador Allende, the president of Chile, or passed any funds to opposition groups in the country. In both cases he gave an unequivocal "No, sir," but it eventually came to light that the CIA had run a major destabilization campaign against the Allende government. For lying under oath to protect CIA secrets, Helms was taken to court in 1977 by federal prosecutors on the charge of perjury. District Judge Barrington D. Parker declared, "You stand before this court in disgrace and shame."[6] Eventually, he cut a deal with the Justice Department that saw him plead guilty to a lesser charge of misdemeanor and escape with a $2,000 fine. Outside the courtroom, his attorney, Edward Bennett Williams, announced that his client would wear his conviction like a "badge of honor."

It thus came as a huge shock when, in the spring of 2003, contrary to every professional instinct and habit, Helms published a memoir of his three decades in US intelligence, titled *A Look over My Shoulder*. "This is a memoir I never expected to write," he acknowledged in the book's preface.[7] Sadly, the aging spymaster passed away six months before publication, meaning that reviewers and commentators were denied the opportunity to question him about his motivation for going into print. Rather unsatisfactorily, all that he had seen fit to reveal in the preface was that the end of the Cold War had allowed the disclosure of some older secrets.

Drawing on the Helms private papers, now available to inspect at the Booth Family Center for Special Collections at Georgetown University, as well as an interview with his widow, Cynthia, this chapter seeks to understand what prompted Helms to pen an autobiography and, ostensibly, renege on the habit of a lifetime.

Three arguments will be made.

One, the decision to write stemmed from a deep and growing concern about how the CIA was viewed, both by the public and by policymakers, in a post–Cold War world. After a short period of celebration following the collapse of the Soviet Union, the 1990s evolved into a decade of anxiety for the CIA. The "peace dividend" raised the specter of budget cuts, and there were even voices suggesting that the defeat of Communism meant that the CIA was no longer needed. Feeding into this broader conversation about the CIA's role and purpose were history books and newspaper headlines that either criticized the CIA's operational record or painted the agency as a bogeyman, subverting American core values. Added to this were self-inflicted public relations disasters, such as the revelation in 1994 that case officer Aldrich Ames had for

Photo 5.1 The Man Who Kept the Secrets: For Director of Central Intelligence Richard Helms (second from left), secrecy was the lifeblood of intelligence work. *White House Photograph Office*

years gone undetected as a spy for the Soviet Union and Russia. During his career Helms had not been overly concerned about the swinging pendulum of public opinion, believing (in his words) that the "nation must to a degree take it on faith that we too are honorable men."[8] His attitude had always been that the CIA could ride out any storm through a combination of secrecy and stonewalling. In the 1990s, however, he came around to the view that lack of public trust in the CIA was a problem that could not be ignored. Without it, he determined, the agency would see its budgets slashed, reducing it to a discussion group on international affairs. He worried that unless public confidence was restored, the CIA would be plagued by self-doubt and struggle to attract talented new recruits. He also feared that without public support, the policymaking community the agency is designed to serve would question its judgments.

Two, it will be suggested that Helms's transformation from secret keeper to espionage town crier was welcomed by the CIA, to the extent that his old employer actually assisted in the memoir's production. Like Helms, in the 1990s the CIA gradually recognized that it was better to contribute to the public debate about intelligence than to sit in silence while it was being contested. By failing to communicate its mission, the CIA realized that it had allowed people to imagine the worst. "We need to take initiatives to share our history," concluded a CIA Task Force on Greater Openness in April 1992.[9] One of the ways it went about this was by working behind the scenes with memoirists it could trust, helping them to produce positive and cheery accounts. *A Look over My Shoulder* was one such project.

And three, while writing a memoir was a big step for Helms, it did not represent a volte-face. Secrets still mattered to him. His memoir was not about baring the secrets of the Company; his sobriquet—"the man who kept the secrets"—remained intact. Rather, the book was about public relations and a shift from what political scientist Peter Gill, speaking in the UK context, describes as a fundamentally "defensive" approach to information management to an "offensive" strategy of "persuasion."[10] It was about dispelling some of the mystery that surrounded intelligence work and defending the CIA's record against snowballing innuendo and inaccuracy. It was about telling the American people that US security from foreign threats demanded a permanent foreign intelligence service, peopled by men and women who worked responsibly, with high risk and little reward. *A Look over My Shoulder* was Helms's way of saying that, in the twenty-first century, the requirements of an intelligence leader had changed. To his successors on the CIA's seventh floor, he was sending a message: as much as it was still necessary to keep secrets, and presumably burn documents as required, public education also mattered.

The Man Who Kept the Secrets

To appreciate just how much Helms's thinking changed during the later years of his life, it is important to take the story back to the spymaster's final years at the CIA. Helms departed the agency in February 1973. Behind him he left an organization that was steadily becoming engulfed in scandal. In February 1967 the underground magazine *Ramparts* had revealed that the CIA had been financing the National Student Association as a front group in the battle to win Cold War "hearts and minds," sparking outrage. Following this, the mainstream media picked up the scent and discovered a trail of CIA money running through labor unions, think tanks, and universities. By early 1973 stories were emerging that linked the CIA with the unfolding Watergate scandal, with the revelation that two of the so-called Plumbers, E. Howard Hunt and James McCord, had worked for the CIA in the past. Writing to a friend, Helms lamented, "I feel like a GI creeping through a mine field. There is no predicting what is going to blow apart next. Not the least of my problems has been to distance the Agency from those scallywags who indulged in the Watergate caper. I wish their previous employer had been the Salvation Army."[11] Helms himself would become Watergate's first casualty. When he refused Richard

Nixon's brazen request to have the CIA block the Federal Bureau of Investigation's investigation into the burglary, the president summoned him to Camp David and fired him. As a consolation prize, he was offered and accepted the position of US ambassador to Iran.

By 1975—often described as the Year of Intelligence—the CIA's reputation had sunk even further, as a combination of press sleuthing and congressional investigations revealed a host of dirty tricks and misdeeds, dating from the CIA's founding in 1947. Although Helms had left the agency, he was caught firmly in the crosshairs. He was personally linked to dozens of covert actions overseas, plus plots to assassinate foreign leaders, including Patrice Lumumba of the Congo, Rafael Trujillo in the Dominican Republic, and most famously, Fidel Castro of Cuba. Helms's signature was shown to have authorized the invasive prying into over 20,000 items of first-class mail. It was revealed that he had overseen a program of mind control and drug testing on unsuspecting US citizens and had been at the heart of the cover-up of the death of Frank Olson, a forty-three-year-old germ warfare specialist who had been given LSD in a glass of Cointreau and who nine days later committed suicide by jumping from the tenth floor of a New York skyscraper. The Senate Select Committee on Intelligence, led by presidential hopeful Frank Church, implied that Helms had carried out certain projects without the president's knowledge, while the President's Commission on CIA Activities, headed by Nelson Rockefeller, criticized him for authorizing the destruction of key evidence, including photographs, transcripts, and tape recordings relevant to the Watergate inquiry. In the eyes of his critics, of which there were many, as best-selling intelligence author James Bamford has written, Helms became the "CIA's Darth Vader."[12]

In spite of all the bad publicity, Helms remained convinced of the need for total secrecy. As mentioned earlier, he took pride in his misdemeanor charge for lying to Congress about CIA malefactions in Chile. As he saw it, there was nothing dishonorable about protecting secrets, and his view was shared by many of his former colleagues. Indeed, after his trial in 1977, he attended a reunion of intelligence veterans who gave him a standing ovation and raised his $2,000 fine by passing the hat. In May 1978 Helms agreed to be interviewed by the British journalist David Frost but was characteristically cagey. When asked the question, "Is it practical that the public be informed of what intelligence is doing in its name?" his response was "I don't see how. . . . It may be possible to tell them about oil imports and wheat estimates and things of that kind, although I happen not to agree even with that."[13]

Helms was appalled by the actions of CIA Director William Colby, who had adopted a policy of controlled cooperation with Congress, acceding to requests from members of Congress for information and giving more than bare-bone answers to their questions. Colby's logic was that if he volunteered what he called "bad secrets" (information about assassination plots, drug testing, etc.), he would feel less pressure to surrender "good secrets," such as information about sources and methods, which warranted absolute protection. Helms was deeply troubled by this. He compared Colby's candid testimonies before Congress to the Bolsheviks' ransacking the tsar's intelligence files after the Russian Revolution, and worried that hostile intelligence services, good at nothing if not patiently looking for needles in haystacks, would find something significant in the publicized material.[14] Colby, he believed, by opening up, had foolishly sucked outside forces into the world of intelligence—career politicians like Church, arguably more interested in making sensational headlines and riding the wave of anti-CIA hysteria to national prominence than in doing what was right for the nation's well-being. Helms's feelings on the matter are encapsulated in a letter he sent to journalist Charles Murphy on March 19, 1975:

> I must say that Colby has done a startlingly successful job at making a total mess. . . . He may have thought he could become the "white hat", but that ploy has surely backfired now and he must look to sophisticated Washington like the biggest jerk on the block. It is all terribly sad and he has brought it all on himself by his mumblings and other matters about which he should have kept his mouth shut. The Agency committed no assassination of foreign leaders, but by the time [President] Ford and Colby get through passing their sentences, they leave the worst possible impression.[15]

It is worth noting that Helms was not alone in thinking this way. Legendary CIA counterintelligence supremo James Jesus Angleton told friends that he wondered if Colby might be working for the "other side."[16] Moreover, many years later, when Colby's body was fished out of a river near his home in Rock Point, Maryland, after he had reportedly suffered a heart attack while paddling his canoe on a late-night boating trip, conspiracy theorists claimed that his death was actually a revenge killing by the CIA's old guard who never forgave his candidness on the witness table.

Fighting Back

The end of the Cold War was a cause for celebration at the CIA. On the historic night of November 9, 1989, as the Berlin Wall came down and people from the east of the city spilled across the border, the CIA had a party at its headquarters in Langley, Virginia. In her memoir retired CIA field operative Melissa Boyle Mahle recollected, "The corridors were alive with people, talking, laughing, and swapping war stories. . . . There was champagne and a sense of camaraderie among the Cold War warriors. The good guys had won."[17] However, the festive mood was short-lived. As the Soviet Union broke up into constituent republics and with Francis Fukuyama famously announcing the triumph of Western liberal democracy and the advent of a post-ideological world, questions began to be asked about the CIA's reason for being.

The most high-profile voice to question the CIA's relevance and purpose was four-term US senator Daniel Patrick Moynihan.[18] Moynihan had two problems with the CIA. One, that it was incompetent. Although later disputed by a number of historians, at the time the agency was widely believed to have failed to foresee the collapse of the Soviet Union, adding to earlier errors such as failing to predict the Arab-Israeli War in 1973 and missing India's first nuclear test a year later. Attempting to predict world events is, of course, not an exact science, but, according to Langley's senior managers, analysis was the agency's greatest strength. Moynihan's second complaint related to excessive secrecy. In 1984 he had resigned in protest as the vice chairman of the Senate Intelligence Committee, citing the CIA's refusal to keep the committee "fully informed" about US support for the contras in Nicaragua. With glasnost and a new spirit of openness sweeping across the old Eastern bloc, he considered the CIA's obsession with secrecy as outdated and dangerous.

In a move designed to make a metaphorical point about the CIA being a Cold War relic, in 1991 Moynihan proposed a bill that would have disbanded the organization and passed its various functions to other departments. A year later two federal lawmakers, US senator David Boren and US representative David McCurdy, chairmen of the Senate and House Intelligence Committees, respectively, introduced two separate bills calling for a major restructuring of the intelligence community. Taken together, the Moynihan and Boren-McCurdy proposals encouraged every American, from the Beltway to the heartland, to think about whether, in a post–Cold War context, it was sensible to keep ploughing money into the CIA. For liberals, a reduced intelligence budget meant better health care. For conservatives, lower taxes.

Not since the dark days of the mid-1970s had the CIA faced a bigger crisis. Mahle remembers seeing cars garlanded with "Abolish the CIA" bumper stickers.[19] In truth the CIA's survival was not at stake; save among individuals of a conspiratorial mien or those operating at the fringes of the political system, there was a general recognition of the need for the United States to have a permanent foreign intelligence agency. However, the prospect of budget cuts and downsizing was very real: even Colby was quoted as saying that it was time to beat swords into ploughshares. As was the possibility of Beltway rivals encroaching on the CIA's territory. The emergence of transnational terrorism, international organized crime, and drug trafficking heralded a new kind of threat that knew no national borders. To eradicate these dangers, national jurisdictions were being asked to work together in real time, meaning that the traditional distinction between foreign and domestic intelligence collection was breaking down. At Langley there was deep concern that it would lose the intelligence turf wars and see its budget, personnel, and prestige diminished.

Although it is the instinct of any bureaucracy to protect its resources, the CIA was genuinely troubled by the impact that cuts would have on its ability to keep the United States safe. Arguably, the New World Order was a more dangerous place than the Cold War, when at least the United States knew who the enemy was and when both superpowers had a mutual interest in avoiding nuclear war. Keeping track of amorphous terrorist groups with no obvious national affiliation posed a serious challenge and required resources. As CIA Director James Woolsey said in his confirmation hearings, the United States had successfully defeated the Soviet dragon but was now living in a jungle filled with a bewildering array of poisonous snakes.

In this context the Helms memoir was born. Like the CIA, the retired spy-master had become increasingly worried by the agency's predicament in a post–Cold War world. A key part of the problem, he determined, was that people, including the denizens of Capitol Hill, had a shockingly poor under-standing of the CIA's operational record, the role of intelligence in national security policymaking, and the danger posed by a myriad of widening threats to national security. In effect, through its own silence, the CIA had allowed itself to become the devil that nobody knew.

According to his widow, Helms spent a large part of his retirement read-ing spy books, the majority of which painted him and the agency in a nega-tive light—organizing secret wars, planning assassinations, and playing court procurer for White House dirty tricks, coupled with bumbling ineptitude.[20] This literature, he concluded, was doing the CIA untold harm. It damaged the morale of intelligence officers and, even more seriously, added fuel to the increasing perception that the CIA was either irrelevant or incompetent and therefore should have its appropriation slashed. "The more he read," remarked Cynthia, "the more he became upset and his views changed."[21] Having been diagnosed with multiple myeloma (a condition he kept secret, even from his son), he decided that he should be a passive observer no more: he and the agency had to fight back.

Helms had been particularly troubled by three books. The first was *War of Numbers*, published in 1994, by the late CIA analyst Sam Adams.[22] Drawing on documents that Adams had secretly taken from the CIA and buried in the woods near his 250-acre farm in Virginia, the book was a blow-by-blow account of Adams's ten years at the CIA, from 1963 to 1973. The bulk of the book was devoted to Adams's belief that, during the Vietnam War, the CIA, together with Gen. William Westmoreland's command staff, had conspired to minimize enemy troop strength in a bid to deceive Congress and maintain public support for the war. Helms was accused of bowing to political pressure and underreporting by as much as half the number of Vietnamese Communists under arms. As a result, charged Adams, US troops had to fight an enemy much larger than they suspected, leading to massive failures, such as fatally misjudging the ferocity of the Tet Offensive in January 1968. In Adams's words Helms's agreement with the military to hide the true size of enemy forces was a "monument of deceit."

The second book to upset Helms was *The Very Best Men*, published in 1995, by Evan Thomas, assistant managing editor and Washington bureau chief of *Newsweek*.[23] The book was an account of the first two decades of the CIA, seen through the actions of four prominent senior officers—Frank Wisner, Richard Bissell, Tracy Barnes, and Desmond FitzGerald. In recounting their intertwined lives and careers, Thomas depicted an organization that was obsessed with covert action, possessing a hubris and swagger totally disproportionate to its achievements. As a reviewer for the *New York Times* commented, with its strong emphasis on amateurish failures in Cuba (namely, the Bay of Pigs), China, and the former Belgian Congo, the book made the CIA "look like the coyote in a Road Runner cartoon, frequently outwitted or foiled by its own feckless enthusiasm for its task."[24] In researching the book Thomas had benefited from Executive Order 12356, giving him access to certain classified documents, on the proviso that he signed a secrecy agreement and submitted his work to the CIA for prepublication review. To Helms's fury, it transpired that the agency not only failed to properly vet the manuscript but gave Thomas far greater access to information than should have been the case, including access to sensitive documents suggesting that Helms, the consummate bureaucratic survivor, had had reservations about certain doomed covert actions but said nothing—hence the in-house joke "Frank the fucker and Dick the ducker."[25] Helms immediately blamed Robert Gates, the CIA director when Thomas began writing, but a subsequent internal investigation claimed that Thomas had inadvertently benefited from the errors of several "lower level people."[26]

The third book to distress Helms was *The Man Who Kept the Secrets: Richard Helms and the CIA*, by Pulitzer Prize–winning journalist Thomas Powers.[27] The book had been published in 1979, but fascinatingly, Helms had never read it. Apparently, he felt he knew the book pretty well, since he and Powers had talked on several occasions during its preparation.[28] In 1995 he finally did read it and was not happy. Although Powers had been generally positive about Helms, presenting him as a good soldier who took his marching orders from one president at a time, the book was highly critical of the CIA as an organization. Powers accused the agency of "intervening callously and recklessly around the world" and claimed that the CIA operations represented a "record of crime, blunder, embarrassment and failure." Like Sam Adams, he also discussed politicization, suggesting that the CIA had routinely "cooked" national intelligence estimates to suit predetermined policy—for example, inflating the strategic threat posed by a Soviet first-strike capability so that the Nixon White House could convince Congress to increase arms spending and thus put pressure on Moscow. According to Cynthia Helms, Powers's book was instrumental in convincing Helms to open up, since he had enormous respect for Powers and was genuinely shocked that someone so knowledgeable could, in his view, get things so wrong.[29]

Helms's new belief that the CIA had to build, not assume, public support was shared by the agency itself. In the 1990s it too had arrived at the view that it could ill afford to be a silent observer in the important national debate about the future of US intelligence. During his Senate confirmation hearings in late 1991, CIA Director Robert Gates testified that the agency "must change and be seen to change, or confront irrelevance and growing sentiment for [its] dismemberment."[30] Less than two weeks after Gates had been sworn in as director, he created a Task Force on Greater CIA Openness to consider ways of "making more information about the Agency available to the American people . . . *to the extent possible* [emphasis added]."[31] On the basis of interviews with CIA employees, but also senior figures within the media, academia, and both the legislative and executive branches, the task force reported, proudly, that "we have an important story to tell, a story that bears repeating."[32] Many Americans, it underlined, "operate with a romanticized or erroneous view of intelligence from the movies, books and newspapers."[33] Too much secrecy, it argued, meant that people made the wrong assumptions about the agency, either that it was doing something bad or doing nothing at all. It concluded, "The CIA will have to work harder at explaining the need for intelligence in a post–Cold War world."[34]

Gates introduced his Openness Task Force with a speech to the Oklahoma Press Association on February 21, 1992. In it he acknowledged that "CIA Openness" was an oxymoron but promised to change this. Over the next few years, Gates and his successors (James Woolsey, John Deutch, and George Tenet) oversaw a range of initiatives designed to make the CIA more visible and understandable. With great fanfare the CIA's Center for the Study of Intelligence released a series of glossy volumes of declassified documents on some of the agency's oldest operations and analytical work. The CIA's in-house journal, *Studies in Intelligence*, had many of its articles declassified, while CIA historians were encouraged to publish unclassified essays and speak at academic conferences. Although the CIA was keen to stress that its declassification program was "warts and all," generally speaking the material focused on successes and avoided "bad secrets." For example, documents were released on the Cuban Missile Crisis, undoubtedly a "feel good" case for the agency, but nothing was volunteered on potentially embarrassing episodes such as the Bay of Pigs. The CIA's bid to give itself a makeover also led to the creation of a new position within the Office of Public Affairs—entertainment industry liaison—tasked with helping filmmakers to produce more accurate cinematic portrayals of the agency. In 1999 the CIA even allowed the makers of the TV series *The Agency* to bring their cameras to Langley and film office staff as extras. Unsurprisingly, help did not extend to projects that demonized the CIA as a rogue outfit, with legions of assassins at its beck and call—for instance, *The Bourne Identity*, starring Matt Damon. To quote Chase Brandon, the agency's first Hollywood liaison, "By page twenty-five [of the script] . . . I lost track of how many rogue operatives had assassinated people. . . . I chucked the thing in the burn bag."[35]

A central component of the CIA's bid to change public attitudes and perceptions was memoirs. The agency had in fact long recognized the importance of memoirs as a powerful social force, capable of shaping the CIA's image with the broad-based American public. One piece of internal correspondence written during the directorship of Adm. Stansfield Turner (1977–81) stated that if the CIA wanted to enhance "attitudinal acceptance by the 'grass roots,'" it should support "first person spy memoirs of a colorful nature."[36] "Memoirs," it continued, "would be a counterforce to destructive, uncontrolled leaks by former employees."[37] Turner enthusiastically supported the idea of assisting memoirists who were, in his phrase, "favorably oriented toward the Agency."[38] Indeed, he even instructed the CIA's Office of Public Affairs to purchase "bulk quantities" of memoirs by loyalists to "nudge [them] in the direction of the bestseller list."[39] One of the beneficiaries of Turner's memoir strategy was former station chief Cord Meyer, who was allowed to inspect CIA records while putting together his 1980 book, *Facing Reality*.[40] However, the tactic of supporting certain memoirists died with CIA Director William Casey (1981–87). A veteran of the "Oh So Secret" days of the wartime Office of Strategic Services (OSS), Casey wanted the CIA to be a "no-profile Agency," meaning that memoirs, however well-intentioned, had to stop.[41] Gates's task force considered this a grave error, as did John Hollister Hedley, who in 1997 became chairman of the CIA's Publications Review Board (PRB), responsible for vetting the nonofficial writings of CIA employees. "Evidence abounds," Hedley has written, "that former CIA officers can offer pertinent and valuable insights without damaging national security in the slightest. Indeed, they can enhance it. Memoirs can help clear the air. They can illuminate and inform.

They can correct misconceptions. They can contribute expert opinions on current issues. They provide insight into what kind of people work for the CIA—people with intellect and integrity."[42]

Accordingly, when Helms notified the CIA of his intention to write a memoir, he found the organization only too happy to help. He was given full access to the CIA's vast archive, including internal histories, and permitted to interview serving personnel. His coadjutor, CIA alumnus William Hood, was afforded the same privilege. Helms was given his own office in the Center for the Study of Intelligence at the CIA and was assigned a research assistant to help him identify relevant archival material, read draft chapters, and put forward suggestions in the service of accuracy and style.[43] Later, Dr. David Robarge, a political analyst who joined the CIA's History Staff in 1996, was given the job of research assistant in addition to his other responsibilities.[44] According to Cynthia, Robarge—a graduate of Columbia University with a PhD in modern American history—was "enormously helpful, talking to Dick all the time and accompanying him on research trips."[45] The avuncular and respected Hedley proved quite helpful as well. For example, in the spring of 1998 Helms applied to the Lyndon B. Johnson Presidential Library in Austin, Texas, asking for permission to inspect still classified records. After this request had been turned down, Hedley appealed to the library's director, Harry Middleton, requesting that Helms be granted "every courtesy and accommodation."[46] "We are excited about the undertaking," he wrote, "and feel certain that when all his research and writing comes to fruition, he will make a unique and valuable contribution to intelligence literature and to the history of the Cold War."[47] The intervention worked: Helms subsequently had no access difficulties with the library.

Unlike many memoirists, who find the prepublication review process time-consuming and exasperating, resulting in books replete with line after line of blacked-out text, Helms had no such trouble. The PRB was punctual in returning chapters, adhering to the legally mandated response time of thirty days and asking for few changes. None of the required deletions were regarded by Helms as being unreasonable. For example, he was asked to remove a reference to a piece of equipment still used in the field. Largely out of character, the PRB was happy to reword objectionable passages rather than take a red pen to the whole page or section, as is often the case. For example, the book revealed the CIA's links with the Israeli intelligence agency Mossad, a relationship that had never been officially acknowledged by either the Israeli or American government. Instead of deleting the entire discussion, the board offered Helms some rephrasing. Thus, "Jim Angleton . . . handled liaison with the Israeli intelligence services" became "Jim Angleton . . . handled some matters with Israel."[48] Similarly, "Jim's liaison with the Israeli services was of exceptional value" became "Jim's interest in Israel was of exceptional value."[49] Fascinatingly, the real "censor" in Helms's case was not the CIA but the publisher, Random House. The PRB had turned a blind eye to the mention of several secret code names, but Random House was concerned that they would alienate the general reader and removed them.[50] The publisher also deleted a fascinating chapter called "Agency Families," in which Helms had recounted stories about women who had bravely assisted their husbands in an operational capacity, including one occasion when a wife had made a dead drop and another when a wife had made a "brush contact" with an agent in place on a "busy street in Warsaw."[51] Such material—caviar to the scholar of intelligence—was strangely dismissed as being boring.

A Look over My Shoulder

Helms, who passed away at age eighty-nine on October 23, 2002, did not live to see the publication of his memoir. Guided into print by Hood in the spring of 2003, *A Look over My Shoulder* was everything Gates's Openness Task Force could have hoped for when, a decade earlier, it had recommended that the CIA "share our history." At the core of the book was a prosaic but pertinent message: human intelligence matters. While Helms valued the contribution of billion dollar satellites and high-tech monitoring equipment— so-called spies in the sky—the book made it clear that signals intelligence was no substitute for traditional human intelligence collection and analysis. Abandoning the old adage that "an intelligence success revealed is an intelligence failure"—a motto Helms had stuck to with theological intensity during his career—the book gave cases in which humans had "made a difference." For example, there was a detailed discussion of Col. Oleg Penkovsky, an agent in place in Moscow (code name Hero) who provided critical information about Soviet missiles and war plans during the Cuban Missile Crisis. "This information," wrote Helms, "was without question a fundamental part of the data that permitted President Kennedy to make the decisions that avoided the possibility of a nuclear showdown and perhaps war."[52] Much was made of the CIA's pride in producing unvarnished and "value free" intelligence assessments, untainted by political considerations or policy preferences. Countering the conventional wisdom that Helms had been so desperate to serve and advance his career that he became a bootlicker of the presidency, the book showed his dogged determination to deliver unwelcome forecasts about Vietnam to Presidents Johnson and Nixon.

The book gave some perspective on the controversial subject of covert action. As discussed earlier, popular discourse was awash with portrayals of the CIA rigging elections, orchestrating coups, and toppling governments like bowling pins. Unsurprisingly, Helms had been nervous about how to handle the subject, as evidenced by a letter he sent to Hood that contained the words: "What in the hell are we going to do?"[53] Fortunately, Hood had a solution. As he saw it, the book had to make three arguments, which it ultimately did. One, covert action was "as old as secret intelligence" and certainly did not originate with the CIA.[54] Hood provided Helms with examples from the era of George Washington, the implication being that if covert action was acceptable to the selfless father of the Republic, it should be palatable to every contemporary American. Two, covert action was a valuable "third option" between doing nothing and engaging national security threats overtly, which in the nuclear age could lead to catastrophic loss of human life. Related to this, it was argued that ethical concerns about covert action are never absolute; rather, they must be weighed against the seriousness of the threat and the viability of other options, including the likelihood of a diplomatic resolution and the wisdom of a military response. And three, covert action was only ever carried out at the explicit request of the president. To illustrate this, the book showed that the CIA had favored a "slow burn" approach to Fidel Castro, but the Kennedy White House had wanted him out of the picture as soon as possible, by any means necessary. It also included a foreword by Henry Kissinger, in which the legendary diplomat and former secretary of state emphasized that "all [covert actions] were approved—and in most controversial cases, ordered—by presidents of every Cold War administration, even when the paperwork was conducted to provide deniability."[55]

On the subject of covert action, Hood saved Helms from potential embarrassment. In a draft chapter, Helms had made the astonishingly frank admission that, in its early days, the CIA had carried out "thousands" of covert actions—a revelation hardly likely to ease public fears that the agency was a squid-like meddler in international affairs. Hood—"so as not to frighten anyone"—changed this to "hundreds."[56] He also quashed Helms's suggestion that the book should address the issue of how a short-term covert action success can become long-term failure. For example, Helms had written a chapter discussing Operation Cyclone, the program to arm and finance mujahideen rebels during the Soviet-Afghan War, in which he argued that a Communist Afghanistan was in retrospect preferable to the repressive Taliban regime that emerged in the country. Probably true, counseled Hood, but to admit this would "simply succeed in giving the Agency a black eye."[57]

As reviewers pointed out, there was nothing revelatory in the book. In the words of the late CIA officer and historian Thomas Troy, "*A Look Over My Shoulder* is definitely not an exposé. . . . Readers looking for 'now it can be told' tales of intelligence derring-do will have to look elsewhere."[58] Helms had adhered rigidly to Gates's instruction letter of November 18, 1991, in which he asked his Openness Task Force to find ways to improve "openness . . . to the extent possible"—the operative words being "extent possible." The book disclosed no new operations, added no names to the list of known spies, betrayed no sources and methods, and revealed no information that might have (to borrow John Prados's expression) "flap potential."[59] The fact that someone who clearly knew so much said so little nevertheless took nothing away from the book. Published eighteen months after the surprise attack of September 11, 2001, during which time the CIA had assumed a lead role in the struggle against Islamist terrorism, his defense of the agency's role in protecting US security, coupled with his unique insights into the structure, use, and development of intelligence, could not have been timelier; he had chosen his moment well.

Conclusion

In conclusion this chapter has tried to shed light on a fascinating final period in the life of Richard Helms. The quintessential Cold War spymaster—who, for some people, was and remains a symbol of all that is wrong about the CIA—Helms spent the majority of his life utterly devoted to keeping secrets. Words like "disclosure," "openness," and "transparency" were anathema to him. His commitment to secrecy was so unwavering that he considered it his duty—and even "honorable"—to lie on Capitol Hill in order to keep CIA activities out of the public eye. A dressing-down from the judge had no effect on him, for he valued his oath to the CIA above the oath he swore to Congress to tell the truth. Accordingly, when, in the autumn of his life, he decided to write a memoir, people were genuinely shocked. Of all the "Company men," Helms was probably the last person anyone expected to go into print.

But write a book he did. Like the CIA, he eventually reached his breaking point with negative and (in his view) inaccurate representations of intelligence work, and he worried that, if left uncorrected, they would continue to harm the morale of intelligence officers and potentially lead to a reduction in the CIA's role, influence, and budget. This concern was particularly acute in the years between the collapse of the Soviet Union and 9/11, a period when defense expenditure was being cut but when new and potentially more dangerous national security threats like Islamist terrorism were arriving on the scene. By constantly circling the wagons, Helms determined, the CIA was doing itself no favors, since silence bred suspicion, helped to blow mistakes out of proportion, and led to ignorance about what threats existed.

What the agency needed was a voice—to convince taxpayers and their representatives that it was ethical, effective, and ultimately worth the enormous outlay of public funds in a security landscape that was far from safe. Writing a memoir was one way to achieve this, representing a "third way" between secrecy, on the one hand, and openness, on the other. Some might interpret the Helms memoir as a sign that the tiger had changed its stripes, but this was not the case. Containing neither "good" nor "bad" secrets, *A Look over My Shoulder* was an exercise in public education by a still passionately secretive man. Given the CIA's role in its production, one might even ask whether it should be classified as a memoir at all. Arguably, a better description would be official history by proxy. Or "unofficial official history."

Notes

Parts of this chapter have already appeared in an earlier publication: Christopher Moran, "From Confession to Corporate Memory: The Memoirs of CIA Director Richard M. Helms," *International History Review* 36, no. 1 (2014): 70–88. I am grateful to Taylor & Francis for permission to reproduce certain elements.

1. John Kenneth Knaus to Scott Breckinridge, 2007MS063, Box 34, Scott Breckinridge Papers, Wendell H. Ford Public Policy Research Center, University of Kentucky, Lexington, KY (hereafter cited as WHF).

2. Thomas Powers, *The Man Who Kept the Secrets: Richard Helms and the CIA* (London: Weidenfeld and Nicolson, 1979).

3. David S. Robarge, "Richard Helms: The Intelligence Professional Personified," *Studies in Intelligence* 46, no. 4 (2002): 35–43.

4. Cameron LaClair, interview by the author.

5. Cynthia Helms, interview by the author.

6. Cited in Joseph Heller, *Good as Gold* (London: Vintage Books, 2011), 341.

7. Richard Helms, *A Look over My Shoulder: A Life in the Central Intelligence Agency*, with William Hood (New York: Random House, 2003), Preface.

8. Richard Helms, "Intelligence in American Society," *Studies in Intelligence* 11, no. 3 (Summer 1967): 1–16.

9. Task Force on Greater CIA Openness to DCI, "Task Force on Greater CIA Openness," December 20, 1991, CIA FOIA Electronic Reading Room (CIAFERR), https://www.cia.gov/library/readingroom/docs/DOC_0005524009.pdf.

10. Peter Gill, "Reasserting Control: Recent Changes in the Oversight of the UK Intelligence Community," *Intelligence and National Security* 11, no. 2 (1996): 313–31.

11. Richard Helms to D. A. Woodruf, August 12, 1972, 8/30/438, Richard Helms Papers, Georgetown University Special Collections (hereafter cited as RH).

12. James Bamford, "Spy vs Spies," *New York Times*, July 18, 1999.

13. David Frost, "An Interview with Richard Helms," *Studies in Intelligence* 25, no. 3 (Fall 1981): 5.

14. Trevor Paglen, *Blank Spots on the Map: The Dark Geography of the Pentagon's Secret World* (New York: Penguin, 2009), 193.

15. Richard Helms to Charles Murphy, March 19, 1975, 9/9/452, RH.

16. Kathryn S. Olmsted, *Challenging the Secret Government: The Post-Watergate*

Investigations of the CIA and FBI (Chapel Hill: University of North Carolina Press, 1996), 92.

17. Melissa Boyle Mahle, *Denial and Deception: An Insider's View of the CIA* (New York: Nation Books, 2004), 56.

18. See Paul McGarr, "'Do We Still Need the CIA?': Daniel Patrick Moynihan, the Central Intelligence Agency and US Foreign Policy," *History: The Journal of the Historical Association* 100, no. 340 (2015): 275–92.

19. Mahle, *Denial and Deception*, 147.

20. Helms interview.

21. Ibid.

22. Sam Adams, *War of Numbers: An Intelligence Memoir* (Hanover, NH: Steerforth, 1994).

23. Evan Thomas, *The Very Best Men: The Early Years of the CIA* (New York: Simon & Schuster, 1996).

24. Richard Bernstein, "Book of the Times: Four Old Boys and Their Adventures at the CIA," *New York Times*, October 4, 1995.

25. Thomas, *Very Best Men*, 151.

26. Robert Gates to Richard Helms, November 1, 1995, 9/17/461, RH.

27. Powers, *Man Who Kept the Secrets*.

28. Helms interview.

29. Ibid.

30. "Mysteries and Secrets," *Los Angeles Times*, April 19, 1992.

31. Robert Gates to Director of Public Affairs, "Greater CIA Openness," November 18, 1991, http://www.namebase.net/campus/pa01.html.

32. Task Force on Greater CIA Openness to DCI, "Task Force on Greater CIA Openness."

33. Ibid. For more information about Hollywood portrayals of the CIA, see Tricia Jenkins, *The CIA in Hollywood: How the Agency Shapes Film and Television* (Austin: University of Texas Press, 2012); Simon Willmetts, *In Secrecy's Shadow: The OSS and CIA in Hollywood Cinema, 1941–1979* (Edinburgh: Edinburgh University Press, 2016).

34. Task Force on Greater CIA Openness to DCI, "Task Force on Greater CIA Openness."

35. Josh Young, "24, Alias and the New Spook Shows: Hollywood Pries Open the Lid on Normally Top-Secret CIA," *Entertainment Weekly*, September 21, 2001, http://www.ew.com/article/2001/09/21/24-alias-and-new-spook-shows.

36. "The Agency Vis-à-vis Academic and Opinion Maker Circles and the Broad Based Public," Date Unknown, CIA Records Search Tool, National Archives II, College Park, MD (hereafter cited as CREST).

37. Ibid.

38. Stansfield Turner to Herbert Hetu, April 5, 1977, CREST.

39. Ibid.

40. Christopher Moran, *Company Confessions: Revealing CIA Secrets* (London: Biteback, 2015), 176.

41. Michael Isikoff, "Keeping the Lid on Tight at the 'No-Profile Agency,'" *Washington Post*, April 29, 1983.

42. Hedley, "Three Memoirs by Former CIA Officers," *Studies in Intelligence* 49, no. 3 (2005).

43. John Hollister Hedley, interview by the author.

44. David Robarge, interview by the author.

45. Helms interview.

46. John Hollister Hedley to Harry Middleton, May 6, 1998, 18/4/714, RH.

47. Ibid.

48. "Chapter 30: Six Days." 4/75/406, RH.

49. "Chapter 28: Beyond X-2." 4/73/404, RH.

50. William Hood to Richard Helms, October 27, 1997, 10/47/531, RH.

51. "Draft Chapter: Agency Families," 10/51/535, RH.

52. Helms, *Look over My Shoulder*, 217.

53. Richard Helms to William Hood, March 16, 1998, 1/28/28, William Hood Papers, Georgetown University Special Collections (hereafter cited as WH).

54. William Hood to Richard Helms, October 9, 1997, 10/42/526, RH.

55. Helms, *Look over My Shoulder*, xii.

56. William Hood to Richard Helms, October 9, 1997, 10/42/526, RH.

57. Richard Helms to William Hood, March 16, 1998, 1/28/28, WH.

58. Thomas M. Troy, "Review," *Studies in Intelligence* 48, no. 1 (2004): 75–84.

59. John Prados, *The Family Jewels: The CIA, Secrecy and Presidential Power* (Austin: University of Texas Press, 2013), 270.

6 "A Jesuit in Reagan's Papacy"

Bill Casey, the Central Intelligence Agency,
and America's Cold War Struggle for Freedom

Andrew Hammond

"His nation and all those who love freedom," remarked President Ronald Reagan, "honor today the name and memory of Bill Casey." On May 6, 1987, the thirteenth director of central intelligence (DCI) died. Casey had been present at the creation of the modern American intelligence community during the dark days of World War II and departed the stage just as that community was entering a bewildering new post–Cold War world. "America has lost a patriot," the president went on, "and the cause of freedom, an able champion."[1]

As an intelligence leader, Casey was nothing if not colorful, aggressive, and divisive. He was unbureaucratic to the core, and the qualities that in many ways made him an effective spy chief also made trouble for the Central Intelligence Agency (CIA), which he led, and the executive branch of the US government, which his agency ultimately served. If Casey was "Reagan's sword," he was a double-edged one.[2] The Iran-Contra affair, of course, comes immediately to mind when considering Casey's service, as does the DCI's legendary hostility toward the media and Congress: two essential constituencies for American intelligence leaders since the press exposed the CIA's "family jewels" in the mid-1970s and the Church Committee subsequently held hearings. A representative on the House Permanent Select Committee on Intelligence, for example, complained that under Casey, "we are like mushrooms. They keep us in the dark and feed us a lot of manure."[3]

Casey has been alternatively called a "crystal-ball in a pin-stripe suit," a "street-fighter," and a "scrappy, street-smart—and ruthless—buckaroo."[4] In the opinion of one former senior career CIA officer who served under him, Milt Bearden, Casey was both the "best and worst director" the agency had ever known.[5] During the Second World War, Casey had been the head of Secret Intelligence in Europe, serving under his idol, head of the Office of Strategic Services (OSS) and "father of American intelligence" William "Wild

Bill" Donovan. Forty years later Casey led that community himself under Reagan, the man whose election campaign Casey had successfully chaired. During those forty years Casey remained rambunctious, driven, irascible, and impatient. "Two vodka martinis," he yelled less than three weeks into his tenure from his seventh-floor office at CIA Headquarters in Langley in 1981. Then, as his former deputy Robert Gates recollects, "without waiting for a response, he slammed the door shut."[6] Although Gates's memoir does not say whether these martinis were to be shaken or stirred, both verbs would be accurate descriptors of the effect that Casey had on the agency he oversaw on Reagan's behalf until just months before his death.

This chapter will examine the role that Bill Casey and the CIA played in the latter stages of the Cold War. Unbeknownst to him at the time, Casey was the penultimate leader of the US intelligence community in that superpower standoff. The Cold War was indeed a war; like World War II, it was explicitly waged by the United States in the name of "freedom."

For a fuller portrait of Casey, we can read the memoirs of Reagan administration officials, such as Al Haig, Reagan's first, short-lived secretary of state (1981–82); Caspar Weinberger, the hawkish secretary of defense (1981–87); and George P. Shultz (1982–89), the man who replaced Haig and went on to become the most important figure in the administration after the president himself.[7] We could also turn to both volumes of *The Reagan Diaries*, Gates's previously mentioned memoir, or Joseph Persico's 1990 biography of Casey.[8] The story of CIA activities under Casey in Central America, meanwhile, has been recounted in Bob Woodward's book *Veil*, and the story of Operation Cyclone, the longest and largest covert operation in CIA history, in Steve Coll's excellent *Ghost Wars*.[9] Alternatively, we could shift our level of analysis upward to consider some of the books that look at the CIA more broadly yet touch on it during the Reagan and Casey years, such as *For the President's Eyes Only*, *The CIA and American Democracy*, or *Executive Secrets*.[10]

Significant blind spots and omissions nevertheless remain. The field of intelligence studies more generally has been characterized, as one recent survey of the field has suggested, by a methodological bent that can perhaps best be described as "hard-core empiricism." At the same time, the study of intelligence has also been a branch of academic inquiry closely associated with narrow "realist" understandings of history and international relations.[11] Not surprisingly, then, most of the works about the CIA and Bill Casey view international affairs from a broadly materialist perspective, a conceptualization of culture that is generally static and defined by things rather than dynamic and defined by relationships. These works attempt to narrate the facts of history without an adequate consideration of the role that meaning, identity, and subjectivity might play in human affairs. As Casey pointed out in 1981, albeit in a different context—during a seminar on national and international affairs—"facts can confuse . . . just as houses are made of stones . . . a pile of stones is not a house."[12]

Through concepts we classify, categorize, and organize the world around us. This in turn profoundly shapes the ways in which we relate to the world and act within it. A story that has not been told, therefore—and the central theme of this chapter—is the role that one particular conceptual category has played in the career of one of the most important and memorable DCIs of modern times.

Specifically, this chapter will suggest that "freedom"—alternatively called America's "master narrative," "ultimate codeword," and "most resonant, deeply held value"—is a powerful and important interpretive frame through which we may profitably understand Casey, the CIA, and US foreign policy.[13] Not "freedom," let us be clear, as a definitive fixed essence, or as an accurate descriptor of agency activities, or as an opposite category through which we may normatively capture the cut and thrust of US foreign policy more generally, but freedom as a locus of historic contestation, as a site where politics takes place, and as a lens through which we might understand the ways in which Casey, the CIA, and America understood themselves, their relationship to others, and their place in history.

In so doing, this chapter will add to our knowledge and understanding of Bill Casey and the CIA. It will provide both a challenge and a modest but necessary corrective to a subfield that has for far too long been stubbornly resistant to broader debates with regard to the role of cultural meaning in the historical profession and the human sciences.[14] At the very outset, though— and to preempt the reductionism frequently proffered to those who take culture, identity, and ideas seriously—this does not mean that materiality, things, and facts are unimportant, marginal, or nonexistent. No competent observer would suggest that the "hard stuff" of international relations—perhaps best exemplified by armored divisions, carrier battle groups, and air expeditionary wings—do not matter. Suffice it to say that the world does not come to us already imbued with significance and meaning. The way we interpret the world and the meaning that we give to it—to materiality, to things, and to facts—matters very much: analytically, historically, and politically.

This chapter, then, will argue that when we study intelligence leadership in the American context, we must bear in mind the profoundly ideational component of American life and in particular the concept of freedom. This concept is deeply embedded in the documentary record and in the very DNA of the American republic. To be clear, I am not suggesting that US foreign policy actually is about freedom (in the way that, say, a Republican presidential candidate might espouse) or that US foreign policy is any less riven by tensions, contradictions, and hypocrisies than that of other comparable political communities. Rather, I am saying that this is a prevailing narrative about America that deserves to be critiqued, analyzed, and evaluated. What role, then, does freedom play in intelligence history and US foreign policy? Is it doing any political or historic work? If so, let us ask not only, what is freedom? but also, what is freedom doing? These are questions that must be reckoned with for any kind of substantive understanding of US foreign policy. For freedom not only predates the founding of the country in 1776 but is woven into every important historical and political juncture in the country's history, including the struggle with the Soviet Union and Casey and the CIA's role within it.

When we think about intelligence leaders and how they differ, therefore, we must try to think of not only the types of political regimes from which they emanate or the ways in which they are affected by economic structures. We must also think about their cultural context—the concepts, ideas, and narratives that they use to understand the world around them. Indeed, as one scholar has pointed out, the United States is the "imagined community *par excellence*."[15] Although this cultural context is central to the entire structure of American history, it has been markedly understudied and misunderstood in the field of intelligence studies. This is all the more so when considering the US role in the international system and the global implications of its power. As Casey's boss noted in his Westminster Address of 1982, political struggle takes place in the realm of ideas, "in the values we hold, the beliefs we cherish, and the ideals to which we are dedicated." By the same token one of Reagan's successors from the opposite side of the bipartisan divide, Bill Clinton, stated that more than anything else "America is an idea"—a sentiment echoed more recently by Anne-Marie Slaughter in *The Idea That Is America*.[16]

Intelligence studies, then, has by and large given us an incomplete picture of American intelligence: something the author aims to humbly address throughout the rest of this chapter. To provide a deeper context, the next section will consider where the CIA as an institution and US foreign policy more generally found themselves on the cusp of the Reagan era. The subsequent section will look at the ways in which freedom was a vital force animating US foreign policy and deeply embedded in the way Bill Casey understood his mission and America's role in the world. The final section, then, will consider some of the implications of this analysis and some of the criticisms that may be made.

US Foreign Policy and the CIA: The Signification Spiral of the 1970s

Upon walking down the presidents' gallery in Langley, opposite the directors' gallery, where Casey's portrait now stands, one sees that on Richard Nixon's portrait the president himself wrote, "The CIA, a vital aid in the defense of freedom."[17] Casey first entered the US government under Nixon and went on to be chairman of the Securities and Exchange Commission (1971–73) and undersecretary of state for economic affairs (1973–74) before he became chairman of the Export-Import Bank under Ford (1974–76). By the time he became DCI in January 1981—he was one of Reagan's most controversial appointments—however, there was a palpable sense that the CIA, US foreign policy, and freedom were on the back foot.

By the end of the 1970s, in the wake of the Watergate scandal, the Vietnam War, Soviet advances in Africa, and economic woes precipitated by the Organization of the Petroleum Exporting Countries (OPEC) oil embargo of 1973, many Americans sensed that the "historic correlation of forces" had shifted—perhaps decisively—against the United States. In 1978 US National Intelligence Estimate (NIE) 11-4-78, *Soviet Goals and Expectations in the Global Power Arena*, stated,

> As it enters the 1980's, the current Soviet leadership sees the heavy military investments made during the last two decades paying off in the form of unprecedentedly favorable advances across the military spectrum, and over the long term in political gains where military power or military assistance has been the actual instrument of policy or the decisive complement to Soviet diplomacy. . . . This more assertive Soviet behavior is likely to persist as long as the USSR believes that Western strength is declining and as it further explores the utility of its increased military power as a means of realizing its global ambitions.[18]

The CIA itself had been beset by difficulties during this time of troubles. Mistrusted by Presidents John Kennedy, Lyndon Johnson, and Richard Nixon during the 1960s and early 1970s,[19] the agency had a series of short-lived directors during a weakened post-Watergate presidency and was wracked by intense public criticism and media scrutiny, not to mention the Church and Pike Committee hearings.[20] During this time the American public viewed the intelligence community as "out of control and a potential menace."[21] As a former Langley legend who was implicated in some of the CIA's excesses, James Jesus Angleton, complained in 1976, "The congressional investigations were like being pillaged by a foreign power, only we have been occupied by the Congress with our files rifled, our officials humiliated and our agents exposed."[22] In a similar vein former DCI John McCone wrote to Casey in 1981 warning that as a result of the hearings, the agency's very existence was under threat.[23] Attacked from both the Left and the Right, the CIA was not immune to criticism from several of the intellectual strands that would subsequently be woven into the Reagan administration's foreign policy (such as the Committee

Photo 6.1 "Captain Queeg": DCI Admiral Stansfield Turner (standing) caused resentment in the ranks by purging some 800 officers from the CIA's Clandestine Service, hence his nickname Captain Queeg, the ironfisted skipper from *The Caine Mutiny*. *Central Intelligence Agency*

on the Present Danger, Team B, and the Coalition for a Democratic Majority).[24] All in all, the CIA seemed like an institution under siege.

The CIA's relationship with the Carter administration had been ambivalent at best. The president himself had come to office with a promise to clean up the agency. At the swearing in ceremony of his DCI at CIA Headquarters, for example, he stressed, "When any impropriety or illegality does occur, I want to know about it immediately because a concealment of a mistake and its subsequent revelation will be a devastating additional blow."[25] President Jimmy Carter nominated to be DCI an old friend from his days as a midshipman at the US Naval Academy, Adm. Stansfield Turner. While Turner shared Carter's technical bent and spearheaded improvements in the agency's technical collection capabilities, he was not viewed with any kind of affection in the Directorate of Operations, the traditional beating heart of the CIA. In fact, Turner oversaw the Halloween Day Massacre in 1977, during which 20 percent of the directorate's covert action and human intelligence operatives were cut. Turner never really found his feet in the administration or at the CIA. National Security Adviser Zbigniew Brzezinski (1977–81) outmaneuvered Turner, in part by giving what amounted to the daily intelligence briefing for the president.[26] As one firsthand observer pointed out, Turner went on to be "regarded with deep hostility and dislike by many in and out of the Agency and intelligence community."[27]

Two events unfolded at the end of the decade, however, that began the process of transforming the CIA's fortunes: the Iranian Revolution and the Soviet invasion of Afghanistan. These events were also the culmination of what we may term the signification spiral of the 1970s, whereby each reverse—real or imagined—fed into a deeper sense of US national anxiety.[28] A signification spiral exists when each signification—a conveyance of meaning with regard to an event—amplifies and escalates that which came before: with the result that the event itself is made to appear even more threatening than perhaps it actually is.[29] This signification spiral, to be sure, was as much as anything else a threat to the American sense of self, national identity, and the nation's core values and way of life. The Cold War contest with the Soviet Union, then, was as much as anything else a struggle over selves.

April 1, 1979, saw the proclamation of the Islamic Republic of Iran and the consolidation of power by Ayatollah Khomeini after two years of domestic unrest directed at the increasingly authoritarian US-backed shah. For the United States the issue came to a head when the deposed shah was allowed to come to New York City in October 1979 for medical treatment. Carter had reservations about the political wisdom of such a move, and there was division within the administration. After some powerful friends, including Henry Kissinger and the chairman of Chase Bank, David Rockefeller, had lobbied on the cancer-stricken shah's behalf, he arrived on Rockefeller's private jet unaware of the coming chain of geopolitical events whose consequences have lasted to this day.[30] Enraged at the decision, hard-line, pro-revolutionary students took fifty-two US diplomats hostage in November, and thus began a 444-day standoff. Needless to say, the hostage crisis did nothing to bolster Carter's flagging national security credentials.[31] At the time, though, it was seen not only as a serious blow to US prestige but also, given Iran's close ties with the United States before the revolution and its geographic location, as an event with potentially serious strategic ramifications.

Then, in December 1979 came an incident that Carter would call the "most serious threat to the peace since World War Two." The northern tier countries included Iran and Pakistan, adjoining US allies that prevented deep Soviet penetration of the Persian Gulf region, and one nonaligned, landlocked Muslim country to the east of Iran and the northwest of Pakistan, a vitally important buffer between these states and Soviet Central Asia: Afghanistan. On December 25, while the US National Christmas Tree sat dark except for the star atop it honoring the hostages, the Soviet Union invaded Afghanistan. "Basically," as Brzezinski said, "it was the first time in the entire Cold War that the Soviet Union overtly used military force to affect a significant geopolitical change and to do so in a region where there were significant American interests involved."[32] Echoing NIE 11-4-78, Johnson's former national security adviser, W. W. Rostow (1966–69), wrote in a letter to Carter, "The impulse to convert their hardware and logistical advantages into direct control over Middle East oil must be considerable. . . . The impulse certainly represents the greatest threat of a Third World War since 1945."[33] In his State of the Union address in January 1980, Carter shared these sentiments with the American people: "Let our position be absolutely clear: an attempt by any outside force to gain control of the Persian Gulf region will be regarded as an assault on the vital interests of the United States of America, and such an assault will be repelled by any means necessary, including military force."[34]

This was the birth of the Carter Doctrine. If détente had been dying a slow, painful death as the 1970s wore on, the Soviet invasion of Afghanistan administered the coup de grâce. Carter's response was multipronged and included withdrawing the second Strategic Arms Limitation Talks agreement (SALT II) from Senate consideration, proposing an increase in defense spending, and strengthening the country's ability to project force into the region through the establishment of the Rapid Deployment Joint Task Force (RDJTF), a precursor to today's Central Command (CENTCOM). Behind the scenes the response involved moving beyond the previously approved nonlethal aid for the mounting insurgency in Afghanistan. A logistical and financial pipeline was put in place that involved a dollar-for-dollar deal with the Saudis to match US funding and a key role for the Pakistanis in distributing money and material to the factional mujahideen groups.[35] The Carter administration also developed a narrative of freedom to accompany its response to the invasion and its covert operation. The Soviet-Afghan War, then, became part of the broader Cold War struggle for freedom, and the mujahideen— many of whom had questionable liberal credentials at best—were routinely characterized as "freedom fighters."[36]

In other words, the essential bedrock of US policy was in place before the Reagan administration came to office: a fact that has usually been overlooked in the highly politicized weak Carter–strong Reagan historiography surrounding this issue. The Soviet invasion of Afghanistan was a rupture in the broader canvas of world politics that represented a genuine turning point in the Carter administration. From that point on the administration was much less conciliatory. The invasion was also a watershed in the Cold War, the history of the broader Persian Gulf, and US foreign policy more generally.[37]

In 1980 Reagan campaigned with a promise to "unleash" the CIA, but Carter had already put the agency on a longer leash. As Senator Daniel P. Moynihan, who sat on the recently established Select Committee for Intelligence, remarked approvingly, "Carter has now discovered that it is *his* CIA!"[38] The

CIA felt as if it was needed again. In many ways it was the ideal institution for a country still jaded by Vietnam; this new war in Afghanistan could be fought with US treasure and Afghan blood. Indeed, the war was often referred to as a chance to give the Soviets their Vietnam.[39]

The Soviet invasion of Afghanistan, then, was not only the culmination of the signification spiral of the 1970s; it was also a turning point in the history of the "time of troubles" CIA. From the invasion onward there was a robust reassertion of the American sense of self that had been slowly eroding in the preceding decade, an erosion symbolized by Carter's so-called malaise speech in 1978. Although we do not know what would have happened had Carter won the 1980 election, we do know that Reagan took the narrative of freedom to new rhetorical heights and built on Carter's policies to oversee the largest peacetime buildup of weapons in US history.[40] We also know that the Afghan operation became the largest covert action in agency history and attained a mythic status in the debates surrounding not only the US role in the Cold War's end but the CIA's understanding of itself.

Bill Casey as Leader, Manager, and Believer

Already weakened in the eyes of the American public, Carter did not survive the twin foreign policy shocks of the Iran hostage crisis and the Soviet-Afghan War and the sense of continuing drift they engendered. The ongoing hostage crisis and a failed rescue attempt in a way indicated that Carter was not the man for the times. If Carter lectured from a position of moral self-righteousness, Reagan reconfirmed for the electorate its own inherent sense of self-worth; if Carter sketched out in painstaking detail the trade-offs that would have to be made, Reagan simplistically promised the people that they could have it all; and if Carter stressed shades of gray and national introspection, Reagan outlined the Manichean nature of the world and America's providential mission. Any foreign policy volte-face, therefore, was too late, and Reagan—whatever one thinks of him politically—had an ability to connect with broad swathes of the American public in ways that Carter simply could not, or at least could not by 1980.

In this context the Reagan administration sought to "put wind in the sails of freedom."[41] Casey had originally hoped for an appointment as secretary of state in the wake of Reagan's Electoral College landslide. But "intelligence is like witchcraft; you have to be accepted by the community in order to practice it. No amount of wishful thinking will gain you entry to the trade." Thus, as part of the original OSS coven, Casey was in many ways well-suited to take over at morale-stricken Langley. Besides his government service during the

Nixon administration, Casey had subsequently pursued a variety of legal, political, and business interests, amassing wealth and connections along the way. Like many other senior Reagan administration officials, Casey fused devout Catholicism, fierce anti-Communism, and a fervent belief in American exceptionalism.[42] A self-made New Yorker from Queens, he came to the Reagan team relatively late, in 1979, when he hit it off with the candidate and was tapped to run the presidential campaign against Carter.[43]

In the Reagan administration's desire to fill out the sails of "freedom," the CIA played a most interesting role. During the Carter era the agency's position seemed ambiguous and prone to vacillation, perhaps because of some of Carter's own shortcomings. But under Reagan the CIA was in some ways the lead agency in the aforementioned endeavor. Whereas Carter had come to office to rein in the CIA, Reagan promised the opposite. Much as it had in the aftermath of the September 11, 2001, attacks, in early 1981 the CIA seemed to have the right skill set at the right time for the right political context; thus, the agency could continue on its rocky path toward national rehabilitation. Whereas Operation Cyclone had grown out of the Carter Doctrine, which securitized the broader Persian Gulf region, the CIA underpinned the so-called Reagan Doctrine, which sought to support anti-Communist insurgents—or, as the administration liked to call them, "freedom fighters"— worldwide. Although the Soviet-Afghan War was the Reagan Doctrine's signature application, the policy also touched operations throughout the third world, in Cambodia, Ethiopia, Mozambique, Angola, and Nicaragua.[44] As Reagan proclaimed in his 1985 State of the Union address, "We must not break faith with those who are risking their lives—on every continent, from Afghanistan to Nicaragua—to defy Soviet-supported aggression and secure rights which have been ours from birth. . . . Support for freedom-fighters is self-defense."[45]

These operations, of course, were not without controversy. As one commentator has noted, the CIA under Casey was in many ways "the arm of government most faithful to the rhetoric of Reagan's uncompromising anti-communism—the Jesuits in Reagan's papacy one might say."[46] As a former division chief in the Directorate of Operations pointed out to this author, there was a "clear uptick" in terms of both morale and funding when Casey took over at the CIA.[47] Indeed, the agency's improved status seemed a reflection of the new DCI's position within the administration. Although he was never one of the original Reagan hands, or as close to the president as popular mythology would have one believe, Casey was the first DCI to take a place in the White House as a fully participating cabinet member. When Casey took over, however, the problems at the CIA were not just limited to its relationships to the executive branch, Congress, the press, and the public.

At this point the agency also faced internal dissention, generational change, and bureaucratic, risk-averse behavior. Casey was not without his detractors; because he had been Reagan's campaign manager, his appointment could hardly be framed as apolitical. Nevertheless, others came to share the division chief's sentiments mentioned previously. US ambassador to Italy Maxwell M. Rabb, for example, sent Casey an *International Herald Tribune* article noting that it "gave me great satisfaction to see the headline, 'Even Critics Give CIA Director Credit for Bringing New Vitality to the Agency.'"[48] The front cover of *Newsweek* in 1983, on the other hand, proclaimed, "The Secret Warriors: The CIA Is Back in Business." "For better or for worse," the article read, "the Company is back in the business of covert action—with a global scope and an intensity of resources unmatched since its heyday 20 years ago."[49]

Intelligence and foreign policy, nonetheless, do not take place in a cultural vacuum. While every administration has worked within the context of American political culture, the concepts and narratives that underpin American national identity resounded in the country's political discourse during the 1980s in a way that they had not done for some time—in part owing to evolving structural conditions that are beyond the scope of this paper and in part owing to Reagan's singular ability to communicate with the American public. An ongoing joke at the CIA was that Casey did not need a telephone scrambler because he mumbled, and Haig was infamous for "Haigspeak," characterized by circumlocution and ambiguity. Reagan, in contrast, was direct, clear, and— frustratingly for his critics—simplistic: "America," he pointed out in his final benediction to the nation, "is freedom."[50] This keyword would be a hallmark of Reagan's presidency, from his first inaugural on the western steps of the US Capitol until his farewell address in 1989. Indeed, Reagan appropriated the term so successfully that he markedly changed US political discourse at the domestic level, a change the Democratic Party is still struggling with to this day. Reagan's narrative of freedom, which was characterized by slippages of meaning between the national and international levels, was also propounded by other figures in the administration. Shultz, for example, argued, "There was nothing covert about the Reagan Doctrine. It was an articulated view that we were in favor of freedom."[51]

The DCI likewise saw the struggle against freedom in black and white terms. Quite simply for him, the struggle was between freedom and its enemies. In a speech before the Southern Center for International Studies in Atlanta in 1986, he explained, "Honest men and women can disagree about the proper strategy and tactics to employ in our policy towards the Soviet Union. . . . It is important to understand just how different the Soviets are from us in their history, their culture, and their outlook. . . . We are dealing with a *fundamentally* alien and *totally unpalatable* value system."[52]

On a visit to the Khyber Pass, on the other hand, one State Department official noted that Casey wept tears of joy when he spoke to the Afghan insurgents, or what he termed "his freedom fighters." "The freedom fighters in Afghanistan," he pointed out in a later speech, "have made it as dangerous for a Soviet convoy to stray off the beaten path as it was for the Germans in France in 1944."[53] In a ceremony at CIA Headquarters to sign the new Intelligence Identities Protection Act (1982) into law, meanwhile, Reagan noted that in its new leader the US intelligence community "will never have a better friend or a more able advocate of your mission." Indeed, he told agency employees in his private remarks before his public address, "You and I are involved in perhaps the most important of all the great struggles for human freedom. . . . In this struggle you play a leading role—indeed, you are one of the principle reasons why the forces of freedom will triumph."[54]

Casey compared this struggle for freedom with earlier wars the American republic had waged, whether for its independence during the Revolutionary War (a keen historian, Casey had penned an *Armchair Tour of the American Revolution*[55]) or against the Axis powers during World War II—for example, in remarks at a Veterans of OSS dinner where Prime Minister Margaret Thatcher was to be presented with the William J. Donovan Medal.[56] He also compared it with broader struggles down through the centuries. In a speech at Ashland University in Ohio, he expounded on the struggle between "state despotism" and the protection of "individual freedom," in his mind the highest goal of the state: "We can't make the mistake of putting this conflict in the past tense: the current competition between the United States and the Soviet Union is the latest chapter of the same conflict that pitted Athens against Xerxes and the Persians, and Medieval Europe against Genghis Khan and the Mongols. Unfortunately, this is a history lesson that is not sufficiently appreciated." Then he continued, "I apologize for starting out on this philosophic note, but it is simply impossible to understand why this country needs a strong intelligence capability, if we don't understand why we are engaged in the competition with the Soviets in the first place and what the real nature and historic context of that contest actually is."[57]

In the popular cultural imagination, we are used to thinking of spy chiefs in a number of ways. We may think of them as ruthless (Machiavellian intrigue during the Italian Renaissance), cynical (Harry Lime in *The Third Man*), duplicitous (the "rotten apple" in *Tinker, Tailor, Soldier, Spy*), coldhearted (Edward Wilson in *The Good Shepherd*), or crafty (Dar Adal in *Homeland*), or as unscrupulous Talleyrand-like opportunists, liable to switch sides at the most expedient opportunity (Littlefinger and the Master of Whisperers in *Game of Thrones*). There may even be a degree of truth to some of these assumptions.[58] To a certain extent, we must be careful here. These characters do not exhaust the range of possibilities for thinking about spy chiefs, especially when we consider them in the modern era, leading and managing vast state bureaucracies, often wedded to particular value systems and modes of being (whatever tensions or hypocrisies we may detect therein). So, while we may be used to thinking of them in the aforementioned terms, and while they may indeed be leaders and managers of intelligence agencies, they can also be *believers*—and this is a way in which we are much less accustomed to thinking about them—passionate supporters and exponents of a cause and a way of life. This was certainly the case with Bill Casey. As Gates pointed out in *From the Shadows*, "Casey had not come to CIA with the purpose of making it better, managing it more effectively, reforming it, or improving the quality of intelligence. . . . Bill Casey came to CIA primarily to wage war against the Soviet Union."[59]

We may, of course, disagree with what Bill Casey took "freedom" to be. For example, we may have a different definition of freedom; we may disagree with him politically, or not be as socially conservative as him, or object to his views of the free market; we may not agree with how he led the CIA, the tactics he pursued, or the broader thrust of Reagan's foreign policy or indeed of US Cold War foreign policy more generally. Alternately, we may harbor deep suspicion with regard to his role in the Iran-Contra affair or vilify him for the role we deem he played in propagating the violence that beset Central America in the 1980s. From an analysis of private correspondence, government documentation, and public speeches, however, we cannot be left with anything but the conclusion that freedom was central to Bill Casey's worldview and that he believed in it to the depths of his soul.

Casey's Cultural Operating System

Let us first consider some objections that may be made to the argument advanced thus far before we consider some of its implications. Briefly restated that argument is (a) when we study US intelligence leadership, we must bear in mind the profoundly ideational component of American life, and (b) freedom is a powerful and important interpretive frame through which we might profitably understand Casey, the CIA, and US foreign policy.

The first and perhaps most obvious objection is that freedom is just propaganda, an attempt to pull the wool over the eyes of a supine public. The first and most obvious response is to ask why that would obviate the need to study it. Besides the need to study the phenomenon in its own right, surely we would want to study why governmental elites feel the need to use this term and, indeed, use it perhaps more than any other. Second, it is hard to explain why Reagan administration officials such as Casey used the same term while far from the public's gaze, in their musings, diaries, and personal correspondence, if they were not sincere. We could of course take another step—and a big one at that—and suggest that it was some kind of conspiracy, an attempt to subvert the historical record and to fool future generations of historians and political scientists. The problem is this conspiracy would have to have been a bipartisan intergenerational conspiracy. For example, NSC-68, adopted in 1950, the top-secret blueprint for the opening phase of the Cold War, called freedom the most "contagious idea in history. . . . We have no choice but to demonstrate the superiority of the idea of freedom by its constructive application."[60]

Elites do, of course, recognize the power of concepts, ideas, and narratives and attempt to use them, instrumentalize them, and hide behind them for alternative purposes. They sometimes lie, conceal, and dissimulate. The history of the twentieth century alone should be enough to rid us of any willful ignorance that they do not. Generally speaking, however, if person a foregrounds reason x as why he or she did something—because reason x is more palatable than reason y—this does not necessitate definitively discounting reason x as a motivation. Neither does it inevitably lead to the conclusion that reason x is a value that person a does not believe in (or, if a is a collectivity, that certain individuals within the group view reason x more cynically or instrumentally than others do).[61] It also does not involve discounting reason y as a justification that may be subsumed within a more expansive reason x.

But again, why and how elites justify and legitimate what they do (to themselves, to institutional hierarchies, to interagency interlocutors, and to the general public) seem like legitimate avenues for intellectual inquiry and for scholars of intelligence who are studying spy chiefs' political actions. The United States has always had a strong ideational component to its social and political life. As Richard Hofstadter famously said, "It has been our fate as a nation not to have an ideology, but to be one."[62] When Casey was DCI, moreover, this was especially pronounced as the United States was in a global competition with a power that had a very different conception of the world— and of the right and the good.[63] Intelligence leaders can no more transcend the context of this political culture than the populace from which they emanate.[64]

Was the Reagan administration just an anomaly with regard to freedom? As president, Reagan used the term perhaps as much as, if not more than, any postwar US president.[65] As his preeminent biographer, Lou Cannon, writes in *The Role of a Lifetime*, Reagan relished sounding the "battle-cry of freedom."[66] Nonetheless, he was merely doing what every US president has done since George Washington, going back through Carter, Nixon, Kennedy, Roosevelt, Wilson, and Lincoln, to name but a few.[67] Indeed, a quick keyword search of the American Presidency Project between January 1, 1789, and December 31, 2012, reveals 14,016 hits for "freedom" and 5,283 for "liberty" (a word with which "freedom" is often conflated in US political discourse).[68] In other words, while Reagan may have taken the word "freedom" to more pronounced rhetorical heights, he was merely telling Americans what they told themselves about themselves—and what is more, what they have always told themselves about themselves.

Modern spy chiefs in the Anglosphere have assumed an increasingly public role, and when so doing, they must not only justify the institutions for which they work but legitimate them by grafting their work onto broader narratives of national identity.[69] This they must do by working within the confines and strictures of a prevailing political culture that they claim to represent and serve. Casey was perhaps an anomaly when compared with some of his predecessors, such as his former OSS colleague Richard Helms (1966–73), who lived much more in the shadows, or the technocratic Turner. Nevertheless, Casey's use of the word "freedom" was very much in keeping with the language used by the rest of his colleagues in the Reagan administration. So, although he was hardly a slick public relations man for the CIA's corporate image with regard to the press or Congress—he almost seemed to relish ruffling their feathers—Casey did consistently and forcefully articulate the nature of the struggle the institution was involved in and the ways in which it was taking the fight to the enemy (after the style of his imprudent rule-bending hero Wild Bill Donovan). In a way, then, Casey was appealing to the American people and those who had voted for Reagan over the heads of these institutions rather than through them.

However, why would the Reagan administration use "freedom" and other value-laden concepts? Why would they not just recite the dry facts of domestic politics and policy prescriptions for the national interest? In fact, is policy not really all about the national interest anyway? Was not the American response to the Soviet invasion of Afghanistan, for example, really about oil instead of freedom? Documentation evidences the fact that yes, oil was very much in the minds of US planners and policymakers and of central importance. Think of NIE 11-4-78 or of Rostow's correspondence with Carter noted previously.[70] In early 1981 Albert Wohlstetter sent Casey a classified study titled "Interests and Power in the Persian Gulf," and in this study oil and energy were central. "Nearly 22 of the 30 million barrels of oil consumed every day by the noncommunist world," it pointed out, "come from the Persian Gulf." If the Soviet Union were able to interfere with this flow, "it could pry the American alliance apart."[71] The following year Casey received a letter from Helms in which the former director wrote, "As you know, I follow events in the Persian Gulf very carefully. . . . The future Soviet need for oil will oblige them to play an even harder game in the area."[72] Casey's own view was that the two primary targets of Soviet imperialism since the end of the Vietnam War had been "the oil fields of the Middle East which are the life-line of the Western Alliance and the Isthmus and Canal of Panama" (thereby contextualizing the CIA's operations in Afghanistan and Nicaragua).[73] The aforementioned fears must also be interpreted in the light of the OPEC oil crisis of 1973, Carter's 1977 speech that called the energy crisis "the moral equivalent of war," and intelligence estimates that showed the Soviet Union was increasingly having its own problems in this area. The importance of oil, therefore, seems beyond doubt.

Nonetheless, as recent studies on the Soviet-Afghan War based on Russian archival material have demonstrated, oil was not the Soviet motivation for invading Afghanistan.[74] This illustrates that the national interest is not exogenously given and is much more subjective than realist scholars would have us believe. Indeed, human relations are inherently social and relational, and through this social interaction, we come to understand our identity and interests. Identity and interests, therefore, are inextricably linked—each informs the other. As Melvyn Leffler points out in *For the Soul of Mankind: The US, the Soviet Union, and the Cold War*, "Not only did US and Soviet officials believe that their nations embodied a superior way of life, but their beliefs and memories affected their construction of reality—their perception of threats and opportunities."[75] In the case of Afghanistan, then, we have the same set of events interpreted in quite different ways through US and Soviet prisms of political culture and national identity. In Casey's aforementioned speech about the twin goals of Soviet imperialism, he emphasized that the United States was involved in the "lineal descendent of the same conflict that Western civilization has struggled with for Millenniums—state despotism versus freedom."[76]

How do we square this then: if American support for the Afghan freedom fighters was about oil, does this mean that freedom was epiphenomenal and unimportant? No, access to oil was interpreted within a broader cultural framework in which freedom was, and is still, seen as the cornerstone of US national identity. In other words, for the United States it was about *both*. Oil, grand strategy, and geopolitics were all interpreted within the confines of this intersubjective, institutionalized, historical narrative—all refracted through an omnipresent cultural operating system. The American political economy of freedom, then, relied on access to this oil, and any monocausal materialist answer to this question is not only reductionist but raises many others. So, it is not oil *versus* freedom but oil *for* freedom; it is not materialist explanations *versus* idealist explanations, but raw materials—tangible, touchable, things of this world such as oil—that allow a particular conception of the good life—"American freedom"—to take place. In other words, there is a recursive relationship between oil and freedom.

Motivations for foreign policy are always complicated. It was of course about more than just oil and freedom. Nonetheless, that is why we must be careful when we try to prize oil and freedom apart; why we must consider intersecting, competing, and sometimes conflicting drivers; and why we must beware of throwing out the interpretive baby with any explanatory bathwater. Casey's cultural operating system can no more be definitively divorced from CIA activities and US foreign policy than we can separate the game of chess from the objects with which it is played.[77] Indeed, despite attempts by realpolitik practitioners, hard-nosed realists, and calculating geostrategists to conceptualize the world using a Metternichian schema in which political culture and national identity are entirely absent, American political culture ultimately envelops them back within its ambit. As Kissinger concedes in perhaps his most important book, *Diplomacy*, itself a paean to realism, "Throughout history the American people have found their ultimate inspiration in historic ideals, not in geopolitical analysis."[78] Kissinger's erstwhile boss and the figure with whom he developed détente and triangular diplomacy, however, offered the following while he was vice president in 1960: "The problem of freedom goes deeper than the psychological conditioning of any particular individual. It touches the very root of man's conception of himself."[79] Indeed, in many ways the Reaganite insurgency was a reaction against what one of Reagan's main 1980 foreign policy campaign advisers called "that relativism—that philosophy of a safe, 'pragmatic' middle ground—that has sapped the American spirit." Referring to a speech Kissinger gave in 1980, he continued, "I fear that Henry has misread not only the ethos of the American people but that of the Soviet rulers as well." In fact, he went on, "in his appeal to the ideal of human rights, Carter was closer to the mark than the 'realists' ever were. . . . An American statesman needs . . . to believe in the rightness of his country's cause."[80]

As has been outlined thus far, Casey and Reagan were certainly believers in the rightness of their country's cause. The Reagan administration in which Casey played a prominent and important role, then, sought to regraft CIA activities and indeed weld US foreign policy more generally back onto the founding myths and national narratives that had been undermined and gradually eroded during the signification spiral of the 1970s. Material possibility, then, was linguistically constituted.[81] "It matters deeply," notes Jutta Weldes, "that US state actors are able to interpret and to define world politics in ways that at least significant portions of the US population, and other audiences, find plausible and persuasive."[82] You can talk about freedom all you want, of course, but as Eric Foner has pointed out, if people do not want what you are offering and if social and political reality do not match up with what you are saying, then in the recalibration of power that takes place every four years in America, you are going to be in trouble. Reagan twice gave the American people policies they wanted. (Whether this was for better or worse is a separate debate.) As his chief speechwriter, Anthony Dolan, wrote in a letter to one of Reagan's strongest supporters in the Senate, Reagan provided "an administration that is prepared to lead, to take them somewhere. . . . The American people want to dream and hope and be part of a great mission and cause."[83] In the American context, let us be clear, political culture is not a "decorative addendum" to the harsh realities of the national interest and interstate relations—the "icing on the cake of the material world" at best, a superfluous distraction from the weighty matters of power and politics at worst. On the contrary, it is "absolutely deadly political."[84]

Conclusion

"Freedom," as Michael Oakeshott observed, is a term that provokes "the fever of battle as readily as the detachment of thought." "Often a single situation," he continued, "will provoke both these reactions in different individuals and the result is inevitable misunderstanding and a fruitless controversy of cross-purposes."[85] I am certainly not trying, therefore, to play into some kind of crude and triumphalist narrative in which "freedom-loving" Reagan comes to office and unleashes Bill Casey and the CIA, who supply the mujahideen with Stinger missiles and material support that ultimately leads to the withdrawal of the Soviet Fortieth Army, the collapse of the Soviet Union, and the US winning of the Cold War, with the aid of massive defense spending and the providential hand of God. In other words, what we may call, after a dedication inscribed in one of Tom Clancy's best sellers, the "Reagan was the man who won the war" thesis. How the Cold War ended and the role that Reagan, Casey, and the CIA played in this series of events will be debated for many years to come. I do maintain, however, that the United States has a pronounced ideational component to its politics and its history and that "freedom" is a term that we must deal with carefully given its power and potency in the American political culture—even within the CIA, which is so easy to see as a purely cynical manifestation of a realist worldview.

Let us now further consider some of the implications of the argument outlined previously for intelligence studies. First, if identity and interests are inseparable and if cultural conditions make particular forms of state action possible, then as scholars of intelligence we must reconcile ourselves to taking culture seriously. Not just as a way to give verve and flair to a rather dry chapter of our books based on dusty policy documents (although an admirable aim) or to engage broader audiences (an even more admirable aim), not just as an optional afterthought (a discretionary *dolci* after our *primo* and *secondi*, although of course we may decide we do not have a sweet tooth), but because culture and "the giving and taking of meaning" are central to political life and state activity.

Second, we must be aware that intelligence leaders are increasingly in the public eye and quite frequently need to engage, justify, and legitimate their institutions and actions. When they do so, they will be engaged in intensely cultural and political activities; we therefore need to have a more nuanced understanding of political culture and cultural conditions than the type that one sometimes finds begot of very thin understandings of culture or conceptual lethargy. If people act toward others on the basis of the meaning they have for others, then we have to work a bit harder to find out the types of meaning that intelligence leaders are giving to people involved in events—whether those people be themselves, senior policymakers to whom they are accountable, those who work for them in subordinate roles, or the public more generally. We must understand much better how these narratives of national identity function, what political and historic work they do, and what peculiarities there are as far as how these narratives work with regard to intelligence leaders and spy chiefs—especially in the Anglosphere.

Notes

1. Ronald Reagan, "Statement on the Death of the Former Director of Central Intelligence William J. Casey," May 6, 1987, in Gerhard Peters and John T. Woolley, The American Presidency Project, http://www.presidency.ucsb.edu/ws/?pid=34236.

2. See Robert Gates, "Reagan's Sword: Casey at CIA," in *From the Shadows: The Ultimate Insider's Story of Five Presidents and How They Won the Cold War* (New York: Simon & Schuster, 1996), 198–225.

3. The congressman was Norman Mineta (D-CA), who most recently served as George W. Bush's secretary for transportation (2001–6). Quoted in David M. Alpern et al., "The Secret Warriors: The CIA Is Back in Business," *Newsweek*, October 10, 1981, Folder "The Freedom Fighter," Box 1.15, Roseanne Klass Collection on Afghanistan and the Soviet-Afghan War, Special Collections, Milton S. Eisenhower Library, Johns Hopkins University, Baltimore, MD.

4. Herb Meyer, quoted in Paul Kengor, "Bill Casey's Centennial: Remembering the CIA Director Who Won the Cold War," *American Spectator*, April 5, 2013. http://spectator.org/articles/55841/bill-caseys-centennial; Leonard Bushkoff, "What Made Casey Run? A Profile Probes the Career and Character of the Hard-Boiled CIA Boss," *Christian Science Monitor*, January 9, 1991, http://www.csmonitor.com/1991/0109/dbcasey.html; George Shultz, quoted in Robert D. Hershey Jr.,

"Shultz Memoirs Say Bush Knew of the Arms-for-Hostages Affair," *New York Times*, February 1, 1993, http://www.nytimes.com/1993/02/01/us/shultz-memoirs-say-bush -knew-of-the-arms-for-hostages-affair.html.

5. Milt Bearden, quoted in Steve Coll, *Ghost Wars: The Secret History of the CIA, Afghanistan, and Bin Laden, from the Soviet Invasion to September 10, 2001* (New York: Penguin Press, 2004), 147.

6. Gates, *From the Shadows*, 198.

7. Alexander Haig, *Caveat* (London: Weidenfield and Nicolson, 1984); Caspar Weinberger, *Fighting for Peace: 7 Critical Years in the Pentagon* (New York: Warner Books, 1990); and George P. Schultz, *Turmoil and Triumph: My Years as Secretary of State* (New York: Scribner's, 1993).

8. Ronald Reagan, *The Reagan Diaries*, ed. Douglas Brinkley (New York: Harper-Collins, 2009); Gates, *From the Shadows*; Joseph E. Persico, *Casey: From the OSS to the CIA* (New York: Viking, 1990).

9. Bob Woodward, *Veil: The Secret Wars of the CIA, 1981-87* (New York: Simon & Schuster, 2005); Coll, *Ghost Wars*. See also Andrew Hammond, *Struggles for Freedom: Afghanistan and US Foreign Policy since 1979* (Edinburgh: Edinburgh University Press, forthcoming).

10. Christopher Andrew, *For the President's Eyes Only: Secret Intelligence and the American Presidency from Washington to Bush* (New York: HarperCollins, 1995); Rho-dri Jeffreys-Jones, *The CIA and American Democracy* (New Haven, CT: Yale University Press, 2003); William Daugherty, *Executive Secrets: Covert Action and the Presidency* (Lexington: University of Kentucky Press, 2004).

11. Christopher Moran and Christopher Murphy, "Introduction: Intelligence Studies Then and Now," in *Intelligence Studies in Britain and the United States: Historiography since 1945*, ed. Christopher Moran and Christopher Murphy (Edinburgh: Edinburgh University Press, 2013), 3.

12. William J. Casey, "Speech before the Department of State Executive Seminar on National and International Affairs, Department of State Bicentennial," May 6, 1981, Speech, Folder 4, Box 557, William J. Casey Papers, 1928–1996, Hoover Institution Archives, Stanford University, Palo Alto, CA.

13. Eric Foner, *The Story of American Freedom* (London: W. W. Norton, 1999), xiv; Andrew J. Bacevich, *American Empire: The Realities and Consequences of US Diplomacy* (Cambridge, MA: Harvard University Press, 2002), 230; Robert Bellah et al., *Habits of the Heart: Individualism and Commitment in American Life* (London: University of California Press, 1996), 23.

14. Although see Peter Jackson, "Pierre Bourdieu, The 'Cultural Turn' and the Practice of International History," *Review of International Studies* 34 (2008): 155–81; Scott Lucas, *Freedom's War: The US Crusade against the Soviet Union, 1945–1956* (Manchester: Manchester University Press, 1999).

15. David Campbell, *Writing Security: United States Foreign Policy and the Politics of Identity* (Minneapolis: University of Minnesota Press, 1998), 105.

16. Anne-Marie Slaughter, *The Idea That Is America* (New York: Perseus Books, 2007), 1.

17. Noted during a visit by the author to CIA Headquarters, Langley, Virginia, October 6, 2011.

18. "Soviet Goals and Expectations in the Global Power Arena," NIE 11-4-78, July 7, 1981, CIA FOIA Electronic Reading Room (CIAFERR), http://www.foia.cia.gov/sites /default/files/document_conversions/89801/DOC_0000268220.pdf.

19. Johnson compared the CIA to a cow he milked called Bessie in that like Bessie, who swung her "shit smeared" tail through a fresh pail of milk, the CIA spoiled Johnson's policies. Nixon, on the other hand, famously called the CIA "those clowns out at Langley." See Robert Jervis, "Why Intelligence and Policymakers Clash," *Political Science Quarterly* 125 (2010): 185. See also chaps. 7–10 in Jeffreys-Jones, *CIA and American Democracy.*

20. This was very different from what had come before. In 1973, for example, DCI James Schlesinger went up to Capitol Hill and attempted to tell the chairman of the Senate Armed Services Committee about some of the agency's programs. The response: "No, no, my boy, don't tell me. Just go ahead and do it—but I don't want to know!" Loch Johnson, "The CIA and the Question of Accountability," *Intelligence and National Security* 12 (1997): 180.

21. Phil Davies, *Intelligence and Government in Britain and the United States*, vol. 1, *Evolution of the US Intelligence Community* (Santa Barbara, CA: Praeger, 2012), 264.

22. James Jesus Angleton, quoted in William Colby and Richard Helms, "Oral History: Reflections of DCI Colby and DCI Helms on the CIA's 'Time of Troubles,'" *Studies in Intelligence* 51, no. 3 (1988), https://www.cia.gov/library/center-for-the-study-of -intelligence/csi-publications/csi-studies/studies/vol51no3/reflections-of-dci-colby -and-helms-on-the-cia2019s-201ctime-of-troubles201d.html.

23. John A. McCone to William J. Casey, May 11, 1984, John A. McCone Correspondence, Box 328, Folder 12, Casey Papers.

24. See Anne Cahn, *Killing Détente: The Right Attacks the CIA* (University Park: Pennsylvania State University Press, 1998).

25. Jimmy Carter, "Director of Central Intelligence Remarks at the Swearing in of Admiral Stansfield Turner," March 9, 1977, in Peters and Woolley, The American Presidency Project, http://www.presidency.ucsb.edu/ws/?pid=7141.

26. See Zbigniew Brzezinski, *Power and Principle: Memoirs of the National Security Advisor, 1977–1981* (New York: Farrar, Straus, and Giroux, 1983), 64.

27. Gates, *From the Shadows*, 110

28. "A signification spiral does not exist in a vacuum. It can only work if the connecting links are easily established by drawing on pre-existing ideological complexes or discursive formations." Kenneth Thompson, *Moral Panics* (London: Routledge, 1998), 19–20.

29. Stuart Hall et al., *Policing the Crisis: Mugging, the State, and Law and Order* (Basingstoke: Macmillan, 1982), 223.

30. See Ann McDermott, *Risk-Taking in International Politics: Prospect Theory in American Foreign Policy* (Ann Arbor: University of Michigan Press, 1998), 77–106.

31. Compounded in 1980 by a failed rescue attempt called Operation Eagle Claw. See Betty Glad, *An Outsider in the White House: Jimmy Carter, His Advisors, and the*

Making of American Foreign Policy (Ithaca, NY: Cornell University Press, 2009), 263–69.

32. Zbigniew Brzezinski, telephone interview with author, September 23, 2011.

33. W. W. Rostow to President Carter, January 7, 1980, President's File of Input for 1980 State of the Union Address, Folder 1/23/80, Box 166, Office of Staff Secretary—Handwriting File, Jimmy Carter Library, Atlanta.

34. Jimmy Carter, "State of the Union Address Delivered before a Joint Session of the Congress," January 23, 1980, in Peters and Woolley, The American Presidency Project, http://www.presidency.ucsb.edu/ws/?pid=33079.

35. This would have important effects further down the line. See Coll, *Ghost Wars*; Peter Tomsen, *The Wars of Afghanistan: Messianic Terrorism, Tribal Conflicts and the Failure of Great Powers* (New York: Public Affairs, 2011); Mohammad Yousaf and Mark Adkin, *Afghanistan—The Bear Trap: Defeat of a Superpower* (Havertown, PA: Casemate, 2001).

36. See Hammond, *Struggles for Freedom*.

37. See also Nancy Mitchell, "The Cold War and Jimmy Carter," in *The Cambridge History of the Cold War*, vol. 2, *Crises and Détente*, ed. Melvyn Leffler and Odd Arne Westad (New York: Cambridge University Press, 2010), 85.

38. Daniel P. Moynihan to President Carter, January 10, 1980, Box 166, Folder 1/23/80, President's File of Input for 1980 State of the Union Address, Office of Staff Secretary—Hand-writing File, Jimmy Carter Library, Atlanta.

39. Congressman Charlie Wilson, for example, told the *Washington Post*, "There were fifty-eight thousand dead in Vietnam. . . . I have a slight obsession with it, because of Vietnam. I thought the Russians ought to get a dose of it." Charlie Wilson, quoted in Bob Woodward and Charles R. Babcock, "US Covert Aid to Afghans on Rise," *Washington Post*, January 13, 1985, Box 1, Folder 47, Charlie Wilson Papers, East Texas Research Centre, Stephen F. Austin State University, Nacogdoches, TX.

40. For an argument that Reagan's words and deeds emboldened Kremlin hard-liners rather than created the space necessary for "new thinking," see James Graham Wilson, "Did Reagan Make Gorbachev Possible?" *Presidential Studies Quarterly* 38 (2008): 456–75.

41. Ronald Reagan, "Address before a Joint Session of Congress on the State of the Union," January 27, 1987, in Peters and Woolley, The American Presidency Project, http://www.presidency.ucsb.edu/ws/index.php?pid=34430.

42. Others in this category included Richard Allen, the first of Reagan's six national security advisers; Bill Clark, who succeeded him and was one of Reagan's closest political friends; and Secretary of State Al Haig.

43. Interestingly, Stansfield Turner, in *Burn before Reading: Presidents, CIA Directors, and Secret Intelligence* (New York: Hyperion, 2005), subtitled his chapter on Casey and Reagan "The Resurrection of 'Wild Bill.'"

44. See James M. Scott, *Deciding to Intervene: The Reagan Doctrine and American Foreign Policy* (Durham, NC: Duke University Press, 1996).

45. Ronald Reagan, "Address before a Joint Session of the Congress on the State

of the Union," February 6, 1985, in Peters and Woolley, The American Presidency Project, http://www.presidency.ucsb.edu/ws/?pid=38069.

46. James Cooper, "The Reagan Years: The Great Communicator as Diarist," *Intelligence and National Security* 23 (2008): 898.

47. Former senior CIA Directorate of Operations officer, off-the-record interview with author, August 20, 2011.

48. Maxwell M. Rabb to William Casey, November 25, 1981, Box 564, Folder 15, Casey Papers.

49. Alpern et al., "Secret Warriors."

50. Ronald Reagan, "Farewell Address to the Nation," January 11, 1989, in Peters and Woolley, The American Presidency Project, http://www.presidency.ucsb.edu/ws/?pid=29650.

51. George Shultz, "Interview with George P. Shultz—Presidential Oral History Programme," Miller Centre of Public Affairs, December 18, 2002, http://web1.millercenter.org/poh/transcripts/ohp_2002_1218_shultz.pdf.

52. Emphasis in the original. William J. Casey, speech at the Southern Centre for International Studies, Atlanta, November 8, 1986, Box 314, Folder 1, Casey Papers.

53. Coll, *Ghost Wars*, 100.

54. Ronald Reagan, remarks by President Reagan—CIA Bill Signing Ceremony (Private), June 23, 1982, Box 91372, Folder "CIA (04/21/1982-08/07/1982)," Executive Secretariat, NSC: Agency File, Reagan Library, Simi Valley, CA.

55. William J. Casey, *Where and How the War Was Fought: An Armchair Tour of the American Revolution* (New York: Morrow, 1976).

56. William J. Casey, remarks by William J. Casey at the Award of the Donovan Medal to the Prime Minister of Great Britain Margaret Thatcher, February 28, 1981, Box 556, Folder 6, Casey Papers.

57. William J. Casey, lecture at the John M. Ashbrook Center for Public Affairs Lecture, Ashland College, Ashland, OH, October 27, 1986, Box 313, Folder 8, Casey Papers.

58. *The Third Man*, directed by Carol Reed (1949; Burbank, CA: Warner Home Video, 2002), DVD; John Le Carré, *Tinker, Tailor, Soldier, Spy* (1974; London: Penguin Books, 2011); *The Good Shepherd*, directed by Robert De Niro (2006; Universal City, CA: Universal Studios, 2010), DVD; Howard Gordon and Alex Gansa, Homeland, season 4 (2014; Century City, CA: 2015), DVD; David Benioff and D. B. Weiss, *Game of Thrones*, season 1 (2011; Burbank, CA: Warner Home Video, 2015), DVD.

59. Gates, *From the Shadows*, 199.

60. Since the end of the Cold War, scholars have also found that what Soviet leaders said in public they routinely said in private. Politburo stationery, for example, bore the heading "Proletarians of the World Unite!" Quoted in Robert Jervis, "Identity and the Cold War," in *The Cambridge History of the Cold War*, vol. 2, *Crises and Détente*, ed. Melvyn Leffler and Odd Arne Westad (New York: Cambridge University Press, 2010), 33. See also Leffler, *For the Soul of Mankind*, 8.

61. Although there could of course be exceptions.

62. Quoted in Seymour Martin Lipset, *American Exceptionalism: A Double-Edged Sword* (New York: W. W. Norton, 1996), 18.

63. For a comparison, see Jervis, "Identity and the Cold War."

64. This is not to say that through advanced education and practical experience, they may well have come to hold a more sophisticated understanding of the international system or a more nuanced view of American politics and its practicalities.

65. See Kevin Coe, "The Language of Freedom in the American Presidency, 1933–2006," *Presidential Studies Quarterly* 37 (2007): 375–98.

66. Lou Cannon, *President Reagan: The Role of a Lifetime* (London: Touchstone, 1991), 336. Foner, meanwhile, points out that "freedom" is the "heaviest weapon" in a president's "rhetorical arsenal." *Story of American Freedom*, 253.

67. Some, of course, with greater degrees of success than others. Roosevelt was another master communicator, and Kennedy's powers of public speaking were considerable indeed.

68. Searches for "freedom" and "liberty" on the American Presidency Project website (http://presidency.proxied.lsit.ucsb.edu/ws/) excluded documents from the Office of the Press Secretary and election campaign documents. See Foner, *Story of American Freedom*, xiii.

69. For an interesting recent example from a recently retired spy chief, see Eliza Manningham-Buller, "Security," *Security Freedom: 2011; The Reith Lectures*, BBC video, 43:00, September 20, 2011, http://www.bbc.co.uk/programmes/b014pxnq.

70. "We now awake to find that a region largely celebrated in romantic fantasy holds the fate of the world in its hands," wrote Richard Nixon in a chapter titled "The Oil Jugular" in his 1980 *cri de coeur*, *The Real War* (New York: Touchstone, 1990), 71.

71. Albert Wohlstetter, letter with enclosed secret study on behalf of PANheuristics, June 6, 1981, Box 568, Folder 13, Casey Papers.

72. Richard Helms to William J. Casey, August 26, 1982, Box 326, Folder 11, Casey Papers.

73. Casey, speech at the Southern Centre for International Studies.

74. See Rodric Braithwaite, *Afgantsy: The Russians in Afghanistan, 1979–1989* (London: Profile Books, 2011), 332; Gregory Feifer, *The Great Gamble: The Soviet War in Afghanistan* (New York: Harper, 2009); and Artemy M. Kalinovsky, *A Long Goodbye: The Soviet Withdrawal from Afghanistan* (Cambridge, MA: Harvard University Press, 2011), 37–38. This of course is not to say that the Soviets got their strategic, operational, or tactical—or indeed political—cards either right or aligned. See these works for a further discussion.

75. Melvyn Leffler, *For the Soul of Mankind: The United States, the Soviet Union, and the Cold War* (New York: Hill and Wang, 2007), 8.

76. Casey, speech at the Southern Centre for International Studies.

77. See Karen Fierke, *Changing Games, Changing Strategies: Critical Investigations in Security* (New York: Manchester University Press, 1998), 11–12.

78. Henry Kissinger, *Diplomacy* (London: Touchstone, 1994), 735.

79. Richard Nixon, "The Meaning of Communism to Americans: Study Paper by Richard M. Nixon, Vice President, United States of America," August 21, 1960, in

Peters and Woolley, The American Presidency Project, http://www.presidency.ucsb.edu/ws/index.php?pid=25416&st=freedom&st1.

80. Robert Strausz-Hupe to Fred Ikle—Henry Kissinger's Speech, April 22, 1980, Box 12, Folder HKA/Ford, Fred C. Ikle Papers, Hoover Institution Archives, Stanford University, Palo Alto, CA.

81. Fierke, *Changing Games*, 11–12.

82. Jutta Weldes, *Constructing National Interests: The United States and the Cuban Missile Crisis* (Minneapolis: University of Minnesota Press, 1999), 241.

83. Anthony Dolan to Senator Paul Laxalt, July 25, 1984, Box 323, Folder 8, Casey Papers.

84. Stuart Hall, "The Meaning of New Times," in *Stuart Hall: Critical Dialogues in Cultural Studies*, ed. David Morley and Kuan-Hsing Chen (London: Routledge, 1996), 232; Stuart Hall, "Subjects in History: Making Diasporic Identities," in *The House That Race Built*, ed. Wahnemma Lubiano (New York: Pantheon Books, 1997), 290.

85. Michael Oakeshott, *Early Political Writings, 1925–1930* (Exeter: Imprint Academic, 2010), 164.

7 To Command or Direct?

DIRNSAs and the Historical Challenges of Leading the National Security Agency, 1952–2014

Betsy Rohaly Smoot and David Hatch

> I was horrified and disappointed when General Collins, then Chief of Staff of the Army, told me I was to take this job, but I must now confess that I have thoroughly enjoyed these past five years.
> —Gen. Ralph J. Canine, first director of the National Security Agency

The National Security Agency (NSA), while part of the US Department of Defense (DOD), is largely staffed and managed by long-tenured civilian personnel in conjunction with a complement of military personnel, both officers and enlisted. Military personnel assigned to the agency generally serve three-year tours. In many ways NSA has been run more as a corporation than as a military command, and that circumstance has often stymied the flag-rank officers who arrive expecting to be commanders.

Agency directors must balance the needs, and react to the perceptions, of three constituencies: their masters within the executive branch, especially the DOD and the intelligence community (IC) bureaucracy; the NSA workforce, particularly the senior civilian leadership; and outsiders in the form of the legislative branch and the public at large. Most of the senior leaders at NSA in the 1950s and 1960s acted as if their departments within the agency were fiefdoms; in fact, these department leaders were often nicknamed "warlords." Because most directors of the National Security Agency (known to insiders as DIRNSAs) were unfamiliar with NSA's internal operations and personnel practices, the warlords often ran the agency without great regard for the directors' ideas. They were quite happy for a director to deal with management matters external to NSA and engage in ceremonial activities inside, but through bureaucratic impediments, they were able to delay or deny implementation of decisions on internal change. The relative emphasis given to these three constituencies changes over time; in recent decades the push for openness and transparency of government have become factors that DIRNSAs have had to weigh against the need for secrecy in the agency's operations.

This survey of the past DIRNSAs examines the leadership qualities they demonstrated while in office. It is necessarily limited by classification restrictions; however, much still can be said on the basis of public knowledge to demonstrate the impact of the DIRNSAs on NSA, the IC, and national security. We will look at factors that have been important in leading NSA and will try to understand what the DIRNSAs have done to benefit the agency and influence internal senior leaders and how the position of director has changed over time.[1] Some useful material discussing the tenure of DIRNSAs does exist in books examining the history of NSA, but this assessment relies primarily on our knowledge of the historical corpus within the agency and agency-produced materials that have been declassified and are now available to the public.[2]

Understanding NSA

NSA was established in 1952 and has two primary missions: signals intelligence (SIGINT) and information assurance (IA). The SIGINT mission encompasses collection, processing, and dissemination of intelligence information from foreign signals, not just for intelligence and counterintelligence purposes but also to support military operations. The IA mission has the goal of preventing foreign adversaries from gaining access to sensitive or classified national security information. NSA also has a strong research component that supports both missions.[3] Taken collectively, the work of the agency is that of cryptology.[4] The secrecy of its mission has sometimes been reflected in the joke that NSA stands for "No Such Agency."[5] Before the formation of NSA, US government cryptology was centered on the short-lived Armed Forces Security Agency (AFSA), formed in 1949 to coordinate and supplement the cryptologic work of the US military services. The second director of AFSA was also the first DIRNSA.

Within NSA, the armed services contribute to national cryptologic work through their respective service cryptologic components (SCCs).[6] In 1972 the Central Security Service (CSS) was established to combine the work of NSA and the SCCs into a unified effort. The DIRNSA also serves as director of the CSS.[7] A related, but distinct, military organization is the US Cyber Command (USCYBERCOM), created in 2010. From 2010 until the time of this writing, the commander, USCYBERCOM, has also served as DIRNSA.[8]

Overview of the DIRNSAs

The DIRNSAs have had widely differing backgrounds, which makes it difficult to express general characteristics that describe them as a class. In many cases they were suitable candidates for the job because they possessed specific leadership or technical talents. In some cases individuals seem to have been given the job in order to diversify their personal experience and to prepare them for an even more senior position. Few seem to have sought the position directly. Some may have had the experience that Gen. Ralph Canine expressed in the epigraph. At the same time some who came to the job eagerly left it with disappointment and dismay. There are no clear criteria for the selection of directors aside from the requirement that the position be filled by a military officer. The position is a three-star one with a term of three to four years and the understanding that it will rotate, if somewhat unevenly, among the military services. Directors are appointed by the secretary of defense, so the position is a civilian political appointment that requires Senate confirmation.[9] As a rule the director is very different from the majority of those in the agency he leads. Until the selection of Adm. Michael Rogers in 2014, no director had been a career cryptologist. Only a few had prior NSA service, and the position cannot be attained by working one's way up through the ranks at the agency. Almost by definition the role is for an outsider. While the first director of AFSA and the seventeen DIRNSAs to date have been white men, they have showed great diversity in other domains.

- Ten attended military service academies, while the others received their undergraduate education at nonmilitary schools and came to the military via reserve programs, Officer Candidates School, or direct commissioning.
- Two had engineering backgrounds (Phillips, Allen).
- Two were present in Hawaii at the time of the Japanese attack on December 7, 1941 (Stone, Blake).
- Seven served in combat positions (Canine, Frost, Gayler, Phillips, Inman, McConnell, Minihan).
- Five had a tour at NSA or in an SCC before they became director (Frost, Inman, McConnell, Minihan, Rogers).
- Four, however, came to the job having never served in any intelligence position (Canine, Blake, Gayler, Phillips).
- Seven went on to higher positions either immediately after they had left NSA or at some point after their retirement (Gayler, Phillips, Allen, Inman, Studeman, McConnell, Hayden).

It is convenient to break this study into chronologically distinct eras of NSA's history and examine the directors of these eras with those whose challenges were similar.

Establishing NSA

Lt. Gen. Ralph J. Canine, USA   November 1952–November 1956
Lt. Gen. John Samford, USAF   November 1956–November 1960
Vice Adm. Laurence H. Frost, USN   November 1960–December 1961

Even after the passage of the National Security Act of 1947, the US government struggled to organize a national cryptologic service. The creation of AFSA in 1949 was an attempt to consolidate military cryptologic functions. It was somewhat successful, but perceived inadequacies with the organization's work led to the establishment of NSA in 1952. NSA was made a national organization to serve the entire executive branch of the government, not just the armed forces. In its first ten years, the young organization worked to capitalize on previous American cryptologic successes and make a place for itself within the DOD and the new IC. The focus of these directors was largely on the executive branch and the workforce.

AFSA was cobbled together in 1949 primarily from the cryptologic elements of the armed services. Its director (DIRAFSA) was of two-star rank; the position was to rotate in succession among the services every two years. The director was an administrator, with little authority to decide policy. That was the province of the AFSA Advisory Board (AFSAAB), a contentious group of service representatives who seldom agreed on anything.

When AFSA needed to replace its first director, Rear Adm. Earl Stone, in early 1951, it was found that no formal mechanism had been provided for leadership transitions. Therefore, Stone proposed to the AFSAAB that a special committee, composed of two flag-rank officers from each of the services, be formed to consider the candidates nominated by each service. AFSAAB readily agreed to this plan. The succession proved easier than expected. Because an admiral was the sitting director, the navy declined to nominate anyone; when the air force found the army nominee acceptable, the air force leadership declined to submit a name. Thus, army major general Ralph Canine became the second director of the AFSA.

It is unclear why Major General Canine was nominated to be director of a central cryptologic organization; he lacked experience in either intelligence or communications, much less cryptology. Perhaps there was a desire to bring strong leadership to what was perceived as a faltering organization. If so, Canine was the man for AFSA. He was old-time army, a veteran of both world wars. In World War II he had been chief of staff of a corps subordinate to George Patton's Third Army. Many of Canine's leadership actions reflected not only Patton's style and blunt language but also his forward-thinking approach.

One of Canine's first major actions caused chaos and controversy at AFSA, but it left no doubt that a strong leader had taken charge. When he became director, the agency was split between two major military posts, the army's Arlington Hall Station in Northern Virginia and the Naval Security Station in the District of Columbia. Its development from wartime units had given it a hodgepodge of furniture made from different materials and in different colors. Canine ordered that all offices had to be uniform in their furniture type and color. The disruption caused by the moving and painting of furniture impeded the mission and damaged morale for a time but eventually was appreciated for its contribution to the employees' pride in their organization.[10] Later, as plans were made for NSA's new building at Fort Meade, Maryland, Canine was even concerned about the paint colors for the walls. In this and many other ways, he demonstrated concern for the well-being of his highly specialized workforce.

AFSA had problems beyond just paint schemes and morale, however. Hence, President Harry Truman, responding to complaints from civilian departments and military commanders in Korea, implemented a number of reforms to AFSA in 1952. Among these changes were elimination of the AFSAAB, the granting of more authorities to the director, and the designation of the director's job as a three-star position with a four-year term.[11] Presumably it seemed unwise to change directors again after barely a year, so Ralph Canine was promoted and became the first director of the National Security Agency, a new organizational name chosen to reflect a new era in American cryptology.

When AFSA made the transition to NSA, Canine, newly promoted to lieutenant general rank, was quick to take advantage of his new authorities. He proved remarkably open to new ideas and plans and successfully lobbied the Defense Department and Congress to improve NSA. He sought and obtained appropriations for research into communications and the new field of computers and cultivated the new NSA Science Advisory Board as a source of fresh direction for a technically oriented organization. In addition, he argued for and got the authority to promote cryptologists into the highest ranks of the civil service. Finally, he used both good arguments and his military bearing to bring the service cryptologic agencies (SCAs) into greater cooperation with the central organization.[12]

An important aspect of Canine's leadership, as it was for many DIRNSAs, was his cultivation of senior managers. He often called for briefings on particular subjects and took note of those who knew their subject. Canine believed that many NSA personnel, even in the higher grades, had not had sufficient education in federal service, so he arranged for opportunities for advanced schooling, with the most senior going to the National War College. He rotated the most senior personnel among the top jobs so that any of them would be prepared to step into any position as needed.

He also paid substantial attention to the rank and file. A very high percentage of the workforce, both civilian and uniformed, had been in the army or navy cryptologic organizations during World War II, and those organizations had not cooperated well with each other. Knowing this, Canine insisted that his workers were all NSA employees, not representatives of their service. However, what most won the admiration of the workforce was his management style. Despite his gruff demeanor he was a "people person." He made surprise visits to offices, and soon amusing stories began to circulate about civilian employees who had failed to recognize him or his military rank. As he walked the hallways, he was usually willing to let an employee buttonhole him and explain a problem or offer a new idea. When he heard about an obstacle to a mission, he often took matters into his own hands, eliminating bureaucratic bottlenecks.[13]

When Canine retired in 1956, he left an NSA that was a much more effective organization than the one he had first encountered. He had become a revered figure whose reputation only grew in later years. At a symposium in 1991, a number of retired NSA senior officials, who had known most of the great persons of American cryptology and were themselves the heroes of the current generation, were asked who their own heroes were. Two names surfaced among this elite group: William Friedman, who founded modern American cryptology, and Ralph Canine. Canine is the only DIRNSA to receive a retrospective moniker: "The Great Unifier."[14]

Canine was succeeded by Lt. Gen. John Samford. It is unlikely that Samford was selected as the second DIRNSA because of his personality, but this became an important factor in his success at the job. His predecessor, Canine, had molded NSA into an effective and respected organization, but at the same time Canine's rough manner had irritated many people with whom he dealt, particularly in organizations outside NSA. Samford's more conciliatory style of leadership brought individuals and the SCAs a stronger sense of community.[15]

Vice Adm. Laurence H. Frost, Canine's chief of staff from 1953 to 1955, replaced Samford in 1960. He became interested in cryptology early in his career at a time when junior officers on a ship would often handle communications and crypto.[16] Frost was the first director to deal with a public scandal—the defection of two civilian NSA cryptologists, William H. Martin and Bernon F. Mitchell, in September 1960. He oversaw a significant reorganization of the internal structure and organization of the agency, and the core principles of that structure were retained until the early 1990s.[17] However, his tenure as the third DIRNSA was cut very short, apparently owing to disagreements with the Pentagon during a reorganization directed by Secretary of Defense Robert S. McNamara.[18] Frost's experience does suggest that prior NSA experience is no guarantee of success in the top spot.

NSA was truly shaped by the leadership of Canine and the consolidation of goodwill effected by Samford. Together they accomplished the task of shaping an agency that had the strong centralized control that AFSA had lacked. But Frost did not lack influence as his structural reorganization was sound and carried the agency through the 1960s. The founding directors established NSA's home on the Fort Meade campus, allowed a strong senior civilian leadership to exert considerable authority over the direction of the agency, established the mission-focused esprit de corps of the workforce, and set many of the cultural patterns for employees that would linger until the end of the twentieth century.

Integration into the IC

Lt. Gen. Gordon A. Blake, USAF	*January 1962–June 1965*
Lt. Gen. Marshall Carter, USA	*July 1965–August 1969*
Vice Adm. Noel Gayler, USN	*August 1969–July 1972*
Lt. Gen. Samuel C. Phillips, USAF	*August 1972–July 1973*

As the Cold War heated up and US involvement in Vietnam grew, NSA capitalized on the organization's capability and moved from being a lesser part of the Defense Department's intelligence structure to a more significant part of the IC. The agency's increased prominence in intelligence decision making was due in no small part to the efforts of its directors who fought for a larger role and greater recognition.

Lt. Gen. Gordon Blake was a quiet leader who was genuinely liked by the workforce. Within months of assuming office, he was faced with the Cuban Missile Crisis, and he used this tense period to raise the IC's awareness of the agency's work and to improve NSA's crisis response posture. Internally, he showed himself willing to do whatever it took to get the job done, including subsuming his rank to perform the menial task of manning the phone when the crisis manager needed more people to come to work.

While cooperation between NSA and the IC evolved at a steady albeit slow pace under Blake's command, Lt. Gen. Marshall S. Carter expanded the extent of the agency's participation in community matters significantly. Carter had been a protégé of Gen. George C. Marshall, having been his military aide in

China after World War II and again when Marshall was secretary of defense and then secretary of state. Later, Carter served as deputy director of central intelligence (DDCI) from 1962 until 1965, immediately preceding his appointment at NSA. As DDCI he had had an excellent opportunity to observe and learn about the relationships of all IC elements. Long a deputy or a chief of staff, Carter saw the directorship of NSA as an opportunity for him to be in command of an organization.

As DIRNSA Carter was intent on posturing NSA as a "national" agency and having the agency participate in discussions and decisions as a full member of the IC. At a large gathering in the NSA auditorium early in his tenure, Carter made it clear to senior managers that NSA was a national agency and that it would act like one in its dealings with the US Intelligence Board (USIB) and the DOD.[19] Until that time NSA was considered only a subset of the DOD intelligence structure, was a lesser participant in discussions at the USIB and its subordinate committees, and could participate in IC discussions only if the topic at hand involved SIGINT or NSA. Carter insisted that NSA representatives to the USIB keep abreast of all IC issues and participate in all discussions, not just NSA-related ones. Symbolic of the changed thinking was the agency seal, which read, "National Security Agency—Department of Defense." In 1965 Carter had it redesigned. He gave it a more powerful-looking eagle and changed the logo to read, "National Security Agency—United States of America." He had the new seal quietly substituted for the original in the USIB conference room.[20]

By this time it had become clear that NSA and the IC were acting in new ways toward each other. While Carter did not have a very good relationship with the Defense Department or the military services, and left the position feeling that DOD had diluted the effectiveness of the cryptologic effort through budgetary cutbacks that forced him to reduce collection against certain targets, the NSA workforce appreciated him as a champion of the institution.[21]

Carter was followed by Vice Adm. Noel Gayler, a highly decorated World War II aviator. While Carter had been popular with his subordinators, Gayler was tough on them; he disliked paperwork and frequently just dumped it on his immediate staff. He was especially tough on briefers.[22] Not surprisingly, he did not have a close relationship with the civilian leadership of NSA, with the exception of one subordinate.[23] Also in distinction to Carter, Gayler operated with a view to approval from the Pentagon because he did not intend to end his career at NSA, as most of his predecessors had. While Gayler did not have a great relationship with the DOD or the armed services, he was politically astute and able to deal with some of the authority and procedural problems between the services and NSA.[24]

Gayler was probably the first director to get deeply involved in technical operational details of collection systems. This was perhaps because Gayler recognized that satellite collection was the way of the future. While the earliest SIGINT satellites were launched during Admiral Frost's tenure, they were run by the navy, and NSA had little influence in their operation.[25] Gayler, however, wished to exert NSA's authority over development of such systems.[26] He was the first DIRNSA to have a full-time seat on the National Reconnaissance Program's Executive Committee, which was chaired by the deputy secretary of defense and managed the budget of the National Reconnaissance Office, the agency that launches and flies US intelligence satellites.[27] He pushed for this position because he believed that as satellite systems became more important in the production of intelligence, a major change in resource allocation, operations, and management was needed. Gayler was intimately involved with planning the number of and targeting details for the burgeoning SIGINT satellite programs.

In late 1969 or early 1970, Gayler got a tough assignment from the administration of President Richard Nixon: create a "National Cryptologic Command," a unified command consisting of NSA and the SCCs (then called cryptologic agencies). Since this involved far-reaching changes that affected the parent military services and tactical communications intelligence (COMINT) support to operations, the task proved to be impossible from a political standpoint. Gayler, however, was able to broker a compromise, giving the DIRNSA more authority over the SCCs. The result was the CSS.[28] While the CSS gave NSA greater operational control over service cryptologic assets deemed national, it left most tactical assets untouched and ignored SIGINT assets of the Central Intelligence Agency (CIA).[29] When Gayler received a fourth star and departed for a higher command, he left behind an NSA workforce that believed in agreeing to the CSS compromise. Gayler had arranged a lesser deal than expected in exchange for his promotion.

The next DIRNSA was Lt. Gen. Samuel C. Phillips, who was sent to NSA in August 1972. Phillips was a World War II veteran and an engineer. Before he became DIRNSA, he had been a missile officer who had worked much of his career with nuclear systems. In 1964 Phillips was assigned to the National Aeronautics and Space Administration as director of the Apollo Manned Lunar Landing Program. He also commanded the Space and Missile Systems Organization of the Air Force Systems Command. Phillips was told when he came to NSA that he would serve there only a year, after which he would receive his fourth star and move on back into the technical side of the air force. Phillips came to NSA with a very specific agenda to reduce the size of the agency, a move made necessary by government-wide reductions in light of the drawdown of US forces in Vietnam. As part of his charge, he introduced a system of incentivized early retirements that avoided a reduction in force or the firing of civilian personnel. In August 1973 General Phillips received his promotion and assignment as commander, Air Force Systems Command, resuming a distinguished technical career. While he ably accomplished the mission he was sent to complete, his directorship had very little long-term impact on the direction of NSA.

NSA serves two masters: the Defense Department and the IC. During the period of 1962 to 1973, the adolescent agency asserted its independence and importance within the defense system by reaching for more authority and demanding attention and a primary role within the intelligence system. Blake's tenure and leadership inaugurated this coming of age by calling attention to NSA's skills and relevancy. Carter championed SIGINT within the IC. Gayler healed some of the breach with Defense and gained ground in the IC, while Phillips quietly and competently worked to consolidate the mission in light of the Vietnam drawdown. NSA had stood up for itself with both masters, and while not yet completely satisfied with its role in the IC, it was starting to come into its own.

Tearing Down and Building Up

Lt. Gen. Lew Allen, USAF   *August 1973–July 1977*
Vice Adm. Bobby Ray Inman, USN   *July 1977–April 1981*
Lt. Gen. Lincoln D. Faurer, USAF   *April 1981–April 1985*
Lt. Gen. William E. Odom, USA   *April 1985–July 1988*

The 1970s and 1980s were marked by wild swings in budget—downsizing as a result of post–Vietnam War budget cuts and then dramatic increases during the presidency of Ronald Reagan. During this time NSA needed to modernize technologically to keep up with the growth of computing as well as find ways to accomplish its mission under the new regime of oversight in the wake of the congressional investigations led by Senator Frank Church and Representative Otis Pike.

Gen. Lew Allen was the first director of NSA who was not a World War II veteran. Like his predecessor Phillips, he came to NSA with an impressive technical résumé, including a doctorate in physics. He also brought IC credentials to the job, having served briefly at the CIA as the deputy director for the IC. A protégé of James Schlesinger, Allen was appointed DIRNSA shortly after Schlesinger became secretary of defense in July 1973.[30] Schlesinger was convinced that NSA was too large and too expensive and asked Allen to look into this problem. Allen, while he thought that NSA harbored "ambitions for responsibilities that somewhat exceeded the grasp," told Schlesinger that his belief was unsubstantiated.[31]

One of Allen's most important legacies was to institute a planning mentality where one had not previously existed. He inherited a DOD mandate for severe budget and personnel cuts, including a proposal to cut the cryptologic budget by 3 percent. The "Clements Cuts," named for then–assistant secretary of defense William P. Clements, specified that reductions should come from management efficiencies, technological efficiencies, and mission reductions. Allen believed that cutbacks in technological innovation were risky and in a bold move instead relied on well-reasoned mission reductions, both at NSA and in the field, to accomplish the mandated cuts.[32]

Allen was the first DIRNSA to testify in an open congressional hearing with his October 29, 1975, testimony to the Church Committee. In dealing with Congress in the wake of IC abuses that came to light in the 1970s, he set standards for cooperation that enhanced NSA's reputation on Capitol Hill and that continue to serve as models within NSA and the IC.[33] He was also the first director to confront the logistical challenge of declassifying and releasing large volumes of NSA documents in response to the 1974 Freedom of Information Act.[34] When Allen left NSA, he received his fourth star and moved to senior assignments in technical operations. His final assignment was as chief of staff of the air force.

Vice Adm. Bobby Ray Inman became DIRNSA early in the Jimmy Carter administration. He had a strong background in naval intelligence that made him well qualified, but the possibly apocryphal story is that he got the job because decision makers in the Carter administration heard his slight Texas accent, observed his Southern-sounding name, and assumed the admiral was another "good ol' boy." Inman is generally remembered as a successful DIRNSA. One personal characteristic that abetted this success was his photographic memory. He had phenomenal recall of documents, briefings, and people he had met. This allowed him to give complex lectures or congressional testimony without notes and to charm visitors by remembering not only their names but a wealth of personal detail.[35] In effect it reduced Inman's need for a large staff—he did not need the support.

When Inman became the director, he was satisfied that the current senior leadership and the generation coming up behind it were highly qualified. However, he worried about the generation after that. He returned to Canine's philosophy of rotating mid-level personnel in order to prepare them for promotion into the senior ranks. To this end, he formed a committee to identify NSA mid-level managers with the potential to move into senior positions. He then insisted that all persons on the list be transferred within the year.

His rotation policy was an important factor in developing well-rounded leaders, ready for higher things. In fact, virtually all the people on the list ended up in the most senior NSA offices. Not only did this policy prepare a strong generation of future leaders, but it also undercut the power of the warlords. This practice has continued and been codified into specialized programs for preparing promising employees to move up, effectively ending the warlords' stranglehold on the agency.[36]

Lt. Gen. Lincoln Faurer, who succeeded Inman, was a pilot with advanced degrees in both engineering management and international affairs. His tenure was marked by the dramatic increase in defense spending initiated by the Reagan administration. NSA's budget and personnel hiring increased rapidly and required extensive construction of additional buildings and leasing of others. During his time as director, he was highly effective in strengthening NSA's foreign partnerships.

Faurer also concentrated on internal management issues as well as an expansion of NSA's mission on the defensive side. Whereas Inman had not needed a staff system, Faurer, modeling his approach on the behavior of successful corporations, tried to rebuild NSA using new management principles that emphasized cooperation and corporate decision making. While he was a leader at applying innovative management techniques within the federal government, he was not entirely successful in convincing the entrenched NSA bureaucracy of their value.[37]

Faurer valued accommodation and collegiality and used his skills in planning to encourage innovations in communications and computer security. He was a champion of participative management at all levels and efforts that supported his belief in the great potential of individual agency employees. During his term computer security (COMPUSEC) was added to the traditional communications security (COMSEC) mission of NSA, and Faurer had a role in the establishment of the National Computer Security Center, which brought computer security products to nonnational security organizations.[38] In addition, his actions in creating Project Gunman were extremely important in discovering eavesdropping devices in the US embassy in Moscow.[39]

Lt. Gen. William E. Odom was the next DIRNSA (see chapter 8). On the surface Odom, a scholarly army Soviet specialist who had a PhD in political science and spoke Russian and German, might appear to be a good fit for NSA and its cadre of well-educated Soviet specialists. He had served on the National Security Staff in the Carter administration, and National Security Adviser Zbigniew Brzezinski respected his views and considered him an innovative strategic thinker.[40] Some of NSA's senior civilians who worked for him also thought that he was a considered thinker.

Most of the agency, however, perceived Odom as reactive and dictatorial. Odom never adapted to NSA's method of doing business, which differed greatly from a military command system and sought to enhance the independence of the office of the director by building a command staff that would allow him to manage actions and verify information independently from the senior leadership. Odom battled the system for his entire term and ultimately left in 1988 without feeling that he had a made a dent in the way the system operated.[41]

Nevertheless, Odom did understand NSA's mission, as his "Ten Thrusts" initiative showed. The initiative was a set of goals designed to maintain NSA's edge in various technical disciplines, to sharpen the agency's focus on customer support, and to enhance its capabilities in providing information assurance.[42] He also launched initiatives to physically decentralize the cryptologic system to increase the chances of its survival in the event of disaster or war. In addition, he followed in Faurer's footsteps by encouraging the continued expansion of NSA's new role in computer security within the national security community.[43]

Modernization is not exclusive to any one era, but changes in both technology and outlook particularly characterized this period. The directors who served between 1973 and 1988 made valiant efforts to update not just planning for how technology should be improved but for human resource changes such as succession planning. They dealt with dramatic shifts in resources, from the sharp cuts and downsizing of the post-Vietnam period to the remarkable funding and resulting growth during the Reagan administration. The need for increased openness and disclosure following the Church-Pike investigations challenged a bureaucracy long accustomed to silence and the leaders who had to begin to balance openness and secrecy.

Facing the Challenges of the Post-Cold War World

Vice Adm. William O. Studeman, USN *August 1988–May 1992*
Vice Adm. J. Michael McConnell, USN *May 1992–February 1996*
Lt. Gen. Kenneth A. Minihan, USAF *February 1996–March 1999*

The men charged with leading NSA out of the Cold War era were all career military intelligence professionals cognizant of the need for the agency and its workforce to change. They each grappled with decreased funding and downsizing of operations and staffing, shifting geopolitics, and most critically, rapid technological changes in computing and communications. The turbulent 1990s disrupted the agency's operations on every level. In addition, NSA's visibility and openness increased incrementally during this period. While Studeman, McConnell, and Minihan each made improvements and steadied what some perceived as a sinking ship, they did not effect change on a grand scale.

Vice Adm. William O. Studeman was in charge when the Berlin Wall came down and the Soviet Union fell. With his background in naval intelligence, he was "intelligence community–minded" and sought ways to work more closely with NSA's sister agencies. During Operation Desert Storm Studeman took initiative to create interagency fusion cells where representatives of intelligence agencies could collaboratively support military operations. Possibly because of these efforts and his broad perspective on intelligence issues, Studeman left NSA in 1992 to serve as deputy director, and later acting director, of the CIA.[44]

Like many of his predecessors, Studeman had some troubles coming to a modus vivendi with the civilians who worked for him. At a staff meeting early in his tenure, Studeman agreed almost immediately with a certain proposal presented to him. He was amazed and not a little annoyed to find that the civilians who had made the proposal continued to press for the airing of many different points of view about the issue in order to clarify the decision. For weeks afterward he complained that people at NSA would "argue with you even when you agree with them!"

While the DIRNSAs of the 1970s and 1980s had been forced to be more open with Congress and the public, Studeman was the first to try to get out in front of the openness issue. With the end of the Cold War, Studeman recognized the need for the public to better understand NSA's raison d'être, and he acted to raise the agency's public profile. Not only did he make public appearances, he sent NSA mathematicians to support local schools with presentations and as tutors, an educational outreach effort that continues to the present day. With Studeman's support, work began on the creation of what eventually became the National Cryptologic Museum, an open and free public institution that today serves more than 50,000 visitors a year.

Studeman was succeeded in 1992 by Vice Adm. J. Michael McConnell, who on paper had a similar profile. McConnell also had a background in naval intelligence but, unlike Studeman, had served a tour as a mid-level manager at NSA. His public profile was a bit higher from the start of his directorship owing to his service as J-2 and Pentagon briefer during Operation Desert Storm. McConnell would also go on to higher office in the IC, being recalled from retirement in 2007 to serve as the director of national intelligence.

Inman had started to position the agency in the public's eye, foreseeing that difficult times would follow the end of the Cold War. However, McConnell was obliged to deal with the harder task of downsizing the agency at the behest of a Congress that sought a "peace dividend." A number of major and minor reorganizations marked McConnell's tenure as the agency struggled to balance increasingly sparse staff and equipment resources with the demands of mission. Some of these realignments changed structures (and power bases) that had been in place for more than two decades, unsettled senior management, and displaced many in the workforce. McConnell worked hard to juggle cuts in funding and personnel with the need to provide both SIGINT and IA support to US forces deployed (rather surprisingly) in the Balkans and eastern Africa.

The 1990s were a time of accelerated change in computers, communications, and encryption technology. The world began to move to fiber-optic cable and away from more easily accessed long-distance microwave technology. Encryption techniques and devices were increasingly available from commercial sources and no longer the province of governments alone. Foreign companies challenged the virtual monopoly that American corporations once had on cutting-edge communications technology. This rapid move away from technologies well-understood by NSA combined with the greater public availability of encryption threatened NSA's core mission. Both the "downtown" Washington, DC, customers and overseers and the media perceived that NSA was losing its technical edge and that the agency's internal processes were stuck in the Cold War.[45]

Lt. Gen. Kenneth A. Minihan, the director of the Defense Intelligence Agency, found his tenure there cut short in favor of an assignment to NSA to deal with these problems. Like his two immediate predecessors, he was a career intelligence professional. Like McConnell, he had done a tour as a mid-level manager at NSA. Minihan, however, was known as an aggressive manager. He sought to revitalize the workforce and have it accept the fact that change was required to survive. His October 1996 "Future Day" effort, a stand-down day during which the agency workforce examined issues of change and preparation for new technologies and new challenges, set the stage for change despite receiving some gentle ridicule and resistance from cynical members of the workforce.

Change took the form of the *National Cryptologic Strategy for the 21st Century*, a declassified version of which was released publicly.[46] Minihan's intent was to put NSA in a position to provide information dominance for the United States and its allies, to protect the integration of COMINT and COMSEC, and to transform both the workforce and the workplace. Recognizing that the interdependence of these various missions was not understood in some pockets of the workforce, much less outside NSA, Minihan coined the vision statement "One Team, One Mission" to describe the agency. Although many employees grew weary of the constant repetition of this theme, the phrase did help promote positive awareness of the agency's reason for being and its ultimate unity. To put the US government in a better position to deal with threats to information technology, Minihan stood up the Information Operations Technology Center, a joint IC venture collocated with NSA.

The 1990s were perhaps the most traumatic decade in the history of NSA up to that time. The agency was faced with the rapid change of computer technology that culminated in the availability of computer communications to the masses of the world, the fiscal cuts of the "peace dividend," the challenge of taking on cryptologic missions that differed greatly from the problem of the monolithic Soviet threat, and all the resulting morale issues for the workforce. Three able and well-liked directors grappled to realign an agency built on the successful practices of the post–Cuban Missile Crisis Cold War into a flexible and responsive instrument that could be leveraged against unexpected crises in regions where institutional knowledge might be less than robust. There was some success and increased openness. However, even more change was needed and would first come in the form of a new leader.

Confronting Terrorism and the World of Cyber

Lt. Gen. Michael V. Hayden, USAF   *March 1999–July 2005*
Gen. Keith B. Alexander, USA   *August 2005–March 2014*

While as of this writing it may be too early for a true historical look at the tenures of Generals Michael V. Hayden and Keith B. Alexander, there are some important issues regarding their leadership in this period that already merit consideration.

It is significant that before taking his appointment as DIRNSA in 1999, Lt. Gen. Michael Hayden consulted only one former director, Adm. Bobby Ray Inman. The former director told Hayden about the ways in which NSA senior managers would seek to limit the internal changes that directors sought to make. Hayden came away from the meeting determined not to allow himself to be isolated or to be merely a figurehead.

In fact, Hayden, like Minihan, came to NSA to make changes. Hayden initially was bemused, if not stymied, by NSA's corporate culture. Despite having served as a military attaché at the US embassy in Bulgaria, he was used to, and more comfortable with, the military culture of respectful discussion before a decision, followed by leadership unanimity of speech and action afterward. As did Studeman, he found that many senior civilian leaders continued to pursue their own lines even after the DIRNSA made a decision.

Many people in the defense and intelligence communities thought that NSA had let itself fall behind in the use of technology in an era of rapid technological change; even the public media repeated comments that reflected adversely on the agency's abilities. Whatever he believed personally, Hayden told NSA employees that they were at the top of their game but that changes in many areas of endeavor would be required to keep pace with global events.

He explained that not only was technology advancing rapidly but that new adversaries were as technologically savvy as Americans were.

Hayden moved boldly not only to implement change but to be seen by the public and the national security elites as doing so. Early in his tenure, Hayden established two panels—one composed of insiders, the other of members of the wider IC—to make recommendations on needed changes and reforms.[47] He began to increase NSA's visibility to the outside world through a strategy of media engagement, becoming the most well-known DIRNSA since Lew Allen (who had been the first director to testify in open session before Congress).

Hayden's changes were both wide and deep. On November 10, 1999, he announced his "100 Days of Change" and began promulgating a series of messages called "DIRGRAMS" that would convey his ideas and direction to the workforce through his tenure. These messages eventually numbered in the hundreds.[48] Among his most important moves was to streamline NSA's table of organization. The new organization reflected mission priorities by downgrading the status of or even eliminating support elements. To reduce time away from mission, Hayden abolished moss-encrusted and complicated personnel procedures for promotions and assignments, replacing them with processes similar to those found in the military.[49] He also brought outside experts into senior positions.

However necessary the changes might have been, many sectors of the workforce did not deal well with their wide-ranging nature or their rapidity of implementation. Hayden, however, proved to be a master at communications. The workforce was inundated with information delivered by memos, electronic articles, and videos explaining the benefits of change itself as well as the reasons behind the specific changes at NSA. As one of the most articulate men in public service, Hayden met frequently with the workforce for free-flowing question and answer sessions at which he defended his decisions and explained the thinking behind them. If this did not satisfy all elements in the agency, the efforts did bring the workforce successfully through the changes.

Change, particularly technological change, can be expensive, and it is often impeded by bureaucratic practices. One solution to this was Hayden's decision to outsource many aspects of NSA's mission. Hayden reduced the size of the NSA workforce by offering incentives for early retirement. These workers were replaced (not necessarily on a one-for-one basis) by contract personnel. By and large, contractors were not cheaper than federal employees, but Hayden believed that a contract force would be more agile; that is, as skill needs changed, the makeup of the contract workers could also be changed quickly through new or altered contracts in ways that would be impossible for federal employees.

The terrorist attacks of September 11, 2001, occurred near the end of what would have been a normal three- to four-year tenure as DIRNSA, although at the time it was not clear whether Hayden would have left the post in early 2002. Hayden's actions during the crisis, well communicated to NSA employees, helped reassure the workforce that senior management would do whatever it could to support their efforts. He was also the beneficiary of the workforce's keen understanding of the importance of their mission and their willingness to make personal sacrifices to accomplish it. As a result of the attacks and the need for continuity in light of the new mission, Hayden remained in the job until July 2005, at the time a record for service as a DIRNSA. After leaving NSA, Hayden was appointed deputy director of national intelligence, then director of the CIA. After his retirement from government service, he took a vigorous role in public debates about numerous intelligence and SIGINT issues, and in 2016 he became the first DIRNSA to publish an autobiography.[50]

Gen. Keith B. Alexander was a unique DIRNSA in a number of ways. He served as director for four years before he was appointed in 2009 to concurrently serve as commander of the newly created USCYBERCOM. He also received an unprecedented fourth star halfway through his record-setting nearly nine-year term. Alexander's background in intelligence and deep interest in things technical meant that, more than other directors, he sought out opportunities to sit with analysts and learn how to use frontline analytic tools. The Alexander years were marked by a series of unauthorized disclosures about the agency's work and mission, and as a result General Alexander probably spent more time in congressional testimony—both open and closed—than any other DIRNSA in history.

Increased public scrutiny in both the Hayden and Alexander eras has changed the role of the director as leader of NSA, and far from the days of "No Such Agency," it seems unlikely that the position will ever revert to one that required (or allowed) minimal interaction with the world at large.

The Leadership of Deputies

Dr. Louis Tordella	*August 1957–April 1974*
Ann Z. Caracristi	*April 1980–July 1982*
William B. Black	*September 2000–August 2006*
John C. "Chris" Inglis	*August 2006–December 2014*

DIRNSAs are assisted by a deputy director (DDIR). The best of the deputies used their insider leadership perspective to enhance the work of the director they served.

Today we take it for granted that the DDIR of NSA is the highest-ranking civilian in the agency, but it was not always so. DIRNSA Canine did not want a civilian deputy and had three successive "vice directors," all military flag officers—Rear Adm. Joseph Wenger, Brig. Gen. John Ackerman, and Lt. Gen. John Samford. When Samford took over from Canine and Ackerman was his vice director, two air force officers were in charge of NSA. This led to the promulgation of National Security Council Intelligence Directive 6, which mandated a civilian DDIR of NSA.[51]

DIRNSA Samford did not share Canine's prejudice against civilian deputies and first attempted to bring in a different perspective by hiring a former CBS Television executive, Joseph H. Ream, for the job. This was in line with the Eisenhower administration's policy to bring outside expertise into government operations. However, the position was not a good fit for Ream or his successor, a longtime cryptologic program manager named Dr. Howard Engstrom.[52]

Ideally, however, civilian deputies have the ability to assist the director they served, being "of" the agency rather than the "outsider" brought in to fill the main leadership role. The third civilian DDIR was a good fit for the job and complemented the seven DIRNSAs from Samford to Allen for whom he worked over a remarkable period of nearly seventeen years. Louis Tordella, a professor of mathematics at Loyola University of Chicago, joined the navy in 1942 and was part of that service's code-breaking operation during the war. As a civilian member of AFSA, he made a name for himself as program manager for a successful secure communications security device, the AFSAM-07.[53]

An early advocate of the use of computers for cryptology, Tordella forged a close working relationship between NSA and the American computer industry. His technical expertise and broad understanding of the agency's work meant he was trusted not only by the closest of the cryptologic partners, the United Kingdom, but by the DOD and Congress. Senator Leverett Saltonstall once said, "If Lou Tordella says it's OK, that's good enough for me."[54] Tordella was a decisive, authoritative leader and guided the agency (and its transitory directors) through many perilous days of the Cold War. He had two nicknames within the workforce. He was known familiarly as "Dr. T" by most employees. However, his tight control over budget matters led to the moniker "Dr. No" among senior managers.[55] He built on the cryptologic legacy of World War II and ensured NSA moved into the modern technological era. He was part of the fight to have SIGINT considered a full intelligence source within the IC.

Tordella's long tenure as DDIR did not set a precedent for the office. For the next thirty years, the deputy's term ran between two and four years, and departing deputies almost automatically were rewarded with a term as the senior agency representative in the United Kingdom if they wanted the position. Some of them, however, were notable for reasons other than longevity.

This was particularly true of Admiral Inman's deputy, Ann Caracristi, who had a long tenure at the agency and a depth of expertise on the Soviet problem that Inman lacked. Caracristi was one of the small number of women to rise to a supervisory position during the war and was the last of the cryptologic veterans of World War II to be deputy DIRNSA. She was well versed in the technical and analytic aspects of the day-to-day work of the agency. Caracristi's professionalism in responding to tough intelligence problems contributed to her advancement at NSA. While DDIR she advocated customer support and good IC relationships. She was particularly respected by the workforce and in some intangible way bridged a gap between the old and new, from the cryptologic success of World War II to those of the Cold War.

Of more recent DDIRs, two are notable for changing the definition of the job and their differing leadership qualities, in addition to their longer-than-usual tenures. William B. Black was a longtime agency leader who was involved in an influential study of SIGINT support to the military.[56] He retired in 1997 to work in private industry but then returned to serve as DDIR in 2000, a time of marked transformation of the agency's operations and policies. A career SIGINT professional, Black championed the need for cryptologic centers outside the Washington region. His depth of knowledge of NSA's inner workings combined with his experience in private industry provided needed support to DIRNSA Hayden in the years following the terrorist attacks of September 2001. He was kept in the position longer than anticipated to provide stability and continuity during that time of change.

John C. "Chris" Inglis came to the job from a very different perspective and was the first of the baby boomer generation to fill the DDIR position. Inglis, a graduate of the US Air Force Academy and a pilot, began his NSA career as a civilian information security analyst and rapidly moved into the ranks of management. His technological background combined with his adaptability to other areas of operations resulted in a calm, empathetic style of leadership appreciated by the workforce. With DIRNSA Alexander "dual-hatted" as commander of Cyber Command, Inglis functioned as the self-described "chief operating officer" of NSA.

The role of the DDIR of NSA has changed over time. In the post-Tordella era the civilian deputies have supported the DIRNSA by contributing expert knowledge of the agency's policy, procedures, and workforce. After the terrorist attacks of 2001, the tenure of deputies has lengthened; with the creation of USCYBERCOM, the role has taken on increased responsibilities. It remains to be seen if these trends will continue.

Conclusion

NSA has always had to contend with a number of contradictory requirements, both internal and external to itself. In balancing the organization's three natural constituencies—the executive branch, the workforce, and the "outside," in the shape of the legislative branch and the public, DIRNSAs have expended time and energy in a variety of directions depending on the issues of their day. The 2009 creation of USCYBERCOM and the demands for openness and transparency, starting in the 1970s but accelerating rapidly in the years following the terrorist attacks of September 2001, have changed the game, requiring the director to manage the agency in an increasingly outward-focused manner.

NSA has always struggled for some degree of autonomy from its two parents: the DOD and the IC. This struggle often consumes a great deal of the director's time and political capital. The directors of the 1960s, during the post–Cuban Missile Crisis Cold War, strove to solidify NSA's role within both structures and to make sure that the agency had a seat at the table for policy and planning that influenced the course of the SIGINT mission. In the 1970s DIRNSAs struggled to accomplish their mission despite the personnel drawdowns after the Vietnam War and resulting budget cuts; their successors in the 1980s faced the challenge of managing a massive influx of funds and personnel as the Cold War ramped up during the administration of President Ronald Reagan.

The DIRNSA is a senior military officer coming to the agency from the outside who must lead a large civilian workforce that is generally quite accustomed to its own ways. In the early years of NSA, Canine, Samford, and Frost, but most particularly Canine, exerted considerable influence over the morale and culture of the workforce and the working structure of the bureaucracy. However, at the same time, Samford's selection of the powerful Tordella to serve as DDIR inadvertently in the long term resulted in an entrenched internal civilian bureaucracy loyal to the DDIR that would often hinder future DIRNSAs.

It has been difficult for the director to implement change when he is a transitory figure, particularly given that the senior civilians under his command have a vested interest in maintaining a system that benefits their control and their understanding of mission and operations. At times the NSA internal bureaucracy—from senior leaders to the workforce—seems to have continued on its own course, confounding any attempts made by DIRNSAs to guide or influence its actions. This is evident particularly in the short tenure of Phillips but also in a degree of resistance to change that confronted Studeman, Mc-Connell, and Minihan during the turbulent 1990s.

Some directors have been genuinely liked by the workforce and a few have been reviled, but there has been no evidence that this affects their ability to get things done. Far more meaningful has been the ability to find ways to work with or around the entrenched senior bureaucracy. Some directors have been successful in effecting changes or achieving goals by working with the existing internal power structure, despite the costs incurred. A powerful and like-minded DDIR has proved to benefit the work of a director in this regard.

Several directors, however—Canine, Inman, and Hayden among them—made profound and positive changes at NSA through confrontation with the senior management that was accustomed to running the agency. A common characteristic for these DIRNSAs was an understanding of what needed to change and a willingness to confront entrenched subordinate leaders, replacing them if necessary. Canine and Hayden also sought to outflank the "warlords" by mobilizing support for change from within the workforce.

It is not clear whether prior service at NSA has been to a director's advantage or not. Hayden liked to joke that the first time he set foot in NSA, he was the DIRNSA, yet he successfully led the most far-reaching internal changes in NSA's history and kept morale high within the workforce as the agency responded to the 2001 terrorist events. Many other directors without prior NSA experience had successful tenures in their own times. Moreover, there are no clear-cut examples in which directors with prior NSA duty drew on that experience to achieve their goals. Some directors benefit from their time at NSA more than NSA benefited from their service. Since Gayler's promotion to commander in chief, US Pacific Command, more directors have gone on to higher positions than have gone into retirement.

By and large, the early DIRNSAs were anonymous men. However, since the end of the Cold War, perhaps even from the time of the congressional hearings of the 1970s, directors have had to add "media smarts" to their skill mix. All have had to adopt far-reaching policies for interactions with the public and with public media; a few have had the ability to participate in media events successfully themselves. In the more recent era of transparency—not all of it voluntary—and subsequent to the creation of USCYBERCOM, the focus of the DIRNSA has been increasingly turned away from NSA. The civilian DDIR, acting in a "chief operating officer" function, now must often take the lead in dealing with the demands for leadership, guidance, and direction from the internal constituency at the agency.

The nature of the position of DIRNSA has been evolving rapidly since the 1990s and will continue to change at a fast pace. DIRNSAs in the future must be politically adept at dealing with the DOD and the IC behind closed doors. They must, as well, be able to interact with Congress and provide the American people with a degree of transparency regarding the agency's mission that will sustain the public's faith in the lawfulness of the work of NSA. Simultaneously, they need the ability to understand and direct a dizzying array of rapidly developing high technology programs. Finally, they must be the rare military leaders who know how to lead a large civilian workforce. The DIRNSA of the future will need to be cognizant of the lessons of his (or her) predecessors to succeed.

Notes

This essay is entirely the work of the authors. It does not necessarily represent the opinion of the National Security Agency or the Department of Defense. It has, however, been reviewed by the National Security Agency for security purposes.

Epigraph: Canine's remarks to the secretary of defense upon his departure from NSA, unpublished notes held by the Center for Cryptologic History, Fort Meade, MD.

1. Much of the source material for this article can be found in the redacted version of Thomas R. Johnson, *American Cryptology during the Cold War* (Fort Meade, MD: Center for Cryptologic History, 1999), https://www.nsa.gov/news-features/declassified-documents/cryptologic-histories/. Where possible, sources available to the public have been noted.

2. James Bamford and Matthew Aid discuss both biographical detail of NSA directors and offer some insight as to their leadership during their time at the agency. James Bamford, *The Puzzle Palace: A Report on America's Most Secret Agency* (Boston: Houghton Mifflin, 1982); Matthew W. Aid, *The Secret Sentry: The Untold Story of the National Security Agency* (New York: Bloomsbury Press, 2009).

3. National Security Agency, "National Security Agency Mission Statement," accessed June 11, 2015, https://www.nsa.gov/about/mission/index.shtml.

4. Cryptology encompasses the science of making codes and ciphers (cryptography) and breaking codes and ciphers (cryptanalysis). In this chapter "cryptologic" refers to SIGINT and IA (what in years past was known as communications security).

5. This play on NSA's initials was likely born from the fact that it took some time for NSA to show up in Defense Department directories. The delay can be attributed to normal lags in the typesetting era of printing rather than a desire to obscure the agency's existence.

6. SCCs were previously called service cryptologic agencies (SCAs) and service cryptologic elements (SCEs).

7. The two elements are commonly referred to as NSA/CSS.

8. Commander, USCYBERCOM, is a military four-star position and DIRNSA is a three-star position. To date two DIRNSAs have commanded USCYBERCOM, but it is expected that the positions will eventually be split.

9. While the position of DIRNSA does not require confirmation, promotion to the rank of three stars does, as does appointment to command USCYBERCOM, and to date the two jobs have been linked by the fact that the same individual holds both at the same time.

10. Barry Wells, unpublished recollections, 2002, Center for Cryptologic History. This was the text of a briefing based on Wells's personal experiences that was never delivered.

11. Directors' terms began as four years and then began to vary. Canine, Samford, Carter, Allen, Inman, Faurer, Studeman, and McConnell had four (or nearly four) years; Frost and Phillips had very short tours. Blake, Gayler, Odom, and Minihan had three-year terms. This pattern would shift after the terrorist attacks of September 2001.

12. Johnson, *American Cryptology*, 1:67.

13. Name Redacted, "Glimpses of a Man: The Life of Ralph J. Canine," *Cryptologic Quarterly* 6 (1987): 31–38.

14. Discussion, Cryptologic History Symposium, National Security Agency, Fort Meade, MD, 1991.

15. Johnson, *American Cryptology*, 1:269.

16. Laurence H. Frost Oral History Interview, 1970, John F. Kennedy Oral History Collection, John F. Kennedy Presidential Library and Museum.

17. Ibid.; Johnson, *American Cryptology*, 2:294.

18. Laurence H. Frost Oral History Interview; Johnson, *American Cryptology*, 2:338; Memoir of a retired NSA senior, unpublished, Center for Cryptologic History, NSA, Fort Meade MD.

19. Established in 1957 by President Dwight D. Eisenhower, the USIB served as a focal point for discussion of intelligence issues between the director of central intelligence and the heads of US intelligence agencies.

20. Johnson, *American Cryptology*, 2:358.

21. Ibid., 392, 359.

22. Ibid., 478.

23. This individual was described as "Machiavellian" by someone who served as one of Gayler's military aides; it was a trait that appealed to Gayler.

24. Johnson, *American Cryptology*, 2:370, 469, 478.

25. Ibid., 406–9.

26. Ibid., 408–10.

27. Bruce Berkowitz, *The National Reconnaissance Office at 50 Years: A Brief History* (Chantilly, VA: National Reconnaissance Office, 2011), 14, http://www.nro.gov /history/csnr/programs/NRO_Brief_History.pdf.

28. Johnson, *American Cryptology*, 3:359, 360.

29. Ibid., 63–64.

30. Schlesinger brought Allen into the CIA during Schlesinger's short five-month tenure as director of central intelligence. Allen was not confirmed by Congress owing to a feud between Congress and Schlesinger as to whether the position he filled

should be civilian or military. Thus, when Schlesinger became secretary of defense, he asked Allen to take the DIRNSA position, which did not require confirmation. Ibid., 89.

31. Ibid., 90.

32. Ibid., 24–26.

33. Ibid., 96–99.

34. Ibid., 109–12.

35. Ibid., 190.

36. Ibid., 191.

37. Johnson, *American Cryptology*, 4:266–68.

38. Ibid., 292. Also see Michael Warner, "Notes on the Evolution of Computer Security Policy in the US Government, 1965–2003," *IEEE Annals of the History of Computing* 37 (2015): 9–18.

39. Sharon A. Maneki, *Learning from the Enemy: The Gunman Project* (Fort Meade, MD: National Security Agency, 2012), 3.

40. Johnson, *American Cryptology*, 4:267–68.

41. Ibid., 269.

42. Ibid.

43. Ibid., 294. Also see Warner, "Evolution of Computer Security Policy."

44. William O. Studeman, "Farewell," April 8, 1992, National Security Agency, https://www.nsa.gov/public_info/_files/directors_misc/Director_Farewell.pdf.

45. Tom Bowman, "Air Force General to Head NSA," *Baltimore Sun*, January 25, 1996.

46. *National Cryptologic Strategy for the 21st Century*, 2002, http://fas.org/irp/nsa/ncs21/index.html.

47. New Enterprise Team, *The Director's Work Plan for Change*, October 1, 1999, https://www.nsa.gov/news-features/declassified-documents/directors-misc/assets/files/Directors_Work_Plan.pdf.

48. A list of DIRGRAMs is available at http://www.governmentattic.org/4docs/73NSA-DIRgrams_1999-2001.pdf.

49. One change was to the promotion process. Each mid-level organization and above had boards of up to a dozen members that met several times each quarter. Eliminating boards and moving the promotion process to an annual cycle in which decisions were made by a small number of managers freed hundreds of lower-level managers and technical experts to spend additional hours on mission.

50. Michael V. Hayden, *Playing to the Edge: American Intelligence in the Age of Terror* (New York: Penguin Press, 2016).

51. David P. Mowry, "Major General John B. Ackerman, USAF," *Cryptologic Almanac 50th Anniversary Series*, 2003, https://www.nsa.gov/news-features/declassified-documents/crypto-almanac-50th/assets/files/major-general-john-b-ackerman.pdf.

52. Johnson, *American Cryptology*, 1:231.

53. David Hatch, "The Education of a Deputy Director," Tordella memorial book

(1996), https://www.nsa.gov/about/_files/cryptologic_heritage/publications/misc /tordella.pdf.

54. Gene Becker, "If Lou Tordella Says It's OK, That's Good Enough for Me," *Cryptolog* 22 (1996): 25–27.

55. For more on Dr. Tordella, see *Cryptolog* 22 (1996).

56. Johnson, *American Cryptology*, 3:66.

8 The Intellectual Redneck

William E. Odom and the National Security Agency

Richard J. Aldrich

At three o'clock in the morning on November 7, 1979, Lt. Gen. William E. Odom made a phone call. Odom was military assistant to National Security Adviser Zbigniew Brzezinski, and it was his somber duty to inform his boss that Moscow had just fired more than 200 nuclear missiles at the United States. Both knew that President Jimmy Carter's response time was less than seven minutes. A startled Brzezinski asked for confirmation before he conveyed the fateful news to Carter. Odom checked and called back, explaining in his low Tennessee drawl that they now believed that no fewer than 2,200 missiles were inbound for the American homeland, heralding an all-out attack. Just as Brzezinski was about to call the president and advise retaliation, Odom rang again to say that he was now suspicious because some warning systems were reporting no Soviet launches at all. They later discovered that someone had mistakenly put military exercise tapes into the computer system. It was a false alarm.[1]

William E. Odom, known as Bill, was at the center of national security affairs for much of the late twentieth century. A senior security official under President Jimmy Carter and then Ronald Reagan, he later served as an adjunct professor of political science at Yale. Odom initially rose to prominence as Brzezinski's military assistant. But the peak of his career was a decade of intelligence leadership under Reagan. Odom led military intelligence as the army's assistant chief of staff for intelligence from 1981 to 1985 and then ran the National Security Agency (NSA) until August 1988, presiding over all US signals intelligence (SIGINT) and communications security (COMSEC) activities. He finally retired from the army in 1989. Thereafter, he went on to serve on various blue-ribbon panels intended to overhaul intelligence and continued to undertake classified advisory roles into the 1990s.

Always outspoken, Odom remained in the spotlight until his death in 2008. He was a vocal critic of the invasion of Iraq in 2003. This was not because he

Photo 8.1 The Intellectual Redneck: The dictatorial style of Lt. Gen. William Odom, pictured here in 1983, caused him to clash with many of the National Security Agency's senior civilian managers. *US Department of Defense*

feared intervention generally; indeed, in the 1990s he was keen to see American troops deployed to the Balkans. However, he was a persistent critic of the George W. Bush administration's neoconservative determination to create democratic governance in other countries by a mixture of coercion and military action. In 2005, as a former SIGINT chief, he offered striking criticism of the American decision to engage in mass collection of the communications data of American citizens without a warrant (as required by law) that caught public attention. The top American legal minds have also concluded that this action was illegal. Odom argued that the call data collection program, known as Stellar Wind, was not only unlawful but also largely ineffective, something that the serving Federal Bureau of Investigation (FBI) director later confirmed in congressional testimony.[2]

In exploring the career of an intelligence leader, it is worth asking what, in essence, they considered themselves to be. Throughout his career Odom defined himself as a scholar and an area studies expert on the Soviet Union. At Yale Odom offered an undergraduate seminar on Russian political theory and was awarded the Lex Hixon Prize for Teaching Excellence in the Social Sciences. He was renowned for giving time generously to his students. Russia and the eastern bloc were the constants in his early career. In the mid-1960s he served in the US liaison mission to the Soviet forces in East Germany. Odom then served as a military attaché at the American embassy in Moscow from 1972 to 1974. Odom earned an MA in Russian studies at Columbia in 1962 and completed a doctorate there in 1970. Columbia was where he met Brzezinski, who took him into the Carter administration as a hawkish Soviet expert. Odom's frequent interface with things Russian led him to entertain doubts about the détente policy pursued by the West throughout the 1970s, and he saw the Soviet invasion of Afghanistan in December 1979 as a vindication of his beliefs in a Moscow that was fundamentally aggressive.[3]

Odom also conceived of the Soviet Union as simultaneously dangerous and fragile. He was convinced that its inability to reform opened up the possibility of eventual collapse. Observing the instability in Poland and the rise of Solidarity during late 1980, he reflected, "The Soviet Union, however militarily strong it is, suffers enormous centrifugal political forces. A shock could bring surprising developments within the USSR, just as we have seen occurring in Poland. The dissolution of the Soviet Union is not a wholly fanciful prediction for later in this century." Along with the specialist journalist Timothy Garton Ash, he was one of the few to recognize the importance of Solidarity as a pre-tremor that foretold the earthquake that was to come with Perestroika five years later. Ironically, however, the same belief in the rigidity of the Soviet system rendered him overly skeptical of the importance of Gorbachev as a reformer and the ability of the Soviet Union to change.[4]

Known for his distinctive Tennessee drawl, Odom described himself as an "intellectual redneck" and prided himself on both straight talking and challenging conventional thinking—a formidable combination. Odom wrote no fewer than seven books. An outstanding scholar with a profound understanding of Russia, he ranks as perhaps the most overtly intellectual intelligence chief of the Cold War.[5] Yet at the same time he struggled to reconcile martial and intellectual values, and while brandishing his undoubted academic skills in the context of Beltway battles, he nevertheless could prove remarkably intolerant of open debate if things were not going his way.

Odom was ultimately a somewhat paradoxical character. He believed in public engagement for the sake of promoting public trust in the mission. Yet he disliked civilians and is certainly remembered as one of the more acerbic and volatile directors of NSA.[6] He fought vigorous battles inside NSA while also fighting on behalf of NSA against other agencies. His aggression, directness, and preference for radical solutions did not diminish with the years:

in the second edition of his book outlining reforms for the US intelligence community, published in 2004, he argued that both the Central Intelligence Agency (CIA) and Defense Intelligence Agency (DIA) should be abolished.[7]

Odom as Head of Army Intelligence

Appointed as the army's assistant chief of staff for intelligence in 1981, Odom appeared more soldier than academic. He pushed for more technical collection and focused on war fighting. He was also keen to develop a stronger independent intelligence capability for the army, convinced that the CIA was not able to support the military in the increasing numbers of low intensity and special operations that it had to carry out in the Middle East and Latin America. This reflected a genuine need to fill the gap of short-range emergency tactical collection, but it also fed Odom's prejudices in favor of militarized intelligence. The CIA regarded him as smug, self-important, and incapable of believing that the agency could "possibly understand anything about any army, US or Soviet."[8]

Nevertheless, the CIA's failure to adequately support special operations was an objective fact. This had become clear during the disastrous efforts to rescue the Iran hostages in 1979–80. The military need detailed, operational, on-the-ground intelligence, and the CIA could not deliver it or move fast enough. As a result, in August 1980 Secretary of Defense Harold Brown set in motion the creation of Field Operations Group, a mixed group that gradually became the army's "Mission Impossible" team. By 1981 this group had been renamed Intelligence Support Activity (ISA) and was embedded in Army Intelligence and Security Command (INSCOM). Odom was an enthusiastic developer of this project, and it soon included over three hundred people.[9]

ISA was a strange creature, sitting somewhere between intelligence and special operations. In its vast hangars at Fort Belvoir in Virginia, it boasted a hot air balloon, a Rolls Royce, a dune buggy, and a fire engine. Its eccentricities and black budget caught the attention of the next secretary of defense, Caspar Weinberger, who decided the unit should be liquidated. Together with Frank Carlucci, his deputy, Weinberger feared that the Pentagon had secretly created a largely "uncontrolled" mini CIA that was in danger of repeating some of the excesses that had damaged the agency a decade before, leading to a season of inquiry on Capitol Hill and notable press hostility. Through intense lobbying, Odom persuaded Weinberger to reverse the decision, and ISA survived. Its mission was made more defined, and the unit was rendered more accountable. It was now focused on clandestine military operational support in peace and war, and especially on close-range human intelligence (HUMINT) and SIGINT collection in response to emergency requirements.[10]

Under Odom ISA saw action all over the world. Its close-range SIGINT operators listened in on Salvadoran rebels and Sandinista forces in Central America in support of El Salvador and Honduras. It provided personal protection to the Saudi royal family against assassination. In 1982 ISA also went to Khartoum to guard the Sudanese president, Gaafar Nimeiry, against Libyan insurgents. It surveyed American installations across the Middle East after the bomb attacks in Lebanon, but sadly its warnings of further terrorist threats and the vulnerabilities of US facilities were neither shared nor acted on. Odom initially encouraged ISA to try to infiltrate agents into Middle Eastern terrorist organizations, but when the head of ISA explained that part of the terrorist initiation process involved murder, Odom quickly backed away. Thereafter, ISA became more wary and took to asking Odom to set out his orders in writing with his signature at the bottom.[11]

Odom's persistent interest in ISA improved his knowledge of SIGINT, and he became a forceful advocate of short-range collection as a tactical device. This was the wave of the future, and Odom was an important innovator in this respect throughout the 1980s. In December 1981 Brig. Gen. James Dozier, working at the Southern Command of the North Atlantic Treaty Organization (NATO), was kidnapped in Verona by the Red Brigade terrorist group. Odom used ISA close-range SIGINT teams to help locate Red Brigade groups. Teams in helicopters found the origins of the radio transmissions together with a fleet of vans and informed the efforts of the Italian security agencies.[12] ISA's importance was partly symbolic, indicating a growing awareness of the need for a greater counterterrorist capability.

Odom's interest in SIGINT was well-known in Washington. Accordingly, in 1985, when NSA was in need of a new director, his name was in the frame. Bill Casey, as Reagan's director of central intelligence, took a strong interest in the appointment and collided with Weinberger, who thought it was more a decision for the chairman of the Joint Chiefs of Staff (JCS). All agreed that it should be someone with some SIGINT background, and Odom soon emerged as one of the top candidates. Casey preferred Vice Adm. Edward Burkhalter, who was a senior CIA official, and argued that Odom would actually be better as the next head of the DIA. Robert McFarlane, the president's national security adviser, agreed. Casey's persistent efforts to secure the post for Burkhalter also caused a row with his former deputy, Adm. Bobby Ray Inman. In the past Inman had himself served as director of NSA, and he strongly believed that Casey was trespassing on the turf of the Joint Chiefs and the secretary of defense, who owned NSA. Eventually Reagan settled the matter and backed

Weinberger, the Joint Chiefs, and Inman in their preference for Odom. To Inman's delight Casey was defeated. All this was not without irony since, over the next five years, the Pentagon often found Odom to be a maverick. Moreover, Inman was horrified by Odom's subsequent decisions at NSA, which included reversing many of the reforms Inman had implemented at NSA a decade earlier.[13]

Odom and NSA

Accordingly, in April 1985 Gen. Bill Odom arrived as the new director of NSA at its vast headquarters located at Fort Meade, a few miles north of the Beltway. Odom already enjoyed a reputation as a tough-talking army officer with an extremely abrupt manner. He saw himself as a new broom, complaining that his predecessor "would not favor radical change" and that the staff at NSA was "too laid back."[14] He also looked afresh at the various allied SIGINT relationships and was deeply unimpressed, observing that "the name of the British game is to show up with one card and expect to call all the shots."[15] Ingenious old-fashioned British cryptanalysis was being overtaken by the raw power of America's Cray supercomputers, and this had been underlined by remarkable NSA breakthroughs with some Soviet high-grade diplomatic traffic in the late 1970s.[16] Again Bill Odom noted, "What the British brought in World War Two, they do not bring any more. . . . Today, this business requires huge investment and Britain doesn't have that." Britain's subsequent decision to buy its own Zircon spy satellites signaled a renewed commitment by Government Communications Headquarters (GCHQ) to spend big money on SIGINT and could be seen as an effort to push back against Odom's noisy unilateralism.[17]

Bill Odom's first year as director at NSA was a traumatic one. Washington soon dubbed 1985 the Year of the Spy since it brought the exposure of Ronald E. Pelton, a damaging mole within NSA who worked in A5, the sensitive Soviet section. With a photographic memory, Pelton proved even more disastrous to Western code breaking than GCHQ's Soviet mole Geoffrey Prime. At almost the same time, the Walker ring, a whole group of spies working within US naval intelligence and communications, was uncovered. Edward Lee Howard, a CIA officer, was also revealed to be working for the Russians. To cap it all, in November 1985 the Americans discovered Jonathan Pollard, a Mossad spy inside the Office of Naval Intelligence handing over sensitive material to the Israelis. Even so, the Americans had not yet uncovered the two best covert sources employed by the Soviets—namely, a CIA officer named Aldrich Ames and an FBI officer named Robert Hanssen.[18] These frightening cases of KGB espionage had a direct impact on Odom. They also affected the British, since they made Bill Odom all the keener to see the polygraph deployed by GCHQ at Cheltenham.[19]

Ronald Pelton had learned Russian in the US Air Force from 1960 to 1964 and soon found employment with NSA, where he worked for fifteen years. He was at the heart of the effort to decrypt Soviet communications and knew many of America's most closely guarded secrets. He was forced to leave NSA in 1979 after bankruptcy, and with mounting family problems, Pelton opted to sell his secrets to Moscow in January 1980. His phone calls to Soviet diplomats were intercepted, but he was not identified at the time. Over the next three years, Pelton met with his handlers in Vienna and was questioned at length. He received $35,000, a paltry sum given the fabulous value of the intelligence he handed over. He was finally uncovered when a Soviet defector exposed him in 1985.[20]

One of the results of the Ronald Pelton espionage case was to plunge Odom and Casey into a war with the press. There were a variety of SIGINT-related issues in the Pelton case that NSA did not want reported, and specific legislation passed in 1950 to protect SIGINT information from newspaper revelations seemed to deem such publication illegal. But government lawyers were reluctant to trespass on issues related to the First Amendment, which gave journalists strong protection. Nonetheless, Odom and Casey were strident and claimed that the intelligence leaks had cost "both human lives and billions of taxpayer dollars." Journalists took this badly and accused Odom and Casey of trying to tear up the First Amendment and reduce the freedom of the press.

Casey and Odom had initially hoped that NBC News would be prosecuted for reporting that Pelton revealed an expensive technical method of eavesdropping involving the use of American submarines in Soviet harbors. US Navy submarines working with NSA had attached listening pods to undersea cables in an operation code-named Ivy Bells. But days later Odom backed off and admitted that he would only recommend prosecution of journalists with "the greatest reluctance" and that the combination of the law and his oath to protect intelligence sources presented him with "a very uncomfortable dilemma."[21]

Instead, Odom and Casey held several private meetings with *Washington Post* editors, persuading them to delete several technical details concerning the Ivy Bells system from their coverage—other newspapers then followed suit. However, a 1987 book by veteran *Washington Post* journalist Bob Woodward, called *Veil*, gave a remarkably detailed description of the Ivy Bells project. Perversely, Woodward insisted that Casey himself was the source of the sensitive information. Privately, Odom was furious. An internal NSA security bulletin published at the time lumped American traitors, Soviet spies, investigative journalists, and book writers together as enemies of America. James Bamford and Seymour Hersh were viewed as being no less guilty than Ronald E. Pelton in collectively creating an unwelcome climate of "exposure" for NSA.[22]

Odom and the New Zealand Cutoff

Alongside Soviet bloc espionage, another big issue for Odom was relations between the Western SIGINT allies. In 1985 the United States cut off the intelligence flow to New Zealand, one of the second-party members of the UKUSA alliance. Rather like the cutoff that Kissinger had imposed on Britain in 1973, this was triggered by wider defense issues rather than SIGINT specifically.[23] New Zealand was sensitive about nuclear weapons, given that the Southwest Pacific had been used for many years by both the Americans and the French as an atomic testing zone. In 1985 New Zealand's Labour government, led by Prime Minister David Lange, introduced a general ban on ships carrying nuclear weapons entering New Zealand's harbors. This effectively excluded many American naval vessels, which routinely carried nuclear depth charges. Washington was keen to deter other countries from following a similar course—perhaps creating a Pacific nuclear-free zone—and so earmarked the New Zealanders for exemplary punishment. Intelligence was the chosen instrument to remind this small country of its place in the international order.[24]

At first Odom was not involved or even consulted in this remarkable confrontation. Prime Minister Lange met with Paul Cleveland, the American ambassador in Wellington. Cleveland informed Lange that henceforth he would not be receiving NSA's precious SIGINT jewels. Lange responded tartly, saying that they were not jewels by any means and the intelligence cutoff was probably a good thing, since he would now have "more time to do the crossword."[25] Paul Cleveland was flabbergasted by Lange's sangfroid and so got to work on some of Lange's cabinet colleagues. Cleveland next asked David Caygill, the government's finance minister, whether he realized quite how important the intelligence issue was. Caygill recalls, "I asked him what he meant," and Cleveland responded that it was all about "trust." He explained that the UKUSA intelligence alliance was all about mutual confidence, and now that had completely evaporated. "We have not spied on each other," continued Cleveland. "If you go ahead with your policies we will not be able to trust you." Caygill later explained to Lange that the American ambassador had meant that the United States would no longer feel any inhibition in conducting intelligence-gathering operations against the New Zealanders as unreliable allies and potential neutralists.[26]

All this was a problem for Odom. Hitherto, relations between New Zealand's Government Communications Security Bureau (GCSB) and NSA had been rather close.[27] Working in partnership with NSA and GCHQ, the New Zealanders were actually devoting much of their time to spying on allies, friends, and neutrals with the Americans. In 1985 New Zealand was reading diplomatic telegrams and telephone satellite communications from France, Japan, and the Philippines, as well as a host of South Pacific island states. It was also intercepting the communications of some United Nations organizations in the Pacific, together with the communications of nongovernmental organizations such as Greenpeace, the environmental protest group.[28]

The Americans often used their superior platforms to capture "raw traffic" that was of interest to the New Zealanders or that matched their translation skills. Lange's own papers show that a great deal of attention had been given to Japanese communications by the three partners. New Zealand's GCSB had produced 238 intelligence reports on Japanese diplomatic cables, using "raw traffic from GCHQ/NSA sources." However, the bureau lamented that the recent implementation of a new Japanese high-grade cipher machine had seriously reduced its output. Diplomatic traffic from Fiji, Vietnam, and Laos was being intercepted. The bureau was also working on South African military traffic and Argentinean naval traffic. New Zealand's GCSB relied heavily on the collection capabilities of its British and American allies to provide French communications on its behalf that were out of range of its own monitoring stations. American overhead satellites, including the new Orion, were crucial in this respect. After the Greenpeace ship *Rainbow Warrior* was attacked in Auckland harbor by the French secret intelligence service, GCSB set in motion a special collection effort in the region. NSA and GCHQ were asked to monitor targets in France, including certain Paris telephone lines. In short, all three allies worked closely together on a wide range of targets, and so, despite Lange's sangfroid, New Zealand had in fact lost valuable material as a result of being banished in 1985.[29] However, both GCHQ and the Australian SIGINT agency, the Defence Signals Division (DSD), worked hard to undermine the American SIGINT ban by providing the New Zealanders with national intelligence from their own sources.[30]

Remarkably, Odom saw the ban as detrimental to NSA's interests. Thus, he also worked gently to subvert it, and indeed over time he came to ignore it. In return New Zealand agreed to host more elaborate satellite-receiving stations on behalf of NSA. Nevertheless, in the short term, this confrontation had profound effects on all the venerable Commonwealth countries that helped to found the UKUSA SIGINT alliance and that were known as the second parties. Odom now pondered big questions and wrote in his notebook: "If 2nd party status disappears—What then?" He complained that Britain, Canada, and Australia had made a fuss and tended to "over do [the] banishing of NZ," but he also understood that they wished to be supportive of their Common-wealth ally.[31] On the ground the ban created fiendishly complex operational problems because UKUSA SIGINT had become so closely wired together in the 1980s. Peter Hunt, director of Canada's SIGINT agency, the Communica-tions Security Establishment (CSE), asked Odom's advice about what to do with "integrees"—in other words, people on loan from the GCSB who were embedded in the headquarters of his own organization in Ottawa.[32]

Although NSA did not like the Pentagon decision to cut New Zealand off, in the 1980s there was nevertheless general American disillusionment with all the UKUSA second parties—especially Canada. In the summer of 1985, Peter Hunt confessed to Odom that he had been having great difficulty persuading Canadian policymakers of the value of CSE's SIGINT product, although this situation was now improving. The CSE had been helping NSA and GCHQ with increased covert collection from Canadian embassies, but when Odom met with officials from the US embassy in Ottawa to discuss intelligence coop-eration, they all agreed "how poor the Canadian effort is!"[33] By contrast, NSA was increasingly impressed by the Western European third parties, such as the West Germans, who were achieving very good results against the diplo-matic traffic of Eastern Europe countries like Czechoslovakia, using ground stations.[34] All prompted Odom to seek substantive changes.

Odom, GCHQ, and Europe

The director of NSA (DIRNSA) is an intelligence leader in several respects—not only as the national lead on SIGINT and COMSEC but also the fig-urehead of a global SIGINT alliance. Odom had spent some of his military career in Germany and was impressed by the West German armed forces and their intelligence services. In 1985 he decided to make improved NSA rela-tions with the West Germans a high priority. Hitherto, NSA had hesitated since the German foreign intelligence service (BND) was known to be pen-etrated by eastern bloc spies. But after the Geoffrey Prime affair in Britain and indeed the damaging Pelton, Walker, and Howard cases in the United States, the German security problems seemed less unique. "Sure we knew they were leaky," recalled Odom, "but we felt we had a way of compartmen-talizing SIGINT carefully to deal with this." What mattered to Odom was that the Germans were investing more and more in money in SIGINT and were becoming a bigger player in Europe. They had already demonstrated their technical proficiency in some excellent electronic warfare projects con-ducted jointly with Israel. In the rather pragmatic world of SIGINT alliances, diversifying partners made perfect sense. However, GCHQ "went up the wall" when it heard about Odom's efforts with the West Germans, Odom recalled with a wry grin, "since it undermined their specialness."[35]

Predictably perhaps, Bill Odom took an initial dislike to his opposite number at GCHQ, Peter Marychurch, whom he referred to as "the Sheep." Indeed, Odom hated all the qualities that had prompted Whitehall to choose Marychurch as director of its biggest intelligence agency. Following the tenure of his gung ho predecessor, Brian Tovey, GCHQ wanted a more stable and avuncular figure. Marychurch was not a great intellectual, but he was an effective administrator and a good diplomat. After his initial career working on Soviet naval traffic and then a period as GCHQ's representative in New Zealand, some were surprised to see him rise to rank of director. Unlike many of his contemporaries, he had spent little time in London, Brussels, or Washington, and so he seemed rather disconnected from the big defense debates of the day. By contrast, Bill Odom prided himself on his intellectual toughness and his ability to talk global strategy and the language of the National Security Council.[36]

There was also a clash between soldier and civilian here. Odom was always thinking about frontline military operations. He was especially interested in the idea of using national strategic intelligence assets to push information forward to operational units and thought that NATO armed forces in Europe had long been starved of SIGINT. To an extent this was true. Both GCHQ and NSA had historically seen themselves as serving Whitehall and Washington first and foremost. Under existing rules, only when war actually broke out would high-grade SIGINT from UKUSA be released to the Western Europeans and also pushed forward to commanders on the front line. The lack of current SIGINT support for frontline units was causing problems not only in Germany. One of the commanders of the main US SIGINT station in South Korea confided to Bill Odom that there too "the requirements of the field commander were their lowest priority." He added that "NSA fought every attempt to collect and disseminate 'tactical' intelligence" to military formations. Because Bill Odom was a soldier's soldier at heart, he wanted current SIGINT to reach those who would be on the front line if a major war ever occurred in either Europe or Asia.[37]

During late May 1985 Bill Odom traveled to Europe to probe this issue. Accompanying him was Pete Aldridge, director of the National Reconnaissance Office, the agency that provided America's spy satellites. On June 7, 1985, they met Peter Marychurch in Cheltenham and discussed progress on Britain's own Zircon SIGINT satellite. Marychurch was forced to admit that GCHQ was already hitting problems, partly of cost and partly of competency. He explained that this was likely to delay the Zircon project and also pushed the British toward the use of more US contractors, for which he needed to ask their permission.[38] One of the ironies of so-called British space defense projects was that although they were supposed to increase national "independence," in reality they often needed backdoor American technical support to get them off the ground.[39] There were other irritants in the relationship. NSA's largest base overseas, Menwith Hill, a remote spot on the Yorkshire moors, was proving to be an especially unpopular posting with NSA personnel, and Bill Odom noted there were too few volunteers and too many draftees.[40] The "substantial" cost of NSA SIGINT bases in Britain was a further factor that pushed him away from Britain toward continental Europe, since the price of operating from West Germany seemed more reasonable.[41]

Although Odom complained loudly about Britain's poor spending record in intelligence, he did not like GCHQ's plans for its own Zircon SIGINT satellite. A few days after his meetings with Marychurch, he chewed over the whole matter of the Anglo-American relationship in a lengthy discussion with Dick Kern, a senior staff officer at NSA. Odom expressed the view that the relationship with GCHQ "had grown too big" and "needed to be managed better." They both agreed that Britain's new Zircon satellite program was an "unwanted intrusion" into the realm of space that they did not want to share with any of their allies, and so this was viewed as "a problem." Ultimately, NSA wanted to monopolize the Western flow of SIGINT from space, giving America the "potential to turn off the flow in future." Odom and Kern agreed that they now needed to reconsider certain areas of cooperation with GCHQ, including the "integration of personnel." All this was to be offset by improving relations with third parties such as the Germans.[42]

In the summer of 1985, Odom attended the annual gathering of all the SIGINT chiefs in Western Europe, hosted that year by the Norwegian chief of intelligence, Rear Adm. Jan Ingebrigtsen. Significantly, the members of this elite club only stretched as far south as France since NSA equated the reliability of SIGINT partners in Europe as a function of their distance from the Mediterranean. The Greeks ranked bottom in this hierarchy since their communications were known to be horrifically insecure.[43] Odom was like a social anthropologist and enjoyed recording the "traditional national suspicions and jealousies" displayed by the cast of characters in his daily log. He liked his Norwegian host, whom he found "pleasant, dignified, and pro-American." He warmed to the Germans, who had come forward with a "most constructive proposal" that most of the group was ready to accept. However, the British, he noted, "can't accept happily their own loss of pre-eminence in this business."[44] Odom was especially fond of the German chief, Eberhard Blum, remarking that he and Blum "had a good talk, some good laughs, and a few reminiscences." Blum, he noted, was inclined to defend NSA, even when other West German government officials complained of the US "Big Brother" approach, arguing that in fact the Americans had always dealt fairly and generously with their smaller SIGINT partners. However, Blum was coming up for retirement, and Odom noted sadly that while his German colleagues shared his views, they were rather more hesitant when it came to "putting down the British."[45]

Because of his emphasis on military SIGINT, Odom had encouraged the German BND to bring forward proposals for a scheme code-named Sigdasys, which aimed to improve the flow of operational SIGINT among NATO's frontline commanders in Europe.[46] Peter Marychurch was dead against it since the British had long been hesitant about sharing SIGINT with frontline commanders.[47] Ironically, Sigdasys was just what the British Army's electronic warfare operators of the front line had been requesting for years. This was because their own short-range "Y" units were having a tough time listening in on the Soviets, since Warsaw Pact radio security had continually improved, making eavesdropping activities difficult. "Traditionally," they noted, "the signal intercept service has been the primary source of tactical intelligence," but now its value was fading as Soviet divisional headquarters improved their communications security.[48] By the 1980s tactical listening was reduced to direction-finding work against frontline formations.[49] GCHQ's trenchant opposition to the German proposals at Bergen intensified Bill Odom's intense dislike of Peter Marychurch. On June 11 Odom went home and penned his thoughts on the various European SIGINT chiefs, including the director of GCHQ: "Peter Marychurch, my UK counterpart, is the least attractive of the lot."[50]

Yet while Odom was an intelligence expert and an excellent linguist, he was not a lifelong SIGINT specialist. By contrast, the affable Peter Marychurch had spent decades at GCHQ and knew more about the hazards of working with the West Germans. Only a month later, Odom's close friend, Eberhard Blum, retired as president of the BND and was succeeded by Heribert Hellenbroich, the long-serving and respected head of Germany's domestic security service, known as the BfV. At forty-eight years old, Hellenbroich seemed set to follow an upward path, not dissimilar to Britain's famed spymaster Dick White, who had successfully headed MI5 and then SIS. Alas, this was not to be. On August 27, 1985, Hellenbroich's old service, the BfV, was hit by an extraordinary spy scandal. One of his immediate subordinates in the BfV, and a close friend, defected to East Germany. This triggered a general panic, with some of the West's most valuable agents in East Germany hurriedly defecting westward for fear that their identities had been compromised and their lives were in danger. The West German premier ordered an inquiry and discovered that Heribert Hellenbroich had kept his friend in his post despite his notoriously heavy drinking and personal problems. Hellenbroich was summarily dismissed and became the shortest-serving BND chief in the agency's history.[51]

Remarkably, Odom was not deterred by these serious security problems within the West German intelligence services and continued to press ahead with his German plan. There were bureaucratic obstacles, since the German BND was engaged in a fierce turf battle over tactical SIGINT with the West German army, which closely resembled the electronic warfare tussles between NSA and America's own armed forces.[52] Nevertheless, by the summer of 1986, NSA, BND, and indeed GCHQ were building the new Sigdasys system proposed by the Germans, which gave a better supply of SIGINT to NATO operational commanders and allowed partners to pool their military SIGINT on the Soviets. The costs were split three ways among the British, Americans, and the Germans, with the French joining soon after.[53] In September 1987 Peter Marychurch suggested the Swedish National Defense Radio Establishment (FRA) join as a "sleeping partner" since Sigdasys was saving costs for everyone by eliminating overlap.[54] The Americans continued to be impressed by the BND's aggressive and expanding global SIGINT program—for example, its cooperation with the Chinese Nationalist code-breaking agency in Taiwan.[55]

Sadly, in terms of the Cold War, Odom's desire to deliver more SIGINT to frontline divisions in Europe was twenty years too late. By 1986 the new Soviet premier, Mikhail Gorbachev, was already beginning to transform world affairs. In the Pentagon and in the UK Ministry of Defence, Gorbachev was welcomed with cautious optimism. Observers were not only watching Gorbachev but the "exceptionally able" Russian ambassador in Washington, Anatoly Dobrynin, who was also a natural diplomat.[56] Meanwhile, the Middle East and Africa were now becoming more important to NSA together with thematic subjects such as terrorism. All eyes were on the conflict between the Marxist regime in Angola and rebel forces of Joseph Savimbi, who received support from both the South Africans and the CIA. By July 1986 NSA was pondering how to expand coverage of sub-Saharan Africa. At a meeting with his senior staff on July 16, Odom expressed high hopes for an ambitious new GCHQ covert collection operation that was being mounted from within the British embassy in Luanda, the Angolan capital.[57]

Odom may have been overfocused on the remote possibility of conventional military conflict with the Soviet Union. But in other ways Odom was ahead of his time. Odom was right in asserting that the civilian specialists at NSA were not always familiar with the SIGINT requirements of military combat operations. Moreover, a number of crises, including the Libyan raid in 1986, the 1991 Persian Gulf War, and the fighting in the former Yugoslavia during the 1990s, underlined the importance of using tactical SIGINT assets—and indeed using all strategic assets—to push intelligence forward to local commanders. By 2003, with the Afghan War in full swing, all this had changed. Odom, now in retirement, was able to comment that NSA could bring to bear "the entirety of the signals intelligence system—space-based collectors, collection sites far from the zone of military operations, and cryptanalytic and linguistic skills that military services cannot afford or maintain—for support to tactical operations."[58]

Odom and Iran-Contra

During the Reagan era Odom was privy to some remarkable secrets that almost no one else knew. Colin Powell, who was then serving as military assistant to the secretary of defense, Caspar Weinberger, recalls that a senior officer in the JCS organization named Vice Adm. Arthur Moreau had privately shared with him some rather odd NSA intercepts, some of which related to Israel. Moreau's NSA material also showed that, although NSA was controlled by the Pentagon, Weinberger was being cut out of some of NSA's most interesting intelligence products. When Powell probed the actual content of the messages, they concerned the fact that various foreign intermediaries were "cooking up an arms deal" between Reagan administration officials and the alleged Iranian moderates.[59]

Powell had uncovered Oliver North's Iran-Contra operation. Both Powell and Weinberger knew that this had been a plan originally proposed by Robert McFarlane, the national security adviser, but until now they were completely unaware that it had actually been put into action. Powell shared this explosive material with Weinberger, but each time Weinberger made inquiries, McFarlane remained elusive. Eventually Weinberger instructed Powell to call Bill Odom "and remind him who he works for." When Powell spoke to Odom, he "sensed the discomfort of a man being tossed between two reefs." McFarlane had ordered Odom to give these intercepts the narrowest possible circulation. Weinberger could do little at that point about Iran-Contra other than observe that it had "attracted the sleaziest sort of rug merchants" and warn that the White House that it was courting political disaster, which indeed it was.[60]

Iran-Contra exploded into the public domain in late 1986 and resulted in an inquiry by Senator John Tower in 1987. There were few reverberations for Odom and NSA until his last eight months in office. The big issue was NSA COMSEC assistance to Oliver North's Iran-Contra program, which involved the supply of two KY-40 laptops with encryption keys to send secure e-mails.

Odom was incensed that his COMSEC staff had assisted North's operations without his knowledge and singled out John Wobensmith, a senior officer in the Communications Security organization, for special punishment. Alongside this issue Odom was now openly fighting with many of the civilian officials promoted during the Inman period. Remarkably, Inman, who had initially supported Odom's nomination, now testified against Odom at congressional hearings and also briefed against him in the press.[61]

Odom was notably keen to distance himself from Oliver North and used the episode to underline the distance between NSA and Iran-Contra. Odom asserted that he personally had steered his agency clear of the whole episode. "You didn't hear the name of this agency come up in the hearings," he said. "Do you know why? The reason was I understood Oliver North's ilk long before most others did. I made damn sure this place was straight."[62]

On August 1, 1988, Odom was replaced by Adm. William Studeman, who immediately cut one of Odom's pet projects: an expensive program to make SIGINT satellites survivable in a future war with Russia. Odom had fought his staff over this elaborate program because most of his underlings preferred to spend the money on actual collection operations rather than war preparations. Studeman agreed with Odom's underlings and redirected the money.[63]

Odom as Intelligence Reformer and Bush Critic

After NSA, Bill Odom headed for Yale University. From there, in the late 1990s, he energetically joined the intelligence reform debate.[64] In 1997 he prepared a report for the National Institute for Public Policy suggesting radical structural changes for the intelligence community. These suggestions were largely ignored. A few years later, in the wake of the September 11, 2001, terrorist attacks, he revisited his findings, updating them for a world hungry for change in the realm of intelligence. He rightly observed that despite major problems in the US intelligence community, there had been no deep structural change for almost forty years. Many blue ribbon panels had come and gone, but for the most part they had attempted "to doctor the symptoms not treat the illness."[65] His observations were not unlike those made by Amy Zegart in her analysis of 9/11, which argued that structural change and organizational patterns really matter.[66] Odom had watched CNN scoop the US intelligence community during the bombing of Libya in 1986, and now he urged reformers to look at the massive shift that had occurred in the global media business and compare it with the glacial pace of change in systems for the provision of government information.[67]

More interested in wiring diagrams than intelligence culture, Odom nevertheless anticipated many of the changes later grudgingly instituted by the Bush administration between 2003 and 2008. Odom wished to see the role of the director of CIA and director of central intelligence disaggregated and a proper head of the intelligence community created, adding predictably that it would need to be a figure from the armed services if the army, navy, and air force were not to withdraw their assets.[68] He argued for a single community lead for each of three main intelligence disciplines: HUMINT, SIGINT, and imagery. At the time of his commentary, only imagery had moved toward adopting a single disciplinary structure. He was conscious of the overlap, duplication, and at times sheer childishness of the Beltway battles that characterized Washington, though in his own time he had been an eager and sometimes devious participant in budgetary games between the agencies.[69]

Odom employed his characteristically outspoken language, asserting that "the current arrangements border on the criminal."[70] He was even willing to see the CIA take over the broad direction of all US HUMINT but argued that the CIA did covert action badly and that the CIA should, in return, surrender this to the Pentagon. Odom admitted that the evidence for the first years of special operations in Afghanistan as yet remained unclear but clearly retained an affection of ISA, the special unit he himself had nurtured and protected while overseeing US Army intelligence in the early 1980s.[71] In practice however, he doubted that any national HUMINT service would be interested in the vast volume of low-level agent work required to support the Pentagon's military units in the field.

As we have seen, one of Odom's greatest passions was using national assets to support operational and even tactical commanders. In this respect Odom had always been years ahead of his contemporaries and to some extent even anticipated aspects of the Revolution in Military Affairs. The lesson that Odom took away from the first Gulf War in 1991 was the idea of distributed processing. He did not see why battlefield commanders should wait for the Washington agencies to offer their final judgment on intelligence after lengthy all-source analysis. Instead he wanted raw intelligence from satellites and other assets pushed direct to local military hubs. This had been done temporarily during the first Gulf War, and Odom wished to see this happen routinely—despite the misgivings of both the CIA and DIA.[72]

Odom's other great passion was counterintelligence. He lamented the way in which the United States, including the FBI and the security services of the air force and the navy, saw law enforcement and counterintelligence as the same thing. He wished to see the United States develop its own counterintelligence service—akin to the UK's MI5—that was capable of playing the game "long" rather than seeking immediate prosecutions. Law enforcement, he insisted, was "hopeless" at catching spies. His passion for counterintelligence extended through all of government, and Odom nurtured a particular animus against the State Department. Like so many of his reforms, these reflected personal experience and in this case the refusal of George Shultz to think seriously about Soviet technical and physical penetration of the American embassy in Moscow during the 1980s. Here again, Odom's visceral pleasure in delivering uncomfortable truths resonated, and at the time of his final publications in 2007, the United States was still losing several diplomatic officers a year in Moscow to Russian honey trap operations.[73]

During his final years Odom's public profile had never been higher. He became one of the most vociferous critics of the Bush administration's policy in Iraq, penning eye-catching newspaper commentaries with titles such as "What's Wrong with Cutting and Running?" In 2007 he was invited by the Democratic Speaker of the House of Representatives, Nancy Pelosi, to offer a reply to President Bush's weekly radio address. His last column, coauthored in May 2008 with Brzezinski, advocated renewed American engagement with Iran. A constant critic of keeping US troops in Iraq, he pointed out the contradictions in Bush's stated war aims. He advocated a staged withdrawal as a way to salvage American policy in the Middle East.[74]

Yet the attack on the Iraq War was not Odom's most vigorous intervention against Bush. In late 2005 Jim Risen published a book titled *State of War: The Secret History of the CIA and the Bush Administration.* The book detailed the illegal wiretapping activity allegedly authorized by NSA director Michael Hayden and various American telecommunications companies at the direction of Bush and Cheney. The *New York Times* had sat on the story for a long time, squirming over the possible national security consequences, but the impending publication of the Risen book prompted the newspaper to reveal the story in December 2005. Thereafter, the Bush administration struggled to defend a warrantless eavesdropping program that was an obvious violation of the Foreign Intelligence Surveillance Act (FISA), which forbade eavesdropping on Americans without a court warrant.

Odom was seething with rage. On January 4, 2006, as he waited to be interviewed by George Kenney, a former US diplomat, he blurted out, "Hayden should have been court martialed" and then added that President Bush "should be impeached." Odom refused to discuss the warrantless eavesdropping during the interview, realizing that he was beyond anger and might not be able to control himself. But in a later interview he again expressed amazement that Bush had not been impeached. His predecessor as DIRNSA and long-term sparring partner, Adm. Bobby Ray Inman, shared his feelings, having helped to draft the 1978 FISA as DIRNSA. Inman asserted publicly and unequivocally that there "clearly was a line in the FISA statutes which says you couldn't do this." Inman and Odom were very different men, but both had seen the consequences of intelligence excesses emanating from the White House over previous decades and so firmly believed that procedure was there to protect personal freedom of ordinary citizens from those at the top. Accordingly, Odom closed one of his last public interviews by quoting Ben Franklin's famous observation that "somebody who values security over liberty deserves neither."[75]

Conclusions

On September 26, 1986, Ronald Reagan attended a dedication ceremony at an impressive new NSA headquarters building at Fort Meade, north of the Beltway. Covered in striking mirror-black glass and often described as a "dark Rubik's Cube," it added another sixty-eight acres of office space to Odom's already considerable SIGINT empire. There, in the unseasonably warm weather, the president joined Bill Odom and Bill Casey on the podium. He told the assembled NSA staff that before setting out that morning, he had asked Odom and Casey for directions to the landmark new building. All they would say, he quipped, was, "Mr President, leave the White House, go to 17th and K, and wait for the phone to ring." After making a further joke at the expense of the KGB's "intellectuals," Reagan then proceeded to praise the staff of the agency. He added that neither he nor Secretary of State George Shultz nor Caspar Weinberger could do their jobs without the support of NSA. He congratulated all those who, together with Casey and Odom, "co-operated so effectively" to produce America's intelligence. But beneath the jokes, congratulations, and mutual pleasantries, one wonders what Odom and Casey were really thinking at this point. The Iran-Contra explosion was just days away. On November 5 a covert supply aircraft was shot down over Nicaragua; five days later, Oliver North began shredding documents. Although outspoken and volatile, Odom held a strong belief in lawful intelligence activity and respect for the American constitution.[76]

In some ways Odom was little different from a long line of tough American military leaders, from Curtis Le May to Chester Nimitz, who boasted a hot temper and did not hesitate to give their superiors and subordinates the "hairdryer" treatment. Yet Odom was distinguished by his penetrating intellect. Perhaps it was a little self-conscious: in common with many academics, he derived enormous pleasure from small intellectual victories. Yet all across Washington there was respect for his fabulous cerebral capability. Duane R. Clarridge, a CIA division chief, remembers him as "an acute observer" whose passing observations during a dinner thrown by Casey resolved long-standing conundrums about the nature of intelligence management and organizational culture. He also believed in connectivity between the world of intelligence and the world of intellectuals. One of the most admirable things about America is the ease with which capable leaders can move back and forth between the world of the practitioner and the world of academia, carrying with them fresh ideas. Odom, for all his testiness, exemplified this more than any other intelligence leader of the Cold War.[77]

Notes

1. Robert M. Gates, *From the Shadows: The Ultimate Insider's Story of Five Presidents and How They Won the Cold War* (New York: Simon & Schuster, 1996), 114.

2. J. F. Matlock, "William Eldridge Odom," *Proceedings of the American Philosophical Society* 154, no. 3 (September 2010): 355–58.

3. Matthew Aid, *The Secret Sentry: The Untold History of the National Security Agency* (New York: Bloomsbury, 2009), 181–87; Matt Schudel, "William E. Odom, 75; Military Adviser to 2 Administrations," *Washington Post*, June 1, 2008.

4. "Lieutenant-General William Odom," *Telegraph*, June 23, 2008. Private information.

5. His writings include *America's Inadvertent Empire*, coauthored with Robert Dujarric (New Haven, CT: Yale University Press, 2004); *Fixing Intelligence for a More Secure America* (New Haven, CT: Yale University Press, 2003); *The Collapse of the Soviet Military* (New Haven, CT: Yale University Press, 1998); *America's Military Revolution: Strategy and Structure after the Cold War* (New York: American University Press, 1993); *Trial after Triumph: East Asia after the Cold War* (New York: Hudson Institute, 1992); *On Internal War: American and Soviet Approaches to Third World Clients and Insurgents* (Durham, NC: Duke University Press, 1992); *The Soviet Volunteers* (Princeton, NJ: Princeton University Press, 1973); *Commonwealth or Empire? Russia, Central Asia, and the Transcaucasus*, with Robert Dujarric (New York: Hudson Institute, 1995).

6. Aid, *Secret Sentry*, 181–87.

7. Interview by the author with an anonymous source.

8. Edward Mickolus, ed., *Stories from Langley: A Glimpse inside the CIA* (Lincoln: University of Nebraska Press, 2014), 64.

9. Jeffrey T. Richelson, "Truth Conquers All Chains: The U.S. Army Intelligence Support Activity, 1981–1989," *International Journal of Intelligence and CounterIntelligence* 12, no. 2 (1999): 168–82.

10. Steven Emerson, *Secret Warriors: Inside the Covert Military Operations of the Reagan Era* (New York: Putnam, 1988), 20–21.

11. Smith, *Killer Elite*.

12. Richelson, "Truth Conquers All Chains," 182–88; Emerson, *Secret Warriors*, 209–32.

13. Douglas F. Garthoff, *Directors of Central Intelligence as Leaders of the US*

Intelligence Community (Washington, DC: CIA, Center for the Study of Intelligence, 2005), 161–63.

14. Odom (NSA) Daily Log, May 10, 1985, Box 25, File 5, Odom Papers, Library of Congress.

15. M. Urban, *UK Eyes Alpha: The Inside Story of British Intelligence* (London: Faber and Faber, 1996), 60.

16. This was known as "success with the A5 problem" after the part of NSA that worked on Soviet diplomatic traffic. Aid, *Secret Sentry*, 165.

17. Urban, *UK Eyes Alpha*, 60.

18. V. Cherkashin, *Spy Handler: Memoir of a KGB Officer* (New York: Basic Books, 2005), 224–25.

19. Odom, daily log, November 8, 1981, Box 20, File 3, Odom Papers.

20. Sharon LaFraniere and Susan Schmidt, "Accused Spy Ronald Pelton Was Preoccupied with Money," *Washington Post*, December 7, 1985.

21. Michael J. Sniffen, "Urgent CIA and NSA Chiefs Appeal for Media Cooperation in Keeping Spy Secrets," Associated Press, May 29, 1986.

22. Stephen Engelberg, "N.S.A.: Slamming the Press, in Daylight," *New York Times*, October 14, 1987.

23. Richard J. Aldrich, *GCHQ: The Uncensored Story of Britain's Most Secret Intelligence Agency* (London: Collins, 2011), 277–98.

24. Alan Cranston, "US Signals Intelligence to New Zealand Blocked," *Jane's Defence Weekly* 2 (February 16, 1985): 243; W. T. Tow, "The ANZUS Alliance and United States Security Interests," in *ANZUS in Crisis: Alliance Management in International Affairs*, ed. J. Berkovitch (London: Macmillan, 1988), 61–66; Thomas R. Johnson, *American Cryptology during the Cold War* (Fort Meade, MD: NSA, 2004), 4:304.

25. Helen Bain, "Lange's Secret Papers Reveal USA's Bully Tactics," *Sunday Star-Times*, January 15, 2006.

26. "Lange Papers Reveal US Spy Threats," *New Zealand Herald*, January 15, 2006. See also "US New Zealand Nuclear Feud Detailed," *International Herald Tribune*, January 15, 2006.

27. The document seems to have been Government Communications Security Bureau 1985/86 Annual Report, which was headed "Top Secret Umbra Handle Via Comint Channels Only."

28. Bain, "Lange's Secret Papers."

29. Ibid.

30. G. Barker, "The Mystery Boats," *Australian Financial Review*, November 28, 2003, 16–18.

31. "New Zealand—Tucker," Odom (NSA) daily log, November 6, 1986, Box 25, File 7, Odom Papers.

32. "Peter Hunt," Odom (NSA) daily log, November 18, 1987, Box 26, File 2, Odom Papers.

33. Conversation with Peter Hunt (D/CSE), Odom (NSA) Daily Log, August 8, 1985, Box 25, File 5, Odom Papers. On embassy collection, see M. Frost, *Spyworld:*

Inside the Canadian and American Intelligence Establishments (Toronto: Doubleday, 1994), 154–78.

34. Odom (NSA) Daily Log, August 1, 1985, Box 25, File 5, Odom Papers.

35. William Odom, interview by the author, 2008.

36. Ibid.

37. Gorman to Odom (ACSI), April 26, 1985, Box 17, File 7, Odom Papers.

38. "GCHQ/ZIRKON mtg. London," Odom (NSA) Daily Log, May 7, 1985, Box 5, File 5, Odom Papers.

39. Record of a mtg. with Weinberger, Odom (NSA) Daily Log, May 31, 1985, Box 25, File 5, Odom Papers.

40. "Jarry Masz—Menwith Hill Station," Odom (NSA) daily log, September 15, 1985, Box 25, File 6, Odom Papers.

41. Odom (NSA) Daily Log, June 11, 1985, Box 25, File 5, Odom Papers.

42. "GCHQ: Post Mortem w/ Dick Kern," Odom (NSA) Daily Log, June 7, 1985, Box 25, File 5, Odom Papers.

43. Odom interview.

44. "Notes & Observation on London and Bergen Mtgs," Odom (NSA) Daily Log, June 11, 1985, Box 25, File 5, Odom Papers.

45. Ibid.

46. The best account of Sigdasys is in C. Wiebes, "Dutch Sigint 1945–94," in *Secrets of Signals Intelligence*, ed. M. Aid and C. Wiebes (London: Frank Cass, 2001), 276–78.

47. Mistakenly, Odom blamed Foreign Office influence on GCHQ for Marychurch's views.

48. ACIC, A/101/5, Annex A, "The Role of Electronic Warfare, 1980–1990," WO 32/21273, British National Archives (TNA).

49. RARDE Technical Report 9/79, "Evaluation of the Warsaw Pact Threat to I (BR) Corps Communications Post 1985," DEFE 15/2582, TNA.

50. "Notes & Observations on London and Bergen Mtgs.," Odom (NSA) Daily Log, June 11, 1985, File 5, Box 25, Odom Papers.

51. M. Johnson et al., "West Germany: Spies, Spies and More Spies," *Time*, September 9, 1985. Private information.

52. Odom (NSA) Daily Log, July 10, 1985, Box 25, File 5, Odom Papers.

53. "Wiek—Issues," Odom (NSA) daily log, September 9, 1986, Box 25, File 8, Odom Papers.

54. "Peter Marychurch," Odom (NSA) daily log, September 9, 1987, Box 26, File 2, Odom Papers.

55. "Wieck," Odom (NSA) daily log, Janaury 23, 1986, Box 25, File 8, Odom Papers.

56. Le Bailly to Whitmore (PUS MoD), June 13, 1986, Box 10, Folder 1, Le Bailly Papers, Churchill College, Cambridge.

57. "G-94 Sub-Saharan Africa," Odom (NSA) daily log, July 16, 1986, Box 25, File 7, Odom Papers.

58. Odom, *Fixing Intelligence*, 118.

59. Colin Powell, *A Soldier's Way: An Autobiography* (London: Hutchinson, 1995), 355. Private information.

60. Ibid., 355–56. Private information.

61. Aid, *Secret Sentry*, 181–88.

62. Stephen Engelberg, "National Security Agency: A Career in Ruins in Wake of Iran-Contra Affair," *New York Times*, June 3, 1988.

63. James Bamford, *Body of Secrets: Anatomy of the Ultra-secret National Security Agency* (New York: Doubleday, 2001), 394.

64. Amy Zegart, *Spying Blind: The CIA, the FBI and the Origins of 9/11* (Princeton, NJ: Princeton University Press, 2007), 68–72.

65. Odom, *Fixing Intelligence*, 7.

66. Zegart, *Spying Blind*, 2–15.

67. Odom, *Fixing Intelligence*, 11.

68. Ibid., xxiii.

69. Ibid., 111.

70. Ibid., xxvi.

71. Ibid., 149, 181.

72. Ibid., xxvi.

73. Private information.

74. Zbigniew Brzezinski and William Odom, "A Sensible Path on Iran," *Washington Post*, May 27, 2008; William Odom, "Cut and Run? You Bet," *Foreign Policy*, May/June 2006; William Odom and Lawrence Korb, "Training Local Forces Is No Way to Secure Iraq," *Financial Times*, July 19, 2007; William Odom, "Victory Is Not an Option: The Mission Can't Be Accomplished—It's Time for a New Strategy," *Washington Post*, February 11, 2007.

75. Ray McGovern, "What's CIA Director Hayden Hidin'?" *Al-Jazeera*, January 18, 2009; Corey Pein, "Reagan's NSA Chief Speaks Out," *Augusta Metro Spirit*, November 30, 2006.

76. "Remarks at the Dedicating for New Facilities at the National Security Agency at Fort Meade, Maryland," September 26, 1986, *Public Papers of the Presidents of the United States: Ronald Reagan* (Washington, DC: US Government Printing Office, 1988), 2:1273–76.

77. Duane R. Clarridge, *A Spy for All Seasons: My Life in the CIA* (New York: Scribner, 2002), 80–82.

PART II

British Spy Chiefs

9 Eric Welsh, the Secret Intelligence Service, and the Birth of Atomic Intelligence

Michael Goodman

Few intelligence officers have divided opinion among colleagues but have achieved so much as Eric Welsh. Variously a member of the Royal Navy, Royal Air Force, and the Secret Intelligence Service (SIS) and a chemist working on maritime paint, Welsh seems to have employed a personal approach in all aspects of his work. Not prepared to suffer fools gladly, he was determined and single-minded in his approach. For Welsh, humor was as much the default position to all human interaction as was secrecy. This style afforded him great access and long-term friendships with a number of the leading physicists of the day, but it also ensured that he created enemies along the way, most notably the founder of scientific intelligence, R. V. Jones. Welsh's relatively aloof approach to his work provided notable successes, but it was recurring bouts of ill health, combined with a fondness for drink, that eventually would prove his downfall.

This chapter explores the life of one of the most important but elusive British intelligence officers of the mid-twentieth century. With problems nationally and internationally, Welsh was exactly the sort of gregarious figure that British atomic intelligence needed. There was tension at home, particularly in the artificial division between atomic and scientific intelligence. More broadly, there were difficulties in ensuring effective cooperation between the intelligence world, the scientific components of government, and the universities. In addition, Welsh proved to be a valuable link between the worlds of intelligence and atomic science on both sides of the Atlantic at a time when technical relations were suspended.

Eric Welsh was born on August 31, 1897, in Newbiggin, a small town on the Northumberland coast in the northeast of England. His father worked for the Prudential insurance company, but little else is known about his early years. In 1914 Welsh joined the maritime paint company International Paint.[1] Now a global corporation, it was started in the 1880s by the Holzapfel brothers,

German by birth but English by adoption. The company began with a shed in the docks at Newcastle, trying to get customers to buy its special waterproof paint. At the start of the twentieth century, it moved to larger premises in Gateshead, and it is highly likely that this is where the teenage Welsh worked before he was called up for the First World War.[2]

Eric Welsh kept a brief diary through the latter half of the war. He seemingly joined the Officer Training Corps before he was called up for entry in March 1916.[3] At the tender age of eighteen and a half, Welsh described his profession as "chemist's assistant." Welsh at this point was seemingly slender of build: he was recorded as being 5 feet 6 inches tall with a 34½-inch chest, brown eyes, brown hair, and a fresh complexion. Given his work with maritime paint, Welsh opted to join the navy, and within ten days he was sent for training. On his entry form under notes, it is simply recorded "signals." Presumably Welsh had some knowledge of this, as he was immediately sent to the Signal School in the Crystal Palace in London. Two months later, he was sent to the Signal School in Chatham, Kent. Thereafter he was sent to a variety of shore-based establishments, including HMS *Victory VI* and HMS *Pembroke I*, both of which seem to have offered further training. He passed out in late July, remarking in his diary that it was "jolly easy."[4] His first proper posting was to HMS *Attentive III* in August 1916, an armed patrol ship in Dover. Two months later, Welsh was back in training on shore, but in December he returned to the patrol ship in Dover. His service record indicates he remained with this ship for the next two years. His diary for 1917 and 1918 records such a momentous occasion as joining the first hunt in Edgbaston and various hospital visits.

In July 1918 Welsh was discharged from the navy and transferred to the Royal Air Force (RAF).[5] Why Welsh made this transition and what he did in the RAF is a total mystery. He does not seem to have remained long in the RAF, though, and is recorded as having left in June 1919. The same month, Welsh, again for reasons unknown, left the UK to move to Bergen in Norway. Until his return to military service in 1940, Welsh spent the duration of the interwar period in Norway working for International Paint. He began as a chemist but rose to be technical director. One of his achievements was creating the yellow paint that used to adorn the inside of sardine tins at this time. While in Bergen between the wars, he mastered Norwegian, married a local girl, and fathered three children.

Eric Welsh's life was, once more, upset by war. On April 9, 1940, the German military machine swept into Norway, with devastating effect. German troops landed in Bergen, and that same day, Welsh left the town with two British naval officers to ensure their safe passage out of the country. The following day, he removed his family too. Immediately, Welsh seems to have switched from being a scientist and corporate figure in a paint company to a military man. How this transformation took place with such vigor and speed is unknown. Welsh's son has questioned whether International Paint was somehow a cover for Welsh's real work in SIS. There is no evidence to confirm or refute this, but on balance it seems unlikely.[6] The more likely explanation is that Welsh left active military service in 1919 but transferred to the Royal Naval Volunteer Reserve (RNVR). This would explain the speed by which Welsh left the military and moved to Norway and the contacts that he maintained; it would also justify his military rank of lieutenant commander in 1940.

That war would come to Norway cannot have been a surprise, even if the actual attack on April 9 was. Although it is not clear in what capacity Welsh, by his own account, had made contact with the Norwegian military, he immediately set to work assisting local communities before he requested permission to "be relieved from his services with the Norwegian army" so that he could make contact with British forces. Welsh managed to return to England on April 29, 1940, and reported to the Foreign Office, Admiralty and War Office. He attempted to join the RAF and Navy but was, in his words, rejected because he "was in a scheduled occupation and registered as a scientific worker." Instead, in December 1940 he was given a commission in the RNVR. Nonetheless, he spent the first two months of 1941 serving first on HM Minesweeping Flotilla, Newcastle, and then as liaison officer at HMS Baldur, a naval base in Reykjavik, Iceland. Welsh's life would change again in March 1941, when he was posted to Naval Intelligence.[7]

It appears unlikely that Eric Welsh actually served in Naval Intelligence, for he was immediately recruited by SIS, or MI6, as it is informally known. Given his linguistic abilities and local knowledge, he was dispatched to the Norwegian Section of SIS.[8] Two months later, in May 1941, Welsh assumed control of this section, eventually subsuming Iceland and the Faroes Islands into his brief. Welsh took over responsibilities from a fellow naval officer, Cdr. J. B. Newill. The secretary in the Norwegian Section, Margaret Reid, has recalled something of Welsh's introduction to life in SIS. "I was sorry for little Welsh," she said; he "was not used to office routine, couldn't bring himself to make notes on a bit of paper or pass money through the accounts."[9] These rather relaxed traits would come to be representative of Welsh's approach to his work.

Welsh's appointment came at a crucial time. The previous year, SIS's network in Norway had been largely wound up, and there was a desperate need to establish new ones.[10] Welsh was involved in a number of ways to restore SIS's eyes and ears on the ground. This first involved training willing recruits in England, getting them into Norway covertly using a variety of fishing vessel from locations in Scotland, and then communicating with them, passing on requirements, and receiving reports.[11] In all these matters, it would seem,

Welsh took an exceptionally personal approach. Here, for the first time, was evidence of Welsh's supreme abilities as an intelligence officer in handling people. The agents in Norway referred to themselves as "Welsh's gang," and as one former member has recalled, Welsh's approach was very successful: "Lt.Cdr. Welsh executed his command in a wise and paternal manner. He required the agents to endure hazards and if need be severe conditions, but he did also the outmost effort [*sic*] to save agents who were chased or in distress. The agents had an immense respect for Lt.Cdr. Welsh and they were devoted to execute his orders."[12]

One of the first orders to be fulfilled concerned the German battleship *Tirpitz*. Working with Maj. Finn Nagell of the Norwegian Ministry of Defence's Intelligence Office, Welsh created a network of resistance soldiers across the Norwegian coast whose task it was to monitor the movement of German ships. One of those spotted was the *Tirpitz*, one of the two largest battleships built by the German Navy at this time. It had been dispatched to Norway in late 1941 to act as a powerful and effective deterrent against an Allied attack and to control the passing of ships to and from the Soviet Union. From Norway's coastlines, Welsh's spotters tracked the ship and reported its movements. Subject to a number of different operations, the *Tirpitz* was finally sunk in 1944.

Welsh's greatest wartime involvement, however, concerned the German atomic bomb; this was the birth of atomic intelligence, and Eric Welsh was the midwife who delivered it into the world. From the outbreak of war, concerned scientists had contacted the British prime minister and American president to warn them about the potential dangers of atomic weapons. The Manhattan Project, therefore, owes its origins to a concern that the Germans might develop such a weapon. The occupation of Norway provided the Germans with a key process in the manufacture of the raw materials necessary for a bomb—the heavy water plant in Vemork. Concealed in a deep mountain cleft where the sun is visible for only six months of the year, this inhospitable venue was used because great pipes fed down from the mountain to the factory, providing water to run the plant.

Although Welsh proved to be an adept officer at stimulating loyalty among his agents, it was his knowledge of Norway and science that enabled him to enhance his position within SIS. One of his first tasks in taking over the Norwegian Section was to meet Leif Tronstad, a prewar professor of chemistry and a member of the British network in Norway. In late 1941 Tronstad escaped to England and briefed SIS on the heavy water plant and about German efforts to harness atomic energy. Rather fortuitously, Welsh was already aware of the Vemork heavy water plant, having provided special waterproof paint for its flooring before the outbreak of war.

In response to Tronstad's information, Welsh suggested that the plant be destroyed or sabotaged.[13] The first attempts were undertaken in late 1942 but ended with the capture and execution of the saboteurs. Over the succeeding years further efforts were tried, resulting in the successful commando attack in 1943, the raid by the US Air Force (USAF) later that year, and the sinking of a ferry carrying barrels of heavy water in 1944.[14] For his wartime efforts in Norway, Welsh was awarded a Knight First Class of the Royal Norwegian Order of St Olav by the king of Norway, and an Order of the British Empire (OBE) from King George VI.[15]

His involvement with atomic matters in Norway meant that Welsh was read into and involved with one of the most secret aspects of the war. Atomic information was held on a similar compartmentalized basis to the hugely sensitive signals intelligence efforts at Bletchley Park; within this atomic intelligence was one of the most tightly guarded components. One of Welsh's many attributes was a dogged determination to control everything that passed through his hands. From the earliest stages of the war, SIS had appointed its first scientific officer on attachment from the Air Ministry. Dr. R. V. Jones, an Oxford physicist, was integral to the efforts to understand and thwart German advances in science. Jones was an intellectual who was perfectly suited to masterminding Britain's scientific intelligence efforts, but his role focused on analysis, interpretation, and countermeasures. Atomic intelligence was a smaller effort but masked by far greater secrecy. This meant that the intelligence officers, agents, and scientists had to work closely together, and therefore this required a more interpersonal approach. Jones would not have excelled at this, but Welsh, less of an intellectual but far more suited to coercing and getting the best out of people, was ideally suited to the task. So it was that Welsh became responsible for SIS's efforts to monitor the German atomic bomb program. A large component of this was in Norway, but by no means was all of it.

British intelligence first made serious efforts to monitor German advances at the end of 1941.[16] Welsh's involvement with atomic matters was threefold: through SIS he was intimately concerned with efforts to gather intelligence, but he was also responsible for the production of assessments and efforts to thwart progress. In 1941 Welsh recruited his best conduit of intelligence, the science publisher Paul Rosbaud, who was influential in obtaining information from Germany.[17] At the end of the war, Welsh would help exfiltrate Rosbaud from the Russian sector in Germany. Rosbaud brought with him a collection of books and, accompanied by German-speaking British military officer Robert Maxwell, started Pergamon Press.[18]

Through his network Welsh, and British intelligence more broadly, seems to have become convinced by 1943 that German efforts would not reach fruition within the timetable of the war. All of the leading figures in the German atomic weapons program, from its scientific head, Werner Heisenberg, downward, were targeted, as were the major locations of research. In late 1943 the United States became far more involved in the intelligence picture, and Welsh became the main point of contact for Gen. Leslie Groves's team (Groves as head of the Manhattan Project but also responsible for intelligence matters). This relationship was crystalized through a joint committee on "T.A. Project, Enemy Intelligence" and through the Alsos mission.[19] Alsos, the Greek word for "grove," was a scientific intelligence mission designed to follow the conquering armies through Europe, gathering scientists and scientific papers and attempting to gauge German progress. As part of the nuclear component of Alsos, Welsh was involved in dismantling the German nuclear pile at Haigerloch. The aftermath of this was Welsh's involvement, albeit at a distance, with the German members of the "uranium club," the leading atomic scientists, including Heisenberg, who were interned at a large country house in Cambridgeshire.[20]

Welsh's other great wartime involvement, related to this work and assisted no doubt by his knowledge of Scandinavia, atomic matters, and the manner in which he built relationships, was his intimate involvement with perhaps the most famous physicist at that time, the Nobel Prize winner Niels Bohr. Welsh had helped mastermind Bohr's escape from occupied Denmark in 1943, and once the physicist was in London, Welsh became Bohr's minder.[21] This continued after Bohr had traveled to the United States, where Welsh acted as courier and censor in all messages sent back to his wife in England.[22] Bohr's son, Aage, has recalled how his father "enjoyed discussing [matters] with Welsh and appreciated his directness and sense of humour. . . . He remained for us a personal connection to the Intelligence service, which turned into a friendship." Aage Bohr's memory of Welsh highlights the important characteristics that he brought to his work: affinity with contacts, a humorous presence but serious undertone, and an ability to ensure that he was central to everything.[23]

By the latter stages of the war, Welsh, now approaching his fifties and rotund in appearance, began to suffer from thrombosis in both legs. His son has recalled that although Welsh had never been a heavy drinker beforehand, he took to drinking whisky to alleviate his pain. The thrombosis was such that he often found it difficult to walk from SIS offices in Broadway to the Thatched House Club on St. James Street.[24] In his correspondence with Niels Bohr, it is clear that Welsh was quite unwell in late 1944, though it is unclear what his symptoms were.[25]

Welsh excelled at his wartime intelligence work. He forged close, personal friendships with many of the scientists he interacted with. He instilled a great sense of loyalty among his Norwegian agents, many of whom saw him as a father figure. Even R. V. Jones, whom he would famously fall out with after the war, complimented his wartime efforts.[26] His love for Norway clearly affected him too. His son has recalled that he was initially against the USAF bombing of Norsk Hydro for fear that it would kill innocent Norwegians (Germans were another matter entirely), and he remained affected by having to send men out to Norway. In fact, he even considered leaving government service to return to Norway in 1945, but the pull was too much.[27] SIS needed Welsh and Welsh needed SIS.

Eric Welsh flourished professionally in the postwar world.[28] From 1945 until his death nine years later, he had two roles: one overt, the other covert. The former was to head the Directorate of Atomic Energy (Intelligence) in the Ministry of Supply. This was an analytical body responsible for the collation and interpretation of reports but not the actual collection of information. Welsh's organization passed its reports to the Joint Intelligence Committee, where they were deliberated and passed up to the Chiefs of Staff. As it was not directly involved in collecting information, the unit was reliant on tasking frontline organizations.

The main body of the unit existed overtly. Although this does not mean that the government admitted to its existence or that its activities were open to other government departments, it was located less secretly within the Ministry of Supply. This small body comprised fewer than ten people (excluding secretaries) and included a liaison officer with the Government Communications Headquarters, a collator, various scientific figures including a physicist and a geologist, a liaison with the Americans, and several seconded RAF officers. Welsh, described by his secretary, Sybil Conner, as "a great character," remained primus inter pares.[29] Unsurprisingly, perhaps, those in the unit proudly referred to themselves as the "slaves." There were annual Christmas parties held at the nearby Adelphi, with special prizes for games and dancing.[30] The unit was located on the fourth floor of Shell Mex House on the Strand, and its home was referred to as "the Cage" because of its secure grille-like housing.[31] To enter, an armed guard had to unlock the entry gate, positioned within a network of horizontal and vertical bars.[32] In fact by the early 1950s, this had begun to cause some problems, for the "close checking at the gate" had created "delays" in admitting visitors to the inner sanctum.[33]

Welsh, however, also wore another hat as he remained an SIS officer. Atomic intelligence within SIS was referred to as Tube Alloys Liaison (TAL). Within an extremely secretive organization, TAL was one of the most clandestine aspects, so surreptitious that "operational officers had only the vaguest understanding of it."[34] Just how secret TAL was is exemplified by the following anecdote from a former TAL member: Welsh often attended the meetings of

SIS directorate heads. At one meeting he was quietly asked by one colleague which directorate he headed as he had never been introduced; Welsh replied that it was too secret to mention. Given the sensitivities, Welsh himself had a direct line of access to "C," the chief of SIS. Similarly, because TAL had its own budget, Welsh could exert a level of influence over the process of selecting intelligence targets for which information was desired.

Although he had no formal scientific qualifications, Welsh incorrectly liked to refer to himself as the only SIS officer with a science degree.[35] This lack of a scientific academic background put him in stark contrast to postwar heads of scientific intelligence, all of whom held doctorates in related disciplines.[36] That this did not hold Welsh back is testament to the way in which he built personal relationships and conducted his work. He maintained excellent personal relations with atomic scientists whom he called on for assistance in scientific evaluations, and by the time of his death, his network of contacts was immense. As one former colleague has recalled, Welsh had an almost "feminine intuition for things" and often followed his hunches. A secretive figure, Welsh wrote everything down in a little black book, much to the consternation of colleagues who could never get near it. Upon his death in 1954, it is rumored that Special Branch raided his house but found nothing.[37]

Given his experience, contacts, and the fact that the structure remained intact, it was perhaps natural that Welsh retained his command of postwar atomic intelligence. Those who worked with Welsh commend his personal qualities as head of the directorate,[38] whereas those who opposed his control saw his leadership as calamitous, relating the fate of atomic intelligence to his inabilities as commander.[39] One of Welsh's major critics was R. V. Jones, the wartime head of scientific intelligence. At the end of the war, Jones had tried— unsuccessfully—to absorb atomic intelligence into scientific intelligence and thus into his jurisdiction. Indeed, there are famous examples of Jones and Welsh having to be kept apart at Chiefs of Staff meetings.[40] For Welsh, the key determinant was his success in tackling the greatest priority of the day: predicting when the Soviet Union would break the American atomic monopoly.

A variety of efforts were undertaken to gather intelligence, but from the outset the immense difficulty of the task was recognized. The Soviet atomic program was one of the most sensitive aspects of a very secretive, highly compartmentalized machine. In 1948, however, an opportunity presented itself that was too good to miss: there was a chance to sabotage it. Located within the Soviet zone of occupation in Germany was Bitterfeld. Here there was an I.G. Farben calcium plant, suspected to be used in the production of uranium for the Soviet nuclear weapons program.[41] By 1948 TAL had a well-placed source within the Bitterfeld plant. Welsh's plan—code-named Operation

Spanner—was given blessing in London by "C." Welsh had been concerned about the details of the plan leaking as a result of what he called "American clumsiness."[42] As we know now, there were, in fact, undisclosed Soviet agents, but these were closer to home, operating within British intelligence, both in London and Germany. Welsh's plan was protected from these individuals by his direct line of communication with "C" himself. Welsh aimed to use his agent to introduce some boric acid to the calcium production process, thereby, in his words, "buggering the works." However, before the plan could be put into action, production at the plant had stopped. Although at the time this produced some concern that the plan had leaked, it is now known that the stoppage was due to the testing of the first Soviet atomic bomb, and so Welsh's sabotage plan was never launched.[43]

From the outset Anglo-American relations were central to Britain's atomic intelligence efforts. Unsurprisingly Welsh positioned himself at the center of matters. In 1946 the United States passed the McMahon Act, designed to end the technical exchange of atomic information. Although the greatest impact was felt among atomic scientists, it was also shared in intelligence circles. Yet in spite of this, the McMahon Act was cunningly circumvented by Welsh, who was able to procure significant information and, vitally, resurrect relations with Britain's most cherished partner. Despite official limitations on what information could be given to the British, certain unofficial lines of access remained. Considerable ingenuity was shown by the British, for as Arnold Kramish, a former senior staff member of the Atomic Energy Commission (AEC) with responsibility for intelligence liaison with the British, has testified, Welsh would often bring a selection of Swiss watches, which he would offer in exchange for snippets of information. Indeed Welsh, who visited the United States with some regularity, was increasingly fond of a few drinks and, at such gatherings in Washington, was "very good at getting stuff out of scientists."[44] Although Kramish rejected such offerings, some of his colleagues were less inhibited. The deputy of the AEC intelligence unit was Malcolm Henderson, and according to Kramish, he "had a big mouth and was most indiscreet." Henderson was eventually sacked for taking home top secret papers, but before his impromptu removal, he had become "one of Eric's best 'American Spies.'"[45] By 1949 intelligence figures in Whitehall were discussing the "special relationship" that existed between Welsh's unit and its American counterpart, and certainly this description was wholly warranted.[46]

To assist matters Welsh had, within his team, an officer based in Washington, DC. According to Dr. Wilfrid Mann, although he occupied the exalted position of atomic intelligence liaison with the Americans, his "sole job" was to notify Eric Welsh and SIS if and when the US detected a Soviet atomic bomb test.[47] On September 3, 1949, a diverted American WB-29 (weather B-29) flying between Japan and Alaska collected routine atmospheric samples at 18,000 feet. These samples revealed an unmistakably higher-than-normal radioactive content and became known as Alert 112—the 112th time such an occurrence had arisen. All previous alerts had proved to be the result of natural phenomena (for example, volcanoes or natural increases in radioactivity), and although it was initially suspected this would once more be the case, ultimately the alert proved to be the real thing.[48] To investigate further, additional samples were collected on a September 5 flight over Japan. Analysis at 3:30 a.m. on September 7 proved that the samples were artificial—that they had been injected into the atmosphere by a nonnatural occurrence, and so, on September 10, 1949, the British were informed.[49]

Sir Michael Perrin, one of Welsh's colleagues on the scientific side who was also part of the intelligence effort, has recalled how "on 10th September I had a telephone call from the US Embassy to go for a top secret 'telex' conference and to bring Commander Welsh of MI6 with me."[50] The Americans asked Welsh if he could arrange a flight to collect further samples. Welsh immediately contacted "C" and the RAF.[51]

The first British confirmation came from a UK-based flight leaving on the evening of September 10. Further flights flown over the next few days established the confirmation.[52] Wilfrid Mann learned about the news at 11:30 p.m. on September 14. "I had one foot in the bathtub," he recalls, "when the telephone rang with a request that I go down to the War Room near the White House."[53] Despite his role, therefore, Mann was far from being the first Briton to learn about the Soviet bomb. At 3:00 a.m. (US time) on September 15, a further telex conference began with Perrin and Welsh at the American embassy in London. Returning to his office in the British embassy, Mann sent a series of telegrams through the secure SIS link. With the help of the SIS liaison officer at the embassy, Kim Philby, Mann spent three to four days in extended communication with London, sending top secret messages to Welsh and even more sensitive messages to "C."[54] One of the messages to "C" advised him that he should inform the prime minister of the news.[55] Accordingly, on September 17 Perrin accompanied "C" to Chequers to tell Prime Minister Clement Attlee "that there was evidence that 'Joe 1' had taken place."[56]

That same day, Dr. William Penney (the head of Britain's scientific efforts to build an atomic bomb) and Eric Welsh arrived in the United States complete with samples collected by the RAF. They had flown across the Atlantic to take part in a conference with American intelligence analysts to investigate and deliberate on the intelligence regarding the Soviet bomb. Their evidence also conclusively pointed to an atomic explosion, and Penney's subsequent report was so sensitive that even he could not read a proof copy.[57]

While in the United States, the "strain" had proved "too great" for Welsh, and in September 1949 he suffered a heart attack. In his memoir Wilfrid Mann commented that the attack was not too severe.[58] This was not immediately clear to Welsh's colleagues at the time, though: in London Welsh's secretary, Julia Alloway, recorded the event in a letter to Sam Goudsmit, the wartime scientific head of the Alsos mission: "You will remember when I saw you I said that he was not very well. The doctors took a more serious view, and diagnosed coronary thrombosis and prophesised death; this week they say indigestion and a long life!"[59] Mann recalls in his memoir that he "is almost certain" that Philby visited Welsh in the hospital at this time.[60]

Welsh was flown back to the UK by the USAF. An intensely private individual, Welsh was keen to maintain an aura of mystery about his role in the government. He must have been shocked, therefore, to discover that while he was in transit, a newspaper article appeared in England discussing how a "Mystery Navy man flies home on a stretcher." Fortunately the article continued, "To all questions officials replied that the Commander's name could not under any circumstances be disclosed and that he came under the category of 'top secret.'"[61]

Still recovering from his heart attack, Welsh was back at work by November 1949. Despite suffering from recurring bouts of ill health, including pleurisy, he continued working.[62] The doctors in SIS urged him to take time off and slow down.[63] By this point the British and Americans had agreed that the Soviet test had unquestionably been an atomic detonation, probably caused by a plutonium bomb.[64] In fact the bomb was remarkably similar to the wartime device exploded over Nagasaki and to the first one that Britain would test in 1952. In a postmortem of the British intelligence failure to forecast the Soviet atomic test in 1949, members of the scientific intelligence community observed, "In the last year or so a number of reports dealing with Russian progress in the development of atomic weapons had been largely discounted because they were low grade. It is now assumed that many of these reports were truer than was at first thought." Accordingly, it was felt necessary to have an evaluation by Welsh's unit as to the "reasons for the Russian success."[65]

Welsh strongly associated the test with espionage. In a communication to Wilfrid Mann in Washington, he mentioned how the latest information indicated that the Soviet bomb "was stolen from Leslie Groves." Indeed, Welsh was left in no doubt as to the particular source of this information: referring to Perrin's meetings with the atomic scientist Klaus Fuchs, he mentioned that it was "confessed to some of *our* experts."[66] Although some questions were asked of Welsh's unit, these never resembled an in-depth intensive evaluation of Britain's atomic intelligence apparatus, something that would not happen until 1954. Despite failing to predict the primary reason for his organization's existence, therefore, Welsh was not castigated.

Eric Welsh continued to head both the overt and covert aspects of atomic intelligence, retaining responsibility for everything from defining collection targets to conducting detailed, scientific analysis of Soviet test debris. In the 1952 New Year's Honours, he was awarded an Order of St Michael and St George (CMG).[67] Welsh was, in fact, a very shrewd civil servant. He was able to repel all attempts to unseat him through increasing the prestige, purview, range of activities, and efficiency of his unit so that any proposed alternative to his control would be untenable. He was supported in his position by those in Whitehall who believed that atomic relations with the Americans would be harmed if British atomic intelligence were not kept separate from the conventional scientific intelligence organization.

During this period, from 1950 to 1954, the cornerstones of the Anglo-American atomic intelligence "special relationship" of the 1950s were laid. Through various operations Britain was able to retain a vital foothold in the American nuclear weapons program. Crucially this was a genuine two-way street, based on what information the British could learn not only from the Americans but from the value and importance the Americans attached to British views.[68]

Strengthening Welsh's position was the fact that the Americans appeared to be on Welsh's side. During his visit to the United States in late 1950, Dr. Bertie Blount, the head of British scientific intelligence, had attempted to discuss British and American estimates of the Soviet nuclear weapons stockpile but without success. Though the Americans had themselves been willing to discuss the matter with Blount, they had first inquired through Wilfrid Mann whether Blount was cleared and authorized to discuss the matter. The response from London, no doubt originating from Welsh, was "negative."[69]

In 1954, with the transfer of the civilian and military aspects of atomic energy out of the Ministry of Supply, atomic intelligence underwent a comprehensive evaluation, conducted by Adm. Sir Charles Daniel. Central to his review were Welsh's organizations and the critical role of Welsh himself. His "overt" body in the Ministry of Supply was under the overall command of Sir Frederick Morgan. In his evaluation Morgan was quite unequivocal in his opinion:

> The peculiar virtue of this small body of people lies in its leader, Lieutenant Commander Eric Welsh, who is not only a natural born genius of precisely the type required for the work in hand but who has, over the years, built-up a truly astonishing network of personal contacts up to the highest, not only in

this country but in the United States of America and in Canada. . . . The ramifications of Commander Welsh's activities are world wide and he seems able to command the services of practically anyone.

In offering his opinion of the past record of Welsh's unit, Morgan maintained that "considering the enormous difficulties of obtaining secret intelligence on any target in Russia, the results we have obtained on atomic energy are comparatively good." Thus, in making his recommendations, Morgan concluded, "It could be disastrous to British Atomic Intelligence if Welsh's background, experience or contacts in this subject were lost."[70]

However, Morgan continued, "here is a key man if ever there was one which is partly, of course, a matter for congratulation but also a grave potential source of weakness."[71] In this Morgan had identified the primary concern of those asked to offer their opinions on Welsh: that no one was totally clear on what Welsh spent his money on or what he precisely he did—this was certainly the view expressed by William Penney.[72] It also highlighted the fact that Welsh was something of a one-man band. In fact Claud Wright, the assistant secretary to the minister for defence, warned Daniel that Welsh "serves too many masters" and that "in the political and negotiating fields his influence is probably very dangerous and he must be brought under control."

In his briefing Daniel was also informed that part of the problem he would face in his evaluation was the fact that Welsh "insist[ed] on treating the whole of AEI [atomic energy intelligence] as a special mystery."[73] One explanation for this mysticism was provided by a former member of his team, who emphasized how Welsh "had a feeling about something and followed it." This was put more powerfully once more by Morgan, who commented on how Welsh's "training and common sense tell him where to plant the goods and so far this seems to have been done with remarkable accuracy."[74] The subsequent report concluded that, in fact, the organization should remain under Welsh, though a high-level committee was to be instigated, in part to control his power.[75]

Known to many as a keen drinker, by mid-1954, just as the new changes in structure were taking place, Welsh had started to have "difficulty in keeping himself on his feet."[76] On Sunday, November 21, 1954, Eric Welsh died from a heart attack. His death certificate lists "alcoholism" as a cause, a problem it seems he had suffered from for some time. In keeping with his sense of secrecy, only the briefest of obituaries appeared in *The Times*, listing his awards but not mentioning his work or why he had received them.[77] Within Whitehall and Washington Julia Alloway wrote to many of Welsh's contacts to inform them of the news. Tributes to Welsh and his work quickly followed. Wilfrid Mann described him as one of the "outstanding secret intelligence officers of the middle decades of this century."[78] Goudsmit, who had worked with Welsh during the war and who had remained in contact since, remarked how "few people would understand how great a loss it is. . . . No one can take his place."[79]

The death of Welsh in many respects was not a momentous event simply because by late 1954 his organization, which he had built and defended since the end of the war, was both comprehensive and successful. His legacy was intact. Welsh's successor seems to have merely maintained his hard work. Thus, through this organization and the links it maintained in the lean years of atomic collaboration, Britain could in 1958 ultimately achieve what it had always desired since 1946—resumption of technical relations with the United States.

Eric Welsh was a unique intelligence officer. Although he was absorbed into intelligence work by circumstance, he was able to become the father of atomic intelligence and one of the pioneers of scientific intelligence. His leadership characteristics of humor, personality, secrecy, personal affiliation with agents, and a natural inclination to take charge of everything ensured that he remained liked and admired with a loyal staff. Yet, as revealed in the inquiry into his organization in 1954, these same traits and general aloof nature ensured that he was not entirely trusted as a government employee. He retained a natural affinity for Norway and could never quite forget the sacrifices that he had made during the war. His health was omnipresent in his work, as was his increasing fondness for alcohol, and ultimately, these would prove to be his downfall.

Notes

This paper is drawn only from released official records and published sources, and the views expressed are mine in my capacity as an academic historian. They do not represent the views or carry the endorsement of the government.

A version of this chapter was previously published in *War in History*. I am grateful to Keith Jeffery and Christian Bak for comments on an earlier draft of this article. I am also grateful to Paul Maddrell for comments on this version.

1. A 1956 history of the company, *Seventy-Five Years of Paint-Making, 1881–1956*, includes a plaque identifying Welsh as one of the individuals who had completed twenty-five years of service for the company. It lists his start of employment as 1914. I am grateful to the company archivist for a copy of this booklet.

2. Akzo Nobel, "It Began in 1881," accessed 2012, https://www.akzonobel.com/international/system/images/AkzoNobel_It_began_in_1881_tcm46-14318.pdf.

3. I am grateful to Eric Welsh's late son, John Welsh, for allowing me access to the diary.

4. Eric Welsh diary, entry for July 24, 1916.

5. Details on the preceding paragraphs taken from his "Enrolment Form," ADM 337/78, British National Archives (TNA); and "Sea Service," ADM 339/1, TNA.

6. John Welsh, interview by the author, September 28, 2009.

7. E. Welsh, notes made on "Lieut-Commander Eric Welsh, RNVR," October 20, 1943. I am again indebted to John Welsh for allowing me to see his father's papers.

8. Christian Bak asserts that Welsh was brought into SIS as the SOE/SIS naval operation to Norway from the Shetland Islands expanded and as its previous head moved to other tasks. Correspondence with the author, 2014.

9. Reid to Jan-Hermann, November 6, 1970, MS 708.14, Margaret Reid Papers, Brotherton Library, University of Leeds.

10. Keith Jeffery, *The History of MI6* (London: Bloomsbury, 2010), 374.

11. For examples, see the various wartime experiences of Oluf Reed-Olsen (Papers at the Imperial War Museum) and various correspondence in folder SISA, Norwegian Home Resistance Museum.

12. O. Snefjella, "Secret Intelligence Operations in Occupied Norway during World War II—Reporting of German Naval Forces and Merchant Ships" (unpublished manuscript). I am indebted to John Welsh for a copy of this memoir.

13. Jeffery, *History of MI6*, 375.

14. A great number of books exist on these raids. See, for instance, Thomas Gallagher, *Assault in Norway: Sabotaging the Nazi Nuclear Program* (London: Lyons Press, 2002); also Per F. Dahl, *Heavy Water and the Wartime Race for Nuclear Energy* (London: Taylor & Francis, 1999).

15. Norges Statskalender: 1947, 1050. I am grateful to Egil Vindorum, head of Chancellery, the Royal Norwegian Order of St. Olav, for this information. E-mail to the author, April 28, 2004. On the OBE, see *Supplement to the London Gazette*, June 10, 1944, 2670. Welsh is described as being "employed in a Department of the Foreign Office."

16. M. W. Perrin and R. R. Furman, "T.A. Project, Enemy Intelligence," November 28, 1944, CAB 126/244, TNA. "T.A." referred to Tube Alloys, the British code name given to the atomic bomb.

17. For more, see Arnold Kramish, *The Griffin: The Greatest Untold Espionage Story of World War II* (Boston: Houghton Mifflin, 1986). Some of Kramish's content and conclusions needed to be treated with care.

18. Robert W. Cahn, "The Origins of Pergamon Press: Rosbaud and Maxwell," *European Review* 2, no. 1 (January 1994): 37–42.

19. On the former, see details in CAB 126/244, TNA.

20. Mary A. McPartland, "The Farm Hall Scientists: The United States, Britain, and Germany in the New Atomic Age, 1945–46" (PhD thesis, George Washington University, 2013). I am grateful to Dr. McPartland for a copy of her unpublished thesis. For more on Farm Hall, see Charles Frank, *Operation Epsilon: The Farm Hall Transcripts* (Bristol: Institute of Physics, 1993); and Jeremy Bernstein, *Hitler's Uranium Club: The Secret Recordings at Farm Hall* (New York: Springer, 2001).

21. For details, see AB 1/40, TNA.

22. For more details, see CAB 126/39, TNA.

23. A. Bohr, letter to the author, January 10, 2003.

24. Welsh interview. See also Charles I. Campbell, *A Questing Life: The Search for*

Meaning (Lincoln, NE: iUniverse, 2006), 80. Campbell was a US intelligence officer working on atomic matters.

25. Bohr to Welsh, August 22, 1944, Denmark: Political Correspondence, 3.2, Niels Bohr Archive, Denmark.

26. This is taken from notes of David Irving's interviews with Jones in the mid-1960s. David Irving Collection, Material gathered for his book, *The German Atomic Bomb*, American Institute of Physics, Centre for the History of Physics, Niels Bohr Library, College Park, MD.

27. Welsh interview.

28. For more details on all aspects of the proceeding material, see Michael S. Goodman, *Spying on the Nuclear Bear: Anglo-American Intelligence and the Soviet Bomb* (Stanford, CA: Stanford University Press, 2007).

29. Sybil Conner, letter to the author, November 16, 2004.

30. See various correspondence in AB 8/27, TNA.

31. Frederick Morgan, *Peace and War: A Soldier's Life* (London: Hodder and Stoughton, 1961).

32. Charles Perrin, son of Sir Michael Perrin, interview with the authors, May 17, 2004.

33. "Memorandum by R.E. France [Assistant Secretary/Atomic Energy (S)1]," May 9, 1953, AB 8/27, TNA.

34. P. H. J. Davies, e-mail to the author, August 25, 2003.

35. Nigel West, *MI6: British Secret Intelligence Service Operations, 1909–1945* (London: Weidenfeld and Nicolson, 1983), 163. Also Stephen Dorril, *MI6: Fifty Years of Special Operations* (London: Fourth Estate, 2000), 134. It is unclear why exactly Welsh took this line.

36. Dr. R. V. Jones, for instance, was a physicist, while Dr. Bertie Blount was a chemist, both of some renown.

37. I am grateful to various former members of British atomic intelligence for interviews and correspondence, particularly one interview with a former member of Directorate of Atomic Energy (Intelligence), February 21, 2003.

38. Wilfrid B. Mann, *Was There a Fifth Man? Quintessential Recollections* (Oxford: Pergamon Press, 1982), 62.

39. Anthony Cavendish, *Inside Intelligence: The Revelations of an MI6 Officer* (London: HarperCollins, 1997), 192. Also Reginald V. Jones, *Most Secret War: British Scientific Intelligence, 1939–1945* (London: Hamish Hamilton, 1978), 308–9.

40. For example, "H. Parker to Brownjohn," October 24, 1953, DEFE 7/2105, TNA.

41. For more, see Paul Maddrell, "British-American Scientific Intelligence Collaboration during the Occupation of Germany," *Intelligence and National Security* 15, no. 2 (2000): 74–94.

42. This was a reflection of similar concerns in London in the immediate postwar period, when there were serious (albeit unfounded) doubts about US security. More detail is in Michael S. Goodman, *The Official History of the Joint Intelligence Committee*, vol. 1, *From the Approach of War to the Suez Crisis* (London: Routledge, 2014).

43. Henry Lowenhaupt, "Chasing Bitterfeld Calcium," *CIA Studies in Intelligence*

17, no. 1 (1996). All the preceding information on the plant comes from this eyewitness account.

44. Arnold Kramish, e-mail to the author, January 14, 2003.

45. Arnold Kramish, e-mail to the author, March 21, 2003.

46. B. Blount [head of scientific intelligence], "Organisation of Scientific Intelligence—Deficiencies of the Present Organisation," October 1949, DEFE 40/26, TNA.

47. Wilfrid Mann, interview with C. Ziegler, 1990. I am grateful to Professor Ziegler for providing some details of the interview.

48. See the September 9, 1949, memo by DCI Hillenkoetter, Box 250, PSF: Intelligence File, Harry S. Truman Presidential Library, Kansas, MO (hereafter cited as HST).

49. D. L. Northrup and D. H. Rock, "Detection of Joe 1," *CIA Studies in Intelligence*, Fall 1996, 30.

50. "Letter from Perrin to R. C. Williams," [1984?], Box 2, Folder 1, Robert C. Williams Papers, Niels Bohr Library.

51. "Letter from Perrin to R. C. Williams," August 14, 1984, Box 2, Folder 1, Williams Papers.

52. William Penney, "An Interim Report," Box 173, PSF: Subject File, 1945–53, HST.

53. W. B. Mann, "Sixty Years In and Out of Physics." I am grateful to Kris Mann for a copy of her father's 1990 lecture.

54. A. Cave Brown, *Treason in the Blood: H.St.John Philby, Kim Philby, and the Spy Case of the Century* (London: Robert Hale, 1994), 400.

55. Mann, "Sixty Years."

56. "Letter from Perrin to R. C. Williams," August 14, 1984. See also H. Montgomery Hyde, *The Atom Bomb Spies* (London: Sphere, 1980), 143–44. Joe-1 was the code name given to the Soviet test.

57. Mann, *Was There a Fifth Man?* 68. Mann had helped draft it.

58. Ibid., 69.

59. "Alloway to Goudsmit," October 3, 1949, Box 23, Folder 254, Goudsmit Papers, College Park, MD. See also the correspondence in Box CHAD IV 11/54, Sir James Chadwick Papers, Churchill College Archives, University of Cambridge.

60. Mann, *Was There a Fifth Man?* 70.

61. Cited in ibid., 69.

62. "Welsh to O. Frisch," February 18, 1954, Otto Frisch Papers, Box F.138, Trinity College Archives, University of Cambridge.

63. Welsh interview.

64. "BJSM to P.M.," September 19, 1949, FO 115/4477, TNA.

65. "JS/JTIC(49)32nd Meeting," September 28, 1949, DEFE 41/73, TNA. It was therefore considered necessary to reevaluate Soviet progress in other fields of defense research and development.

66. "Welsh to Mann," December 30, 1949. Emphasis in the original. I am indebted to Professor Kris Mann for allowing me access to her father's private papers, which

includes considerable correspondence between Mann and Welsh. Fuchs had confessed to Perrin.

67. *Supplement to the London Gazette*, January 1, 1952, 5.

68. Details are in Goodman, *Spying on the Nuclear Bear*.

69. ANCAM 391 "BJSM to Cabinet Office," November 20, 1950, CAB 126/338, TNA.

70. "Morgan to Brownjohn," September 21, 1953, DEFE 7/2105, TNA.

71. "Morgan to Brownjohn," September 21, 1953, DEFE 7/2105, TNA.

72. "Note by W. G. Penney for Adm Daniel," December 20, 1953, DEFE 19/38, TNA.

73. "Wright to Daniel," December 5, 1953, DEFE 19/38, TNA.

74. "Morgan to Brownjohn," September 21, 1953, DEFE 7/2105, TNA. Author's interview with a former member of Atomic Energy Intelligence Unit (AEIU), February 21, 2003.

75. For more detail, see M. S. Goodman, "The Daniel Report on Atomic Intelligence," *Intelligence and National Security* 18, no. 3 (2003): 154–67.

76. "Alloway to Goudsmit," November 23, 1954, Box 23, Folder 254, Goudsmit Papers.

77. *The Times*, November 23, 1954.

78. Mann, "Sixty Years."

79. "Goudsmit to Alloway," January 4, 1955, Box 23, Folder 254, Goudsmit Papers.

10 "C" and Covert Action

The Impact and Agency of Stewart Menzies in Britain's Secret Foreign Policy

Rory Cormac

Intelligence has consistently shaped international history in numerous and important ways. In the British context, scholars have perceived this as a predominantly passive process, whereby intelligence informs the policymaking process.[1] Intelligence, however, can also have a more active and direct impact on international affairs. This is achieved through covert action—a state's intervention in the affairs of another in a plausibly deniable manner. Given the potential impact, it is important to determine the role of intelligence leaders in proposing, planning, and executing such interventionism.

Covert action is a field that blurs the traditional divide between intelligence and policy. This raises key questions about the extent to which intelligence leaders adopt a policy role when considering covert action. Do (unelected) intelligence leaders become policy entrepreneurs? What is their relationship with the elected policymakers? Such issues are far from unimportant: they shed light on the foreign policymaking process and highlight the competing pressures of democracy, secrecy, and national security contained therein.

American covert action garners the lion's share of scholarly as well as public attention. As a result, histories of covert action are replete with tales of CIA directors ordering daring operations and directly shaping international affairs from Latin America to the Middle East and Afghanistan.[2] Such activity, however, is not merely an American field. The British, through the Secret Intelligence Service (SIS), have long conducted covert operations too—albeit not to the same extent or scale as their American counterparts. This gives the chief of SIS, long known as "C," the power to intervene in foreign affairs. Examples include conducting Operation Valuable in Albania in the late 1940s, overthrowing the Iranian prime minister in 1953, attempting to undermine President Nasser of Egypt a couple of years later, plotting assassination in Syria in 1957, arming rebels during the 1960s Yemeni civil war, and conducting black propaganda in Indonesia at the same time.

Photo 10.1 The Clubbable Chief: SIS head Stewart Menzies (right) used his social and political connections to advance the interests of the service. He is pictured here with his brother, Keith, in 1914 during the First World War. *Wikimedia Commons*

The United Kingdom still uses covert action today. We have seen a bungled attempt to make contact with Libyan rebels during the Arab Spring, followed by a more successful operation in which covert forces provided assistance in the ensuing civil war.[3] We have heard the then chief of SIS, John Sawers, talk fairly candidly about the role of British covert operations in stalling Iranian nuclear capabilities.[4] Meanwhile, documents stolen by Edward Snowden reveal the recent turn of the Government Communications Headquarters (GCHQ) toward the realm of online covert action. Traditional tradecraft, from disruption to false flag activity, has been given a twenty-first-century cyber twist.[5] And British use of covert action will only increase, not least because the new British national security machinery institutionalizes regular contact between the prime minister and his intelligence chiefs. In a world of military, economic, and political constraint, it seems eminently logical that policymakers would use this forum to ask the intelligence leadership to "do something." The United Kingdom has long used, and will continue to use, covert action as a means to plug the gap between perceived responsibilities and diminishing capabilities.

This chapter uses recently declassified archival files to examine the role and impact of one particular British intelligence chief in covert action: Maj. Gen. Sir Stewart Menzies. Chief of SIS from 1939 to 1952, Menzies oversaw the transition from war to peace and from peace to Cold War. He also oversaw the dissolution of the wartime Special Operations Executive (SOE) and the rise of covert operations against the Soviet Union. The Menzies era therefore forms an important case study in understanding the role an intelligence chief can play in determining British covert action—and interventionist—strategy.

This chapter examines the evolution of Britain's covert action strategy in the transition from war to Cold War. It seeks to isolate the role of C and examine his agency and impact within the policymaking system. It is impossible and counterproductive to consider the escapades of SIS—or indeed the CIA—in isolation from the broader government system. This chapter argues that Menzies's personal impact was constrained by international and bureaucratic systems and that covert action was a political resultant.[6] Nonetheless, his influence did increase by 1950, allowing C to play a central part in formulating Britain's strategy. Challenging the popular "James Bondian" perception of SIS as rogue elephants, analysis of the bureaucratic level reveals that C was tied to the highest levels of policymaking, especially the foreign secretary.

Covert Action and Foreign Policy in the British Tradition

Traditionally, Britain has understood covert action as somewhat straddling the spheres of intelligence and policy. It is something conceptually distinct from the intelligence cycle. Covert action is a means of executing policy that, in addition to being informed by intelligence, directly draws on intelligence assets, structures, and personnel. Former SIS officer John Bruce Lockhart sums up British thinking nicely: covert action is "the extension of government policy by secret and non-attributable means."[7] Conceptualized in this manner, covert action takes on an almost Clausewitzian character.

Scholars have long emphasized the link between covert action and policy in the British tradition. Mark Lowenthal, for example, has argued that the government used to refer to covert action as special political action deliberately to emphasize the link between intelligence and policy.[8] Although in reality special political action formed one type of covert action, Lowenthal's analysis was certainly borne out by the close links between SIS's Special Political Action section and the Foreign Office in the 1950s.[9] Similarly, the late 1950s and the 1960s saw diplomats and intelligence officers brought together when proposing, discussing, and scrutinizing covert action. As Richard Aldrich has argued, during the Cold War "all aspects of the British Secret Intelligence Service stayed firmly under the control of the Foreign Office in a manner that was quite different to the position of the CIA in the United States."[10] SIS was a tool of (or means of executing) foreign policy, whereas the CIA was, and remains, a tool of the president. Relations with the Foreign Office were important; to be successful, covert action must necessarily be conducted in harmony with publicly stated policy objectives and embedded in, or an adjunct to, a broader strategic policy.[11] Indeed, back in 1967 Burke Trend, the cabinet secretary, explicitly criticized the American divide between intelligence and covert action on the one hand and policy on the other. He wrote to Harold Wilson, then prime minister, "This rather arbitrary divorce between intelligence and policy-making is not only inefficient but, if it extends into the field of covert action as distinct from mere intelligence, can also be disastrous, as was evidenced by the Bay of Pigs episode."[12]

At the end of the Second World War, British conceptualizations of the relationships among intelligence, policy, and covert action were fluid. Nonetheless, the British tradition clearly allows scope for C to become a policy actor—potentially by advocating and instigating policies, even becoming a "policy entrepreneur." Indeed, Menzies certainly had control over information and control over resources to carry out certain actions.[13] Before we examine the ability of C, as an intelligence leader, to actively shape international relations, some brief context on SIS is needed.

SIS was, and remains, responsible for British intelligence activity overseas. It reports to the Foreign Office, with C accountable to the foreign secretary. Ernest Bevin, a bullish man with a strong personality, held this position for most of Menzies's postwar tenure. Bevin exercised his influence over SIS from the start, insisting that "no action should be taken, except after consultation with the Foreign Secretary."[14] C also had right of access to the prime minister, Clement Attlee, and sent him a weekly report. In practice, however, he had most regular personal contact with the permanent undersecretary at the Foreign Office, Britain's most senior diplomat. After the Second World War, SIS absorbed the remnants of the SOE (Britain's wartime sabotage and special operations body), thereby demonstrating further Foreign Office control over clandestine activities overseas. In addition, until 1956 C was also responsible for the Government Code and Cipher School (GC&CS), Britain's signals intelligence agency, renamed GCHQ in 1946. SIS had a tense relationship with MI5, its domestic counterpart, and also with elements of the military—some of which pushed for a more aggressive approach to covert action and were bitter about the demise of the SOE. This led to numerous Whitehall battles over jurisdiction. And there is certainly some validity in the argument that (para)military special operations capabilities should be housed within the military. SIS activities were funded by an opaque "secret vote" associated with prime ministerial authority and approved with minimal scrutiny by Parliament. From late 1951 the vote was overseen by what would become known as the Permanent Secretaries on the Intelligence Services (PSIS) committee, which included the permanent secretaries from the Foreign Office, Home Office, Ministry of Defence, and Treasury.[15] In postwar times of austerity, budgets proved a contentious issue. This was the context in which C operated.

Stewart Menzies as C: From War to Peace to Cold War

Stewart Menzies became C in 1939—just two months after the outbreak of the Second World War. He retired to his twin passions of horse racing and hunting in the summer of 1952, after a remarkably long stint in his post. Following the tradition of his predecessors, and unlike current chiefs, Menzies was a military man. After leaving Eton, where he had excelled at sports, he joined the Grenadier Guards before transferring to the Life Guards. Fluent in French and German, he gradually moved into the intelligence world during the First World War when, after recovering from a gas attack, he acquired a counterintelligence role under Field Marshal Douglas Haig. Adept at the art of discretion, Menzies was a rare example of a successful whistle-blower who went on to be promoted after outing intelligence malpractice.[16] In 1919 he served another intelligence role, this time with MI1(c), the organization that would become MI6 or SIS, soon finding himself part of the British delegation to the Versailles conference. And so began a long and successful career with the service.[17]

Menzies demonstrated a remarkable work ethic, stamina, and toughness during the war. Winston Churchill, the wartime prime minister, would call on him night or day, and he soon became an increasingly privileged member of Churchill's inner circle. Menzies's influence was undoubtedly aided by his ability to provide Churchill with valuable signals intelligence in the form of Ultra decrypts.[18]

While he was mentally tough, C was seemingly also reasonably approachable. Although he rarely left his office at Broadway, individual officers maintained right of access to their chief. As his organization grew, so too did the queue outside his door.[19] Like his predecessor, Adm. Sir Hugh Sinclair, Menzies had an informal managerial style and seemingly paid little attention to the formalities of hierarchy. Perhaps as a testament to this attitude, he allowed his senior secretary, Miss Pettigrew, to keep a parakeet in her room adjoining his private office.[20]

Menzies drew contrasting opinions from those with whom he served. Victor Cavendish-Bentinck, for example, the wartime chairman of the Joint Intelligence Committee (JIC), once described him as "not a very strong man and not a very intelligent one."[21] This judgment seems a touch harsh. Menzies would surely not have stayed in post for as long as he did—through such turbulent times—if it were true.

A successful intelligence leader must be adept at playing high-level politics. Alongside forming a close relationship with the prime minister and foreign secretary, politicking can be even more important than a real knowledge of the intricacies of espionage. After all, power is "an elusive blend of at least three elements: bargaining advantages, skill and will in using bargaining advantages, and other players' perceptions of the first two ingredients."[22] Menzies was adept at bureaucratic intrigue. John Bruce Lockhart claimed that he "didn't know much about spying but had a good instinct for Whitehall politics."[23] Similarly, Kim Philby, who served under Menzies, thought that his "real strength lay in a sensitive perception of the currents of Whitehall politics, in an ability to feel his way through the mazy corridors of power."[24] Both Menzies's biographer, Anthony Cave Brown, and SIS's official historian, Keith Jeffery, agree. C possessed an "unsurpassed reputation for surefootedness in a tricky world."[25] That SIS so successfully navigated the Whitehall Darwinian jungle is testament to Menzies's fancy footwork.[26] Although Patrick Reilly, the Foreign Office's liaison to SIS, later emphasized C's "considerable flair for intelligence work" over administration,[27] most evidence suggests that Menzies was a considerable Whitehall maneuverer. As we shall see, his skills allowed him to enhance his reputation and navigate the Whitehall bureaucracy to shape international relations.

The Second World War transformed SIS's standing in Whitehall. It started as a small and underfunded body but ended with a great deal of prestige. By extension, the war significantly enhanced Menzies's personal standing too. In fact, Churchill told the king, in front of Menzies, that Ultra had won the war. Ultra certainly aided Menzies's rise, but there was more to SIS's wartime contribution than taking credit for signals intelligence. Menzies had managed the Ultra material effectively, liaised impressively with foreign intelligence organizations and governments in exile, laid excellent foundations for the Anglo-American intelligence relationship that would become so important in the postwar world, and oversaw his service's important contributions to the various deception operations.[28]

With Churchill praising him in front of the king, Menzies's reputation, "and that of the office of 'C', had never stood higher." Menzies was at the pinnacle of British intelligence and a key adviser to a victorious government. With seemingly nowhere else to go, he apparently intimated to Alexander Cadogan, the permanent undersecretary at the Foreign Office, that it was time for him to resign. Cadogan resisted. He insisted that it was Menzies's duty to remain in post and oversee the transition from war to peace.[29] C agreed and found himself well placed to lead his service into the difficult transition from hot to Cold War.

As the Second World War wound down, Whitehall debate turned to the Russians. After some rather acrimonious discussions about the severity of the threat, the military and the Foreign Office eventually agreed that the next war would be with Moscow.[30] Thus Menzies and SIS returned to the foe of the interwar era, Soviet Russia. C supported a vigorous intelligence offensive against the Russians in an attempt to contain their growing influence. In doing so, he was keen to work with the Americans and proved a firm believer in the Anglo-American intelligence relationship. He knew that SIS did not have the power to fight the Russians worldwide alone but also realized that the Americans needed the UK too. He presciently knew that SIS's experience and overseas installations would prove invaluable.[31]

As an intelligence leader, Menzies had to balance competing obligations and priorities. He was expected to advise the foreign secretary and prime minister. He was expected to work closely with similar ranking officials in the Foreign Office, MI5, and military—who had their own competing interests. He was expected to oversee intelligence-collection efforts. He was expected to oversee covert operations. He was expected to liaise with counterparts in foreign intelligence services, such as the nascent CIA. C had to balance these roles simultaneously, and his performance in one affected his credibility and power in the others.

Nonetheless, Menzies navigated the postwar bureaucratic flux admirably. At the end of the war, C had acquired an irrefutable position within Whitehall. His service had fended off proposals to merge with MI5. It still controlled GC&CS (for the time being). It had absorbed the remnants of the SOE and seen off an attempted military takeover. Such was the mutual trust between Menzies and the Foreign Office that he was even allowed to draft the terms of reference for his own position.[32] Such trust is crucial to an intelligence leader, and Menzies had ensured SIS was at the heart of the foreign policy making process.

Menzies and Special Operations

Menzies's personal opinions are important in determining his impact on British approaches to covert action. Values and interpretations can be just as important in determining a leader's input over, say, more traditional bureaucratic forces.[33] C did not seem to have particularly strong personal opinions about covert action. The available records suggest he had an ambivalent wartime attitude to the SOE and to special operations more broadly. As C, he had had no responsibility for such activity during the war. Instead, he merely observed the activities of SOE, which, established in 1940, was independent from SIS. Although plenty of tension existed between the two secret services, Menzies was less hostile than some of his subordinates were. He tended to limit his criticism to resources, security issues, and the difficulties of liaison. Moreover, Menzies did not openly state a desire to run SOE-style activities himself but instead appeared cautious about their utility. For example, he expressed reservations about the use of targeted killing or assassination during the war. This was driven by practical rather than ethical considerations. He worried, for example, about Nazi retaliation and sought clear political guidance about what was to be achieved by plans to kill certain collaborators. He warned that killing targets such as political figures and transport chiefs would have had little impact on the German war effort because it was too highly organized.[34] According to the head of the SOE, Menzies was also neither "enthusiastic [nor] optimistic" about Operation Foxley, the secret plans to kill Hitler. There is little evidence of his organization actively aiding SOE in its 1944 effort.[35]

Menzies's caution continued after the war. He supported increased Foreign Office control over all overseas activities—including special operations.[36] Consequently, he supported the absorption of SOE into his organization. This was likely driven by bureaucratic factors and C's desire to gain control of a moribund, but related, organization at a time of bureaucratic uncertainty rather than any desire to engage in special operations. Control of SOE-type capabilities (however residual) enhanced Menzies's position on the Whitehall chessboard. Moreover, special operations can cause problems for intelligence agencies, far outweighing the benefits of bureaucratic empire building. Perhaps, on some level, Menzies supported absorption of SOE remnants under Foreign Office control to keep a lid on potential "blowback" tendencies.

As a man born of privilege and of a certain time, Menzies was likely a firm believer in Britain's global role and in the British Empire. Unlike others (especially in the military) who shared this outlook, however, there is no evidence of Menzies's passionately advocating covert action and special operations as a means of maintaining this global role.

By January 1948, as the Cold War heated up, C envisaged only a modest level of commitment to psychological warfare and special operations. Over lunch with John Slessor, head of the Royal Air Force, he suggested an annual budget of £0.5 million. Slessor, who thought £10 million would be more appropriate, was outraged. While this may suggest a lack of enthusiasm for such activity, Menzies had in fact quietly begun limited planning for special operations in the context of a future war.[37]

C's List

This chapter will now focus on the period between 1948 and 1951 in order to isolate C's impact on the policy arena. By 1948 Menzies had grown more assertive. He was particularly concerned with planning for future war and believed that political restraints prevented him from adequately preparing his special operations capability. He felt he could construct only "paper plans."[38] By the following year, Menzies effectively overruled the cautious foreign secretary, Ernest Bevin. Sending the diplomats into a spin, C declined to accept Bevin's refusal to authorize special operations planning in a future war and set about liberally interpreting the foreign secretary's decision to allow greater scope for action.[39] Here, then, is a clear example of an intelligence leader pushing the boundaries set by the democratically elected minister. By the 1950s Menzies had successfully established a Special Operations Targets Committee, which planned for "clandestine sabotage" in a future war with Russia.[40] Planning wartime special operations was pretty cheap and largely hypothetical, however, perhaps explaining how C got away with it.

Covert action in peacetime is more interesting—and dangerous. It removes the conjectures of war planning and seeks to make a more immediate, real, and perhaps physical impact. Here, government and bureaucratic politics came to the fore in shaping British approaches. The Chiefs of Staff were very keen to increase peacetime political warfare and special operations against the Soviets. They believed that "every weapon should be used." However, they also knew that such intensification would have serious political implications and that the Foreign Office would need to be involved. Therefore, the Chiefs of Staff vigorously pressed the diplomats to step up the effort and create a "world wide political warfare plan," in conjunction with relevant military actors.[41] They tasked the Joint Planning Staff to consider appropriate types of activity.[42]

The report reached the Foreign Office at the start of 1948. Orme "Moley" Sargent, its permanent undersecretary, called on C. He asked Menzies to examine the peacetime possibilities and implications of increasing political warfare and special operations.[43] A wily bureaucratic player, C made sure his reply highlighted the potential financial costs and competition for resources. He cleverly based his response on the assumption that he would receive adequate funds.[44] Like most Whitehall actors, Menzies was unlikely to pass up an opportunity to increase his organization's budget and was acutely aware of the need to balance competing obligations.

C was also aware of the interplay between covert action and intelligence. In January 1948 Menzies advised that SIS needed to "collect and collate the maximum possible intelligence regarding [Soviet] Political Warfare methods, her weaknesses and her fears." Acting on this intelligence, Britain "must wrest the initiative from Russia and keep it by constantly watching Russian tactics, seeking openings, assessing her intentions and forestalling her moves while making her react to ours." He maintained that clandestine propaganda can be "far more forceful than overt propaganda," before listing measures that "could be attempted by this Service." The measures ranged from spreading rumors to covertly controlling radio stations.[45] Beyond political warfare, he went on to list possible special operations, from framing diplomats to disrupting Communist Party meetings. In terms of economic warfare, Menzies's options ranged from instigating "go-slow" campaigns to bribery. Finally, paramilitary action ranged from sabotage all the way up to the "liquidation of selected individuals"[46]—a quite striking phrase to see in the British National Archives.

As noted previously, Sargent explicitly tasked Menzies with providing a list of possibilities. C's response clearly fulfilled this task, although it stopped short of considering their implications (other than financial). Menzies was not advocating particular operations, and it is unclear exactly what he personally hoped to achieve, other than securing more financial support for SIS and a general need to tackle Russian ascendancy. He therefore seemingly had little direct impact on policy and, if anything, acted as an intelligence chief cum good civil servant. His letter served more as a menu to aid the Foreign Office in thinking how best to shore up its capabilities while maintaining control in the face of military pressure. Interestingly, something similar happened some twenty-four years later when another C was asked to come up with a list of possible covert operations to be conducted against the Irish Republican Army.[47]

How was Menzies's list received? What impact did it have on policy discussion? Two levels of analysis offer insight. The first is the international. The global system was changing. The Soviet threat had solidified, thereby fixing the idea of Cold War bipolarity. Britain's foreign policy thinking, including covert intervention, inevitably began to reflect this shift (as did the United States'). Indeed, C's political masters—namely, Ernest Bevin—had shown some inclination to ease the restraints on subversion. At the start of 1948, Bevin established the Information Research Department (IRD) and a new propaganda directive—one which he acknowledged was offensive.[48] His change of heart was influenced by international developments: the formation of Cominform the previous year, its declaration against the Marshall Plan in November, and the advantage it provided Vyacheslav Molotov, Bevin's Soviet counterpart. At one level then, C's input came as part of a response to changes in international relations.

The bureaucratic level of analysis offers other insights into British approaches to covert action and the context in which C operated. First, the military had stepped up its campaign against the diplomats to intensify Cold War planning. An increase in special operations formed a significant part of this. Consequently, in what would become a pattern throughout the Cold War, the diplomats needed to appease the military voice while also protecting their own interests, emphasizing caution, and maintaining overall control. C soon found himself in the middle of this battle but seemingly sided with the Foreign Office—unsurprising given SIS's connections with it. Second, Bevin's slightly increased proclivity toward intensifying underhand tactics ignited a further debate about what else could be done. The military sensed a way in. Such pulling and hauling between the military and the Foreign Office forms a classic example of action being a result of political bargaining. Both sides fought for their own interests but also for what they believed was right.[49]

Against this background C's letter made an instant impact on the diplomats. Given his personal status—and that of his organization—within Whitehall, it is unsurprising that the letter ignited debate. C may not have advocated each and every item put forward, but they did somewhat provocatively counter Bevin's existing policy, which opposed attempts to incite rebellion behind the Iron Curtain. By simply bringing these options, including the idea of assassination, to the table, Menzies had (unwittingly or otherwise) reframed the debate. He had provided ideas that sparked conversation. Even if done merely to appease military voices, the discussion of such operations shaped the atmosphere inside the Foreign Office.

Many diplomats were unimpressed at the "confused and repetitive" list. Christopher Warner, overseeing propaganda, for example, thought it strategically flawed. If executed, C's options would incite rebellion behind the Iron Curtain, which Britain would be unable to back up with military force.[50] Warner expressed grave doubts about certain aspects and sought to press C for much more detailed proposals.[51] Interestingly, the list of potential operations soon became known as "C's proposals" and perceived as covering what C envisaged.[52] Regardless of whether he advocated them, Menzies therefore took ownership of these issues by default. William Hayter, the chairman of the JIC, agreed with Warner that such activity risked raising false hope among local dissidents. It could have led to violent Russian reprisals, which would have set back potential resistance.[53] Traditionally, the Foreign Office had been opposed to such activity, largely on pragmatic or strategic grounds. There is a sense in the files that many diplomats thought such dirty tricks had no place in peacetime. Perhaps this also formed part of an organizational identity within the Foreign Office favoring the more honorable methods of traditional diplomacy.

Meanwhile, the Air Ministry had received word that the Foreign Office was discussing the topic. It continued to pile on the pressure, asking for updates and complaining that "nothing [was] being done."[54] On February 13 C met with senior diplomats to discuss planning. His document formed the basis for discussion.[55] Sargent and Menzies then informed the military that steps were being taken to enhance political warfare capabilities. However, they were prepared to go only so far and, playing for time, stated that "special operations other than propaganda raise extremely difficult problems in peace-time" but were "still under consideration" in the Foreign Office.[56] This was technically true—and perhaps the construction of this list was only ever designed as a sop to military pressure. Either way, the Chiefs of Staff's reply made sure the diplomats knew that the military would not forget about it.[57]

Importantly, Hayter placed Menzies's options in their political context. He insisted that such activities should not represent an end in themselves but must be achieved in support of existing overt policy.[58] This was a crucial point in demonstrating C's role. C came up with a list of possible options but, given that he was the head of SIS and not a policymaker, these were inevitably divorced from policy. It was the role of the Foreign Office therefore to bridge the covert action–policy divide.

Attlee and Bevin agreed that the foreign secretary would decide "the extent to which 'black' propaganda methods" were to be used. They also acknowledged that some sort of official machinery may be needed to allow the Chiefs of Staff to make their contribution.[59] This, however, was swiftly dismissed by the Foreign Office officials.[60]

Sargent raised C's list of non-propaganda special operations with Bevin. He recommended that SIS "be given a free hand to carry out such special operations as are possible in the Soviet Union itself and in the Soviet Zones of Germany and Austria." These operations would aim to "transfer and dislocate the economy and administration of the country and to keep the Russian authorities on tenterhooks." As for the satellite states, Menzies should have power to establish "a nucleus organisation for subversive activities."[61] Sargent remained cautious, however, and recommended "only minor diversionary activities." "Even if we wished to," he told Bevin, "we could not overthrow Soviet control by special operations."[62]

Bevin was unimpressed with the idea of undertaking even "minor diversionary activities." He scribbled "grave objections" to "letting loose forces difficult to control." Bevin was "quite definite that nothing should be done" along these lines.[63] The various staffers and policy chiefs had not been able to persuade he who mattered most.

Bevin's rejection reveals two factors about the role of C. First, C (and his service) was not a rogue elephant. Operations needed Bevin's approval, and his perception of the external Soviet threat had not yet intensified to the required level to necessitate covert action.[64] Second, C played an advisory role—perhaps more akin to a staffer than a policy chief. This gives fresh insight into his responsibilities as an intelligence chief. Nonetheless, Menzies's list had an impact, and senior diplomats (under pressure from the military) continued to press Bevin on cautious and unprovocative plans.[65]

Albania and Operation Valuable

By the end of 1948, Whitehall's planners agreed to consider more ambitious operations designed to liberate Soviet satellite states. This approach culminated in Operation Valuable, the failed mission to liberate Albania. Through close analysis of recently released files, it is again possible to determine the role and influence of Menzies in the policymaking process.

Two factors had shaped the policy context and allowed such a seemingly ambitious operation to come into being. Neither involved C. First, the changing international system shaped the British response. The Cold War intensified throughout 1948. As a result of the coup in Czechoslovakia and the start of the Berlin blockade, JIC assessments of Russian expansionism toughened.[66] The perceived threat increased, and the international system became more divided and more dangerous. Reflecting these changes, Britain's foreign policy machinery hardened too. Covert action became a more amenable option for Britain's senior politicians and diplomats.

Second, bureaucratic politics had a discernible impact. The Foreign Office and Chiefs of Staff continued their long battle over approaches to, and control of, covert operations. The military continued to express frustration at the lack of a Cold War planning staff. Under pressure the Foreign Office was forced to play its hand. To fend off the military, Ivone Kirkpatrick, head of the Foreign Office's German Section, finally informed a surprised military audience about the existence of the Russia Committee. He described the top secret Foreign Office body, which had been established back in 1946, as, in effect, Whitehall's Cold War planning staff. This, however, was an overstatement, perhaps designed to appease the military. Significantly, Kirkpatrick invited the Chiefs of Staff to send a representative—an offer that was swiftly accepted—but he warned them not to get their hopes up in terms of ambitious new operations.[67]

This concession had immediate implications. The Chiefs of Staff sent Arthur Tedder, chief of the Air Staff, as their representative. It is perhaps therefore of little surprise that his very first meeting saw liberation operations on the table for the first time. Tedder and his new colleagues pondered the merits of proactively starting a civil war behind the Iron Curtain. They agreed that "our aim should certainly be to liberate the countries within the Soviet Orbit by any means short of war."[68] Albania seemed the most appropriate target, owing to its isolation from the Soviets following Moscow's schism with Yugoslavia.

Although the Chiefs of Staff strongly supported the idea, it was initially floated by Kirkpatrick. Importantly, Menzies had no say at all. He was not a diplomat and was therefore not present at the Russia Committee meeting. Consequently, C was initially a reactive player in the Albania discussions. He had no involvement in the overarching foreign policy but also, and unlike earlier in the year, was not asked to provide a list of ideas to frame the debate. He merely found a role in advising the policymakers after the idea had already been floated.

With Clement Attlee's and Ernest Bevin's approval in principle, SIS began planning. Again, C's organization was no rogue elephant. The initial plan placed primary focus on relieving pressure on Greece, which was in the middle of a civil war, by attacking targets in southern Albania.[69] Kenneth Cohen of SIS suggested that he had an agent "ready and willing to go" who could be infiltrated into Albania in 1949 in order to assess the potential for special operations.[70] Menzies proposed this to Sargent, but the latter was unimpressed and requested a further paper on Albania.[71] By February 1949 the plan had evolved into fomenting insurrection in parts of Albania, weakening Soviet authority, and potentially even detaching Albania from the Soviet orbit altogether.[72] Worried that the Americans might have been planning something along similar lines, Menzies insisted that a note about the necessity of coordination be included in the plan. He then approved the proposed operation.[73]

Unfortunately for Menzies, it was more ambitious than the Foreign Office would have liked.[74] The diplomats did, however, offer a "constructive" response whereby an official in their Southern Department developed a counterplan along similar lines to those laid out by SIS. The difference, however, was that the Foreign Office emphasized intelligence gathering. The diplomats stressed to Menzies the importance of establishing a solid intelligence-gathering network before attempting operations. Menzies was told that Bevin would need to be assured that conditions on the ground were ripe before he offered final approval.[75]

C welcomed the suggestion. Demonstrating his leadership role in balancing intelligence gathering and covert action, however, he pointed out a flaw in the Foreign Office's two-step approach of intelligence followed by covert action. In practice, C informed William Strang (who had replaced Sargent as permanent undersecretary), the two activities overlapped. It was impossible to gather intelligence on resistance merely by inserting a few agents into the country. SIS could know for sure whether there was substance behind the words only by using more "direct methods of probing." Small-scale operations were therefore necessary to test local preparedness to take action, and these in themselves were a form of intelligence collection. For Menzies, therefore, agents had a dual role: intelligence gathering and event shaping. Menzies added that if such probing achieved satisfactory results, then the operation could move on to the next phase.[76] Interestingly, American intelligence leaders were simultaneously coming to the same conclusion. Allen Dulles, director of the CIA, also believed that "secret operations particularly through support of resistance groups, provide one of the most important sources of secret intelligence, and the information gained from secret intelligence must immediately be put to use in guiding and directing secret operations."[77]

Bevin agreed with Menzies and approved the approach in April 1949. Strang informed C of Bevin's agreement to "set up an intelligence system in Southern Albania" to test local preparedness for action. If the outcome was "encouraging," then SIS could "infiltrate instructors in modern guerrilla warfare, in order to recruit, arm, feed, clothe and train anti-Communist supporters for military operations against Greek rebel bases and lines of communication." Bevin decided to leave the possibility of extending the operation to insurrection across Albania for a later date. It depended on progress in the south.[78]

Whitehall therefore opted for an incremental approach. Given the ultimate failure of the operation, this turns out to have been wise. Yet there were disadvantages, as Menzies himself pointed out. If the initial operation was not extended, then any losses incurred in the preliminary stages would have been in vain. Menzies questioned whether it was worth incurring the risk of setting up an intelligence organization unless the operation was definitely going to be followed through.[79] And yet with hindsight, starting on such a small scale likely saved many more lives than it cost.

Menzies's input fades out of the declassified records after Bevin authorized the operation. We now know that although Valuable was unsuccessful, it lingered on in some form into the mid-1950s. As yet, however, there is little evidence of Menzies's role in this. Nonetheless, the declassified documents on Albania reveal the role of C as an intelligence leader. He was relatively passive or reactive. The context for liberation operations had been shaped by international developments and bureaucratic wrangling. The Russia Committee had suggested Albania, while C's subordinates had drawn up the plan. At this point, Menzies became involved in all three elements of policymaking. He looked downward for options, sideways to help build a coalition of support within the Foreign Office, and upward to gain Bevin's confidence. Menzies did have personal impact in shaping the plan and liaising with the Foreign Office at the most senior levels. He offered his experience in understanding the relationships among intelligence, operations, and policy—and in balancing competing priorities. Finally, Menzies's input was explicitly heeded by both Strang and Bevin. His was a powerful Whitehall voice and directly shaped the operation. Nonetheless, final approval quite rightly lay with Bevin and Attlee. SIS, and its chief, was tied to the core executive. It is crucial to note, however, that Bevin's options had been shaped and narrowed by the policy processes taking place beneath him, leaving him with what political scientists would call bounded rationality.

Pinpricks

Following the failure of liberation, Britain opted for a more cautious approach in 1950, known as "pinpricks." Once again, the approach reflected recent changes in the international system. Although the international balance of power remained similar to what it had been in 1948, the Soviets had acquired the nuclear bomb. This created issues of deterrence and escalation that inevitably shaped foreign policy—and approaches to covert action. At the substate level, pinpricks reflected the outcome of institutional learning within Whitehall alongside compromise between the diplomats and the military. Most interestingly within the context of this study, however, pinpricks demonstrated evidence of a more active and autonomous role for C as an intelligence leader.

The new pinprick approach had its roots in Menzies's 1948 list of potential special operations. While assassination schemes unsurprisingly fell by the wayside, less controversial proposals involving the spread of discord and nuisance held more weight. The pinprick approach had a dual function: to use small-scale pilot schemes to test conditions for covert action while gradually chipping away at Soviet authority. A pattern of limited strikes against limited targets in individual countries would sow the seeds of dissension. It would ultimately make the orbit a liability rather than an asset. Moreover, pinpricks would also decrease the risk of escalation to a nuclear war.[80]

Menzies appears to have been a driver of this approach, and for the first time he might be considered a sort of policy innovator. The plans ultimately approved were very similar to the ideas he had put forward back in 1948. For example, one plan involved measures to "incriminate the senior [Communist] officers in the eyes of the Russian security police."[81] Other aspects included economic warfare, black propaganda, and whispering campaigns, again easily traced back to Menzies's list.[82] Meanwhile, C had drafted another, more recent memorandum on Cold War possibilities in Europe. It suggested "minor" activities that might be termed "pinpricks." Senior diplomats argued that "it might well be worth while to try certain minor practical activities, such as had been suggested in Sir Stewart Menzies' paper. There was nothing to lose by such activities, and, if successful, they might well throw grit into the machine of the Communist regimes." This was, of course, subject to ministerial approval.[83] Menzies did not limit his attentions to Europe. He pressed for "clandestine propaganda" in southern China to promote dissension between the various sections of the Communist Party.[84] By mid-1950 propaganda was said to be having a "considerable effect" in Burma and making "a contribution" in Siam.[85] Proposals were described as "necessarily limited in scope" and "in the nature of an experiment."[86] Menzies's tone, between 1948 and 1950, had shifted from one of passively providing options toward one of greater advocacy. The proposals directly influenced discussions by senior diplomats inside the Foreign Office, including the heads of both the Northern and Southern Departments.

The pinpricks strategy gained approval in another new body, the Official Committee on Communism (Overseas).[87] The AC(O), as it was (perhaps slightly illogically) known, brought together only a handful of the most senior cold warriors from the Foreign Office and military. Although not a member of the Russia Committee, C was a member of the AC(O). The minutes suggest that Menzies was generally quiet during these meetings, but he did now sit on the most senior Cold War planning body. This consequently afforded C the scope to engage in policy discussions and become more of a policy actor than hitherto when he was excluded from the Russia Committee. Despite not being particularly vocal, C maintained an ability to shape the approach and frame the agenda as a member of the AC(O). Given his status and bargaining skills, he therefore held an important voice in formulating proposals for covert action. The AC(O) submitted the pinprick plans to Attlee and Bevin. By the end of 1951, they had been approved with little fuss—although it remains clear that ministerial approval was vital.[88] Again, however, the choices available to ministers had been severely constrained by bureaucratic politics.

The pinprick approach was a product of its time and context. Menzies's ideas held more sway in 1950 than in 1948 for four reasons. First, the intensified international system necessitated a tougher response. Second, the Foreign Office needed to engage in some sort of covert Cold War activity to appease the increasingly vocal military. This bureaucratic bargaining created a compromise of relatively unambitious operations. Third, Whitehall had learned from the mistakes of Albania and was now more receptive to Menzies's ideas.

Fourth, Menzies remained a key voice inside Whitehall, with a very strong personal and institutional standing. It seems that his second round of suggestions was more a recommendation than the first, which had served merely as a menu. Accordingly, perhaps they were taken more seriously.

Conclusions and Broader Implications

This chapter has focused in depth on one particular intelligence leader, Stewart Menzies. In doing so, it has raised some broader issues surrounding the role of intelligence leaders more generally and their place in the policymaking process. Questions regarding the nature of the position, the skills required, the influence held, and the impact on democracy of their engagement in what some have described as secret foreign policy can and should be asked of other intelligence leaders in Britain, the United States, and beyond.

It is important to consider the qualities necessary in an intelligence leader. Menzies demonstrated that an ability to navigate the bureaucracies and corridors of power is essential. This is perhaps even more important than a detailed knowledge of espionage. As C, Menzies had a strong reputation within Whitehall built on his wartime successes, but he also possessed adeptness at political maneuverings. This ensured that he had the ear of senior policymakers. Given the blurred lines among covert action, intelligence, and policy, C had theoretical scope to become a quasi-policy entrepreneur and drive British covert action and potentially interventionism.

One must therefore consider how much power an intelligence leader actually has. In the case of Menzies, he could (and did) offer suggestions, frame issues, and shape approaches to covert action. However, he did so as part of a broader process involving the Foreign Office and foreign secretary. Indeed, SIS was close to the Foreign Office system, and there was a great deal of discussion, liaison, and compromise between the two organizations. This might have been different in the United States, where the CIA was, and remains, independent. In terms of authorization, British operations had to be approved by the foreign secretary and often the prime minister. This is important, for it constrained the power of the intelligence leader and prevented SIS from becoming a rogue elephant or engaging in wild operations (as often depicted in popular culture). Of course, this role is entirely appropriate in a democratic society, and there can be little place for headstrong intelligence leaders engaging in their own secret foreign policy without the knowledge of elected representatives. That said, C, as part of the bureaucracy, did constrain choices and frame the debate for Bevin.

It must also be remembered that an intelligence leader is just one actor in a broader and complex bureaucracy. Menzies was skilled at navigating this but still found himself constrained by bureaucratic politics. It is difficult to separate agency from structure, but the effectiveness of his input was often at least partially shaped by the ongoing battle between the Foreign Office and the military, which framed the agenda and sought compromises. Such constraints shape the impact of any intelligence leader, as all must work alongside leaders of other government organizations and departments.

C's place in the policymaking process is testament to Menzies's leadership and elevated place in the Whitehall bureaucracy. By contrast, for example, his successor, John Sinclair, lacked many of Menzies's political attributes, and the 1950s accordingly saw Sinclair occasionally bypassed by his own officers. Anthony Eden's personal use of SIS over Suez forms a prime example.[89] Menzies's standing in Whitehall afforded him a voice and ensured that SIS was well integrated into the broader machinery.

A final question concerns the ability of an intelligence leader to shape international relations. At one level leaders' individual agency will always be constrained by international structural factors. As neorealist scholars would argue, foreign policy (and by extension covert action) is a dependent subsystem of the international global system. This was certainly apparent in the early Cold War as Britain's proclivity toward covert operations closely mirrored the evolving Soviet threat, intensifying bipolarity and deterrence. As advocates of foreign policy analysis would argue, however, such an approach underplays both human agency and bureaucratic bargaining. Intelligence leaders operate within this context. They are theoretically able to affect international relations and even become policy entrepreneurs. However, they are prisoners of the broader bureaucracies in which they serve. In Britain especially they are integrated into the Foreign Office's policymaking process. Covert action is therefore unlikely to be the product of one man, bypassing the machinery to deal with the prime minister directly.

Notes

1. For examples, see Michael S. Goodman, *The Official History of the Joint Intelligence Committee*, vol. 1, *From the Approach of the Second World War to Suez* (London: Routledge, 2014); Keith Jeffery, *MI6: The History of the Secret Intelligence Service, 1909–1949* (London: Bloomsbury, 2011); Christopher Andrew, *Defence of the Realm: The Authorized History of MI5* (London: Allen Lane, 2010); Percy Cradock, *Know Your Enemy: How the Joint Intelligence Committee Saw the World* (London: John Murray, 2002); Richard Aldrich, *GCHQ* (London: HarperPress, 2011).

2. See, for example, William Daugherty, *Executive Secrets: Covert Action and the Presidency* (Lexington: University Press of Kentucky, 2009); Loch Johnson, *America's*

Secret Power: The CIA in a Democratic Society (Oxford: Oxford University Press, 1989); Gregory Treverton, *Covert Action: The Limits of Intervention in the Postwar World* (New York: Basic, 1987).

3. See Matthew D'Ancona, *In It Together: The Inside Story of the Coalition Government* (London: Penguin, 2014).

4. Christopher Hope, "MI6 Chief Sir John Sawers: We Foiled Iranian Nuclear Weapons Bid," *Daily Telegraph*, July 12, 2012, http://www.telegraph.co.uk/news/uk news/terrorism-in-the-uk/9396360/MI6-chief-Sir-John-Sawers-We-foiled-Iranian -nuclear-weapons-bid.html.

5. Rory Cormac, "GCHQ's Cyber Offensive: Online Covert Action," *Ballots and Bullets* (blog), February 13, 2014, http://nottspolitics.org/2014/02/13/gchqs-cyber -offensive-online-covert-action/.

6. Graham Allison and Philip Zelikow, *Essence of Decision: Explaining the Cuban Missile Crisis* (New York: Longman, 1999), 302.

7. John Bruce Lockhart, "Intelligence: A British View," in *British and American Approaches to Intelligence*, ed. Ken Robertson (Basingstoke: Macmillan/RUSI, 1987), 37.

8. Mark Lowenthal, *From Secret to Policy*, 3rd ed. (Thousand Oaks, CA: Sage, 2006), 57.

9. Philip Davies, *MI6 and the Machinery of Spying* (London: Frank Cass, 2004), 227–28.

10. Richard Aldrich, *The Hidden Hand: Britain, America and Cold War Secret Intelligence* (London: John Murray, 2001), 14.

11. James Scott and Jerel Rosati, "Such Other Functions and Duties: Covert Action and American Intelligence Policy," in *Strategic Intelligence*, vol. 3, *Covert Action, behind the Veils of Secret Foreign Policy*, ed. Loch Johnson (Westport, CT: Praeger Security International, 2007), 101; Arthur Hulnick, "What's Wrong with the Intelligence Cycle," *Intelligence and National Security* 21 (2006): 971.

12. Burke Trend to Harold Wilson, March 13, 1967, PREM 13/268, British National Archives (TNA).

13. Allison and Zelikow, *Essence of Decision*, 300.

14. Jeffery, *MI6*, 620.

15. Richard Aldrich, "Counting the Cost of Intelligence: The Treasury, National Service and GCHQ," *English Historical Review* 532 (2013): 599–602.

16. Anthony Cave Brown, *C: The Secret Life of Sir Stewart Graham Menzies, Spymaster to Winston Churchill* (London: Macmillan, 1988), 82–98.

17. *Oxford Dictionary of National Biography*, s.v., "Menzies, Sir Stewart Graham (1890–1968)," 2004, http://www.oxforddnb.com/view/article/34988.

18. Ibid.

19. Nigel West, *At Her Majesty's Secret Service*, 55; Jeffery, *MI6*, 478.

20. Cave Brown, *C*, 689.

21. Quoted in West, *At Her Majesty's Secret Service*, 54.

22. Allison and Zelikow, *Essence of Decision*, 300.

23. Jeffery, *MI6*, 742.

24. Quoted in Stephen Dorril, *MI6: 50 Years of Special Operations* (London: Fourth Estate, 2000), 5.

25. Cave Brown, *C*, 685.

26. Jeffery, *MI6*, 748.

27. Ibid., 742.

28. Ibid., 747.

29. Cave Brown, *C*, 672, 677.

30. See Cradock, *Know Your Enemy*, 25–50.

31. Cave Brown, *C*, 688.

32. Jeffery, *MI6*, 725, 628.

33. See for example, Mark Bevir, Oliver Daddow, and Ian Hall, "Introduction: Interpreting British Foreign Policy," *British Journal of Politics and International Relations* 15 (2013): 163–74.

34. Jeffery, *MI6*, 539.

35. Mark Seaman, *Operation Foxley: The British Plan to Kill Hitler* (London: PRO, 1998), 15.

36. Jeffery, *MI6*, 628.

37. Ibid., 660–61.

38. C to Hayter, November 2, 1948, FO 1093/373, TNA.

39. C to Hayter, March 15, 1949, FO 1093/475, TNA.

40. Colonel G Gordon Lennox to Brig C Price, May 5, 1950, DEFE 11/279, TNA.

41. Stapleton, Secretary of the Chiefs of Staff Committee, to Sargent, December 23, 1947, FO 1093/375, TNA.

42. Joint Planning Staff, "Special Operations," JP (47)118, December 17, 1947, FO 1093/375, TNA.

43. Sargent to Stapleton, January 9, 1948, FO 1093/375, TNA.

44. C to Sargent, January 20, 1948, FO 1093/375, TNA.

45. C, "The Capabilities of Secret Service in Peace in Support of an Overall Political Plan," January 20, 1948, FO 1093/375, TNA.

46. C, "The Capabilities of Secret Service in Peace in Support of an Overall Political Plan: Annex B—Special Operations Other Than Clandestine Propaganda," January 20, 1948, FO 1093/375, TNA.

47. Interview with a retired intelligence officer.

48. Circular telegram from Foreign Office to His Majesty's representatives abroad, January 23, 1948, FO 1093/375, TNA.

49. Allison and Zelikow, *Essence of Decision*, 303.

50. Warner to Sargent, January 24, 1948, FO 1093/375, TNA.

51. Warner to Sargent, February 6, 1948, FO 1093/375, TNA.

52. See, for example, Hayter to Sargent, March 9, 1948, FO 1093/375, TNA.

53. Ibid.

54. Air Ministry to Hayter, February 6, 1948, FO 1093/375, TNA.

55. "Clandestine Support for Anti-Communist Propaganda," Minutes of meeting, February 13, 1948, FO 1093/375, TNA.

56. Sargent to Stapleton, February 27, 1948, FO 1093/375, TNA.

57. Stapleton to Sargent, March 5, 1948, FO 1093/375, TNA.

58. Hayter to Sargent, March 9, 1948, FO 1093/375, TNA.

59. Brook to Attlee, "Anti-Communist Propaganda," March 1948, FO 1093/375, TNA.

60. Brook to Hayter, March 23, 1948, FO 1093/375, TNA.

61. Sargent to Bevin, March 30, 1948, FO 1093/375, TNA.

62. Ibid.

63. Notes on Sargent to Bevin, March 30, 1948, FO 1093/375, TNA.

64. Handwritten note by Bevin on Sargent to Bevin, March 30, 1948, FO 1093/375, TNA.

65. Orme Sargent to Hayter and Warner, May 13, 1948, FO 1093/375, TNA.

66. Cradock, *Know Your Enemy*, 6–27.

67. Confidential annex to CoS(48)139th Meeting, September 29, 1948, FO 1093/370, TNA.

68. Russia Committee, Minutes, November 25, 1948, FO 371/1687, TNA.

69. "Notes on Counter Guerrilla Action in Albania," December 20, 1948, FO 1093/452, TNA.

70. Jeffery, *MI6*, 713.

71. Ibid.

72. "Communist Action in Albania," February 3, 1949, FO 1093/452, TNA.

73. Jeffery, *MI6*, 713.

74. Ibid.

75. Ibid.

76. C to Strang, March 4, 1949, FO 1093/452, TNA.

77. See James Lockhart's chapter in this volume.

78. Jeffery, *MI6*, 714.

79. "Policy towards Albania," March 21, 1949, FO 800/437, TNA.

80. Rory Cormac, "The Pinprick Approach: Whitehall's Top-Secret Anti-Communist Committee and the Evolution of British Covert Action Strategy," *Journal of Cold War Studies* 16 (2014): 5–28; AC(O) Minutes, February 15, 1950, AC(O)(50)4th Meeting, CAB 134/4, TNA.

81. "Proposed Activities behind the Iron Curtain," November 1950, AC(O)(50)52(Third Revise), CAB 21/2750, TNA.

82. Ibid.

83. AC(O) Minutes, February 15, 1950, AC(O)(50)4th Meeting, CAB 134/4, TNA.

84. AC(O) Minutes, June 7, 1950, AC(O)(50)19th Meeting, CAB 134/4, TNA.

85. "The 'Cold War' in the Far East," July 19, 1950, AC(O)(50)31, CAB 134/3, TNA.

86. "Proposed Activities behind the Iron Curtain" (Third Revise), November 1950, AC(O)(50)52, CAB 21/2750, TNA.

87. AC(O) Minutes, February 15, 1950, AC(O)(50)4th Meeting, CAB 134/4, TNA.

88. Prime Minister's Office to Cliffe (Secretary of AC(O)), December 21, 1950, PREM 8/1365, TNA; "Anti-Communist Activities in Europe," December 22, 1950, AC(M)(50)2, CAB 134/2, TNA.

89. See discussion in Goodman, *Official History of the Joint Intelligence Committee*.

11   What Chance for Leadership?

Patrick Dean, Chairman of the Joint Intelligence
Committee, and the Suez Crisis

Danny Steed

In the world of spy chiefs, focus is generally placed on the leaders of the operational intelligence services. In Britain this focus results in examinations of the leaders of the Secret Intelligence Service (SIS), the Government Communications Headquarters (GCHQ), and the Security Service (MI5). Frequently neglected, however, is consideration of the chairman of the Joint Intelligence Committee (JIC). This omission is curious as the JIC dates back to 1936 and, having been established "to remedy the lack of co-ordination in the British intelligence community,"[1] it has been an increasingly important part of the architecture of British intelligence ever since. The JIC as a whole has suffered from a lack of understanding that has been present even in contemporary times. The current chairman of the JIC, Jon Day, states that the genesis of Michael Goodman's recent official history of the JIC was in the Butler report that was commissioned to examine the use of intelligence before the start of the 2003 Iraq War. Day says that before this time "little had been published or was known outside of Whitehall and a few academic institutions about the workings of the JIC."[2] If there is a general lack of understanding about the JIC as a whole, it follows that there will also be a lack of engagement and analysis about the role that the chairman of the JIC plays in intelligence. This chapter begins to address that shortcoming through an examination of one of the JIC's most notable chairmen.

Of all the men who have held the post of chairman, few are as fascinating as Sir Patrick Dean. Dean served in this post from 1953 until 1960, but his experiences at the time of the Suez Crisis in 1956 provide ample material to consult with regard to intelligence leadership. He can be seen as a man for all seasons in intelligence scholarship. W. Scott Lucas suggests that Dean represents the missing link in the historiography of the Suez Crisis, with little progress made on establishing his full role in the events of 1956 for two main reasons.[3] First, he "wrote no memoirs, gave few interviews and, to my knowledge, left no private papers for others to consult."[4] When interviewed he gave precious little away to researchers. This is best shown in his interview for the Suez Oral History Project, compiled in the late 1980s. Dean's answers were brief, and he went so far as to say he had little recollection of the discussions with Guy Mollet and Christian Pineau or of any discussions related to the covert Omega program.[5] When he was asked about the joint Anglo-American covert plan for regime change in Syria, Operation Straggle, he responded, "That's news to me."[6]

The second reason for historians' inability to determine Dean's full role in the Suez Crisis lies in his total devotion to the Official Secrets Act. This position is clear in a 1976 letter Dean wrote to Selwyn Lloyd, foreign secretary during the Suez Crisis, concerning Chester Cooper, a researcher who was visiting London seeking interviews for his book *The Lion's Last Roar*.[7] Dean wrote, "In spite of our [Dean and Cooper's] close friendship, we have never discussed this in any detail and I have always taken the line with him as others that I consider myself bound by the Official Secrets Act, and that at the relevant time I was acting on instructions and have no more to say."[8] The difficulty of ascertaining Dean's specific actions in the Suez Crisis is made all the more intriguing by a cryptic statement made by Frank Cooper, who has declared, "The only chap who knew everything was Pat Dean."[9] Nevertheless, by considering his role throughout the Suez Crisis much can be gleaned about intelligence leadership.

This chapter will look at Dean's role in the run-up to the Suez Crisis, through the crisis itself, and after the crisis. It will show that Dean had precious little room before and during the crisis to display any real leadership. This was due to the constrained position that the JIC held as a Chiefs of Staff (COS) body within the architecture of the British government. Dean was also guilty of falling prey to the politicization of intelligence processes in December 1956. Despite this Dean showed significant leadership in the year following the Suez Crisis, in securing and overseeing the transfer of the JIC from the COS and into the Cabinet Office structure. This centralization of British intelligence remains one of the most underrecognized changes to the structure of British intelligence that has occurred in its history.

Ultimately, through this case study of Patrick Dean, it will be shown that intelligence leaders occupy an inherently fragile position. Dean was quietly effective during the Suez Crisis, but the JIC as a body was also largely marginalized. Dean led the JIC but also became an active (albeit uneasy) participant in the collusion policy of Prime Minister Anthony Eden.[10] Dean then led the move that transformed the JIC into a truly centralized structure, a structure that endures to this day. The leadership dynamic in the JIC is clearly different from those in the operational services, but engagement with the Suez Crisis alone reveals that there is much to be considered for leadership at the level of the JIC.

The Run-Up to the Suez Crisis

In the run-up to the Suez Crisis, precious little opportunity presented itself for real intelligence leadership on Dean's part. The JIC has typically been credited with producing good reports during the Suez Crisis,[11] but ultimately, it also suffered from being "marginalised and unheard."[12] While these analyses are no doubt correct, they fail to engage critically with the weaknesses of JIC assessment at the time, which can be described only as falling evermore prey to a dominating assumption in Eden's government, that the leader of Egypt, Gamal Abdel Nasser, was increasingly a puppet of the Soviet Union.

The reason such criticism has not been raised is that in April 1956 the JIC issued an assessment saying that while Egypt was clearly becoming dependent on Russia, this "does not mean that Nasser has consciously resigned himself to becoming an instrument of Soviet policy."[13] However, the JIC changed its analytic line thereafter and increasingly echoed the dominant British position that Nasser was becoming a Soviet vassal. Historians Richard Aldrich, Rory Cormac, and Michael Goodman state that by the time the Suez Canal Company was nationalized, the JIC "immediately equated nationalist uprisings with communist-inspired insurrections: it was unthinkable to have one without the other."[14] Former JIC chairman Percy Cradock also notes that in any event it has to be doubted whether by the spring of 1956 JIC assessments were consulted by or had any influence on Eden.[15]

The JIC's lack of policy impact does not, however, represent any failure of leadership by Dean. Instead it is reflective of the structural limitation that the JIC suffered with at that particular time. To understand that limitation, it is necessary to consult the JIC charter from the 1950s:

The Joint Intelligence Committee is given the following responsibilities under the Chiefs of Staff:

(i) To give higher direction to, and to keep under review, intelligence operations and defence security matters.

(ii) To assemble, appreciate and present intelligence as required by the Chiefs of Staff and to initiate such other reports as may be required or as the Committee may deem necessary.

(iii) To keep under review the organization and working of intelligence and defence security as a whole at home and overseas so as to ensure efficiency, economy and a rapid adaptation to changing requirements, and to advise what changes are deemed necessary.

(iv) To co-ordinate the activities of Joint Intelligence Committees under United Kingdom Commands overseas and to maintain an exchange of intelligence with them.

(v) To maintain liaison with appropriate intelligence and defence security agencies in the self-governing Commonwealth countries and the United States and other foreign countries, and with the intelligence authorities of international defence organizations of which the United Kingdom is a member.

(vi) To report progress in the spheres of its responsibility.[16]

The second of these allocated responsibilities reveals the inherent structural limitation that impeded the JIC. The requirement to present intelligence "as required by the Chiefs of Staff" shows clearly that the JIC was unable to provide intelligence *directly* to cabinet-level policy deliberations. Instead the JIC was simply an intelligence body housed within the military command structure, the dissemination of whose product could only be guaranteed to reach the COS. There could be no guarantee that JIC product would always reach the cabinet. The only JIC product that can reliably be asserted to have enjoyed regular broad circulation beyond the COS was the *Weekly Review of Current Intelligence*. Marginalized and unheard, the JIC found its position during the crisis thus stemming not from any lack of leadership on Dean's part but instead from structural limitations that went hand-in-hand with its position in the architecture of government. This position, as a COS body, conditioned and restricted the impact that the JIC could hope to have far more than the actual quality of the material it ultimately produced. Whatever its intrinsic merits or demerits, the intelligence that reached the cabinet had questionable impact owing to the increasingly bellicose attitude of Eden toward Nasser before the latter nationalized the Suez Canal in July 1956.

The Suez Crisis

During the Suez Crisis itself, Dean's actions and the JIC's performance did not coincide. Because Dean acted as an active policy participant in the Sèvres collusion and because he tried in December 1956 to drive a political agenda of intelligence collection and analysis, consideration of his role needs to be, in regard to at least these two events, treated separately from consideration of the intelligence body that he led.

A trend is immediately apparent in the JIC's performance during the crisis. In the run-up to the nationalization of the Suez Canal Company in July 1956, the JIC indeed produced some reports of policy relevance. From that time on, however, the stream of JIC material became increasingly focused on the preparation of military operations against Egypt. In sum the JIC transitioned from informing policy development to supporting agreed policy. One JIC document mattered to policy-level deliberations at the outset of the crisis: *Egyptian Nationalisation of the Suez Canal Company.*

The report began by assuming that the British government would seek to reverse Egyptian actions; it did not challenge that view or present any alternative options. Instead it offered financial options that it assessed as open to London and Paris for use against Egypt, notably that two-thirds of canal revenue was paid directly to London and Paris instead of remaining in Egypt.[17] The report most notably provided a calculation of the believed effects that Western action might have on other Arab states:

(a) If steps taken by the West were to lead to an early change of Government in Egypt and a settlement satisfactory to the West, the other Arab States who have a natural admiration for strength, would probably swing in our favour. . . .

(b) Should Western military action be insufficient to ensure early and decisive victory, the international consequences both in the Arab States and elsewhere *might give rise to extreme embarrassment and cannot be foreseen.*[18]

In (b) the JIC provided what was, in retrospect, a most prescient warning.

Despite this vital warning to British policymakers, the significance of the report lies not with any of its contents but instead with the date on which it was circulated. Although the report was produced on August 3, the COS did not approve it for distribution until August 10, one week after its production and a full two weeks after the cabinet had agreed on a policy response. The JIC was able to provide good analysis, but it was unable to provide timely analysis. This can be said with certainty given the knowledge that Britain had agreed in cabinet on July 27 on a policy course of action that sought to reverse the action of nationalization, "with force if necessary."[19] This position is also noted in the diary of Eden's wife, Clarissa: "Anthony and the Cabinet decide to fight, if necessary alone."[20] The JIC had missed its one real window of opportunity to affect the development of British policy, and from August onward its analytic focus became one of supporting the military planning cycles in the development of Operation Musketeer.

At this stage, Dean's specific actions need to be disentangled from the JIC's output, for two of his actions during the crisis raise serious questions about the role that an intelligence leader should play in relation to the policy masters. First, Dean contributed to a closed architecture of decision making in the

British government. Dean was not alone in contributing to this architecture; he, Sir Ivone Kirkpatrick (Dean's immediate superior as permanent under-secretary of the Foreign Office), and Prime Minister Eden together achieved an effective circumvention of the broader Whitehall machinery that closed off any effective open challenges to Eden's Suez policy before it was executed.

Eden is well-known for having had a successful career in foreign policy and for never having held any domestic post before he became prime minister. This long affiliation with foreign affairs, however, left Eden disinclined to delegate tasks,[21] meaning that his appointee for foreign secretary, Selwyn Lloyd, was "bound to be a second-in-command. He was not subservient, but he knew that in major issues he had to carry the Prime Minister with him without any question."[22] During the crisis the significant restriction on the flow of information around government worried many officials. Sir Frank Cooper, the head of the Air Staff Secretariat, said he was "increasingly aware that people had been hiding things, in particular that you could not trust a damn thing that the top politicians or those in the know at the Foreign Office said."[23] Cooper added that normally open channels of communication suddenly became much more constricted. Sir Archibald Ross explains the actions of Eden thus: "I think the fact is that at certain points Eden simply circumvented everybody!"[24] Eden was able to circumvent the normal machinery of government and use a closed channel of communications based on the Permanent Undersecretaries Department (PUSD) because, according to Douglas Dodds-Parker, "if you are in a position of power as Prime Minister or even as Foreign Minister, knowing your way around, [you] get hold of two or three key people and keep everybody else from finding out."[25] Ivone Kirkpatrick and Patrick Dean were Eden's two people of choice.

Kirkpatrick was a natural choice for two reasons: first, he was endlessly loyal to Eden's position on Suez, and second, his position formally controlled PUSD (although Geoffrey McDermott was the director of PUSD at the time, McDermott was subordinate to both Kirkpatrick and Dean). PUSD was a secretive communications link between the Foreign Office and the intelligence services. Its communications were secret, and therefore, it was a perfect vehicle to exclude the broader Foreign Office from policy discussions. Dean was the final link in this chain of circumvention in Whitehall; he was an essential liaison between the policy world and the covert world. Dean's usual role of overseeing intelligence operations was expropriated along with PUSD in order to facilitate closed discussions. Dean was uniquely important, as he was the supervising official in PUSD, directly subordinate to Kirkpatrick. If matters were important enough for Kirkpatrick's attention, Dean said, they "would go up to him through me."[26]

Dean's participation in this rump group showed that he had become politicized. In leadership terms Dean not only failed to challenge what was clearly an inappropriate use of the PUSD channels, but he also became a willing participant in closing down other channels of communication when they were needed most. Sir Patrick Reilly, Dean's immediate predecessor as the chairman of the JIC, told the Suez Oral History Project that every morning Dean received a series of telegrams that were kept out of all normal channels of distribution. These telegrams, Reilly asserts, contained references to the pretexts for using military force against Egypt.[27] Meanwhile, Kirkpatrick has been criticized by both contemporaries and historians who express dismay at his "connivance at the exclusion of the Foreign Office from the decision-making process."[28] Dean has so far escaped even acknowledgment of his role in this, let alone any criticism. That role must be both recognized and criticized as a failure by the chairman of the JIC to challenge inappropriate use of intelligence structures for purposes not directly related to intelligence matters.

A further example of Dean's politicization during the crisis can be seen in his actions at a special meeting of the JIC on November 16. This followed the November 11 distribution of *Soviet Designs in the Middle East,* a report that reiterated the JIC's view of Nasser as a tool of Soviet policy.[29] At that meeting Dean said that "he thought it was important that every effort be made to find evidence to give to the United States that proved that Nasser was a tool of the Soviets."[30] The JIC agreed with Dean's position and "invited Departments to see what fresh evidence they could find."[31] Dean's statement and the JIC report of November 11 reveal that both Dean and the JIC broadly had become influenced by political pressure to find evidence of Soviet conspiracy in the Middle East. That pressure not only distorted analysis in JIC products but was now also advocated by the committee's own chairman to the point of determining what kind of evidence should be sought. Moreover, this evidence was sought not for the provision of objective analytic judgment but instead to impress the American ally.

The second action that must be examined is Dean's role in the Sèvres collusion with France and Israel. On October 22 Foreign Secretary Lloyd and his assistant private secretary, Donald Logan, met with the French and Israelis in Paris to discuss military planning. Following the meeting, Logan recounted that a second visit was needed to continue the discussions. Dean was summoned to Downing Street and instructed to accompany Logan to Sèvres for this second meeting, which took place on October 24. Logan has written categorically, "Patrick Dean at that point knew nothing of the contacts earlier in the week. He was not involved in the detailed planning mechanisms."[32] This point is corroborated by Dean himself, who, in a rare written recollection of the affair, stated that he knew little of the specific planning details, particularly of any joint discussions with the French or Israelis.[33]

Dean recounted that he visited the prime minister early on the morning of October 24. Eden impressed on Dean "his great anxiety about Nasser's policy and aims and his fear that he intended and was able to inflict great damage on British interests in the Middle East."[34] Dean was instructed to attend the meeting between the French and the Israelis in Paris that afternoon "and make it absolutely clear to both of them what the British attitude and intentions were and to obtain their acceptance of them."[35] Then Dean offered several points that conveyed his own understanding of his participation in the affairs:

> At this point I should make it clear that:
> (a) although the Prime Minister had told me that he agreed with the French and the Israelis about the possibility of military action being required . . . I was told and knew nothing about any previous personal contacts or meetings at any level between the British, French and Israelis beyond the fact (which was common knowledge) that he and the Secretary of State had had a meeting with the French, M. Mollet and M. Pineau, in Paris on October 16th. . . .
> (b) I had no written instructions whatever and only knew what the Prime Minister had told me. My knowledge that some plans had been for some time under consideration within the Ministry of Defence was, as I have said, only general. So at this stage was my knowledge (? lack of knowledge) of political contacts with France and Israel. I was in no position to relate the one to the other.
> (c) I regarded my mission—and regarded it throughout—purely as a part of a military contingency plan upon which the Prime Minister wished to make sure that the other parties fully understood and accepted the two essential points upon the basis of which any plans for possible British military intervention would have to be drawn up.
> (d) I never at any time regarded what the Prime Minister asked me to do as authorising me to conclude in any sense a formal inter-Government agreement constituting a Treaty or anything like it between Governments, but merely as an occasion to make sure that British intentions were properly understood and embodied in any military contingency plan which might be drawn up.
> (e) I also regarded the Prime Minister's insistence on secrecy as being the normal adjunct of all forms of military planning.[36]

Dean and Logan subsequently went to the meeting at which the infamous Sèvres Protocol was written. Dean noted that while both he and Logan were surprised at the sudden production of a document, he believed that "it enabled me to make an accurate report to the Prime Minister on the precise intentions of the other two Governments." Dean initialled each page of the protocol and signed it at its end, but "I made it clear that I was signing *ad referendum*."[37] After having returned to London, Dean and Logan were instructed by Eden to return to Paris and request that all copies of the document be destroyed. They returned and made the request on October 25 to no avail.

Dean's participation in the Sèvres affair raises a dilemma about the role of an intelligence leader that is perhaps unique to the JIC: Did Dean in this instance act as chairman of the JIC or as an assistant undersecretary in the Foreign Office? The chairman of the JIC typically carries other responsibilities beyond the JIC itself, and in this instance it is hard to judge Dean as an intelligence leader on the basis of the knowledge of his participation at Sèvres. Indeed, with regard to Sèvres, Dean in many respects simply acted as instructed by the prime minister. While Dean's leadership of the JIC during the Suez Crisis itself can be criticized, Dean had no chance for leadership in the most infamous incident of all, at Sèvres. He should instead be recognized only as the man chosen to accompany Logan for one of the most troubling assignments in contemporary British foreign policy.

After the Suez Crisis: Centralizing British Intelligence

The year 1956 was turbulent for British intelligence, especially for SIS, which endured a change in leadership just days before the Suez Crisis began. The changes that were ongoing at SIS, and the turbulent year that the service endured, have been well covered in the historiography, notably by Davies and Dorrill.[38] Throughout 1957, however, change would also come to the JIC, as it was transferred from the COS and into the Cabinet Office. This transfer was motivated by a three-part rationale. First was the acceptance, by both the intelligence services and the wider government, that intelligence activities had developed a broadened scope beyond merely military issues. The JIC itself had noted that although it had previously performed its role primarily for the COS, "intelligence had spread increasingly into the political, economic and scientific fields."[39] The JIC was producing intelligence products that went beyond the military needs of the COS, resulting in an inconsistency between what the JIC produced and what its customer needed.

The second rationale was the inverse of the first: the JIC was being prevented from producing some useful analyses of which it was perfectly capable because they would not be useful to the COS. Dean stated that although the COS performed many functions, "they exclude a number of increasingly important topics which call for policy decisions in spheres beyond those which directly concern the Chiefs of Staff."[40] Therefore, the JIC was unduly restricted because the COS "may exclude a number of increasingly important topics covering Soviet and Communist activities and other developments which threaten our national interest and security."[41] Dean outlined to Allen Dulles, the US director of central intelligence (DCI), that the current JIC position underneath the COS might "unduly restrict our activities both in the reporting field and in our availability to all Departments of Government as a source of fully-collated intelligence."[42]

The third rationale was the desire to remove a clear constitutional restriction on the JIC. This had come to be labeled as a "practical limitation" by the JIC because the COS was "the sole constitutional recipient of its product."[43] Cradock notes that by this point the JIC had "outgrown its old framework" of operating.[44] Wider use would enable both the commissioning of JIC reports as well as their consumption across a broader range of Whitehall recipients than had before been the case.

Given these considerations, the JIC recommended its transfer to the Cabinet Office with two objectives:

(i) to encourage Ministers and Departments, in addition to the Chiefs of Staff, singly or jointly, to ask for studies by the JIC on matters of concern to them, whether or not such studies have "Service" implications;

(ii) to allow of the submission of JIC studies, whether requisitioned by a Department, the Chiefs of Staff, or initiated by the JIC itself, direct to the Ministers and Departments primarily concerned, as well as to other interested Departments.[45]

To achieve the above objectives, the JIC issued the following list of full recommendations:

(a) the JIC should be placed within the Cabinet Committee structure;

(b) the requirements upon the JIC should be set in part by the Minister of Defence and the Chiefs of Staff as heretofore, and in part by the Cabinet or individual Ministers;

(c) JIC reports should be passed to the Cabinet Office except that, in order to meet the special requirements of the Chiefs of Staff, reports of a mainly military nature should be submitted, as hitherto, direct to them in the first instance;

(d) the decision to circulate JIC reports to the Cabinet or to individual Ministers should rest with the Secretary to the Cabinet or the Chiefs of Staff, as appropriate, or, in cases where any Minister has a predominant interest in the substance of a report, with the Minister concerned.[46]

The transfer of the JIC into the Cabinet Office took effect on October 14, 1957.[47] Before the transfer many consumers could ask the JIC to produce intelligence reports, but the JIC's product could be passed only to the COS, which then could clear the product for broader distribution. As a result of the transfer, as Davies rightly notes, the JIC had been made "genuinely *central* at last."[48] Following the transfer the JIC's services were more "readily available to Ministers."[49] But the JIC was now also much more able to push its material to a wider consumer base, having had the restriction of being subordinate to the COS removed.

So important was this change that Cabinet Secretary Norman Brook wrote to Dean to convince him that the JIC, "as a demonstration of their new status" within the Cabinet Office, needed to be "asked fairly soon to do something directly for Ministers." Specifically, Brook requested the timely production of an assessment of the strength of nationalist movements in the Middle East.[50] This example clearly indicates the enthusiasm that the JIC transfer evoked in the Cabinet Office. Secretary Brook acted to push the services of the JIC to ministers as quickly as possible in order to impress on them that the JIC was at their service and was of use and to edify ministers about what the JIC could actually do.

Dean's role in overseeing the transfer must be judged as an understated triumph of intelligence leadership. Although the successful transfer does not compare to operational intelligence successes, such as the Double-Cross System or the Ultra secrets of the Second World War, architectural changes that take place in intelligence structures and place intelligence services on a more steadfast, more centralized platform to do their work are significant in their own right. Before the transfer the JIC was vulnerable to being marginalized, with the Suez Crisis being merely a potent example of this type of situation. But after the transfer the JIC established itself in the position of centrally overseeing the broad direction of intelligence efforts. It also became immediately accessible to the ministerial level, removing the constitutional restriction that undoubtedly resulted in JIC product being unavailable for essential policy discussions at the crucial moments of the Suez Crisis.

Patrick Dean deserves much credit for this transfer; he oversaw the conception of the idea, secured the agreement of his superiors to allow the transfer to happen, and articulated the details of the change and the rationale motivating it both within the British government and internationally to key intelligence partners through broad correspondence. His quiet success helped place the structure of British intelligence into a centralized footing that not only was crucial in focusing intelligence efforts for the broader Cold War but also established the fundamental structure for British intelligence that endures to the present. Clearly in this instance, Dean displayed great skill in leadership that went beyond the standard view of intelligence leadership in operational matters. He recognized the strategic shift in the role that intelligence plays—the broadening of its scope beyond the military sphere of interests—and took action to ensure that the JIC was in the best possible position within the governmental architecture to cope with this shift.

Conclusion

To conclude, the case of Patrick Dean highlights several issues of intelligence leadership for the JIC. In 1956 Dean displayed little evidence of leadership when it mattered most—with the expropriation of PUSD and its utilization for purposes other than intelligence liaison. He was also a victim of a structural restriction that prevented him as the chairman of the JIC from displaying leadership. JIC's existence as a COS body created a fundamental vulnerability in that the JIC could easily be marginalized, as was the case in 1956. During that time the JIC found itself only in a position to support policy rather than play any real role in informing its development.

Dean's experience also raises two fundamental issues about the JIC in particular and intelligence in general. First, the place that intelligence bodies hold in government is of crucial concern. The JIC in 1956 was marginalized, not ignored, and this was simply a function of its place in the British government. The place held by an intelligence body will fundamentally condition the impact that it as a body and its leader can ultimately generate. With this in mind one must empathize somewhat with Dean in 1956; he had precious little opportunity to display any leadership because the JIC as a whole was not in a position to take the lead on informing policy over the Suez Crisis. Moreover, Dean's and the JIC's succumbing to the Eden government's belief that Nasser was a Soviet vassal reveals the enduring fragility that intelligence bodies have with regard to their political masters. Bodies such as the JIC are vulnerable to the implicit and explicit political pressures of their masters, which shape and interfere with their efforts. The lack of a more robust challenge to the belief of Nasser's complicity is evidence of a gradual shift in attitude within the JIC from its balanced April 1956 judgment to Dean's extraordinary instruction in November 1956 for the JIC to find fresh evidence of conspiracy. Political pressure can result in an outright acceptance of political views within intelligence bodies themselves, which appears to have been the case with the JIC in general, and most certainly in particular with Dean, as the Suez Crisis progressed.

Beyond these issues, however, Dean should be recognized for the leadership he displayed in the transfer of the JIC into the Cabinet Office in 1957.

This transfer has remained one of the unrecognized events in the history of British intelligence, partly because it was a bureaucratic affair and not an operational one (and therefore somewhat boring by comparison), but more likely because the full range of papers related to the transfer were not available at the National Archives until 2006. Despite this lack of familiarity, Dean's quiet yet effective leadership in the transfer placed British intelligence onto a permanently established centralized footing for the first time in its history, a position that both endures and is seen as a method of best practice in intelligence organization.

The final question must, however, be this: When it comes to intelligence leadership, which scholars usually judge with regard to operational matters, how do we value and judge the leadership of the chairman of the JIC? The role must be clearly acknowledged to be different to the operational leadership required by the chiefs of SIS, MI5, and GCHQ. But nonetheless, the fact that the JIC has not only remained an intelligence body but also evolved into a central hub of the British intelligence machinery must now surely permit intelligence scholarship to consider the role that its chairman plays in intelligence leadership broadly. The time has come to identify the full range of expectations we have of those who hold that chair in order to be able to fairly assess the leadership brought to the role.

Notes

1. Michael S. Goodman, *The Official History of the Joint Intelligence Committee*, vol. 1, *From the Approach of the Second World War to the Suez Crisis* (Abingdon: Routledge, 2014), 1.

2. Jon Day, foreword to ibid.

3. W. Scott Lucas, "The Missing Link? Patrick Dean, Chairman of the Joint Intelligence Committee," in "Whitehall and the Suez Crisis," special issue, *Contemporary British History* 13 (1999): 117–25.

4. Ibid., 123.

5. Patrick Dean, interview transcript, File no. 5, Suez Oral History Project, Liddell Hart Centre for Military Archives (LHCMA), King's College London, 2, 4.

6. Ibid., 4.

7. Chester L. Cooper, *The Lion's Last Roar: Suez 1956* (London: HarperCollins, 1978).

8. Patrick Dean to Selwyn Lloyd, October 4, 1976, SELO 6/318, Churchill Archives Centre (CAC), Churchill College, Cambridge University.

9. Frank Cooper, interview transcript, File No. 4, Suez Oral History Project, LHCMA, 8. Most intriguing about the remark was that it was a response to a question that was not specifically about Patrick Dean. The question put to Cooper was trying to establish the role and knowledge of Richard Powell; the quote in the text was the complete response from Cooper to that question.

10. Goodman, *Official History*, 401.

11. Ibid., 408.

12. Richard J. Aldrich, Rory Cormac, and Michael S. Goodman, *Spying on the World: The Declassified Documents of the Joint Intelligence Committee, 1936–2013* (Edinburgh: Edinburgh University Press, 2014), 242.

13. *Factors Affecting Egypt's Policy in the Middle East and North Africa*, JIC (56) 20 (Final), April 4, 1956, para. 3, CAB 158/23, British National Archives (TNA).

14. Aldrich, Cormac, and Goodman, *Spying on the World*, 240.

15. Percy Cradock, *Know Your Enemy: How the Joint Intelligence Committee Saw the World* (London: John Murray, 2002), 116.

16. *Charter for the Joint Intelligence Committee*, Confidential Annex, JIC/1525/56, June 15, 1956, CAB 21/3622, TNA.

17. Egyptian Nationalisation of the Suez Canal Company, JIC (56) 80 (Final), August 3, 1956, p. 2, para. 5, CAB 158/25, TNA.

18. Ibid. 5, para. 12. Emphasis added.

19. *Cabinet Conclusions*, C.M. (56) 54th Conclusions, July 27, 1956, p. 5, CAB 128/30, TNA.

20. Cate Haste ed., *Clarissa Eden, A Memoir: From Churchill to Eden* (London: Weidenfeld & Nicolson, 2007), 235.

21. Dennis Kavanagh and Anthony Seldon, *The Powers behind the Prime Minister: The Hidden Influence of Number Ten* (London: HarperCollins, 2000), 59.

22. Frederick Bishop, interview transcript, File no. 3, Suez Oral History Project, LHCMA, 8.

23. Cooper interview transcript, 8.

24. Archibald Ross, interview transcript, File no. 19, Suez Oral History Project, LHCMA, 3.

25. Douglas Dodds-Parker, interview transcript, File no. 6, Suez Oral History Project, LHCMA, 9.

26. Dean interview transcript, 1.

27. Patrick Reilly, interview transcript, File no. 18, Suez Oral History Project, LHCMA, 3.

28. *Oxford Dictionary of National Biography*, s.v. "Kirkpatrick, Sir Ivone Augustine (1897–1964)," 2004, http://www.oxforddnb.com/view/article/34339.

29. *Soviet Designs in the Middle East*, JIC (56) 117 (Final), November 11, 1956, CAB 158/26, TNA.

30. Minutes of Special Meeting Held on Friday, November 16, 1956, JIC (56) 109th meeting, p. 2, para. 4, CAB 159/25, TNA.

31. Ibid.

32. Donald Logan, *Meetings at Sèvres, 22–25 October 1956*, October 24, 1986, p. 5, CAB 164/1359, TNA.

33. Dean wrote this recollection on the advisement of Burke Trend in 1978 in order to set down fully his role in the Sèvres affair. Dean's candor results presumably from his expectation that the file would never be released into the public domain. John Hunt

to Sir Michael Palliser, May 24, 1978, FO 73/205; and Patrick Dean, untitled Sèvres narrative, 1978, p. 1, FO 73/205.

34. Dean, untitled Sèvres narrative, 2.

35. Ibid.

36. Ibid, 3–4.

37. Ibid, 6.

38. Philip H. J. Davies, *MI6 and the Machinery of Spying* (London: Frank Cass, 2004); Stephen Dorrill, *MI6: Fifty Years of Special Operations* (London: Fourth Estate Limited, 2000).

39. *History of the Joint Intelligence Organisation*, JIC (57) 123, November 29, 1957, p. 4, para. 22, CAB 163/50, TNA.

40. Patrick Dean to C. A. Gault, June 26, 1957, CAB 163/9, TNA.

41. *Joint Organisation for Intelligence*, JIC (57) 40, April 5, 1957, p. 1, para. 2, CAB 158/28, TNA.

42. Patrick Dean to Allen C. Dulles, June 25, 1957, CAB 163/9, TNA.

43. *Joint Organisation for Intelligence*, 1, para. 2.

44. Cradock, *Know Your Enemy*, 262.

45. *Joint Organisation for Intelligence*, 2, para. 4.

46. Ibid.

47. *Notice to Secretaries of Committees*, October 1, 1957, CAB 163/9, TNA.

48. Davies, *Machinery of Spying*, 254. Emphasis in the original.

49. Norman Brook to Harold Macmillan, December 6, 1957, PREM 11/2418, TNA.

50. Norman Brook to Patrick Dean, November 22, 1957, CAB 21/4739, TNA.

12 Who Is "M"?

Michael L. VanBlaricum

Ian Fleming's James Bond is one of the best-known and enduring characters in popular culture. Bond is possibly rivaled only by Arthur Conan Doyle's Sherlock Holmes. When one thinks of Sherlock Holmes, one automatically thinks of his iconic sidekick and biographer, Dr. Watson, and, interestingly enough, his archenemy, Moriarty. Similarly, thanks in part to the Bond films by EON Productions, it is difficult to think of James Bond without thinking of Miss Moneypenny, "Q," and "M."

Miss Moneypenny is M's private secretary and was first introduced in chapter 3 of Fleming's first Bond novel, *Casino Royale*:

"What do you think, Penny?" The Chief of Staff turned to M's private secretary who shared the room with him.

Miss Moneypenny would have been desirable but for eyes which were cool and direct and quizzical.[1]

Moneypenny, played by Lois Maxwell, makes an appearance in 1962's *Dr. No*, the first James Bond film.

Q, as Fleming uses the letter, is the Section or Branch headed by the quartermaster, responsible for provisions and supplies.[2] In the same chapter in *Casino Royale* in which Miss Moneypenny is introduced, Fleming refers to Q when M says to Bond: "Have a talk to Q about rooms and trains, and any equipment you want."[3] In the James Bond films, the name Q is first used in the third film, *Goldfinger*, and does refer to the individual character.[4]

Both Moneypenny and Q, as well as James Bond himself, work directly for M. But who is M? What organization is he in charge of? Why does Fleming use the letter *M* to represent a person? Who does Fleming base M on? And how is M represented in the books and films? Before we look at the answers, or at least speculate about the answers to these questions, we need to look at the background of Ian Fleming, the man who created M.

Who Is Ian Fleming?

Ian Lancaster Fleming, the son of a World War I hero, was a journalist, a playboy, a book collector, a soldier, a spy, an adventurer, a poet, a travel writer, a publisher, and a novelist. The second of four sons, he was born in 1908 in the Mayfair section of London to Valentine and Evelyn Fleming. Ian's father was a banker who worked for Robert Fleming and Company, the bank his Scottish father, Robert Fleming, had founded.

In 1910 Valentine "Val" Fleming was elected as a conservative member of Parliament. He was wealthy, handsome, intelligent, and patriotic and loved the outdoors. Ian's mother, Evelyn "Eve" St. Croix Rose, was of Scottish, Irish, and Huguenot ancestry. She was a beautiful, strong-willed woman who loved music, art, and literature. In 1917 Val, now a major in the Oxfordshire Hussars, was killed in the French trenches of World War I, and Eve was left to take care of her four young sons. Val's close friend Winston Churchill wrote his obituary in *The Times*.[5] Ian idolized his father and saw him as a symbol of chivalry and moral goodness. There is no doubt that losing his father just as he neared his ninth birthday, and subsequently being raised by his now-single mother, had a strong impact on Ian's mental state and lifelong view of the world.

At age seven Ian started his formal education at Durnford, a preparatory school in Dorset. At Durnford School the headmaster's wife, Ellinore Pellatt, would read adventure stories to the boys each evening. These included Anthony Hope's *The Prisoner of Zenda*, J. Meade Falkner's *Moonfleet*, and Sapper's *Bulldog Drummond*.[6]

At age thirteen Ian was enrolled in the elite British public (meaning private) school Eton. While he did not enjoy his time there, he made a personal mark with his athletic prowess. He was named Victor Ludorum (champion of the games) at Eton in both 1925 and 1926 and was only the second person ever to achieve this feat. Like his creation James Bond, Ian never finished Eton. In the fall of 1926, he enrolled at the Royal Military Academy Sandhurst. He did well at Sandhurst but left in September 1927 without taking his commission because he claimed that he did not want to be part of the new "mechanized" army. In actuality Ian's mother convinced him to resign following a few months of sick leave due to a bout of gonorrhea and his general malaise.[7]

Once Ian had resigned from Sandhurst, Eve sent him to Kitzbühel in the Austrian Alps to study at a finishing school, the Tennerhof. The Tennerhof was run by Ernan Forbes Dennis, a former English diplomat-spy, and his

American wife, the novelist Phyllis Bottome. In Austria Fleming read voraciously, became proficient at foreign languages, and brushed up his technique on the ski slopes as well as his way with the girls. During this time he also developed his love for writing. A Fleming short story, perhaps his first, is the only one that survives from his period at Tennerhof. This story, "A Poor Man Escapes," dated 1927, displays an early sense of Fleming's succinct yet descriptive writing style.[8] After Kitzbuhl Fleming continued to study languages in Munich and then Geneva in preparation for a possible career in the Foreign Service. In 1931 Ian took the Foreign Office exams but failed to earn a place.

After he had failed the Foreign Office exam, his mother pulled a few strings, and in October 1931 Ian took his first paying job working as a journalist with Reuters News Agency, a competitor of United Press International. In March 1933 Ian broke a story about six British engineers who were accused of spying in Moscow. Fleming traveled to Moscow by train to cover the trial for Reuters. While there he requested an interview with Joseph Stalin, who declined by sending him a signed note.[9] Writing for a news service required Ian to be fast, concise, and accurate, and the facts he gathered had to be colorful if they were to be noticed. What Ian learned at Reuters served him extremely well when he started writing fiction. In addition, the journalism job introduced him to foreign travel and international politics, both of which greatly colored the James Bond novels.

Despite Fleming's success as a journalist, he resigned from Reuters in 1933 at the age of twenty-five and took a job as a banker. It is fairly clear that family pressures and Ian's need for more income than he could earn in journalism led him in this direction.[10] The banking business ultimately did not suit him, so he moved into the stock brokerage side of the financial world. From 1933 to 1939 Fleming led what, to him, was a boring existence during his working hours. However, he made up for it on his own time. He continued to keep company with several women, and his long-standing interest in book collecting was revitalized. With money he made from a particularly successful stock deal, Fleming asked London rare book dealer and his friend from Kitzbuhl Percy Muir to start acquiring books that had been responsible for technical and intellectual progress since the year 1800. This collection now resides at the Lilly Library at Indiana University.[11]

In 1939 Fleming's life took a turn that allowed him to fully engage his personality and interests. In July 1939, just a few weeks before Britain declared war on Germany, Ian became a lieutenant in the Voluntary Reserve of the Royal Navy. He was approached by Rear Adm. John Godfrey, the new director of naval intelligence (DNI), and given the job of personal assistant to the DNI. Fleming was much more than just an aide to Admiral Godfrey. Fleming became the front man for the Naval Intelligence Division (NID) and rapidly advanced to the rank of commander (James Bond's rank). He was a liaison with the Special Operations Executive (SOE), the group responsible for sabotage, subversion, and work with resistance movements, and the Special Intelligence Service (SIS)—also commonly known as MI6 for Military Intelligence Section 6—which was to be the home of Fleming's James Bond. Fleming worked on propaganda with the Political Warfare Executive (PWE), and he coordinated with the press. Godfrey also allowed Fleming to hatch his own ideas for plans. Fleming's plans were usually never hampered by reality or practicality. His charge was to create elaborate espionage plans; others were responsible for turning them into reality if they were deemed appropriate.

British intelligence wanted the United States to set up an intelligence agency that would work closely with them. In 1941 Gen. William Donovan of the US Army was asked by President Roosevelt to establish the American Office of Strategic Services (OSS). This organization was the predecessor of the Central Intelligence Agency (CIA), which was formed in 1947. In May 1941 Admiral Godfrey and Fleming arrived at New York's LaGuardia flying boat dock on Pam Am's *Dixie Clipper*.[12] They had traveled from London to New York via Lisbon, the Azores, and Bermuda. After meeting in New York with Sir William Stephenson (code name Intrepid and head of British intelligence in the Western Hemisphere), the two traveled to Washington, DC, where they first met with FBI chief J. Edgar Hoover and then with General Donovan. Godfrey returned to London, but Fleming stayed in Washington until late July to aid Donovan in drawing up the plans for the new organization. During this time Fleming wrote at least two memos to General Donovan. One signed by Fleming on June 27, 1941, is particularly interesting because it starts by encouraging Donovan's celerity: "I have prepared some steps which will have to be taken at an early date in order that your organization can be set up in time to meet war before Christmas."[13] Basically, Fleming was telling Donovan to have his organization ready for war by Christmas. America was attacked at Pearl Harbor on December 7, 1941, and entered the war the next day.

Later in 1941 Fleming created one of his most renowned contributions to World War II British intelligence—the Number 30 Assault Unit (30 AU).[14] This group of intelligence commandos specialized in cleaning out Nazi hideouts after the facilities had been captured. The men of the 30 AU were trained in unarmed combat, code breaking, safecracking, and other crafts needed by crack intelligence forces. Ian worked closely with the 30 AU and picked up a lot of knowledge that would prove to be useful to Bond in his future fictional exploits.

After the war Fleming returned to journalism and became foreign manager for the Kemsley Newspaper Group, which included the *Sunday Times*. As foreign manager Fleming had as many as eighty correspondents around

Photo 12.1 Ian Fleming's home in Jamaica, Goldeneye, where all of the James Bond novels were written. *Photograph by Mary Slater. Courtesy of Ian Fleming Images / © The Ian Fleming Estate*

the world. Many of these stringers were intelligence agents who, after the war, were sent overseas as reporters for the newspaper. When Fleming took the job with Kemsley, he negotiated two months off each year to spend at the house he was building on the north shore of Jamaica.[15] He named his house Goldeneye after (depending on whom you believe) Carson McCullers's novel *Reflections in a Golden Eye*, a military operation he was instrumental in planning called Operation Golden Eye, or the simple fact that the nearest town to his house was Oracabessa, which means "golden head" in Spanish.

Fleming spent January and February each year at Goldeneye. Following the same pattern each day, he would try to write 2,000 words. He would first swim naked in the cove below his house to help clear his hangover from the night before and then eat a breakfast of scrambled eggs. Following breakfast he would sit at his typewriter and, using six fingers, type out 1,500 words. After lunch and a nap, he would return to his typewriter and produce another 500 words and then quit for the day.

James Bond, as Fleming told the story, was named after the ornithologist of the same name who wrote the book *A Field Guide of Birds of the West Indies*,

Photo 12.2 Fleming at his desk in Goldeneye in January 1963 working on the James Bond novel *You Only Live Twice. Photograph by Mary Slater. Courtesy of Ian Fleming Images /* © *The Ian Fleming Estate*

which Fleming kept by his desk at Goldeneye.[16] Fleming later said that he had wanted the dullest, plainest-sounding, unromantic, Anglo-Saxon, masculine name he could find. In all, Fleming wrote fourteen Bond novels, including two collections of short stories.

Ian Fleming died of a heart attack in August 1964. He lived long enough to see two of his books made into movies and *Casino Royale* made into a CBS Television special. He saw the release of twelve of his fourteen Bond books. *The Man with the Golden Gun* and *Octopussy and the Living Daylights* were published after his death. To date there have been twenty-four James Bond films produced by EON Productions. In addition, there was the 1967 farcical film *Casino Royale* by Columbia Pictures and the 1983 Warner Brothers remake of *Thunderball, Never Say Never Again*. There was, as already mentioned, the 1954 "Climax!" presentation of *Casino Royale* on CBS television. In addition, Fleming's only children's book, *Chitty Chitty Bang Bang*, was released as the popular 1968 musical film and became a stage musical in the West End in 2002 and on Broadway in 2005. On top of Fleming's fourteen Bond novels, there have been twenty-six continuation novels added to the James Bond canon, as well as three short stories and seven screenplay novelizations. In nearly all of the Bond stories, novels, and films, M is present.

Why M?

In chapter 1 of *Casino Royale*, M is first introduced to the world in the sentence: "Paris had spoken to London where Clements, the head of Bond's department, had spoken to M, who had smiled wryly and told 'The Broker' to fix it with the Treasury." Then a few paragraphs away at the beginning of chapter 2—"Dossier for M"—the narrator explains that M is the head of the Secret Service, which is an adjunct to the British Defence Ministries. However, since M is head of the Secret Service, why did Fleming use the letter *M* and not *C*, which is commonly what the head of SIS is called? Or for that matter, why not some other letter of the alphabet?

Part of this answer can be inferred by close examination of Fleming's original first draft typescript for *Casino Royale*. On page three of his foolscap typescript, when Fleming typed the sentence quoted in the previous paragraph, he initially typed: ". . . had spoken to the Chief who had smiled wryly." But while his typewriter was still on this line he backspaced and typed over "the Chief" with nine lowercase *m*s and then typed the letter *M*.[17] As stated above, it is common in the SIS to refer to its head as Chief or simply as C. Fleming would have known that because of his wartime experience. However, in 1952 SIS had not been officially recognized, and Fleming's knowledge of the organization would fall under the Official Secrets Act.[18] Fleming likely would also have known that in 1932 the novelist Compton Mackenzie had been prosecuted for revealing in his book *Greek Memories* the letter code name "C" and the person to whom it referred, Sir Mansfield Smith-Cumming.[19]

It is interesting to note that in Fleming's unpublished short story, "The Shameful Dream," he refers to Lord Ower, the owner of the fictional newspaper *Our World*, as "the Chief" and has him sign a memo to Mr. Bone, the story's main character, as "O."[20] This story was written around 1952, which was the same time he was writing, or at least contemplating writing, *Casino Royale*. Fleming's style of using a letter to refer to the head of an organization was likely influenced by his years in the intelligence community.

Fleming's use of a single letter to denote the head of a newspaper company, O, or the head of the Secret Service, M, was probably heavily influenced by W. Somerset Maugham's 1928 novel *Ashenden: Or the British Agent*, which is considered the beginning of modern spy fiction.[21] In this loosely connected set of stories, Ashenden is the British agent, and the head of the Secret Service is his cynical and devious boss "R." In fact, the first chapter in *Ashenden* is titled "R." Maugham was in the British Secret Service in World War I and certainly would have known that its chief was known by the letter *C*. Fleming read Maugham's Ashenden stories when he was young and eventually became a friend of Maugham after he had published *Casino Royale*.

Sir Mansfield Smith-Cumming was the first chief of SIS and signed his correspondence "C." Since then, all chiefs of SIS have signed "C." *M*, like *C*, is a letter, but this does not explain why Fleming used M as the name of his Secret Service chief. There are many logical explanations or perhaps theories for this. Gen. Sir Stewart Menzies was the spy chief of the SIS from November 1939 to mid-1952. Hence, he was C during the war years, while Fleming was the liaison between the DNI and SIS, as well as at the time of the writing of *Casino Royale*. So Fleming may have thought of Menzies and used his initial for his fictional spy chief.

Some claim that Maj. Charles Henry Maxwell Knight, known commonly as Maxwell Knight, who was MI5's chief agent runner against the Communist Party, was M or at least part of M in the way Fleming constructed him. Maxwell Knight did sign his memos "M." It is logical that Fleming and Knight would have known each other during World War II and possibly worked together hatching schemes. There does not seem to be much evidence, however, to the effect that Fleming used Knight as a model for M as proposed by Anthony Masters in his book *The Man Who Was M*, but certainly Fleming would have known about Knight's use of "M."[22]

Ben Macintyre, in his book produced during Ian Fleming's centenary celebration, points out that during the war Maj. Gen. Sir Colin McVean Gubbins was a director of the SOE in charge of operations and training.[23] Gubbins was an expert in guerrilla warfare and was, as would be expected in his role, tough and brilliant. Gubbins signed his memos by his middle initial, "M," because "G" is used for army abbreviations and "C" was already taken. Because Fleming was a liaison from the DNI to SOE, he would have known Gubbins and known that he signed his name "M."

William Melville ran Scotland Yard's Special Branch from 1893 to 1903. In 1903 he left Scotland Yard and began leading an intelligence section in the War Office. It is claimed in Andrew Cook's biography of Melville that he lobbied to set up, and ultimately founded and became head of, the British Secret Service, now known as MI5. He used the pseudonym William Morgan and the code name M.[24] Since most of this information did not become publicly available until the 1990s, it is not clear if Ian Fleming was aware of William Melville's role in MI5 or his use of the code name M. Whether Fleming knew it or not, it is an interesting coincidence.

In John Pearson's biography of Fleming, *The Life of Ian Fleming*, he points out that Fleming called his mother M.[25] He goes on to effectively argue that the similarities between Bond's relationship to the character M and Fleming's relationship to his mother are very similar:

> There is reason for thinking that a more telling lead to the real identity of M lies in the fact that as a boy Fleming often called his mother M. There seem to be distinct parallels between the demanding old autocrat in Universal Export bestowing on James Bond his grudging praise, his terrifying blame, and the way Mrs. Val Fleming tended to treat her son Ian during various crises in his life. While Fleming was young, his mother was certainly one of the few people he was frightened of, and her sternness towards him, her unexplained demands, and her remorseless insistence on success finds a curious and constant echo in the way M handles that hard-ridden, hard-killing agent, 007. Never has a man who slaughtered so mercilessly taken orders so meekly. Never has such cool ingratitude produced such utter loyalty.

Finally, in looking at a possible reason why Fleming used the moniker "M" for his spy chief, we acknowledge Frederick Forsyth's reasoning as being quite clever, if not totally logical. In chapter 5 of Forsyth's *The Fourth Protocol*, the author writes, "Oddly, although MI5 has a Director-General, MI6 does not. It is a Chief, known throughout the intelligence world and Whitehall simply as "C", whatever his name may be. Nor, even more oddly, does "C" stand for Chief. The first head of MI6 was named Mansfield-Cummings [*sic*], and the "C" is the initial of the second half of that name. Ian Fleming, ever tongue-in-cheek, took the other initial, "M", for the Chief in his James Bond novels."[26] We have to keep in mind here that Forsyth writes fiction, and hence his statements do not have to have any basis in fact. However, it is just Fleming's style and wry sense of humor that might have led him to choose "M" as Forsyth speculates. After all, we have already seen that Fleming did initially type "the Chief" before he typed "M," indicating that he may have, indeed, been thinking of Mansfield Cumming. Although, it also has to be pointed out that the original C's name was George Mansfield Smith-Cumming, and he used Mansfield as his primary given name and not part of his last name as Forsyth implies.

Does M Have a Name?

The thought that Fleming may have been influenced by the name "Mansfield" when he chose the name M for his spy chief makes one wonder if Fleming had an actual name for his character M in mind when he first introduced him in *Casino Royale*. Whether he had one in mind from the outset of his writing the Bond novels will never be known (unless, of course, we find a note or letter in which Fleming states explicitly what he had in mind). In chapter 4 of his third novel, *Moonraker*, Fleming starts hinting at M's actual name when he has Bond thinking to himself while watching M play Patience (Solitaire):

> "Admiral Sir M—M—: something at the Ministry of Defence." M. looked like any member of any of the clubs in St James's Street. Dark grey suit, stiff white collar, the favourite dark blue bow-tie with spots, rather loosely tied, the thin black cord of the rimless eyeglass that M. seemed only to use to read menus, the keen sailor's face, with the clear, sharp sailor's eyes. It was difficult to believe that an hour before he had been playing with a thousand live chessmen against the enemies of England; that there might be, this evening, fresh blood on his hands, or a successful burglary, or the hideous knowledge of a disgusting blackmail case.[27]

This passage not only lets us know that M's first and last name start with *M* but also gives us a very good description of M's looks, his clothing choices, and the stress of his job. Later in the same chapter, Fleming lets us know what M's first name is when the chairman of the gentleman's club Blades, Lord Basildon, and M are discussing Hugo Drax's cheating at bridge: "'Made nine tricks straight off. How he had the face to open Three No Trumps I can't imagine.' He calmed down a little. 'Well, Miles,' he said, 'has your friend got the answer?'" M is called Miles one more time in this chapter by Lord Basildon and then not again in the book.

It is not until Fleming's penultimate Bond book, *The Man with the Golden Gun*, which was published after Fleming's death, that he finally identifies M's full name. This occurs in chapter 1 when Bond, whom Special Branch had as "missing believed killed" after his adventures at the end of *You Only Live Twice*, is trying to convince Captain Walker over the phone that he is, indeed, James Bond:

> Captain Walker's voice came over at full strength. "I'm so sorry. Now then. This man Mr. Em you want to talk to. I'm sure we needn't worry about security. Could you be more specific?"

James Bond frowned. He didn't know that he had frowned, and he wouldn't have been able to explain why he had done so. He said, and lowered his voice, again inexplicably, "Admiral Sir Miles Messervy. He is head of a department in your Ministry. The number of his room used to be twelve on the eighth floor. He used to have a secretary called Miss Moneypenny. Good-looking girl. Brunette."[28]

Hence, according to Fleming, M is Adm. Sir Miles Messervy. M is not only an admiral but has also been knighted.

What Is M's Personality?

Fleming depicts M in his Bond novels as a stern, sometimes curmudgeonly, head of the British Secret Service. Stern and curmudgeonly are probably what one would expect from a leader who not only has the lives of the agents he is in charge of on his shoulders but also is partially responsible for the safety of the free world. However, despite his gruffness, he does come across, at times, as caring if not a bit Victorian.

In chapter 2 of *Casino Royale*, we get our first insight into M's cold and crusty personality: "'What the hell does this word mean?' He spelt it out. . . . 'This is not the Berlitz School of Languages, Head of S. If you want to show off your knowledge of foreign jawbreakers, be good enough to provide a crib. Better still, write in English.'" In *Doctor No* M is even more crusty, short, and antagonistic: "M snorted. 'Anyway, you asked about Strangways's last case and that's it.' M leant forward belligerently. 'Any questions? I've got a busy day ahead.'"[29] But in the short story *For Your Eyes Only*, M is more reflective and fatherly:

> "Dammit," M's eyes glittered impatiently. "That's just what I mean! You rely on me. You won't take any damned responsibility yourself." He thrust the stem of his pipe towards his chest. "I'm the one who has to do that. I'm the one who has to decide if a thing is right or not." The anger died out of the eyes. The grim mouth bent sourly. He said gloomily: "Oh well, I suppose it's what I'm paid for. Somebody's got to drive the bloody train."[30]

Certainly, M does not approve of Bond's dalliances, whether they be golf or womanizing. In *Goldfinger*, when Bond proposes to M that he should play Goldfinger in a game of golf, we see M respond, "'Fine way for one of my top men to spend his time.' The sarcasm in M's voice was weary, resigned."[31]

While M never came out specifically and spoke against Bond's womanizing, he showed his disdain in *From Russia with Love* in an interchange with Bond about his relationship with Tiffany Case:

> "Do you mind if I ask you a personal question, James?" M never asked his staff personal questions and Bond couldn't imagine what was coming.
>
> "No, sir."
>
> M picked his pipe out of the big copper ash-tray and began to fill it, thoughtfully watching his fingers at work with the tobacco. He said harshly: "You needn't answer, but it's to do with your, er, friend, Miss Case . . ."
>
> ". . . Fine girl, but she's a bit neurotic. We had too many rows. Probably my fault. Anyway it's over now."
>
> M gave one of the brief smiles that lit up his eyes more than his mouth. "I'm sorry if it went wrong, James," he said. There was no sympathy in M's voice. He disapproved of Bond's "womanizing," as he called it to himself, while recognizing that his prejudice was the relic of a Victorian upbringing.[32]

In *On Her Majesty's Secret Service*, we get a more detailed look at M's personal life (what there is of it), but we still see his disdain for Bond's romances. In chapter 20, "M en Pantoufles," M reads Bond's report about his exploits in Switzerland and asks Bond about Tracy, whom, unbeknownst to M, Bond had just asked to marry him: "'You were lucky to run into this girl. Who is she? Some old flame of yours?' M's mouth turned down at the corners."[33]

As for M's overall demeanor, it is instructive to look at a series of response descriptors from chapter 2, "Choice of Weapons," in *Doctor No*:

> M frowned irritably.
> M said gruffly, . . .
> M said abruptly, . . .
> M gave a curt laugh.
> M said shortly, . . .
> M's voice was businesslike, cold.
> M's voice was casual.
> M raised ironic eyebrows at Bond.
> . . . said M dryly.
> M's voice was final.
> M's voice was testy.[34]

And finally, when he took Bond's Beretta away, "'Sorry James,' he said, and there was no sympathy in his voice."

Kingsley Amis, in his book *The James Bond Dossier*, gives us a whole chapter devoted to an analysis of M and his relationship with James Bond. He has analyzed M's demeanor or voice through the first twelve Bond novels. His summary is thus: "His demeanor or voice is described as abrupt, angry (three times), brutal, cold (seven times), curt, dry (five), frosty (two), gruff (seven), hard (three), impatient (seven), irritable (two), moody, severe, sharp (two), short (four), sour (two), stern and testy (five), which divides out as an irascibility index of just under 4.6 per book."[35] It needs to be mentioned that M was not always at work irascibly running the Secret Service. In *On Her Majesty's Secret Service*, Bond walks into M's country house and finds M painting:

> M had one of the stock bachelor's hobbies. He painted in water-colour. He painted only the wild orchids of England, in the meticulous but uninspired fashion of the naturalists of the nineteenth century. He was now at his painting-table up against the window, his broad back hunched over his drawing-board, with, in front of him, an extremely dim little flower in a tooth-glass full of water. When Bond came in and closed the door, M gave the flower one last piercingly inquisitive glance. He got to his feet with obvious reluctance. But he gave Bond one of his rare smiles and said, "Afternoon, James." (He had the sailor's meticulous observance of the exact midday.) "Happy Christmas and all that. Take a chair."[36]

Whom Is M Based On?

While we have speculated on why Fleming used the initial "M" to identify the chief of the Secret Service in his Bond novels and have identified what M's actual name was, as well as looked into M's personality and management style, we have discussed only briefly whom the character M may have been based on. It is important to remind the reader at this point that M is a fictional character and, like James Bond, comes from Fleming's imagination and experiences. Hence, M is an amalgam of potentially many people whom Fleming knew in his life. Despite that caveat it seems clear that the two main authority figures in Fleming's life—his mother, Eve Fleming, and his DNI in World War II, Rear Adm. John Godfrey—are the predominant influences from which Fleming draws M's character and traits.

We have already quoted a previous section from John Pearson's biography of Fleming in which he gives a good argument of why Fleming may have used his mother's characteristics and influence to paint some of the characteristics of M. There is not much to be added to Pearson's concise explanation.

Photo 12.3 The HMS *Repulse*, Godfrey's ship, docked at Haifa, 1938. *Eric and Edith Matson Photograph Collection, Library of Congress*

Adm. John Godfrey is undoubtedly the main model for Bond's Secret Service spy chief. Fleming hints at this strongly in *On Her Majesty's Secret Service* when Bond goes to the door of M's country house and rings the bell: "These thoughts ran again through Bond's mind as he swung the clapper of the brass ship's-bell of some former HMS *Repulse*, the last of whose line, a battle-cruiser, had been M's final sea-going appointment."[37] The HMS *Repulse* was, in fact, the last ship Godfrey commanded as Captain Godfrey, before he became the DNI.

John Henry Godfrey was captain of the battle cruiser HMS *Repulse* from 1936 to 1939. In 1939 he was promoted to rear admiral, and he served as the DNI from 1939 to 1942. Donald McLachlan, who was on Godfrey's staff along with Fleming, describes Godfrey: "For the man behind the baize door in the first three years of the war, Rear-Admiral John Godfrey was exacting, inquisitive, energetic, and at times a ruthless and impatient master. Like the driver of a sports car in a traffic queue, he saw no danger or discourtesy in acceleration; with his own quick and penetrating mind he expected other minds to keep up."[38] Interestingly, in 1967 *Newsweek* published an article titled "The Man Who was 'M'" under the column "Where Are They Now." *Newsweek* states that Admiral Godfrey is M:

Secrecy still surrounds the long career of Adm. John Henry Godfrey, but old hands in Britain's World War II spy network have leaked one significant fact about the man with the piercing blue eyes. Godfrey, director of British naval intelligence from 1939 to 1943, is "M"—the real-life model for the stern and unflappable secret-service chief who sent James Bond on improbable missions in the books of the late Ian Fleming. Top sources in Britain's super secret MI6 decided to set matters straight following some recent bad guesses by the London press on just who really was "M". (Sir Stewart Menzies, wartime chief of MI6, was the leading candidate.)[39]

It is nice to think that an article in a nationally respected news magazine based on unnamed sources would be the definitive proof that Admiral Godfrey was Fleming's model for M. However, the only true proof would be the word of Ian Fleming himself. Fortunately, we have what is probably the closest to that proof we will ever have—Fleming inscribed Admiral Godfrey's personal copy of *Thunderball* as "To John, So much alias 'M'! from Ian." But more important, Fleming inscribed Godfrey's personal copy of *On Her Majesty's Secret Service* with "To John, Who appears in more detail! From Ian."

And as we showed in the previous section, *On Her Majesty's Secret Service* is quite well-known for its detailed descriptions of M. This is probably as close as we will ever get to being able to say QED.

Notes

1. Ian Fleming, *Casino Royale* (London: Jonathan Cape, 1953).

2. John Griswold, *Ian Fleming's James Bond: Annotations and Chronologies for Ian Fleming's Bond Stories* (Bloomington, IN: AuthorHouse, 2006), 25–26.

3. Section Q is actually mentioned first at the end of chapter 2.

4. In the two films before *Goldfinger*, *Dr. No* and *From Russia with Love*, Q is present. He is called the armorer in *Dr. No* and the equipment officer in *From Russia with Love*.

5. Winston Churchill, "Obituary of Valentine Fleming," *The Times*, Late War Edition, May 25, 1917.

6. It has been widely referenced, starting with John Pearson's *The Life of Ian Fleming*, that Ellinore Pellatt read *Bulldog Drummond* to the boys shortly after Ian started at the school. However, it needs to be noted that *Bulldog Drummond* was not published until 1920, and Ian started at Durnford School in 1915.

7. Andrew Lycett, *Ian Fleming* (London: Weidenfeld & Nicolson, 1995).

8. Ian Fleming, "A Poor Man Escapes," in *Talk of the Devil* (London: Queen Anne Press, 2008).

9. Henry Chancellor, *James Bond: The Man and His World* (London: John Murray, 2005).

10. Raymond Benson, *The James Bond Bedside Companion* (New York: Dodd,

Mead, 1984), 46; and Ben Macintyre, *For Your Eyes Only: Ian Fleming and James Bond* (London: Bloomsbury Publishing, 2008), 39.

11. The Ian Fleming Collection of 19th–20th Century Source Material Concerning Western Civilization, Lilly Library, Indiana University, Bloomington, http://www .indiana.edu/~liblilly/etexts/fleming.

12. Commander Fleming and Admiral Godfrey landed in New York on May 25, 1941, on Pam Am's *Dixie Clipper*. They wore civilian clothes because this mission was quasi-covert. Noted French clothing designer Elsa Schiaparelli was on the same flight and was photographed as she left the plane. The next day, May 26, 1941, the photo was run in the *New York Times* under the title "MME. Schiaparelli Arrives on Clipper." Admiral Godfrey can be plainly seen right behind her in the photograph—so much for arriving covertly.

13. Ian Fleming to Colonel Donovan, in *Talk of the Devil*.

14. Craig Cabell, *Ian Fleming's Secret War* (Barnsley: Pen & Sword Books, 2008); Craig Cabell, *The History of 30 Assault Unit: Ian Fleming's Red Indians* (Barnsley: Pen & Sword Books, 2009).

15. Ian Fleming visited Jamaica in the fall of 1944 to represent the DNI at an Anglo-American conference to look at the German U-Boat problem in the Caribbean. This conference was held in Kingston, but Fleming and his friend Ivar Bryce stayed at Bellevue, which was owned by Bryce. On the return trip to Washington, Fleming told Bryce that he had decided to live in Jamaica after the war.

16. James Bond, *Field Guide of Birds of the West Indies* (New York: Macmillan, 1947).

17. Ian Fleming, Original first draft manuscript, *Casino Royale*, in private collection, 1952. Private viewing by the author.

18. See Christopher Moran, *Classified: Secrecy and the State in Modern Britain* (Cambridge: Cambridge University Press, 2013).

19. Richard Norton-Taylor, "Mackenzie Memoirs Banned for Spilling Spy Secrets to Be Republished," *Guardian*, November 18, 2011. http://www.theguardian.com /books/2011/nov/18/mackenzie-memoirs-banned-republished.

20. Ian Fleming, "The Shameful Dream," in *Talk of the Devil*.

21. W. Somerset Maugham, *Ashenden: Or the British Agent* (London: William Heinemann, 1928).

22. Anthony Masters, *The Man Who Was M—The Life of Maxwell Knight* (Oxford: Basil Blackwell, 1984), 126–29.

23. Macintyre, *For Your Eyes Only*, 74–81.

24. Andrew Cook, *M: MI's First Spymaster* (Stroud: History Press, 2006).

25. John Pearson, *The Life of Ian Fleming* (London: Jonathan Cape, 1966), 167–78.

26. Frederick Forsyth, *The Fourth Protocol* (London: Hutchinson, 1984).

27. Ian Fleming, "The Shiner," in *Moonraker* (London: Jonathan Cape, 1955).

28. Ian Fleming, "Can I Help You?" in *The Man with the Golden Gun* (London: Jonathan Cape, 1965).

29. Ian Fleming, "Holiday Task," in *Doctor No* (London: Jonathan Cape, 1958).

30. Ian Fleming, *For Your Eyes Only* (London: Jonathan Cape, 1960).

31. Ian Fleming, "Thoughts in a DB III," in *Goldfinger* (London: Jonathan Cape, 1959).

32. Ian Fleming, "A Piece of Cake," in *From Russia with Love* (London: Jonathan Cape, 1957).

33. Ian Fleming, "M en Pantoufles," in *On Her Majesty's Secret Service* (London: Jonathan Cape, 1963).

34. Ian Fleming, "Choice of Weapons," in *Doctor No*.

35. Kingsley Amis, *The James Bond Dossier* (London: Jonathan Cape, 1965).

36. Fleming, "M en Pantoufles."

37. Ibid.

38. Donald McLachlan, *Room 39* (New York: Atheneum, 1968).

39. "The Man Who Was M," *Newsweek*, January 23, 1967.

13 The Man behind the Desk and Other Bureaucracies

Portrayals of Intelligence Leadership in British Television Spy Series

Joseph Oldham

This chapter will provide a broad overview of how intelligence leaders have been portrayed across the history of the British television spy series, an area that has been largely overlooked in the extensive body of critical work on these programs. Initially, I will look at the formative spy series of the 1960s and 1970s, separating these along the traditionally accepted dichotomy of "romantic" and "realist" traditions, and indeed I will argue that the representation of spy chiefs in fact provides a crucial marker of the distinction between these categories. I will explore how the "romantic" tradition, which on television usually takes the form of the espionage-themed action series, most typically positions an omniscient, paternalistic "man behind the desk" in the central authoritative role. By contrast, the "realist" or "existential" tradition of spy drama generally favors a more complex and ambivalent portrayal of the intelligence bureaucracy, offering this as one of its key signifiers of realism.

Finally, I will look at the more recent series *Spooks* (BBC 1, 2002–11, broadcast in the United States as *MI-5*), which presents something of a convergence of these traditions. I will examine how it reworks the "man behind the desk" figure within the context of an office environment marked less overtly by hierarchy and more by community, while also situating him against an increasingly emphasized bureaucratic structure of the wider state apparatus. I will explore how this shift in the representation of leadership responds to developments both within television drama, employing new narrative conventions associated with the precinct drama, and also in the wider political world, with *Spooks* responding to the increased openness and visibility of the real intelligence services during this time.

The "Man behind the Desk" in the Action Spy Series

The most iconic and essentially default image of the spy chief in popular fiction is that of a largely deskbound figure (usually male) issuing instructions to a field agent. Such characters have played a prominent role in television spy dramas over the years, in particular the action-adventure spy series, a subgenre that emerged to great popularity on either side of the Atlantic in the 1960s. Here I will discuss how the "man behind the desk" model, largely drawn from postwar developments in the spy novel, distilled the notion of intelligence bureaucracy down to its most basic form in a manner that was particularly conducive to the generic and formal features of the action series. However, I will also suggest that British television spy series were somewhat slower to adopt this model than their American counterparts, instead often retaining the focus on the "talented amateur" as protagonist from earlier literary traditions of spy fiction.

A major development in the postwar spy thriller in both Britain and America was a change in the role of the protagonist from the "talented amateur" of clubland era writers such as John Buchan to a professional agent of the state, as particularly popularized by Fleming's James Bond novels (beginning with *Casino Royale*, 1953). As John G. Cawelti and Bruce A. Rosenberg argue, Fleming's characterization of the secret service as bureaucracy introduced "the idea of the organization providing the hero with license or legitimation to commit acts which are normally considered crimes for the average man," this replacing the more abstract sense of divine providence that had underpinned the clubland hero's adventures.[1] Yet even as the intelligence bureaucracy came to play a significant role in *motivating* narratives in the new form of heroic spy fiction, it rarely emerged as a direct focal point in itself. Contrasting Fleming's novels with those of John Le Carré, in which the intelligence bureaucracy is a more central site of intrigue (as discussed later), Michael Denning writes that "just as the spy stories of Le Carré tell tales of white-collar work, so Fleming's adventures are really tales of leisure."[2] Thus, the bureaucracy of the Bond stories is simply a starting point for narratives of adventure, travel, and consumerism, serving to license such narratives while not serving as a specific narrative focal point.

For the most part, this is achieved by distilling the intelligence bureaucracy to its simplest form: that of the individual spy chief, "M." In his role as the sole source of authority, Umberto Eco describes how "M represents to Bond the one who has a global view of the events, hence his superiority over the 'hero' who depends upon him and who sets out on his various missions in conditions of inferiority to the omniscient chief."[3] In effect, M condenses whatever varying perspectives or agendas that might exist within the intelligence services and wider state apparatus into a singular, paternalistic viewpoint alongside which the series is always fundamentally aligned, and the effect of this is to close off the need for any fuller interrogation of the political underpinnings behind the agent's missions. Eco famously characterizes the repetitive structural elements of the Bond series as being like the moves in a "game," as "the reader finds himself immersed in a game of which he knows the pieces and the rules—and perhaps the outcome—and draws pleasure simply from following the minimal variations by which the victor realizes his objective."[4] Within the standard Bond novel scheme, M's role can be distilled to a single element or "move," typically located at or close to the beginning of any given novel, in which he "gives a task to Bond," thereby initiating the mission and chain of events.[5] This move usually takes the form of an office-based briefing scene, establishing a paternalistic "man behind the desk" image of the spy chief that would become a ubiquitous convention of spy fiction over subsequent decades, particularly when given an iconic visual rendering as part of the Bond film series. Thus, the simplicity of the "omniscient chief" model serves as the device by which a steady stream of missions can be provided, enabling the individual stories to rapidly depart the office spaces inhabited by the intelligence bureaucracy in favor of licensed adventures in exterior spaces.

A crucial factor in the emergence of Bond as a cultural icon in the late 1950s and early 1960s lies in how the series proved readily adaptable to many of the emergent popular media forms of the postwar period, substantially facilitated by the standardized narratives described by Eco. This included paperback editions of the books by Pan from 1955 onward, the serialization of *From Russia with Love* (1957) in the *Daily Express*, and a series of comic strip adaptations of the novels in the same newspaper from 1957 onward, eventually culminating in the hugely successful film adaptations beginning with *Dr. No* (Terence Young, 1962).[6]

Another form of popular media that was growing in prominence during this period was the filmed television adventure series. While television drama had previously been dominated by practices of live broadcasting, the late 1950s saw an increasing tendency to produce ongoing series on film, opening up new possibilities for shooting on location, editing complex sequences, and selling programs on the international market. This instigated the production of numerous ongoing series with a focus primarily on action and adventure, including American Western series, British "costume swashbucklers," and police/crime series on both sides of the Atlantic. However, in the 1960s there emerged in both countries a new kind of action-based thriller series oriented around narratives of contemporary international intrigue, on which the Bond series was a significant influence.

The most prolific producer of such programming in the UK was the Independent Television Corporation (ITC), which enjoyed particular success with long-running series such as *Danger Man* (ITV, 1960–68) and *The Saint* (ITV, 1962–69). At a time when much of British television drama remained largely studio-bound and shot on videotape, ITC's adventure series were glossy and expensive filmed productions, enabling a greater focus on exterior locations and elaborate action sequences. This style of production was partially employed to enable greater possibilities for international export, particularly to the American market, where film production was the norm, although it was ultimately the Associated British Corporation's *The Avengers* (ITV, 1961–69) that achieved the greatest success in the United States when broadcast on the ABC network. James Chapman describes how "the episodic series represents the *reductio ad absurdum* of generic entertainment patterns" relying on "highly standardized narrative conventions, plotting and characterisation."[7] This Fordist approach to television drama was particularly embraced by the action-adventure spy series in order to fit contemporary orthodoxies of US network programming, and the basic narrative formula of such programs took the form of a regular procession of "mission" scenarios, primarily situated in exterior environments.

Fleming's Bond stories thus provided an obvious model, particularly with an "omniscient chief" generating and licensing such missions. This influence is certainly noticeable in the parallel tradition of American spy series to emerge from the 1960s, which provided significant spy chief characters such as Alexander Waverly (Leo G. Carroll) in *The Man from U.N.C.L.E.* (NBC, 1964–68) and Jim Phelps (Peter Graves) in *Mission: Impossible* (CBS, 1966–73). Yet, as Michael Kackman writes, "the British spy programs, unlike their American counterparts, were much less concerned with forging links to official state agencies," and one consequence of this is that the spy chief is a significantly less prominent figure in the early years of the British television genre.[8] Despite the cultural prominence of Bond in the 1960s, the more traditional model of the spy as "talented amateur" still exercised a substantial influence over the British television spy series, with some programs (most notably *The Saint*) explicitly adopting such a figure as protagonist. Others, such as *Danger Man* and *The Avengers*, featured protagonists who worked for intelligence services in a professional capacity but tended to sideline the intelligence bureaucracy to a much greater extent than Fleming did. Occasional spy chiefs in the "man behind the desk" model appeared in both of these programs but usually in a much more irregular and marginal role, with the agents more commonly simply arriving at the scene of the case, their authority already assumed as self-evident. Eventually, as it reached its increasingly surreal and comic final season (broadcast in 1968–69), *The Avengers* came to feature a more prominent spy chief in the form of "Mother" (Patrick Newell) with whom it parodied the increasingly exaggerated conventions of its US rivals. Whereas U.N.C.L.E.'s headquarters, in which Waverly resided, was accessed through an innocuous tailor's shop, Mother's briefings took place in a range of bizarre and unlikely locations, such as at the top of a double-decker bus or in a swimming pool. Concurrently, some later, more short-lived programs from the ITC stable adopted a more transatlantic style and mimicked the approach of American series with more developed fictional agencies and substantial roles for spy chiefs such as Tremayne (Anthony Nicholls) in *The Champions* (ITV, 1968–69) and Sir Curtis Seretse (Dennis Alaba Peters) in *Department S* (ITV, 1969–70).

The British action spy series entered into a period of decline in the 1970s. By the end of the decade, the most significant such program was *The Professionals* (ITV, 1977–83), which focused on the assignments of two agents for the fictional clandestine organization CI5, Bodie (Lewis Collins) and Doyle (Martin Shaw), and demonstrated some fundamental shifts in the genre. Although it had many points of continuity with 1960s series such as *The Avengers*, particularly in terms of production personnel, *The Professionals* is commonly seen to constitute a point of convergence with the popular British "tough cop" shows of the 1970s, such as *The Sweeney* (ITV, 1975–78). Philip Schlesinger, Graham Murdock, and Philip Elliott also argue that it was significantly influenced by vigilante crime fiction, such as the *Dirty Harry* film series (beginning 1971), writing, "The whole show is based on the premise that exceptional threats to order and democracy require exceptional measures."[9] In terms of the spy genre's broader history, the series' title is significant, indicating a new adherence to professionalism and rejection of amateurism in the context of the "law and order" decade. In particular, *The Professionals* is notable for shifting the action-adventure spy series toward narratives of defeating terrorist threats in the national space, often derived from "headline" concerns, giving the action spy series a newly topical and somewhat reactionary edge.

The discourse of "exceptional measures" is regularly expressed in the series by its chief character, the head of CI5, George Cowley (Gordon Jackson), presented as a much more prominent lead character than any 1960s leader, with third billing in the title sequence, an active role in many episodes, and a particularly brusque, no-nonsense, paternalistic manner in his dealings with Bodie and Doyle. In the voice-over that accompanies the original title sequence, Cowley declares, "Anarchy, acts of terror, crimes against the public. To combat it, I've got special men: experts from the army, the police, from every service. These are the professionals." Establishing the very premise of the series in his own terms, this speech is significant for positioning Cowley as the moral voice of the series, and throughout the program's run he is regularly given speeches about the need to contain threats "by any means necessary." *The Professionals* therefore can be seen as a key moment when the British action spy series abandon amateurism and foreground the figure of the spy chief, creating a far more assertively paternalistic figure than was common in 1960s series, embodying an ideal of the strong state in the context of the 1970s "war against crime." This provides a new model for the action spy series that can be loosely traced through to the depiction of the "war on terror" in *Spooks*, although, as I will discuss, the later series does much to complicate this.

Overall, the action spy series is substantially indebted to the model of spy thriller popularized by the James Bond stories, in particular through their vision of the spy chief as an omniscient "man behind the desk." Such a figure provided a bureaucratic legitimation to the agent's activities, licensing travel and action-based narratives in exterior environments by providing a regular supply of "missions." This model met the specific requirements of the action spy series that emerged in the 1960s, which similarly focused on exterior spaces and intensified the series form to weekly episodic narratives. Yet for much of this decade, British action spy series were more ambivalent than their US counterparts regarding the role of the spy chief, retaining a significant influence from earlier "talented amateur" traditions of spy fiction. Ultimately, it was not until the genre was substantially reconfigured into topical stories of terrorist anxieties toward the end of the 1970s that the spy chief emerged as a particularly substantial figure in British television action spy series.

Intelligence Leadership as Bureaucracy in Existential Spy Drama

In parallel to the rise and fall of the action spy series, an alternative tradition of British spy drama emerged that, by contrast, placed a far greater emphasis on intelligence bureaucracy as a site of drama and intrigue. Here I will examine arguably the two most notable programs in this strand, *Callan* (ITV, 1967–73) and *The Sandbaggers* (ITV, 1978–80), both of which emerged from the alternative tradition of spy fiction to be popularized during the 1960s, generally associated with authors such as John Le Carré and Len Deighton. Such work drew on the earlier existential tales of "innocents abroad" by Eric Ambler and Graham Greene and, in a similar manner to Fleming in the "romantic" tradition, shifted the focus to professional spies and the bureaucratic structures of government agencies. By contrast to the "romance" category often used to describe more heroic or fantastical spy fiction, this strand has traditionally been considered "realist." However, critics such as Denning have problematized this label, arguing that this is more productively conceptualized as a particular set of aesthetic devices that intuitively suggest "reality"—in other words, features designed to make the audience *feel* that what is depicted is more realistic rather than to provide a genuine insight into intelligence activity.[10] Here I will adopt an alternative label that Denning suggests in acknowledgment of the "different ethical structure" of such stories, that of the "existential thriller," which plays on "a dialectic of good and evil overdetermined by moral dilemmas, by moves from innocence to experience, and by identity crises, the discovery in the double agent that the self may be evil."[11] Nonetheless, I will retain a close interest in the aesthetic devices used to construct a sense of "realism" in such programs and indeed argue that these are crucial for understanding the vision of intelligence bureaucracy that they offer.

While Eco characterizes the Bond novels as a "game" in which the reader "knows the pieces and the rules," by contrast Denning argues that one of the key devices by which the novels of Le Carré and Deighton create an impression of "realism" is their resistance to the formulaic structures of the "romantic" thriller: "Formally, we can see that against the highly coded, game-like structures of the romantic thriller, the codes of realism still appear to be a demystifying, decoding operation . . . the rhetoric of the realists of the thriller is entirely in this tone of breaking out of the highly coded—and thus 'unrealistic' worlds of the early thriller."[12] Thus, if the "realist" spy novel is still a "game," it is one in which the rules now are either highly obscured or likely to be violated to shocking effect, which perhaps corresponds with a perception that this is how real-life conflict truly operates. This resistance to coded structures takes two common forms in Le Carré's and Deighton's work, both of which crucially center on the depiction of the intelligence bureaucracy and its leaders. One is how often narrative outcomes that are positive in terms of national interest are juxtaposed with what Denning describes as a "deeper, more critical tale where the real enemy is the organization itself, the organization that never keeps faith, the organization that betrays its own men."[13] This is an element that Le Carré pioneered in the genre to particularly shocking effect in his breakthrough novel *The Spy Who Came in from the Cold* (1963), in which the protagonist, Alec Leamas, is manipulated and betrayed by his service, sparking a chain of events that led to his violent death at the Berlin Wall. Indeed, narratives in this vein became something of a trademark for this author over many subsequent novels.

The other common method by which the coded structure is broken is through the depiction of an intelligence bureaucracy that has become hopelessly corrupted, typically through infiltration by a Soviet mole and the surrounding institutional crisis that this generates (which inevitably carries echoes of the numerous British intelligence scandals of the 1950s and 1960s). An early instance of this is Deighton's debut *The Ipcress File* (1962), in which his unnamed protagonist must discover which of his aristocratic superiors is a traitor. The following decade Le Carré authored what is perhaps the most famous instance of such a narrative with *Tinker Tailor Soldier Spy* (1974), his allegorical treatment of Kim Philby's exposure, which depicts George Smiley's investigation to identify a traitor in the highest ranks of the service.

Although contrasting in many ways, these two narrative models are unified by posing a fundamental challenge to the paternalistic and benevolent "omniscient chief" that provides an ultimately reassuring presence in the Bond stories and action spy television series. Either the intelligence bureaucracy is efficient, but has in the process developed a monstrous and dehumanizing worldview, or else it has declined, becoming inefficient and corrupted.

Spy dramas pursuing this existential identity were a more marginal tradition on British television in the 1960s than those focusing on action and adventure. This can perhaps be attributed to how the conventions of the episodic series ultimately blunt the pessimistic and "rule-breaking" extremes of existential spy novels, as neither the protagonist nor the institution can be placed in such complex and vulnerable positions on a regular basis if the weekly episodic narratives are to function. One series that moved further into this terrain than its contemporaries was *Callan* (ITV, 1967–72), which portrayed the assignments of David Callan (Edward Woodward), a reluctant professional killer working on behalf of a mysterious branch of the British intelligence services known as the "Section." *Callan* was primarily aimed at a domestic rather than transatlantic audience, which substantially freed it from the more standardized narratives necessary for international sales. Furthermore, it was a much more modestly resourced production than the action-adventure series in the ITC or American traditions, made according to a more traditional model of British drama production of shooting primarily on videotape within the television studio with only a limited number of filmed exterior sequences.

In practice, this arguably transformed what might appear as a "limitation" of this mode of production into a style that hugely supports the conventions of the "existential" subgenre, with the technologically determined focus on interiors rather than exteriors enhancing narratives that are more cerebral than action-based. The series adopts a conventional "man behind the desk" model of spy chief, with Callan accepting his orders from a succession of desk-bound men using the code name "Hunter." Here a "psychological ambivalence" that Eco identifies in the Bond-M relationship is pushed to more antagonistic extremes.[14] Callan's relationship with the first "Hunter" (Ronald Radd) is particularly marked by conflict, with the chief repeatedly manipulating and blackmailing his agent into performing off-the-record assassinations, and both characters repeatedly discussing the potential need to kill the other in the future. In fact, it is the figure of "Hunter" rather than Callan who gains a vulnerable status by which the program demonstrates its tendency toward breaking the "rules," with two subsequent occupants of this office successfully assassinated by enemy powers during the course of the series. Later, a story line running over the fourth and final season (broadcast in 1972) depicts Callan himself being reluctantly promoted to the position of "Hunter," although any sense that this will place him in greater control of his own situation is quickly dispelled as he finds himself taking orders from an equally controlling government bureaucrat by the name of Bishop (Geoffrey Chater).

Toward the end of the 1970s, two further notable spy dramas in the existential tradition were produced for British television; both of them more thoroughly challenged the centrality of the "omniscient chief" as part of their generic intervention, albeit in highly contrasting ways. Most famously, a seven-part adaptation of *Tinker Tailor Soldier Spy* (BBC 2, 1979) brought Le Carré's iconic mole-hunt narrative to the small screen. Here the shift to direct adaptation enabled a stronger fidelity to the narrative techniques that the author had developed in the genre, while the presentation of a single narrative unfolding over multiple episodes enabled the development of more complex storytelling than was possible in the episodic narratives of a series like *Callan*.[15] This was followed over the subsequent decade by numerous similar novel adaptations, including of Le Carré's *A Perfect Spy* (BBC 2, 1987) and of Len Deighton's *Game, Set and Match* trilogy (ITV, 1988), which similarly used their long-form complex narratives to portray a more ambivalent view of the intelligence establishment as riddled with moles and paranoia.

The other innovative series in the existential tradition to appear at the end of the 1970s was *The Sandbaggers* (ITV, 1978–80), which I will examine in more detail as its retention of the episodic series form enables a more productive comparison. The series depicts the activities of the Special Operations Section within the Secret Intelligence Service (SIS), its narratives routinely depicting dangerous overseas missions, often behind the Iron Curtain. However, here the leading character is not one of the field agents (the titular "sandbaggers") but instead the director of special operations, Neil Burnside (Roy Marsden), effectively elevating the traditional "man behind the desk" to central protagonist. The effect of this is to shift the entire emphasis of the program, with the focus of any given episode instead placed on concurrent institutional battles in London and Burnside's ongoing conflicts with his superiors and other parts of the state apparatus. Running for three seasons, *The Sandbaggers* was created and almost entirely written by Ian MacKintosh, giving it an unusually strong identity as an "authored" drama, in contrast with other British spy series, which have usually been more collaboratively written.

As with *Callan*, *The Sandbaggers* was largely shot in the studio on videotape with filmed inserts and is even more thorough in its reworking of the spy series as a genre focused on interior rather than exterior spaces. In his original pitch document, it is clear that this is a key component of MacKintosh's concept and the way he differentiated it from previous spy dramas: "SIS has been the subject of many series and many plays; but never has it been portrayed in real documentary terms and never has there been an examination of its methods, priorities, internal struggles and power within the Whitehall structure. Never has the spotlight been turned on the men who make the decisions, who control the agents, who gamble with the precarious peace of cold war."[16] A similar sentiment appears on-screen in a climactic moment of the opening episode, "First Principles," in which Burnside castigates the head of the Norwegian intelligence service with the statement, "Our battles aren't fought at the end of a parachute. They're won and lost in drab, dreary corridors in Westminster." This makes it clear that in MacKintosh's concept, an emphasis on the interior spaces of Whitehall and Westminster is synonymous with the bid for a greater realism or "documentary terms." Here the office space, which typically only served as the starting point for narratives in the action spy series, is instead transformed into the central site of drama and intrigue. *The Sandbaggers* thus works extensively to portray tension in the higher echelons of the service to a far greater extent than any previous spy series, and several regular characters play a significant role in this regard. Sir Richard Greenley (Richard Vernon), who occupies the role of "C" in the first two seasons, is characterized as a well-meaning diplomat who crucially lacks experience of the intelligence world. By contrast, Burnside shares more combative relationships with Matthew Peele (Jerome Willis), the SIS deputy director, and John Tower Gibbs (Dennis Burgess), an old rival who takes over as C for the final season.

Unlike previous spy series, *The Sandbaggers* introduces an even higher level of leadership by focusing on the intelligence services' relationship with elected government and broader state apparatus, a dimension that is traditionally obscured and made redundant by the "omniscient chief" in the Fleming mode and often marginalized even by much "realist" spy fiction. A key figure in this regard is Sir Geoffrey Wellingham (Alan MacNaughtan), permanent undersecretary at the Foreign Office, a cynical, manipulative civil servant who strongly anticipates the more satirical characterization of Sir Humphrey Appleby (Nigel Hawthorne) in *Yes Minister* (BBC2, 1980–88). In addition, many episodes concern the tangible interference of the off-screen government, providing another set of agendas and source of conflict.

A further notable aspect of *The Sandbaggers'* claim to "real documentary terms" is the siting of its narratives specifically within a genuine intelligence service, the SIS, the existence of which was at the time officially disavowed. Contemporary spy dramas, even in the "realist" tradition, had tended to use fictional substitutes such the "Circus" in Le Carré's novels or the "Section" in *Callan*. By comparison *The Sandbaggers* thus makes an unusually direct claim to "realism," and the impression of accuracy is enhanced by the use of genuine intelligence terminology, most notably the use of the name C. Many commentators on the series have connected this to MacKintosh's own biography, which allegedly included intelligence work during a period of service in the Royal Navy from 1961 to 1976.[17] This places MacKintosh alongside the long line of former intelligence officers who subsequently turned to writing spy fiction, including Fleming and Le Carré, although MacKintosh, in a comparatively unusual move, wrote television series instead of novels. This was not a topic of discussion in contemporary promotional discourse surrounding the first season, which, broadcast in autumn 1978, was the only one to air within the writer's lifetime. MacKintosh disappeared and was presumed dead after an unexplained plane crash over the Gulf of Alaska in July 1979. The accident created an irresistible mystique around the program that was incorporated into its promotional strategy by the time it returned for its second season in early 1980 and has served as a key feature of most retrospective discourse.[18]

As it has proved such a point of fascination, it is worth considering what precisely MacKintosh's "authentic" experience of intelligence is imagined to contribute to the series' sense of verisimilitude. MacKintosh's biographer, Robert G. Folsom, describes the program as "a serialized meditation on ethics," a productive interpretation whereby it serves as a device to explore political and ethical issues surrounding a range of hypothetical intelligence scenarios.[19] In this regard, *The Sandbaggers* is particularly well suited to the form of the weekly episodic television series, opening this form out beyond the conventional "case of the week" model into a series of carefully crafted thought experiments about possible intelligence scenarios. The unusually complex view of the intelligence bureaucracy that it provides is highly effective for this approach, enabling it to explore different political and ethical positions in relation to its scenarios that would be impossible with the traditional simplistic and authoritative model of the "man behind the desk."

Thus, existential spy fiction has commonly staked a claim to "realism" through an apparent breaking of the "rules" of the genre, and a recurrent strategy for achieving this has been through the undermining of the figure of the "omniscient chief" and the paternalistic authority that he provided to the romantic tradition. In the formative novels of this strand, this was often achieved through narratives of treachery within the higher echelons of the service or betrayal by the organization as a whole; however, such fundamental existential crises have arguably not proved so readily adaptable to the ongoing episodic television series. *Callan* explored these areas more extensively than most contemporary series of the 1960s, primarily through emphasizing conflict between the titular character and his superiors that regularly threatened to explode into violence. Later, a more fundamental "realist" intervention was provided by *The Sandbaggers*, which, from both technical limitations and a desire to focus on the institutional workings of the intelligence world by MacKintosh, reinvented the genre into a more psychologically based office drama. Here, the singular chief is replaced by a complex bureaucratic apparatus, rendering the role of the government more visible and providing a device by which more complex political and ethical positions in relation to a variety of intelligence scenarios could be explored on a weekly basis.

Spooks: A Convergence of Leadership Traditions

In the final section of this chapter, I will examine the portrayal of intelligence chiefs in *Spooks* (BBC1, 2002–11), the longest-running and most commercially successful British spy series of the "war on terror" period. Through this analysis I will provide an account of how the conventions introduced in the formative programs of the 1960s and 1970s have been adapted to the changing televisual and political contexts of the twenty-first century. *Spooks* was produced by the independent production company Kudos Film and Television and screened on BBC1, standing as one of the channel's flagship dramas across its decadelong run. It followed a team of agents working for the Counter-Terrorism Department (Section D) of MI5 and was keenly engaged with the narrative of the war on terror, its episodic narratives most typically depicting the infiltration of terror cells and neutralization of explosive threats. Following a relative lull for the British spy series over much of the 1980s and 1990s, this series can be seen as by far the most successful attempt to revive the genre and indeed marks a significant attempt to innovate and shift its conventions for the new century, incorporating characteristics of both the action and existential traditions. Furthermore, unlike earlier British spy series, it was broadcast during a period in which the intelligence services had substantially worked to increase their openness and visibility, and I will explore the effect that this had on the program's depiction of intelligence leadership.

In the initial format followed by the first two seasons, the central character is Section Chief Tom Quinn (Matthew Macfadyen), an active field agent in the action spy tradition who coordinates the other officers on missions around the country. Above Tom, fulfilling the traditional role of the omniscient "man behind the desk," is Head of Section D Harry Pearce (Peter Firth), a late-middle-aged deskbound strategist. Fulfilling a paternalistic and licensing role for new action-based counterterror narratives, Harry in some regard fits the reactionary model of spy chief akin to Cowley in *The Professionals*, yet this is offset by the program's depiction of him as a more soft-spoken, cerebral character, prone to wry political commentary and sardonic humor. Such characteristics, combined with his often-emphasized Cold War history, are loosely suggestive of Le Carré's George Smiley. This combination can be read as an attempt by the BBC to rework the spy series for greater crossover appeal, to both traditional viewers of the action series and a notionally more "sophisticated" audience who might be presumed to prefer Le Carré. The series also draws on the existential strand of the spy genre in a number of other respects. First, it places a substantial emphasis on the interior office spaces of Section D's headquarters, the Grid, alongside the emphasis on exterior-based action narratives. Second, it claims its espionage narratives as taking place within real institutions (such as MI5) and real locations (such as Thames House), picking up a tradition of real-world reference points pioneered by *The Sandbaggers*. Thus, part of *Spooks'* innovation in the genre can be seen as an attempt to erode the long-standing dichotomy between the romantic and existential strands of spy fiction.

In addition to this, the series incorporates many new narrative strategies developed in popular television dramas over the decades since the earlier spy series discussed previously, including the use of what Robin Nelson has called "flexi-narratives." This term refers to the practice of weaving multiple ongoing narrative strands focusing on the central characters around the episodic "case of the week" story lines in order to nurture audience loyalty. Through this, the flexi-narrative achieves a "structure which combines the allegedly 'masculine' preference for action and narrative resolution with the supposedly 'feminine' fluidity and open-endedness in story-telling with an emphasis on human interest."[20] Drawing on the narrative techniques of soap operas, this aims to maximize audience appeal and ratings potential. Nelson argues that flexi-narratives were initially developed in the more competitive environment of US television and pioneered in precinct dramas such as *Hill Street Blues* (NBC, 1981–87).[21] Later this influence came to be felt in UK police series such as *The Bill* (ITV, 1984–2010) and hospital dramas such as *Casualty* (BBC1, 1986–) as a consequence of the increasingly deregulated and market-driven British broadcasting landscape over the 1980s and 1990s.

To some extent, earlier existential spy series such as *Callan* and *The Sandbaggers* had anticipated this development through their use of continuing story lines and unresolved character tensions. Yet there such ongoing narratives were largely focused on "masculine" worlds of professional conflict (as in *The Sandbaggers*) or a more existential conflict (as in *Callan*), as particularly emphasized by the overwhelmingly white, male casts. Story lines focusing on the central characters' personal lives were underdeveloped by comparison to later flexi-narrative series, existing largely to illustrate the *impossibility* of maintaining a personal sphere. By contrast, *Spooks* presents the officers of

Section D as a "work family" in the tradition of the precinct series, which works to condense professional and "family" spaces into a single site of drama. The interaction between the central characters is thus typically warmer and more casual, and more attention is given to their private lives beyond the office. Of particular note is that the audience is encouraged to know all of the protagonists by their first names, including even Harry, a striking contrast with the overwhelming tendency of earlier traditions of spy fiction to favor surnames as a short form of address. In addition, the cast throughout *Spooks'* run is considerably more diverse in terms of gender, ethnicities, and ages, providing more points of empathy and identification than its predecessors, although the positioning of Harry, a middle-aged white man with a Cold War history, as head of section still ties the series back to its generic heritage.

The rise of the flexi-narrative precinct drama can be read in part as a reflection of concurrent attempts by many organizations in the 1990s to flatten corporate structures into "networks." Indeed, although the real MI5 provided no assistance in the production of the series, creator David Wolstencroft acknowledged that one of his inspirations for the on-screen depiction of the service was the BBC itself, which at the time was undergoing a much-discussed shift toward reduced administrative structures, more open management, and a greater commitment to diversity under new director general Greg Dyke.[22] This is most visible in the large, open-plan layout of the office space, which Felix Thompson describes as being "like thousands of others. Even the use of high technology—computers and mobile phones in particular—places them [the protagonists] within the aspirational comprehension of the mass audience."[23] While the office spaces in *The Sandbaggers* were similarly ordinary in appearance and would have been recognizable to white-collar workers in the UK at the time, the open-plan design here emphasizes a sense of community much more vividly. The fact that *Spooks*, unlike earlier spy series, could depict MI5 in these familiar terms is indicative of how much public perception of the intelligence services had shifted since the time of *The Sandbaggers*. Unlike the various spy series discussed earlier in this chapter, *Spooks* was created after the service had been placed on a statutory footing by the 1989 Security Service Act and had begun openly advertising for new recruits in newspapers, in effect portraying itself as a professional occupation like any other.

The new community emphasis is particularly apparent in how *Spooks* transforms the spy genre's traditional mission briefing scene. While the Bond stories and action spy series had tended to favor the directly instructive and paternalistic model of the "man behind the desk" issuing instructions to the agent, in *Spooks* the equivalent scenes take place in a large meeting room in which all of the officers gather around a long table, with different characters contributing points of information, expertise, and opinion to the discussion of the case in hand. Harry usually adopts the role of chairman but is presented with less dominance than the traditional "omniscient chief," giving the briefing scene a more democratic and communal atmosphere.

As it progressed, the series underwent something of a shift in emphasis, arguably coinciding with the departure of Tom, the original leading character, in the third season (broadcast in 2004). An immediate consequence is that his position of section chief becomes more transitory, with various characters filling the role over the remaining seasons. As the only constant (indeed the only character who remains with the program across all ten seasons), the originally somewhat aloof Harry is pushed into the foreground, the narratives increasingly focusing on his personal life, relationships, and professional backstory, drawing him further into the conventions of the precinct drama. Concurrently, the series increasingly incorporates narratives that explore the corridors of power in the wider intelligence community more extensively. This sees the introduction of recurring characters such as Chairman of the Joint Intelligence Committee Oliver Mace (Tim McInnerny, seasons 3–5) and National Security Coordinator Juliet Shaw (Anna Chancellor, seasons 4–6), characters whose attitudes often take a more pragmatic, cynical, or authoritarian form than the typically idealistic stances of the Section D protagonists. This revives the focus on bureaucratic power struggles that had previously been central to *The Sandbaggers*. Indeed, here the world of democratic politics comes to be given even greater exposure than in the earlier program, as a notable narrative device introduced intermittently in the fourth season (broadcast in 2005) and more regularly in the sixth (broadcast in 2007) is for Harry to have briefings with a succession of home secretaries. This in effect displaces the traditional "man behind the desk" model of spy chief to a higher level, while also generating tension as the short-term populist agendas pursued by such characters are often positioned as being at odds with the clandestine expertise of Harry and his team.

Yet, in the more heightened register adopted by *Spooks*, such story lines and devices frequently shift beyond the realm of existential spy fiction and into that of the conspiracy thriller. The series notably takes a substantially more paranoid turn in its fifth season (broadcast in 2006), which opens with a two-part story in which senior MI6 officer Jocelyn Myers (John Castle) heads a plot to fake a series of terrorist attacks as a pretext for launching a right-wing coup. Over the next few seasons, Mace, Juliet, and even the longest-serving home secretary, Nicholas Blake (Robert Glennister, seasons 5–9), are all ultimately written out of the series in a range of story lines that implicate them in explicitly malevolent conspiracies. The timing is significant as, while the increased openness of the intelligence services had been greeted with a largely heroic portrayal in the early seasons of *Spooks*, the reputation of the intelligence services and their role in the broader war on terror came to be increasingly mired in controversy as the program progressed. Such controversies concerned the dossiers pushing the case for the Iraq War and resultant allegations that the intelligence services had been politicized, the repeated presentation of controversial and illiberal counterterror bills by the government, and repeated claims emerging from 2004 onward that the UK had been an accessory in a US program of extraordinary rendition.[24] Such anxieties repeatedly find allegorical representation in *Spooks* through conspiracy-themed story lines. Nonetheless, such anxiety is continually displaced onto other parts of the government and secret state. Harry and his team generally remain positioned as the most moral and humanized people within the state apparatus, as facilitated by the flexi-narrative conventions of the precinct drama.

Spooks thus draws together the tradition of the "man behind the desk" legitimating counterterror activity drawn from action spy series such as *The Professionals* and the emphasis on institutional space partially drawn from the existential tradition, reworking both according to the new flexi-narrative techniques of the precinct drama in order to emphasize community and familiarity. That MI5 can be cast in such terms can be seen as indicative of its changing image and increased openness. The gradual shift to a greater focus on Harry and his relationship with the higher echelons of the state apparatus brings in a further point of continuity with *The Sandbaggers*, emphasizing the complexity of intelligence bureaucracy, yet in response to contemporary intelligence scandals and the broader growing disillusionment with the war on terror, this frequently slides into a paranoid register more in line with the conspiracy genre. Thus, increased visibility of the intelligence services has effectively provided the television spy series with new possibilities for both heroism and paranoia in its vision of intelligence leadership.

Conclusion

Before the openness and visibility drives by the intelligence services across recent decades, the British television spy series developed several rich traditions for depicting spy chief characters. Action spy series tended to adopt an omniscient "man behind the desk" largely derived from the "romantic" literary tradition. This provided bureaucratic legitimation for action-based adventure narratives outside the institutional space while condensing the bureaucracy and broader political structures to their simplest form, that of a single paternalistic figure. Nonetheless, British action spy series in the 1960s were initially somewhat ambivalent toward such characters owing to a lingering adherence to the "talented amateur" tradition of protagonist. Indeed, it was not until the reworking of the genre to encompass a greater focus on counterterrorism in the following decade that the role of the chief became more emphasized to embody a paternalistic ideal of the "strong state." Concurrently, the parallel strand of existential spy dramas was rooted in the tendency of their literary influences to assert claims to realism by challenging such simplistic visions of intelligence leadership, although the potential of this on television was ultimately somewhat limited by the form of the ongoing series and its need for a regular, stable format. Nonetheless, *The Sandbaggers* achieved the most thorough reworking of the television spy series in this vein by casting intelligence leadership as a larger bureaucracy and using it as a dramatic device for exploring more complex political and ethical concerns.

More recently, *Spooks* merged characteristics of both traditions into its keen engagement with the topical anxieties of the war on terror and superficial response to the increased openness of the intelligence services. Its early seasons offered a benevolent "man behind the desk" chief in the tradition of the action spy series but situated in an office space rendered in the familiar terms of the precinct drama, giving a human face to heroic clandestine activity in the war on terror. Yet as the war and the role of intelligence became increasingly controversial, *Spooks* responded by placing greater emphasis on broader bureaucratic structures of the state, often portrayed in more elitist and conspiratorial terms. Thus, the increased visibility of the intelligence services in the twenty-first century has proved something of a double-edged sword for the representations of intelligence leadership in British television drama, which have worked both to humanize the spy chief in the context of the office space and "work family" and to dramatize a deeper alienation with the wider structures of power.

Notes

1. John G. Cawelti and Bruce A. Rosenberg, *The Spy Story* (Chicago: University of Chicago Press, 1987), 134.

2. Michael Denning, *Cover Stories: Narrative and Ideology in the British Spy Thriller* (London: Routledge & Kegan Paul, 1987), 101.

3. Umberto Eco, "Narrative Structures in Fleming," in *The Role of the Reader: Explorations in the Semiotics of Texts* (Bloomington: Indiana University Press), 1979, 147.

4. Ibid., 160.

5. Ibid., 156.

6. James Chapman, *Licence to Thrill: A Cultural History of the James Bond Films* (London: I. B. Tauris, 1999), 23.

7. James Chapman, *Saints and Avengers: British Adventure Series of the 1960s* (London: I. B. Tauris, 2002), 4.

8. Michael Kackman, *Citizen Spy: Television, Espionage, and Cold War Culture* (Minneapolis: University of Minnesota Press, 2005), 81.

9. Philip Schlesinger, Graham Murdock, and Philip Elliott, *Televising "Terrorism": Political Violence in Popular Culture* (London: Comedia, 1983), 83.

10. Denning, *Cover Stories*, 25–36.

11. Ibid., 34.

12. Ibid.

13. Ibid., 140.

14. Eco, "Narrative Structures in Fleming," 148.

15. Joseph Oldham, "'Disappointed Romantics': Troubled Heritage in the BBC's John Le Carré Adaptations," *Journal of British Cinema and Television* 10 (2013): 727–45.

16. Ian MacKintosh, "MacKintosh's Outline for *The Sandbaggers*," in *The Life and Mysterious Death of Ian MacKintosh: The Inside Story of* The Sandbaggers *and TV's Top Spy*, by Robert G. Folsom (Washington, DC: Potomac Books, 2012), 166.

17. Folsom, *Life and Mysterious Death of Ian MacKintosh*.

18. Jane Ennis, "Vanished: The Original Sandbagger," *TV Times*, January 26, 1980, 2–3.

19. Folsom, *Life and Mysterious Death of Ian MacKintosh*, 23.

20. Robin Nelson, *TV Drama in Transition: Forms, Values and Cultural Change* (Basingstoke: Palgrave Macmillan, 1997), 39.

21. Ibid., 30.

22. Jeff Dawson, "The Spies Have It," *Radio Times*, May 31, 2003, 19.

23. Felix Thompson, "*Coast* and *Spooks*: On the Permeable National Boundaries of British Television," *Continuum: Journal of Media & Cultural Studies* 24 (2010): 435.

24. Steven Kettell, *New Labour and the New World Order: Britain's Role in the War on Terror* (Manchester: Manchester University Press, 2011).

Conclusion

Intelligence Leadership in the Twenty-First Century

Christopher Moran, Ioanna Iordanou, and Mark Stout

Following the chapters in this collection, we would like to conclude by offering three lessons for the twenty-first-century US and UK intelligence leader.

Image Matters

Being an intelligence leader brings many challenges. For a famous British female spy chief, 2012 was a particularly difficult year. A bungled mission resulted in the disappearance of her best agent and the loss of a hard drive containing the names of every undercover operative embedded in terrorist cells around the world. Although the agent later resurfaced, like the grand old warship in Turner's *Fighting Temeraire* being hauled off to the breaker's yard for scrap, he was written off as old and washed up. Meanwhile, a mysterious cyberterrorist with a personal grudge against the spy chief reduced SIS headquarters to rubble and promised further carnage. To top it off, there was increasing public and political nervousness about espionage in the modern world, and the embattled spy chief was called on the carpet before an acid-tongued and frowny-faced parliamentary committee keen to make her accountable for the service's failings. Upbraided by a grandstanding minister who would have loved to close her department for good, considering it antiquated and not fit for purpose, the spy chief lectured the assembled audience on the importance of traditional intelligence work in fighting enemies who have no borders and hide in the shadows of society and cyberspace.

The intelligence leader in question, of course, was Dame Judi Dench's "M," in Daniel Craig's third outing as James Bond, *Skyfall*. While a fictional representation, M's appearance in front of a public inquiry is grounded in some measure of reality and underscores the first main takeaway lesson of this volume: *Spy chiefs in the United States and the United Kingdom operate in a brave new world where public engagement to promote a positive corporate image is a fundamental part of the job.* This has occurred gradually and not without opposition from traditionally publicity-shy agencies, but it is clear that the era of the anonymous and silent spy chief is over in these countries because the continued effective functioning of intelligence services depends on the consent of the population and of the members of Congress or Parliament for whom the population vote.

In a classic case of life imitating art, in November 2013, amid intense public scrutiny of intelligence work following the leaks of fugitive National Security Agency (NSA) contractor Edward Snowden, Director General of MI5 Andrew Parker, GCHQ Director Sir Iain Lobban, and SIS chief Sir John Sawers took part in an unprecedented public—and televised—hearing, albeit with a two-minute time delay to ensure the transmission could be halted if any secret information inadvertently slipped out. At times their answers bore a striking resemblance to what M had told committee members in Parliament in *Skyfall.* At one point, for example, Sawers said, "It is not like it was in the Cold War. There are not states out there, trying to destroy our government and our way of life, but there are a very wide range of diverse threats that we face."[1] Similarly, M had warned in the hearing room: "I'm frightened because our enemies are no longer known to us. They do not exist on a map. They're not nations, they're individuals. And look around you. Who do you fear? Can you see a face, a uniform, a flag? No. Our world is not more transparent now, it's more opaque. It's in the shadows." It was not the first time in spy thrillers that fact followed fiction.

There are good reasons why the job of spy chief is now a public-facing role, as Moran's chapter about Richard Helms and Smoot and Hatch's chapter about NSA directors explain. Obtaining public and political trust is a vital component of intelligence work in the twenty-first century. Gone are the days of sharply limited public discussion about intelligence. Nor could a director of the Central Intelligence Agency (CIA) today get away with William Casey's calculated strategy of mumbling indecipherably at congressional oversight hearings. Today, spy stories, especially scandals, not only generate newspaper headlines, they are debated by millions on social media. Snowden is testament to this new reality. The *Guardian* and other newspapers wrote the headlines, but fevered commentary in the Twittersphere gave the leaks unprecedented coverage. From Moscow, where Snowden is residing to avoid US authorities, he uses the Internet to tweet about the "surveillance state" and gives Skype talks to his followers and journalists eager to discuss the top secret programs he has revealed. In this context, intelligence and security agencies cannot afford to remain silent. They have to get their message across and protect their corporate image; otherwise, people will assume the worst and falsehoods will harden into fact.

Obviously, there are limits on what spy chiefs can say on behalf of their agencies, but some clarification and reassurance is essential to ensure that taxpayers and their representatives trust them enough to release public funds. Interestingly, in April 2014 GCHQ announced Robert Hannigan as its new director. Neither a career intelligence officer nor a classic "securocrat," Hannigan came from the world of public relations and "spin," having previously been Tony Blair's director of communications for the Northern Ireland Office.[2] Since taking office, Hannigan has given several high-profile speeches, apologizing for the organization's historical prejudice against homosexuals and calling Snowden's revelations about GCHQ's data-mining techniques a "gift" to terrorists. His appointment is probably a sign of things to come.

Corporate image matters not merely in how intelligence agencies relate to external constituencies such as the public, Congress, or Parliament. It also matters to an intelligence agency's workforce. In October 1975, for example, at the height of the so-called Year of Intelligence, the CIA asked a sample of employees what impact the damaging headlines was having on efficiency and morale. Many staff admitted to feeling a "sense of embarrassment and shame," and there were even tragic stories of agency families being ripped apart, with teenage children horrified by reports of what their mother or father did for a living.[3] Indeed, when senior operations officer David Atlee Phillips told his fifteen-year-old daughter that he worked for the CIA, she said to him, "But Daddy, that's dirty."[4]

Corporate image stems to a large degree from how people *perceive* an organization, and this perception is shaped by events and actions. But clearly, the spy chief has an important role to play here.[5] To borrow from the work of management scholar Charles Fombrun, reputation or image is the result of the public's collective judgment of an organization's actions and accomplishments.[6] Spy chiefs—as the "organizational elites" of the institution they represent—have the capacity to define and construct the corporate image they wish to project to both insiders and outsiders of the organization.[7] This image can come from a bona fide attempt to represent essential features of the organization to others.[8] Alternatively, it can involve an effort to communicate a compelling future image of the organization—an intended vision.[9] In short, spy chiefs, by virtue of their position, have a unique ability to shape the present by creating the notion of what is to come, and the corporate image they construct and project plays a vital role in this process.

Context Matters

In the Oscar-winning biographical film *Patton* (1970), US general George S. Patton makes the crude yet rational observation, "Nobody ever won a war by dying for his country. He won by making the other poor dumb bastard die for his country." While this remark is certainly telling about the nature and strategy of war, it is also pertinent to intelligence leadership. It shows that effective leadership means creating the conditions that mobilize others to follow and implement the leader's vision. This encapsulates the second takeaway lesson from this volume: *Successful spy chiefs must construct and legitimize a sociopolitical context that is favorable to their vision and strategy.*

Specifically, leadership entails the social construction of the context that legitimizes a particular action by a group at a specific point in time.[10] Both Allen Dulles and William Casey exemplified this doctrine. As shown in the chapters by Lockhart and Hammond, people bought into Dulles and Casey's vision of the CIA as a key actor in the fight against Communism because they accepted the prevailing discourse that Communism was the greatest threat to American security and freedom. Recognizing this co-constituted relationship, both Dulles and Casey were extremely active in encouraging the drumbeat of anti-Communist sentiment, albeit in different ways. Consistent with his persona as a charming and avuncular professor, Dulles invited members of Congress and journalists to his home, where he would discuss with them how dangerous the Soviet menace had become.[11] (He once told his mistress that his kindhearted demeanor and bonhomie was an act to get people to trust him, explaining, "I like to watch the little mice sniffing at the cheese just before they venture into the little trap.")[12] True to his roots as a gruff street fighter from Queens, New York, Casey had a less subtle approach. If journalists or other key opinion formers deviated from the line that the USSR was anything less than an "Evil Empire," he would ring them up and shout at them: no hard line about Moscow was hard enough. In their own unique ways, therefore, Dulles and Casey made the context as much as the context made them.

Dulles is emblematic of another way in which intelligence leaders can influence, if not construct, the sociopolitical context in which they wish to situate their course of action. This is their ability to successfully silence those voices that present alternative views and opinions. As Lockhart argued, Dulles successfully overcame the reservations of imposing personages such as President Harry Truman and CIA Director Walter Bedell Smith—who believed that the CIA should primarily be about analysis, not action—by speaking a language they could understand: the language of anti-Communism. In this respect, sense making (in its literal form) is not an act of analytic reasoning but an act of power that operates in two dimensions: either spy chiefs silence those actors who resist or they pacify their concerns by means of taking strategic steps to ensure safety and security.[13] In consequence, effective intelligence leaders can mold the context in which they operate through their "persuasive rendition" of the sociopolitical status quo and their "persuasive display of the appropriate authority style."[14]

It follows that the ability to mobilize actors to take action by carefully constructing the need for it is critical for maintaining what leadership scholar Keith Grint has called "the mystique of leadership."[15] Sometimes, in a bid to get people to buy into their vision as quickly as possible and without opposition, they might need to present the context in extreme terms. For example, as Stout showed in chapter 2, to keep his "Pond" in existence after the war, John Grombach systematically exaggerated the achievements of his own organization while simultaneously downplaying and misrepresenting the effectiveness of the CIA. In this respect, the sociopolitical context in which leaders operate is crucial in order for them to justify their decisions. This has serious implications for how contemporary spy chiefs make and, more importantly, justify decisions and actions. While the era of the Twittersphere and Wikileaks calls for more transparency, there is still a tacit romanticism associated with the secret role of the spy chief. Yet the romance of intelligence leadership—the public fascination with spy chiefs—is inadequate to explain and validate their decisions and actions in isolation. This is why the sociopolitical context in which the spy chief operates matters and why any incoming intelligence leader should treat it with caution and thoughtfulness.

Relationships Matter

The final major lesson from this volume is this: *Spy chiefs are only as successful as the relationships they build.* Like every government leader aside from a head of state, spy chiefs must look north, south, east, and west. In other words, they must inevitably deal with their superiors, their subordinates, and their peers. Relationships naturally require careful handling and nurturing, but the examples in this book suggest that few intelligence leaders have managed all directions successfully.

Aldrich provides us the example of the "outspoken" Gen. Bill Odom, the head of US Army intelligence and then director of the NSA (DIRNSA). While indisputably brilliant, Odom was arrogant and combative, and these traits led him into numerous fights with people at all points of the compass. As DIRNSA, Odom had two bosses: the secretary of defense and the director of central intelligence (DCI). While the secretary was not especially interested in the doings of NSA, the DCI was. Yet Odom clashed repeatedly with him. Odom made a habit of clashing with peers as well. The CIA viewed him as "smug," "self-important," and incapable of believing that the agency could understand military issues. Finally, as Smoot and Hatch show us, Odom brought a commander's mind-set to NSA, an only nominal military agency. As a result, he "battled" the "system" there and left without having substantially changed the agency. Arguably, Odom was more effective in retirement as a scholar, educator, and public commentator on intelligence issues, endeavors in which he had untrammeled authority.

William Donovan was more successful in one regard, but in the end he lost decisively as well. As Graziano shows in chapter 1, Donovan's loathing of bureaucratic folderol and red tape, plus his willingness to break the rules and trample over people who stood in his way, ensured that the men who served under him loved him. However, the same qualities also meant that he had terrible relations with his peers in Washington, particularly the heads of the War Department's Military Intelligence Division and J. Edgar Hoover at the Federal Bureau of Investigation (FBI). Moreover, while Donovan's proclivities in this regard meshed nicely with those of President Franklin Roosevelt, they did not appeal to President Harry Truman, who ultimately decided the fate of the Office of Strategic Services (OSS) in the autumn of 1945.[16]

John Grombach—who loathed Donovan and the OSS—presents a similar case. As Stout demonstrates in chapter 2, Grombach endeared himself to his subordinates through his dedication to getting the job done, no matter the long trail of bruised egos in authority he left behind him. However, that same combative attitude to authority, even to the departments that were funding his private-sector espionage operations, eventually ensured that he ran out of patrons and was forced out of business. The fact that he managed to ply his trade for twelve years is a testament to his entrepreneurial abilities and skills as a tactician, but nevertheless, he chose to play a fundamentally losing game, going up against the leaders of much larger agencies. Much like Odom, he was the kind of man who bled needlessly because he could not resist a fight. By the same token, in chapter 13 Oldham gives us the fictional example of Neil Burnside, director of operations at SIS in the TV series *The Sandbaggers* who had much the same quality and whose career suffered as a result.

Donovan, Odom, Grombach, and the fictional Burnside were all deeply flawed leaders, but even the most savvy and wily intelligence leaders have struggled to have good working relations with superiors, subordinates, and peers. Relationships with subordinates can be difficult when leaders must make painful changes, as Stansfield Turner learned when he cut the CIA's Directorate of Operations. Broad societal trends have put leader-subordinate relationships in a period of flux. It is doubtful that the "man behind the desk"–style of leadership, as Oldham calls it, will suffice. Organizations (not just in the intelligence community) are flattening in an effort to become more like "networks," thereby eroding the distinction between leaders and the led. Moreover, the members of the millennial generation have expectations about the workplace that are different from those of their predecessors. Spy chiefs who cannot adjust to these realities are likely to struggle. Sometimes, too, spy chiefs can have difficulties with their subordinates because of their own personal blind spots. For instance, CIA Director John Deutch, at his first town hall meeting after taking over the agency, found himself challenged by a member of the workforce who wanted to know why—of the many Defense Department employees that Deutch had brought over with him from the Pentagon—the only African American was his chauffeur.[17]

In addition, spy chiefs, try as they might to build relationships and appease both the horizontal and the vertical, will sometimes stumble because of circumstances and people beyond their control. Richard Helms is a classic case of this. The "intelligence professional personified," to quote CIA historian David Robarge, Helms was greatly respected by his staff for his dedication to duty and apparent eagerness to keep the game honest and speak truth to power.[18] The ultimate bureaucratic survivor, he knew for a long time what battles to fight with rival departments and what bullets to dodge when they came from the White House. Eventually, however, even Helms could not manage all sides, as illustrated when Richard Nixon fired him for his unwillingness to enmesh the CIA in the unfolding Watergate scandal.

The relationship between a political master and a spy chief can even be harmed (or improved) by the image of the agency itself. Even leaving Watergate aside, Nixon's relationship with Richard Helms was never going to be close given the president's poisonous attitude toward the men and women of the CIA, dating back to at least the 1960 presidential election, which, in Nixon's view, had been swung in Kennedy's favor by "liberal" CIA officers conspiring against him.[19] On the other hand, William Casey benefited from the image of the CIA. As Hammond points out in chapter 6, Casey was never an intimate of Ronald Reagan's, and yet he headed a CIA that Reagan believed had the potential to do great things if "unleashed." As a result, Reagan gave enormous latitude to Casey. In general, they were an effective team in pursuing "freedom" as they understood it.

Ultimately, however, intelligence leaders must recognize that failed relationships are an unfortunate fact of life, and they are particularly common in the inherently competitive environment of the interagency community. The old joke that "if you want a friend in Washington, get a dog," has more than a little truth in it.

On top of all that, even having good relations with superiors can lead to trouble. The danger of groupthink is well-known, and it can apply even at very senior levels, but there are other dangers.[20] The case of Patrick Dean, the chairman of Britain's Joint Intelligence Committee during the Suez Crisis is illustrative here, as Danny Steed's chapter shows us. Trusted by Prime

Minister Anthony Eden, Dean was drawn into policy deliberations that were outside his ken and that led to a politicization of the intelligence process. Similarly, the trust that Reagan had in Casey may have helped set the stage for the Iran-Contra affair. Having the ear of the political elite is no guarantee of success.

Closing Remarks

We introduced this book by asking how much power spy chiefs in the United States and Great Britain really have and what it takes to be an effective intelligence leader. Of course, "knowledge is power," and intelligence agencies often have access to powerful tools such as the capacity to launch covert actions that can lead to regime change and the ability to play (cynically or otherwise) on the fears of policymakers and even the public. Nevertheless, in closing, we would like to suggest that spy chiefs do not have the kind of unrestricted power to manipulate world affairs that James Earl Jones's CIA director had in *The Hunt for Red October*, let alone the kind of superhuman powers that conspiracy theorists imagine. Rather, they are hemmed in on all sides. Moreover, they increasingly operate in a goldfish bowl, their every action liable to scrutiny. It requires a skillful leader just to maintain the position and effectiveness of his or her agency, let alone lead it to success.

The most effective leaders, then, are those who possess three essential skills:

One, the ability to maintain at least neutral and ideally positive relations with the public, plus overseers and appropriators in Congress or Parliament. This can be particularly difficult for spy chiefs who have come up through the ranks. For years they will have been inculcated with the idea that they must maintain a low profile or even "live their cover." As they climbed the escarpments, they will have been repeatedly instructed never, in any context, to say anything that from any angle could be construed as a secret. Time and again, they will have been told to avoid reporters. In the United States it is likely that they would have been repeatedly polygraphed to ensure strict adherence to the rules. In the United Kingdom an officer's duty to keep secrets would have been symbolically underscored by signing the Official Secrets Act.

Today, however, these behaviors and regulations, at least in their strictest form, have become dysfunctional. Publics and legislators demand a degree of transparency that was unthinkable just a generation ago. If scorned, these constituencies can force budget cuts, create vexing legal restrictions, or even induce a president or prime minister to replace a spy chief who has become a liability. That it took Richard Helms decades after his retirement to realize that too much secrecy was counterproductive testifies to the power of the culture of secrecy inside the Anglo-American intelligence world. But evidence suggests that spy chiefs are willing to move with the times, as illustrated by the 2016 memoir of former NSA and CIA director Michael Hayden: "If we are going to conduct espionage in the future," he writes, "we are going to have to make some changes in the relationship between the intelligence community and the public it serves. . . . It can be no other way."[21] As Hayden himself admits, the objective here is not transparency but what Mike Leiter (a former head of the National Counterterrorism Center) calls "translucence"—giving the public just enough information to "make out the broad shapes and broad movements of what intelligence is doing."[22]

Two, the dexterity to mold the agency they lead to fit the broader sociopolitical environment in which they operate. The most successful spy chiefs will also try to shape that environment in a way that is favorable to their strategy. Doing this, in turn, requires vision, a sophisticated understanding of the societies in which they live, and strategic expertise. Future research in this area might delve further into the limiting or empowering impact of institutional structures on the capacity of the intelligence leader to actually lead. In other words, is the leader made by the organization, or is the organization made by the leader?

And three, the skill to tend important relationships with superiors, peers, and subordinates. This requires the aptitude of an accomplished diplomat but also the ability to be a good "mingler" or "people person," equally adept at moving in the highest circles of power as relating to the rank and file who may, themselves, come from many different professional cultures.

Doing all this is naturally a tall order, so tall that no man or woman can reasonably be expected to excel at all aspects. But, then, intelligence leadership—much like intelligence itself—was never meant to be easy.

Notes

1. "Spy Chiefs Public Hearing," *Telegraph Online*, November 7, 2013, http://www.telegraph.co.uk/news/uknews/defence/10432629/Spy-chiefs-public-hearing-as-it-happened.html.

2. Richard J. Aldrich and Rory Cormac, *Spies, Secret Intelligence and Prime Ministers* (London: William Collins, 2016), 475–76.

3. Christopher Moran, *Company Confessions: Revealing CIA Secrets* (London: Biteback, 2015), 155.

4. Christopher Moran, "The Last Assignment: David Atlee Phillips and the Birth of CIA Public Relations," 35, no. 2 (April 2013): 346.

5. Per Olof Berg, "Organization Change as a Symbolic Transformation Process," in

Reframing Organizational Culture, eds. Petr J. Frost, Larry F. Moore, Meryl Reis Louis, Craig C. Lundberg, and Joanne Martin (Thousand Oaks, CA: Sage, 1985), 281–300.

6. Charles J. Fombrun, *Reputation: Realizing Value from the Corporate Image* (Boston: Harvard Business School Press, 1996).

7. David A. Whetten and Paul C. Godfrey, eds., *Identity in Organizations: Developing Theory through Conversations* (Thousand Oaks, CA: Sage, 1992).

8. Dennis A. Gioia, Majken Schultz, and Kevin G. Corley, "Organizational Identity, Image, and Adaptive Instability," *Academy of Management Review* 25 (2000): 63–81.

9. Dennis A. Gioia and James B. Thomas, "Image, Identity and Issue Interpretation: Sensemaking during Strategic Change in Academia," *Administrative Science Quarterly* 41 (1996): 370–403; Gioia, Schultz, and Corley, "Organizational Identity," 66.

10. Keith Grint, "Problems, Problems, Problems: The Social Construction of Leadership," *Human Relations* 58 (2005): 1467–94.

11. See Richard J. Aldrich, "Regulation by Revelation? Intelligence, Transparency and the Media," in *Spinning Intelligence: Why Intelligence Needs the Media, Why the Media Needs Intelligence*, ed. Robert Dover and Michael Goodman (New York: Columbia University Press, 2009): 13–36; Richard J. Aldrich, "American Journalism and Landscapes of Secrecy," *History: The Journal of the Historical Association* 100, no. 339 (April 2015): 189–209.

12. David Talbot, *The Devil's Chessboard: Allen Dulles, the CIA, and the Rise of America's Secret Government* (London: William Collins, 2015), 135.

13. Keith Grint, "The Sacred in Leadership: Separation, Sacrifice and Silence," *Organization Studies* 3 (2010): 89–107.

14. Grint, "Problems," 1477.

15. Grint, "Sacred in Leadership," 94.

16. Douglas Waller, *Wild Bill Donovan: The Spymaster Who Created the OSS and Modern American Espionage* (New York: Free Press, 2011).

17. Personal information.

18. David Robarge, "Richard Helms: The Intelligence Professional Personified," *Studies in Intelligence* 46, no. 4 (2002): 35–43.

19. John L. Helgerson, *Getting to Know the President*, 2nd ed. (Washington, DC: Central Intelligence Agency, 2012), 75.

20. Irving Janis, *Groupthink: Psychological Studies of Policy Decisions and Fiascoes*, 2nd ed. (Boston: Houghton Mifflin, 1982).

21. Michael Hayden, *Playing to the Edge: American Intelligence in the Age of Terror* (New York: Penguin, 2016), 422.

22. Ibid., 424.

CONTRIBUTORS

Richard J. Aldrich is professor of international security at the Department of Politics and International Studies, University of Warwick, and is the author of several books, including *The Hidden Hand: Britain, America and Cold War Secret Intelligence* (2001) and *GCHQ: The Uncensored Story of Britain's Most Secret Intelligence Agency* (2010). His most recent book, *The Black Door: Spies, Secret Intelligence, and British Prime Ministers*, written with Rory Cormac, deals with the relationship between Downing Street and espionage. He has recently spent time assisting the German parliamentary inquiry into the Snowden affair. In September 2016 he began a Leverhulme Major Research Fellowship on the changing nature of secrecy.

Rory Cormac is an associate professor of international relations at the University of Nottingham. His research specializes in British intelligence and covert action. Between 2015 and 2017 he held an AHRC early career fellowship exploring UK approaches to covert action during the Cold War and era of decolonization. He is grateful for this funding, from which this chapter emerged. His most recent book is *The Black Door: Spies, Secret Intelligence and British Prime Ministers*, coauthored with Richard J. Aldrich.

Matthew H. Fay is a foreign and defense policy analyst at the Niskanen Center and a PhD student in the political science program at George Mason University's Schar School for Government and Policy. He has a master's degree in international relations from American Military University and another in diplomatic history from Temple University. He received his bachelor's degree from St. Xavier University. He has previously coauthored an article on nuclear forecasting for the *American Historical Review* and a white paper on US nuclear force structure for the Cato Institute.

Michael Goodman is professor of intelligence and international affairs in the Department of War Studies, King's College London, and visiting professor at the Norwegian Defence Intelligence School. He has published widely in the field of intelligence history, including most recently *The Official History of the Joint Intelligence Committee*, volume 1: *From the Approach of the Second World War to the Suez Crisis* (Routledge, 2015), which was chosen as one of *The Spectator*'s books of the year. He is series editor for Intelligence and Security for Hurst/Columbia University Press and for Intelligence, Surveillance and Secret Warfare for Edinburgh University Press and is a member of the editorial boards for five journals. He is currently on secondment to the Cabinet Office, where he is the official historian of the Joint Intelligence Committee.

Michael Graziano is an instructor in the Department of Philosophy and World Religions at the University of Northern Iowa, where he teaches courses in the humanities and religious studies. His research interests include US religious history, religion and law, and the relationship between religion and intelligence history.

Andrew Hammond is a Mellon Foundation Postdoctoral Fellow at the National September 11 Memorial and Museum, plus New York University. As a scholar in residence at the 9/11 Museum, he is conducting research for his second monograph, a veteran's oral history of 9/11 and the war on terror. His forthcoming book, *Struggles for Freedom: Afghanistan and US Foreign Policy since 1979*, will be published in 2017 in both hardback and paperback. It is based on extensive archival research and over a hundred interviews with key players. Fieldwork for this project was supported by the Arts and Humanities Research Council. His graduate work was funded by a studentship from the Economic and Social Research Council, which he won after being the University of Warwick's entrant into the national competition. He has held visiting fellowships at the Library of Congress, where he was a British Research Council Fellow, and the British Library.

David Hatch received his MA from Indiana University, Bloomington, and his PhD from American University. He has been an NSA employee since 1973. After a career as an analyst, supervisor, and staff officer, Dr. Hatch transferred to NSA's Center for Cryptologic History (CCH) in 1990. Following a convoluted series of retirements and reorganizations, he became the NSA historian and technical director for the CCH. He is the author of many classified and unclassified publications on the history of cryptology and NSA and has lectured widely on these subjects.

Patrick M. Hughes, lieutenant general, US Army (retired), spent more than forty-five years in the intelligence profession, including thirty years in active military service. In recent years he has been a private consultant, the assistant secretary for information and analysis at the Department of Homeland Security, and finally a corporate vice president for intelligence and counterterrorism. His last active-duty assignment was director, Defense Intelligence Agency (DIA), a position he held for three and a half years. Other positions of responsibility included director of intelligence (J-2), the Joint Staff; director of intelligence (J-2), US Central Command; commanding general, US Army Intelligence Agency; commander, 501st Military Intelligence Brigade with service in the Republic of Korea; and Commander, 109th Military Intelligence Battalion (Combat Electronic Warfare and Intelligence), 9th Infantry Division (High Technology Test Bed), at Fort Lewis, Washington. He is a veteran of the Vietnam War (two tours) and other conflicts. His awards and decorations include the MI Corps Knowlton Award, the National Intelligence Distinguished Service Medal (two awards), the Central Intelligence Agency Director's Award, and the CIA Medallion. He is a member of the US Army Military Intelligence Hall of Fame and the National US Army ROTC Hall of Fame.

Ioanna Iordanou is a senior lecturer in human resource management (Oxford Brookes University, UK) and an associate fellow of the Centre for the Study of the Renaissance (Warwick University, UK), specializing in the historical development of managerial/leadership practices and corporate entities in the early modern period. She has published her research in *The Economic History Review* and *Intelligence and National Security*. She is the author of the forthcoming monograph *Venice's Secret Service: Intelligence Organisation in the Renaissance* (Oxford University Press, 2019).

James Lockhart is assistant professor of history at the American University in Dubai and lives in the Emirates. He specializes in American foreign relations, international studies, and intelligence history in the Global South. He served in the infantry in the US Marine Corps (Reserve), and he has traveled extensively in southern South America, East Asia, and Europe. He earned his PhD in US and world history at the University of Arizona, and his first book, *Chile, the CIA, and the Cold War*: *A Transatlantic Perspective*, is forthcoming with Edinburgh University Press.

Paul Maddrell is a lecturer in modern German history at Loughborough University in the United Kingdom. He is a fellow of the United Kingdom's Royal Historical Society and of the Higher Education Academy and a member of the editorial board of the *International Journal of Intelligence and CounterIntelligence*. His principal publications are his single-authored monograph *Spying* *on Science: Western Intelligence in Divided Germany, 1945–1961* (Oxford University Press, 2006) and his edited book *The Image of the Enemy: Intelligence Analysis of Adversaries since 1945* (Georgetown University Press, 2015). He has also published many journal articles and book chapters on the history of intelligence, Germany, and the Cold War.

Christopher Moran is an associate professor of US national security in the Department of Politics and International Studies at the University of Warwick. He is the author of *Classified: Secrecy and the State in Modern Britain*, which won the 2014 St. Ermin's Hotel Intelligence Book of the Year Award, and more recently, *Company Confessions: Secrets, Memoirs, and the CIA*. Between 2011 and 2014 he was a British Academy Postdoctoral Fellow. He is currently writing a new book on the relationship between Richard Nixon and the CIA.

Joseph Oldham is an associate fellow of the Department of Film and Television Studies at the University of Warwick and formerly an Early Career Fellow of Warwick's Institute of Advanced Study. His research works to bridge the gap between cultural and intelligence studies, and his particular research interests are the history of British broadcasting, the spy and conspiracy genres in British television drama, and their intersection with the history of intelligence. His monograph *Paranoid Visions: Spies, Conspiracies and the Secret State* (Manchester University Press, 2017) is adapted from his thesis for which he was awarded a PhD in 2014. He has also published in the *Journal of Intelligence History*, the *Journal of British Cinema and Television, Adaptation: The Journal of Literature on Screen Studies* (article forthcoming), and *The Conversation.* He currently lectures at the University of Hull's School of Drama, Music and Screen.

Betsy Rohaly Smoot is a staff historian at the National Security Agency's Center for Cryptologic History. Her research interests include early female cryptologists, World War I, cryptology during the Cold War, and terrorism. Before she joined the center in 2007, she served in analytic, staff, and management positions with NSA both at Fort George G. Meade and overseas.

Danny Steed, formerly lecturer in strategy and defense at the University of Exeter, is now an independent author and consultant. He has also previously worked for CERT-UK in the Cabinet Office specializing in cybersecurity. Danny's first book, *British Strategy and Intelligence in the Suez Crisis*, was released in 2016 by Palgrave Macmillan. His next book with Routledge, *The Politics and Technology of Cyber Security*, will be available in 2018 and focuses on the evolution and impact of cybersecurity. Danny's publications and research interests lie in strategic theory and concepts, the history of war, technology in warfare both past and present, intelligence operations, and cybersecurity.

Mark Stout is the director of the MA in global security studies and the certificate in intelligence at Johns Hopkins University's Krieger School of Arts and Sciences Advanced Academic Programs in Washington, DC. He previously worked for thirteen years as an intelligence analyst, first with the State Department's Bureau of Intelligence and Research and later with the CIA. He has also worked on the Army Staff in the Pentagon and at the Institute for Defense Analyses. In addition, Dr. Stout spent three years as the historian at the International Spy Museum in Washington, DC. He has degrees from Stanford and Harvard Universities and a PhD in history from the University of Leeds.

Michael L. VanBlaricum of Dogged Research Associates has nearly forty years of research and program and corporate management experience in various electrical engineering specialty areas. He holds a PhD in electrical engineering from the University of Illinois. He has led breakthrough research in the fields of reconfigurable antenna design, transient electromagnetics, radar target recognition, and photonic-based electromagnetic field development. VanBlaricum is the founder and current president of the Ian Fleming Foundation (IFF), a nonprofit corporation dedicated to the preservation of the legacy of Ian Fleming, his literary works, and his impact on the culture of the twentieth century. IFF provides assistance with research and consults on a variety of issues relating to the history of Ian Fleming and his literary and film creation, James Bond. Dr. VanBlaricum has developed a world-renowned collection of the literary works of Ian Fleming and associated James Bond materials, including manuscripts, letters, books, art, recordings, videos, ephemera, toys, and an extensive collection of research books associated with this cultural phenomenon. The major focus of the collection is as a historical / archival research collection of the writings by and about Ian Fleming and the entire James Bond phenomenon.

INDEX

[Page locators in italics signify photos.]